ETHICAL PHILOSOPHIES OF INDIA

ETHICAL PHILOSOPHIES OF INDIA

BY

I. C. SHARMA
Ph.D.
Head of the Department of Philosophy
M.B. College, Udaipur, Rajasthan

EDITED AND REVISED BY

STANLEY M. DAUGERT
Ph.D.
Chairman of the Department of Philosophy
Western Washington State College

JOHNSEN PUBLISHING COMPANY
Lincoln, Nebraska 68501

PRINTED IN GREAT BRITAIN

Dedicated to my respected teacher
Padma Bhushan Shri G. C. Chatterjee
Chairman, Central Board of Secondary Education, New Delhi;
Veteran Educator and Philosopher of India

PREFACE

It is a privilege that I have, as a reader from abroad, to report my enjoyment of this extraordinary volume. To have presented in brief compass the whole course of ethical theory and moral values as they have emerged and found literary expression in India is a rare philosophic treat. I am sure that the book will be used extensively abroad not only as a book for academic studies but also as a great aid for Western publics in their attempts to understand the practical aspects of Indian systems of moral norms.

Whatever may be its informative value for students in India, this history will certainly be appreciated abroad because of its detailed exposition of the positive aspects of the ideals and disciplines inculcated by the Vedas, Upanishads, Laws, Epics, and individual teachers, whose doctrines too often have been presented abroad in their negative, ascetic, self-denying aspects. This history, replete with scholarly evidence and references to the sources, gives a more balanced and reasonable picture of the ethical heritage of the peoples of India and of their two thousand years of philosophical reflection on human nature and conduct, which constitutes one of mankind's most systematically developed funds of moral wisdom.

HERBERT W. SCHNEIDER

Claremont, California
October, 1962

A*

EDITOR'S PREFACE

I have confined my editing and revising as far as possible to matters of form and style to assist Western readers to grasp Dr Sharma's exposition with facility. Occasionally I have had to depart from this aim and suggest substantial textual changes. In such cases I have had the benefit of discussing the issues with the author directly, and he most often found himself in complete agreement with the suggestions. Where he did not, the text was allowed to stand as he wrote it. It should be perfectly clear that my position as editor and revisor implies neither responsibility for authorship nor responsibility for the views propounded or implied in the work.

Thanks are due to the Research and Advisory Committee of Western Washington State College, especially to its chairman, Dr Herbert C. Taylor, Jr., and its secretary, Mrs Jane Clark, for their assistance in getting the manuscript ready for printing. Special thanks are also due to my secretary, Mrs Judith Olson, without whose patient help the publication of this work would have been long delayed.

STANLEY M. DAUGERT

Western Washington State College
Bellingham, Washington

FOREWORD

I am delighted to present *Ethical Philosophies of India* to Westerners in general and to those interested in the comparative study of Indian and Western ethics and philosophy, in particular. This work is an attempt to bring out the ethical and the humanistic elements in Indian philosophy and to lay emphasis on the special characteristics of Indian ethics. These ethics make Indian philosophy a synthesis of spiritual insight into the fundamental unity of the cosmos and encourage a practical pluralistic outlook with regard to the social and ethical aspects of human life. Up to the present, Indian philosophy, particularly the Upaniṣadic philosophy, has been regarded as chiefly monistic to the extent of repudiating the diversity of the mundane material environment in which a normal individual lives, moves and has his being. That is the reason why almost all scholars of Indian philosophy, Indian and Western, have taken it for granted that the ideology of the Upaniṣads is opposed to Vedic thought and culture, and represents a revolt against the ritualism of the Veda.

This mistaken notion, which is almost universal, and which has taken firm root among the scholars of Indology and Indian philosophy, has arisen because of neglect on the part of writers towards the Brāhmaṇa Granthas, or Brāhmaṇas, which form an integral part of Vedic literature. It is a pity that we find much literature in English, Hindi, Sanskrit and other languages on the hymns, or Mantras, and on the Upaniṣads, but not so much on the Brāhmaṇas, which are not only ritualistic injunctions, but philosophical speculations and analytic explanations of the Vedic ideas and terminology. Without a dispassionate study of the Brāhmaṇas the fallacy of regarding Upaniṣadic thought as a revolt against Vedic philosophy cannot be detected. It is only after the study of the Brāhmaṇas that one realizes that this omission on the part of the students of Indian thought and culture has been responsible for the apparent contradictions in the presentation of Indian philosophy, which in fact is a harmonious evolution and an organic whole that gives proper place to the pluralistic nature of the physical universe and to spiritual oneness; to secular ethics and to the transcendental state of self-realization and hence to the relative realism present in the manifested spatio-temporal world and to mysticism, which reveals to the individual the nature of the invisible unity underlying the visible diversity.

But without the missing link available in the Brāhmaṇic literature, the attempt to connect Vedic thought and Upaniṣadic monism would be like cutting off the trunk of the human body and attempting to join the head with its legs. Mistaken conclusions with regard to the relation of the Vedic hymns to the Upaniṣadic utterances are drawn even by eminent scholars and sincere students of Indian philosophy. For instance, H. Zimmer has remarked,

'The philosophical dialogues of the Upaniṣads indicate that during the eighth century BC a critical shift of weight from outer universe and tangible spheres of the body to the inner and the intangible was carrying the dangerous implications of this direction of the mind to their logical conclusion. A process of withdrawal from the normally known world was taking place. The powers of the macrocosm and corresponding faculties of the microcosm were being generally devaluated and left behind; and with such fearlessness that the whole religious system of the previous period was being placed in peril of collapse.'[1]

This generalization is contrary to the historical facts, for the Upaniṣads, and even the orthodox systems of Indian philosophy, earnestly adopted Vedic thought and recognized the Vedas as an authority. They were so recognized not on blind faith but because of their comprehensive knowledge and their scientific exposition of the nature of the physical universe. The Vedic religion never collapsed, but it was strengthened by the Upaniṣads as well as by the six orthodox systems of Indian philosophy. The Upaniṣads do not preach 'the process of withdrawal from the normally known world', but attempt to emphasize the basic unity of the manifested plurality of the spatio-temporal order of the cosmos. This fact becomes evident when we study Indian philosophy with reference to its

[1] Heinrich Zimmer in *Philosophies of India* (edited by Joseph Campbell), second impression, p. 8.

ethical implications and when we do not overlook the explanations given in the Brāhmaṇas. This book is an attempt to bring out the ethical aspect of Indian philosophy right from Vedic times to the contemporary period without overlooking the Brāhamaṇic interpretations.

The reader will find the arrangement of the book purposive, and chronological with the exception of two chapters. The aim of this arrangement is to bring home to readers that Indian ethics, in keeping with the spirit of Indian philosophy, does not divorce theory from practice. On the contrary, it tries to bring about a synthesis of the ideal and the practical aspects of human life. The quintessence of Indian philosophy is Samadarśana, the realization of the oneness of ultimate reality, and Viṣamarvarttana, the differentiation of behavioural response to the varied situations in keeping with ethical ideals. It is in this sense that insight into the spiritual unity of all men and recognition of different duties allotted to men in accordance with their different bents and different professions and occupations are both essential in grasping the import of Indian ethics. The moment we lose sight of these two aspects of Indian philosophy we are apt to misunderstand it and call it either abstract, or superstitious and dogmatic. I have tried to clarify certain ethical notions inherent in Indian philosophy and have also commented upon the evil consequences of the neglect of the real significance of the Vedic and the Upaniṣadic conceptions.

It is difficult to do justice to this almost overwhelming subject in a small book, but I have tried to include as many ethical problems as possible. Since it is the first attempt to present Indian ethics right from the Vedic age to the contemporary period, and since the subject is too vast and the temptation of elaboration is always present, I hope to be excused if I overlook some aspects of Indian ethics especially with reference to contemporary ethics. In spite of these shortcomings I trust this book will serve its purpose of giving readers an insight into the ethical philosophies of India.

If my work provokes the critical interest of scholars, philosophers and intellectual leaders, I would feel amply awarded. If it should be received as a contribution to the evergrowing synthesis between Eastern and Western thought and culture, I would be even more pleased.

It is a pleasure to express my gratitude to persons who have been sources of inspiration and help in writing and publishing this book. I thank His Excellency, Bharat Ratna, Dr Radhakrishnan, the President of the Indian Union, who has been kind enough to go through a few pages of the manuscript and to encourage me in this venture. I am highly obliged to Padma Bhushan, Shri G. C. Chatterjee, the eminent educator of India, whose blessings and inspiration have been responsible for the completion of this book and to whom it is dedicated. His life and yeoman's work will always remain a source of encouragement and inspiration to those who want to dedicate their lives to the noble causes of education and nation-building.

My sincere thanks are due to my wife Mrs Bhagya Sharma, M.A., who like an ideal better-half has helped me in fairing out this book in her own handwriting and has given me most valuable suggestions. I am also obliged to her younger sister, Miss Kailash Manuja, M.A. (Final), who has aided us both in preparing the manuscript for the press.

I am much obliged to Shri Atam Prakash Mehta, M.A., LL.B., Varanasi (U.P.) who discussed with me various important topics concerning contemporary Indian ethics and aided me in arriving at some plausible conclusions. I also acknowledge my thanks to Shri Krishna Chandra Sharma, the son of the late Pandit Motilal Shastri of Jaipur, the great but little known oriental scholar, philosopher and thinker of contemporary India. It was due to the generosity of Shri Krishna Chandra Sharma that I had access to the works of the late Panditji. I am obliged to Dr S. Basu, Reader in Philosophy, B.H.U., Varanas, for her help in reading proofs of the book. I am also highly obliged to Shri S. N. Chatusvedi for his valuable guidance and to Miss Ruth M. Weil of Long Beach, California, for her valuable suggestions. My thanks are also due to Mrs Suzanna Neff for her help in preparing the index. I am grateful to Dr Max H. Fisch, Chairman of the Department of Philosophy, University of Illinois, for encouraging and inspiring me in my academic pursuits. I am particularly thankful to Dr Elizabeth P. Lam, Executive Associate of the Committee of International Exchange of Persons, for philosophical discussions and exchanges of ideas which helped me in improving this book. The completion of this book would not have been satisfactory without the academic facilities provided for me by Dr Anne G. Pannell, President of Sweet Briar College, Dr William F. Quillian, President of Randolf-Macon Women's College, Dr D. F. Anthony, Director of Asian Studies, and Dr O. W. Wake, President of Lynchburg College, Lynchburg, Virginia. I wish also to express my gratitude to the Committee on International Exchange of Persons, The Conference Board of Associated Research Councils, Washington, D.C., for the same reason. Last but not least, I must sincerely thank Dr Stanley M. Daugert for his most valuable help in editing and revising this book. But for him this book would not have appeared in its present form. This philosopher is certainly a bridge between USA and India.

I. C. SHARMA

Claremont, California
September 5, 1963

CONTENTS

CHAPTER I

INTRODUCTION

Need for the Study of Ethics

The layman is undoubtedly familiar with the words 'morals' and 'ethics' but he seldom conjectures whether there can be any systematic study of the subject which can be designated a science in the sense in which physics, chemistry, geology and botany are understood to be sciences. He cannot imagine how much simple matters as the propriety of duty and the desirability of happiness could provoke the greatest and the wisest thinkers to the extent of establishing contending schools of ethics. The critical examination of these schools might lead him to conclude that if morality is a controversy and intellectual quibble, it would be better to lead a normal, peaceful life than to inquire into the nature of the so-called ethical theories propounded by clever philosophers.

Such a conclusion, however, would be uncalled for and inconsistent because reflection on such a simple question as 'What is good?' lands us in the domains of sociology, psychology, economics, political science, religion, and even of logic and metaphysics. A layman might remark that 'pleasure is good' or 'the prosperity of a nation is good' without knowing that these two answers imply psychological and economic interpretations of 'good' respectively. The gravity of the problem arises when we equate pleasure or prosperity with good. It may be agreed that pleasure is one of the good things of life and so is prosperity. But no man with a sane head on his shoulders would assert that good is nothing but pleasure or that prosperity is the definition of 'good'. Similarly from the point of view of political science, adherence to a constitution and the laws of a state is good. At the time of Plato and Aristotle a good man or an ethical man was one who was a good citizen. From the point of view of religion, a good life is the life of faith in God and the resignation of all actions without any expectation of fruit to God. But such a view of good comes into obvious conflict with political and sociological notions of good.

If a man were to resign all his actions to God with full faith in His Divinity or Grace, he might not be able to achieve the political good either for himself or for the state to which he belongs. Religion and politics may have been interrelated in the Middle Ages in Europe, but in the contemporary age of geophysical discoveries, Sputniks and spaceships, not only is a secular attitude toward politics necessary, but it is unavoidable. At the most a politician can advocate humanism as an acceptable philosophy of life. Thus the conflict between the religious notion of good and the political notion of it is bound to cause confusion and misunderstanding.

Logic tells us that a definition ought to be based on the most essential attributes of a thing, namely, its genus, that is, a class which is larger than the term to be defined, and which includes the latter plus the differentia or the distinguishing characteristic of the term to be defined. This characteristic marks off the term to be defined from its genus. For example, the term 'man' may be defined by referring to the term 'animal', which is the genus of the term man, and to rationality, which is the differentia, as it differentiates the term 'man' from its genus, the term 'animal'. Thus the definition of man as 'a rational animal'. If we apply these rules of definition to the term 'good', we shall have to agree with G. E. Moore in holding that good is indefinable and that 'good is good and nothing else'. For good is an elementary entity, an ultimate mode, beyond which and larger than which there is no genus. That is why when we once say that 'pleasure is good' we cannot interchange the subject and the predicate of this proposition so as to affirm that 'good is (nothing but) pleasure'.

Such complications with regard to the definition of the word good have been responsible for the controversial ethical theories of hedonism and rationalism. When only one of the substantives to which the term good is applied is equated with good, there arises the fallacy G. E. Moore has called the naturalistic fallacy. However far-fetched the committal of this fallacy might have been regarded by Moore, it is a fact that such a fallacy does occur and has been the cause of great confusion in the domain of moral science. The very occurrence of these complications and the inability of common sense to solve such problems compel us to subject moral problems to scientific study.

We have seen so far that the notion of good, which is crucial to morality involves or rather presupposes the background of psychology, economics, political science, religion and logic. Since this fact is ignored or overlooked by the man in the street, he considers morality a matter of common sense. Similarly a naïve moralist forgets that if good is taken as an end of human conduct, part of the reason is that human life is one of the realities in the infinite cosmos and this end would have no meaning if it were not in harmony with the ultimate reality. Not only the term 'good', but the terms 'truth 'and 'beauty' also have special connotations, and lose their significance without reference to their metaphysical background. Thus from the theoretical point of view it is essential to study the problem of ethics in a systematic and scientific manner.

Now let us take the practical aspect of the need to study ethics. It may be urged that if ethics is a theoretical study of moral problems, if it only speculates and weighs the pros and cons of an act in the balance of reason and ultimately declares it as right or wrong, good or evil, such a declaration might not have any practical value for the man in the street. Many scholars, literary figures and poets have decried the theoretical study of ethics and even of human nature, because such a study is nothing but 'a mighty bloodless substitute for life'.[1] It is said that experience alone can enrich the ethical aspect of the human mind and that no amount of theoretical knowledge can possibly raise man's ethical standard. Wordsworth has aptly remarked that:

> One impulse from a vernal wood,
> May teach you more of man,
> Of moral evil and of good,
> Than all the sages can.

But reflection on this problem would reveal that even the theoretical aspect of ethics is not only necessary for the practical application of morality to life, but it is an unavoidable condition. Socrates declared long ago that 'virtue is a kind of knowledge'. What he was trying to point out was that no one could be moral by accident or without true knowledge of the nature of a moral act. In Jaina ethics, which is known to be the practical application of non-violence as the highest virtue, it has been

[1] R. L. Stevenson, 'An Apology for Idlers'.

stated that 'knowledge must precede compassion[1]'. These statements are themselves enough to indicate that knowledge of virtue is the very foundation of the practice of virtue. As a matter of fact man's uniqueness as an ethical being is entirely due to the fact that man has the knowledge and the power of discrimination between right and wrong, good and evil. Had man been ignorant of the nature of morality and moral distinctions his behaviour would have been on the same level as that of animals.

Logic, ethics, and aesthetics with their ideals of truth, goodness, and beauty, or Satyam, Shivam, and Sundaram, are the prerogative of man and mark him off from the lower animals who are absolutely ignorant of these ideals and hence need not make efforts to conform to them. Thus the superiority of man over animal lies in living on a higher plane, where he apprehends truth, realizes good, and creates beauty or harmony. A philosophical system that falls short of this threefold realization of human nature cannot be regarded as humanly useful. Since unlike the philosophic development in the West Indian systems took a practical turn, the ideals of truth, beauty, and goodness were regarded as not mere ideals, but actual states of existence to be realized by the aspirant in his practical life. But it should be remembered that, of course, all the theories of Western philosophy, with the possible exception of pragmatism have not been preached and practised in the manner in which the followers of the Indian schools like Jainism, Buddhism, Sāṁkhya, Yoga and Vedānta have preached and practised their philosophies. The intuitive experience in this direction had led the Indian philosophers to the conclusion that ultimately the state of existence which is attained by the aspirant after the spiritual discipline is the state of co-existence and merger of these three ideals in a harmonious manner. This is the state called Jivanmukti, or liberation, which is not eschatological, but of this earth earthy. Jivanmukti undoubtedly is the stepping stone to Videha Mukti, or final liberation, which is the state of Ananta Jñāna, infinite knowledge, Ananta Vīrya, infinite power and Ananta Sukha, infinite bliss.

Thus the theoretical discussion of ethical problems is the very foundation of their application in practical life. Such a discussion is not only necessary from the academic point of view in

[1] Pahdhamam Nāṇam Tao Dayā, *Daśavaikālika Sūtra*, X.

order to decide as to which theory of the moral standard is preferable, but modern conditions of life also warrant that the study of ethics is a most important subject. The modern age is an age of transition and of astonishing contrasts. Man today has reached heights of civilization and culture that he never reached before in the history of human civilization. His scientific progress has given him almost unlimited power to control nature, even to the extent of making successful attempts to cross space and to reach the other planets in the universe. This power and marvellous success have to a great extent led man astray. The result is that he has neglected the ethical aspect of life.

Science has benefited man in developing his material resources, but at the same time it has deprived him of his spiritual and ethical development. The invention of machines, industrialization and complex technology have given rise to a commercial civilization which puts a premium on wealth over finer human values and sentiments. A man in the village who is untouched by this civilization even today values love and affection more than wealth, but the urban population, particularly in the advanced countries of the world, suffers from economic prejudice even when it has to deal with human problems. We may provide here an illustration cited by a Western thinker. Professor W. E. Hocking reports a Chinese writer recently accusing Western Civilization of hypocrisy in the matter of the 'sacred' worth of the individual. This writer noted that while Westerners go to the Orient and talk about the sacred rights of individuals, nevertheless street-car companies in America, which kill a statistical number of individuals per year, have been 'known to decline to install safety-fenders, on the ground that the cost of the fenders would be greater than the annual indemnities for lost life and limbs'.[1] This example has been cited here to point out the negligibility of the ethical aspect of life in economic civilization. We shall refer to it again.

Western civilization in laying more emphasis on material progress, has brought about a disparity between the theory and the practice of philosophy, and has kept science apart from religion, and metaphysics from ethics. This dualistic attitude of the West has been responsible for the social crises and political conflicts that have disrupted the normal life of individuals and have brought man to the brink of committing atomic suicide. In spite

[1] C. A. Moore (Ed.), *Philosophy East and West*, p. 8.

of man's mastery over nature, and in spite of the fact that his dreams of interplanetary travels are about to come true, the common man of the world is not at peace. Doubt, despondency and fear are rife in the world today. The most progressive countries are in the greatest danger of meeting doom if war breaks out. In the face of these circumstances the need of the hour is the spiritual regeneration of human society. There is no doubt that the ethical ideals laid down by Indian sages thousands of years ago are universal standards that can be followed at all times, and are a lasting cure for the evils which have crept into modern society. This is true because these ideals were never regarded as mere theories of morality, but as modes of spiritual life by adopting which the individual and society could develop in a harmonious manner.

But unfortunately even in India, where these sages flourished and practised the spiritual life, this rich philosophy, which was a synthesis of the material and the spiritual, of the mundane and the theological aspects of life, took a one-sided turn due to some unforeseen and unavoidable historical vicissitudes; and there appeared a gap between the theory and practice of the ideals.

Indian philosophy originally accepted the propagation and, practice of the four Puruṣārthas, or the ends of life, namely, Artha, the economic end; Kama, the emotional end; Dharma, the ethical end; and Mokṣa, the spiritual end. As we shall see in the sequel, these four ends of life are respectively associated with the physical, mental, intellectual and spiritual perfection of the individual and of society. But as the time passed and the various systems of Indian philosophy arose, this integrated view of life was neglected. Some systems laid emphasis on the economic and emotional aspects of life, whereas others emphasized the ethical and the spiritual aspects. Asceticism was favoured by those who bade a good-bye to all the ends of life except the spiritual. Thus the partial emphasis on one or two of the four ends of life brought about confusion amounting to conflict between the various schools of philosophy in India. It is due to that confusion that in present-day India we find human values neglected by the majority. Forms and ceremonials have taken the place of religion, and selfishness has suppressed the altruistic feeling which was the special feature of Indian culture. Thus we find that in East as well as in West true ethical life is the need of the hour. This need can be met only when disinterested research in the field of ethics is carried out. The aim of the present work is to unfold the real meaning of Indian ethics. The understanding of every subject requires a critical analysis and pragmatic interpretation in the modern age of rationalism and science. Hence our study of Indian philosophy should be critical as well as comparative.

However, before giving a critical analysis of the ethical philosophy of the great Indian nation from Vedic times to the present day it is necessary for us to explain the nature and the scope of ethics in a general way. It will be admitted that ethics as a separate subject is undoubtedly the product of Western philosophy. It had its origin in ancient Greece. It is a fact that in India ethics was always regarded as part of philosophy and religion, and hence it was never thought necessary to study it separately. This does not mean, however, that Indian philosophy was ever deprived of ethics. On the contrary, we shall find that each and every system of Indian philosophy is replete with ethical attitudes and regards the highest moral life as the only way to attain spiritual perfection, which has always been regarded as the *summum bonum*, or supreme good of life. But for our present purpose we shall have to sort out the ethical aspect of Indian philosophy from its other aspects. Before doing this, we shall have to define ethics from the Western point of view.

First let us clarify the relation of ethics to philosophy. Like all the other sciences, ethics has a limited field of study. Its subject matter is human behaviour and its propriety. In other words it takes into consideration the entire social behaviour of man, raises questions about it and also attempts to answer those questions. Ethics tells us what type of behaviour or conduct can be regarded as moral, and what type of conduct is immoral. It discriminates between the right and the wrong and the good and the evil, and points out what is the supreme good towards which all our life is to be directed. In brief, ethics can be conveniently defined as the study of the ultimate end or the ideal involved in human life. From this point of view, it can be said that ethics is the philosophy of life.

From the Western point of view, philosophy means the love of wisdom. From the Indian point of view, philosophy means realization or experience or perception (Darśana). Thus a philosopher is one who knows reality or who intuits reality. In other words, philosophy's purpose is to understand the fundamental basis of the universe and to explain the meaning and purpose of human life. Philosophy thus concerns itself with the knowledge of the universe and with the purpose of human life. The universal or the theoretical aspect of philosophy is metaphysics, and the practical or the purposive aspect is practical philosophy. Practical philosophy includes the three normative sciences—logic, aesthetics, and ethics, which correspond to cognition, affection and conation, the three aspects of human experience. The purpose of logic is to tell us the ideal of cognition or thinking; aesthetics explains to us the standard of feeling; and ethics propounds the ideal of conduct or action. Thus it is evident that logic, aesthetics and ethics respectively propound truth, beauty and goodness as the subject-matter of their study.

The brief analysis given above makes it clear that ethics is concerned with human life and that it judges human behaviour from the normative point of view. That is why various definitions of ethics have been formulated by various thinkers. Mackenzie points out that 'Ethics is a general study of the ideal involved in human life'. According to Rashdall, 'Ethics is that theory of good and evil which has human well being as its goal'. Dewey says that 'The subject-matter of ethics is to point out what is right and good in conduct'. In like manner, Moore considers supreme good as the subject-matter of ethics.

These definitions of ethics are more or less expressive of the same purpose. All of them indicate that the subject-matter of ethics is the social behaviour of man, judged from the point of view of right and wrong and good and evil. When Mackenzie regards ethics as a study of the ideal or the end involved in human life, he means to say that it studies human behaviour from the point of view of right and wrong and good and evil. Similarly when Rashdall considers ethics as the theory of good and evil with a view to establishing human well-being as the ultimate end of life, he also means to establish that ethics is a normative study of human behaviour. Dewey as well as Moore clearly points out that right and good are the subject-matter of ethics. These explanations clearly suggest that ethics is concerned with the norms of human social behaviour.

Of course, it is very difficult to define ethics, for while giving its definition, we have to establish its limitations. No subject or science can be restricted and reduced to a water-tight compartment. All the sciences overlap one another and their frontiers cannot be strictly demarcated. Especially in the case of ethics, which is concerned with the propriety of human conduct, it is most difficult to draw the lines of demarcation, because behaviour is so vast that it can be studied by various sciences from various points of view. In spite of this, it can be said that ethics is that study of human behaviour which propounds the supreme good or the *summum bonum* of human life, and which formulates the judgments of right and wrong and good and evil. In order to make this definition more explicit, it would be desirable to explain the words 'right', 'good', and 'science' respectively.

The word right is undoubtedly related to character. This word is similar to the Greek word *ethos*, which also means character. Similarly the term 'moral philosophy', which is a synonym of 'ethics', is based on the Latin word *mores*, meaning habits or customs. Thus from the point of view of lexicography, ethics is that science which is concerned with moral behaviour or with the right and wrong and good and evil of human behaviour. Ethics propounds those principles which make our conduct moral. This becomes clearer when we explain the derivation of the words right and good.

The word right is derived from the Latin word *rectus*, which literally means 'straight' or 'according to rule'. Thus when we define ethics as the science of the rightness of conduct, what we mean is that it is concerned with those principles or rules which make our conduct right or straight. The analysis of the word right explains one aspect of ethics. Rules are the means, and wherever there are means, there must be an end or goal as well. If right is the means of conduct, the question arises what should be its end. We get the answer to this question only when we analyse the word good, which is derived from the German word, *gut*. *Gut* means anything useful or serviceable for some end or purpose. When we say that such and such school is good, what we actually mean is that it is useful for the education of children. In our daily life we do not only interpret good as something which is useful for some end, rather we mean by it the end or the goal itself. We consider many actions as good because they are the various aims of our life. If we accept this meaning of the word good, and regard ethics as the science of good conduct, we arrive at the conclusion that ethics is concerned with the end or goal of life. As we know, in our life and in the lives of others there are numberless things that can be regarded as good. Ethics as a science is not concerned with the particular goals of the individuals. On the contrary, it is concerned with that supreme goal or the ultimate end with reference to which the entire life of individuals is directed, the *summum bonum*. In Western ethics, this supreme good has been referred to variously by various thinkers. Rationalism takes reason to be the supreme good. Hedonism regards happiness, and perfectionism considers self-realization as the supreme good. As we shall see, almost all systems of Indian philosophy agree with regard to the nature of the supreme good, because they all consider Mokṣa or liberation as the *summum bonum*. Only the Cārvāka system of Indian philosophy agrees with Hedonism in accepting happiness as the end of life. Thus with reference to the above explanation of the words right and good, we arrive at the conclusion that the subject matter of ethics is the ultimate end or the supreme good of human life. If the ideal of ethics is the ultimate good and if this good is regarded as the basis of human behaviour, it is evident that ethics is a normative science of conduct.

This definition of ethics will remain incomplete unless and until we explain the nature of normative science. A science may be conveniently defined as a systematic, methodical and exhaustive knowledge of a subject. It is in this sense that physics, chemistry, biology, and botany are regarded as the sciences of various subjects. Similarly, logic, economics, sociology, and so on are sciences because they are all systematic, methodical and exhaustive studies of various subjects. Sciences, however, have been classified into two main groups, namely, (1) naturalistic or positive sciences; and (2) normative sciences. Naturalistic or positive science is that science which explains a subject as it is. It does not concern itself with the propriety or desirability of the subject, and does not have any ideal or norm so as to judge the desirability or undesirability of the facts. It is a factual description indifferent to human weal and woe. It observes facts, classifies those facts and propounds the natural laws about those facts. For example, botany is a naturalistic or a descriptive science of plants. Its main purpose is to observe various kinds of plants, to describe and classify them, and to propound the laws which are responsible for their birth, growth and decay. Thus botany is a descriptive science of the nature of plants. The judgments passed in a naturalistic or a positive science are always descriptive judgments. On the contrary, normative science is that science which adopts some standard or norm and pronounces the judgments of propriety or appreciation about its subject-matter. Whereas descriptive science tells us how a particular object is, normative science pronounces how something ought to be. In normative sciences we are always concerned with appreciative judgments, whereas in the natural sciences we are concerned with descriptive judgments. For example, logic is a normative science of thought which tells us what our thought must be to be valid, true or consistent. Thus when we say that ethics is the normative science of conduct, what we mean is that it is concerned with the appreciative judgments of conduct. When we say that ethics deals with the right and wrong and the good and evil of conduct, what we mean is that it gives appreciative judgments of conduct.

This distinction between the naturalistic and the normative sciences can be expressed in a different manner. Naturalistic or descriptive science has the special feature of being a systematic description of facts. Thus such a science can be regarded as factual or phenomenal science and its judgment can be called the factual judgment. On the contrary, normative science is not concerned with the description of the facts but with the values of the facts. Thus the judgments passed in a normative science are value judgments. Hence such a science is called the science of values and a descriptive science is known as the science of facts. On the basis of the classification of the sciences given above we can say that ethics is the science of values, and that its judgments are appreciative judgments or judgments of value. Ethics evaluates human conduct and arrives at the conclusion that good conduct is an intrinsic value.

In order to make the definition of ethics still more explicit and to demarcate its scope and subject-matter, it is necessary to distinguish between the nature of science and art, and decide whether ethics is one or the other. In Western ethics this question has special significance because ethics is concerned with conduct or behaviour, and conduct cannot be limited only to theoretical investigation. Logic may be an abstract theoretical and formal science of thought, but ethics is concerned with the practical life of the individual, and it can never remain a formal or merely theoretical study. That is why the question arises whether good behaviour is an art that may be more or less developed in different individuals, or a body of knowledge whose study might automatically make an individual moral and virtuous. If one individual is considered to be more moral than the other because he has greater skill in being moral, it would mean that ethics is a kind of art.

In giving a brief explanation of the word science we remarked that science was an organized knowledge of a subject. The purpose of science is to propound an explicit, consistent and orderly knowledge of a subject. In other words, it aims at giving us understanding or knowledge. Thus the specialty of science consists in knowing. On the contrary, art is an organized practice or skill and its main concern is with practical application. If science specializes in knowing, art specializes in doing. This difference between science and art indicates that the science of a subject and the art of it may not always co-exist in one person. It is possible for a person to be a scholar of science and yet be ignorant of the art of that very subject. For example, a professor of physics may have theoretical knowledge of the principles of swimming, yet he may not be able to swim himself. If he unluckily falls into a river he may be drowned. On the contrary, an illiterate villager who has never heard of the principles of swimming may be a very good swimmer. Thus science and art may be regarded as separable aspects of life, although they can go together. Even in the sciences which are mainly concerned with practical life, these two aspects may not be correlative. For example, a student of medicine who attains first place in an examination of medical science may not prove to be a successful physician. On the contrary, a student who obtains the lowest rank in the said examination may prove to be a very successful physician. The same is the case in training teachers. Thus we can say that there is no science the theoretical knowledge of which necessarily leads to the practical skill of the subject concerned. In other words a practical skill does not depend on pure science. This difference between science and art compels us to declare that ethics is not an art. The student of ethics need not necessarily become a moralist or a saint. On the contrary, a moralist or a saint who has not studied ethics theoretically may be able to guide the students of ethics in the practice of virtue.

Moreover, ethics can never be regarded as merely an art because conduct depends upon goodwill and not upon any kind of skill. To some extent logic may be concerned with the skill of arguing. Similarly aesthetics, which is closely connected with the fine arts, may also have its practical methods. But since ethics is partly based on the attitude of will, it is absolutely a different kind of science resting on different criteria. An ethical man is not one who *can* act morally, but he is a person who actually does act morally and is inspired by goodwill. On the contrary, a good thinker is one who can think correctly, even though he may not be doing so in his practical life. In the same manner, a good artist is one who has skill in presenting a particular art, even though he may not always be engaged in doing so.

Mackenzie in solving this problem has pointed out that ethics can never be regarded as an art because virtue has two such special features that are not at all significant in art. First of all, virtue implies activity. We cannot regard a man virtuous as long as he is not actually engaged in virtuous activity. A moral person is not one who knows morality, but one who actually practises it. In the case of an art the possession of skill is more important than the actual activity. In the words of Mackenzie: 'A good painter is one who can paint beautifully; a good man is not one who can, but who does, act rightly. The good painter is good when he is asleep or on a journey, or when, for any other reason, he is not employed in his art; the good man is not good when asleep or on a journey, unless when it is good to sleep or to go on a journey. Goodness is not a capacity or potentiality but an activity.'[1]

Socrates considered virtue a kind of knowledge. What he appears to have meant was that knowledge consisted in the practical applicability of virtue because no one could be virtuous if he were ignorant of the nature of virtue. However, we cannot say that the knowledge of virtue is enough to make a man moral. That is why Aristotle pointed out that 'virtue is a kind of habit'. It is a habit of right choice. In other words, virtue is a synthesis of knowledge and habit, consciousness and activity, thought as well as will. That is why a Sanskrit verse points out that an imperfect morality is one-sided. The verse is as follows:

[1] J. S. Mackenzie, *A Manual of Ethics*, Sixth Edition, pp. 8–9.

Jānāmi dharmaṁ na ca me pravṛitti;
Jānāmyadharmaṁ na ca me nivṛitti.

I know virtue but I am not practising it;
I know vice but I am not free from it.

This verse indicates that virtue or morality is not merely concerned with knowledge, but is a behavioural activity. Even in art skill is related to activity, but it is not entirely dependent on activity. Thus ethics is different from an art.

The second characteristic of virtue Mackenzie notes is the attitude of will. A virtuous or moral act is an act which has been chosen voluntarily. If the choice of an act is not based on goodwill, it cannot be regarded as moral or virtuous. There is no doubt that goodwill is central to morality. Kant has remarked, 'There is nothing good in the world and even out of it, that can be regarded good without qualification, but goodwill . . . a good will is good not because of what it performs or effects, not by its aptness for the attainment of some proposed end, but simply by virtue of the volition'. A wicked and evil person can become a good artist; but no one can become a good artist if he has simply a strong inclination towards good behaviour and has always been inspired by goodwill. In art the final judgment is passed on the basis of the skill. In morality an action is judged largely on the basis of volition and intention. This discussion indicates that there cannot be any art of conduct and that ethics can never be regarded as an art. It is undoubtedly a science, but a science whose practice or practical application heavily depends upon a certain indispensable kind of volition.

Ethics and other Sciences

We have said that ethics is a special kind of science, and that it has a normative point of view. Because this science is concerned with human behaviour, and since behaviour is almost the whole of human experience, the subject of ethics is so vast that it touches the boundaries of various branches of knowledge. Most other sciences are concerned only with one particular aspect of human experience, but conduct or behaviour being almost the whole of the human experience makes the scope of ethics very wide. If ethics is defined as a science, it should not be regarded as such from a narrow point of view. As a matter of fact ethics is the philosophy of human conduct, a philosophy related to all the other branches of knowledge dealing with human experience and even with nature. There are some sciences which support ethics and still others which are based on ethics. We shall, therefore, explain the relation of ethics to other sciences in some detail.

Ethics and Physics

Physics is concerned with the nature of matter and the statement of relations ('laws') governing the material world. At first sight one may say that ethics has nothing to do with physics, and that even if there is any relation between the two it must be very remote. In stating the relation between ethics and physics, Mackenzie has remarked, 'Of course, ethics is indirectly related to physical science, inasmuch as a knowledge of physical laws enables us to predict more accurately and certainly than we should otherwise be able to do, what the effect of various kinds of conduct will be. But this knowledge affects only the details of conduct, not the general principles by which our conduct is guided. A wise man in modern times will be less afraid of the sea and the stars, and more afraid of foul air and impure water than a man of similar wisdom in ancient times.'[1] But the progress made in the physical sciences and particularly in the field of astro-physics in very recent times undoubtedly affects the behaviour and morality of man. Because of far-reaching research in the field of physical science today man has amassed such an unlimited power that, were he to use it, might lead to the complete destruction of life on this planet. Atom bombs and hydrogen bombs, the product of physical science, do raise ethical problems. If ethics is neglected, and if the inventions of physical science have nothing to do with moral principles, it is likely that scientific progress might put an end to human civilization and culture. It is evident that physical science cannot proceed without being interested in human weal or woe, and the indifference of physics to morality can prove dangerous to human interests. From our point of view, then, the relation of ethics and physics is so intimate that the neglect of this relation might lead to destruction.

Besides this, physical causation has something to do with ethics. 'Like causes like', but the freedom of the will is an excep-

[1] *Op. cit.*, p. 60.

tion to this law of physical causation. Free will is capable of bringing about changes in the physical world even though will itself is not a physical phenomenon. Thus a non-physical cause can produce an effect in the physical world. Freedom of the will violates the law of physical causation. In order to remove this conflict between ethics and physics it is necessary that both sciences should be closely connected. It is fair to say that physical science helps us in understanding that environment in which we carry on moral effort.

Ethics and Biology

Biology is a natural science, and it aims at describing the nature of life or the living process. Because conduct is the activity of living beings, it is evident that the relation of ethics to biology must be more intimate than the relation of ethics to physics or chemistry. But this does not mean that these two sciences are closely connected. There are various biological and physiological urges of man, and these urges do influence his moral life. For example, the sex instinct of man gives rise to various moral problems. It is with a view to solving such problems that society founded the system of marriage, but this relation of ethics and biology is remote and indirect.

The unprecedented progress in the field of biology during the last century, and the changes that have taken place in this field have great ethical significance. The most important theory that has influenced ethics is the theory of evolution. According to Darwin's theory, man evolved from a mono-celled amoeba to his present complicated individuality, and during a long course of evolution the various tendencies and patterns of complicated behaviour man has acquired are nothing but the means of fulfilling his biological needs. Some scholars are of the opinion that the distinction between good and evil is also related to the evolution of life. Good is that which promotes life and bad is that which hinders it. According to these thinkers, even the lower animals have ethical standards. This alone proves that the theory of the evolution of life has influenced ethics greatly.

Although biology is related to ethics, it can be said that the problems of both these sciences are similar but not the same. We cannot say that the behaviour of the lower animals is moral or ethical. If life-promoting behaviour or activity were to be regarded as moral, then ethics would be reduced to a natural science. It is an error to base ethics solely on biology. Biology is a natural science, and ethics is a normative study of behaviour. Biology is concerned with all sorts of life including that of plant and animal, whereas ethics is concerned with that behaviour of man which can be regarded as right and wrong and good and evil.

Ethics and Psychology

The relation of ethics to psychology is most intimate. Psychology is a very old science originating during the time of Socrates, Plato, and Aristotle, but at the same time it is one of the youngest sciences because at the beginning of the twentieth century it left the parental roof of philosophy and joined the fold of natural sciences. Various definitions of psychology have been formulated by psychologists. According to one of them, psychology is the science of behaviour. Other definitions of psychology agree that the subject-matter of psychology is the activity or the behaviour of human individuals. We know that the subject-matter of ethics is also human behaviour. Thus the definition of psychology and its subject-matter indicate that the relation of psychology and ethics must be very close.

We can say that the relation of ethics and psychology is at least as close as that of logic and psychology, or of aesthetics and psychology. For the sake of simplification, the subject-matter of psychology is usually divided into the following three classes:

(1) Cognitive behaviour (knowing);
(2) Affective behaviour (feeling); and
(3) Conative behaviour (willing or acting).

When psychology asks the nature of cognition or thinking, we proceed to inquire how cognition or thinking takes place. Thus the cognitive aspect of psychology leads us to establish the normative science of thinking, and the aim of this normative science is to point out the consistency and to lay down the standards of thinking. Now this normative science is called logic. In the same manner the feeling aspect of psychology which explains to us the nature of the affective behaviour inspires us to know what our feelings ought to be. Thus this aspect of psychology leads us to propound aesthetics or the science of beauty. When psychology explains to us the nature of spontaneous and voluntary action, we are inspired to know what action we ought to take. Thus the naturalistic study of action gives rise to the science of ethics, which propounds the ultimate end of human conduct.

There is no doubt that logic, aesthetics and ethics are the three value sciences and that their origin is associated with psychology. From one point of view these three normative sciences borrow their subject-matter from the subject-matter of psychology. That is why the relation of these three sciences to psychology has special significance. However, this does not mean that these three normative sciences are merely branches of psychology. While referring to the relation of these three sciences to psychology it should be remembered that psychology is a naturalistic or a positive science, whereas logic, aesthetics and ethics are normative sciences. In spite of the fact that ethics and psychology are intimately related they are in principle distinct from each other. First of all, it can be pointed out that both of them have different points of view. Secondly, the scope of their study is also different. Psychology studies the whole of human behaviour; whereas ethics is concerned to study only the conative behaviour of man.

In spite of these differences, we can say that logic as well as aesthetics may exclude psychology, but ethics can never afford to sever its relations with psychology. A logician may exclude the psychological aspects of thought. In the same manner, a painter need not necessarily explain the emotional aspects of behaviour, but ethics, being concerned with practical life, can never exclude the descriptive science of human behaviour. Psychology tells us the nature of human behaviour, and the limitations of the conduct of man. Ethics points out what should be the aim of the conative aspect of human behaviour. We can never know the ideal of human conduct as long as we are not aware of the capabilities of human behaviour.

The above discussion makes it evident that there are several psychological descriptions which have intimate relations with ethical problems. Before laying down a standard of human conduct it is essential to know the nature of human behaviour. For example, ethical hedonism holds that the aim of human desire ought to be pleasure. Some ethical hedonists support this view on the basis of psychological hedonism. According to psychological hedonism the nature of our desires is such that they always aim at pleasure. The psychological study of desire, wish, will motive, intention, etc., is so important for ethics that some thinkers have included the study of these phenomena as an integral part of ethics. Thus we can say that ethics depends on psychology to a great extent for solving its problems.

Ethics and Sociology

Ethics is also very intimately related to sociology. The purpose of sociology is to study groups of people or communities. This science is of recent growth. Its scope is so wide and its problems are so uncertain that it is very difficult to lay down its frontiers. Very often the problems of political science and economics overlap those of sociology. It can be said, however, that sociology especially studies social institutions, rites, customs, and other social relations and traditions. Its point of view is mostly historical and naturalistic. There is no doubt that ethics as a normative science is distinct from sociology, but in spite of having different points of view their problems are similar. We shall find that customs, manners and the traditional rules of society are the oldest standards of conduct. History testifies that the logical development of moral conduct was of later growth. Therefore, before laying down an ethical standard for the whole human race, it is necessary to know the foundation of the social ethics of human beings right from the very dawn of human civilization. In other words, no theory of ethics can be regarded as final as long as a detailed study of social institutions is not carried out with the help of sociology. From this point of view, ethics depends upon sociology to a great extent.

Ethics and sociology are so intimately related that in almost every detailed book on ethics the sociological aspects of morality form a most important part of its study. But sociology, as is proper, has an almost exclusively social outlook; whereas the point of view of ethics, in spite of being general, is individualistic, because the ideals propounded by it are applicable to the individuals who form part of society. Sociology concerns itself with social customs and manners, but it is not an appreciative science in the sense of declaring the judgements of right and wrong and good and evil. Sociology is not a normative science and is essentially descriptive or naturalistic. The ideals propounded and subjected to criticism in ethics are the means of sublimating the life of each and every individual. If we analyse this purpose of ethics, we shall arrive at the conclusion that individual morality ultimately leads to social morality. The ethical imperative meant for the individual is undoubtedly inspired by social well-being.

The main problem of ethics is in fact a social problem. Ethics lays down duties for each and every individual and also propounds rights corresponding to these duties. These rights and duties represent the relation of individual and society and the responsibility of both. For example, J. S. Mill, a supporter of ethical hedonism, holds that the ideal of life should be the greatest happiness of the greatest number. The ethical hedonistic theory raises the problem of the proportion between the individual happiness and the social happiness. In the same manner T. H. Green's theory of self-realization makes an attempt to solve the problem of the relation of individual and society. When the student of ethics attempts to apply the theories of ethics to his life he faces the social problems of reward and punishment, of suicide, of capital punishment, of marriage, etc. The study of sociology is of great importance for solving these problems.

Ethics and Logic

So far we have been studying the relation of ethics to the natural or positive sciences. All these sciences are related to ethics because ethics gets indirect aid from them in solving some problems. Logic is a normative science which is most intimately related to ethics. It is sometimes held that logic is the basis of all the sciences, because it is the only science which lays down the fundamental principles of valid thought. Each and every science whether it is positive or normative, essentially must employ valid thinking and that is why it has to depend upon logic. But the relation of ethics to logic is so intimate that some thinkers have declared that moral acts must always be based on reason.

Socrates was the first person to draw the attention of philosophers towards ethics. As we have already mentioned, according to Socrates 'virtue is a kind of knowledge', and this knowledge is based on reasoning or intellectual experience. In the same manner, the Stoics believed that reason ought to be the ideal of life. Kant based his entire philosophy on the critical analysis of knowledge and regarded reason as important to ethics. According to him, a moral act is a consistent act. The inconsistent act is undesirable and immoral.

The above discussion indicates that logic and ethics have been closely related. But this intimate relation should not lead us to conclude that these two sciences are one and the same. Ethics is an independent science. Logic is also independent of ethics. Both sciences are undoubtedly normative, but logic is concerned with abstract principles of thought, whereas ethics deals with practical life. Logic is purely theoretical; whereas ethics has a practical outlook. Logic is formal; whereas ethics is concerned with the conscience and the goodwill of man.

Ethics and Aesthetics

Aesthetics is also a normative science, and has a normative outlook like ethics. The difference between the two is that ethics regards good as the supreme end of life, and aesthetics aims at beauty as the ultimate end. As we have already mentioned, logic, ethics, and aesthetics are respectively concerned with the ideals of truth, goodness, and beauty. Good, or supreme good, is the subject-matter of ethics and is related to beauty. A good will is sometimes referred to as 'beautiful will' and moral behaviour is sometimes called 'beautiful behaviour'. The Greek philosophers used the same term to express 'good' and 'beautiful'. In modern times when it is said that a person leads a beautiful life, what is actually meant is that such a person is sublime from the ethical point of view. But when we identify the 'good' and the 'beautiful', beauty does not stand for physical charm. Thus ethics and aesthetics are not related so closely that we may not differentiate between the good and the beautiful. We often experience that whatever appears beautiful is not conducive to moral or spiritual development. If by beauty we mean internal beauty, then the relation of aesthetics to ethics would be very intimate. In fact beauty is chiefly related to the emotional aspect of man; whereas good is related to the conative aspect of man.

The Indian tradition in ethics requires that in the case of a normal person emotion and duty should be balanced, but if there is a conflict between emotions and duty then from the moral point of view duty should be preferred to emotions. That is why an extremely ethical person may have to neglect beauty. The moral idea of Niṣkāma Karmayoga advocates the control of feelings and emotions and considers the disinterested act morally the best act. Thus it is likely that ethics and aesthetics may come into conflict with each other. This conflict is resolved when beauty is not considered as physical but is regarded as spiritual. We should never forget that the life of man is a synthesis of knowing, feeling and willing, and that for the all-round development of personality the three values of truth, goodness and beauty are equally important. The ethical theory of self-realization also expresses such a synthetic view of life. In the Bhagavadgītā, however, the path of knowledge, the path of devotion and the path of action have been propounded with a view to bring about such a synthesis. The path of knowledge considers truth as the basis of life, the path of devotion takes beauty, and the path of action takes goodness as the foundation of human life. In the Bhagavadgītā all the three paths have been considered equally important and not in conflict with one another. The reason is quite evident. Man being a unity of knowing, feeling, and willing, no one of the corresponding ideals can be separated from the other two. That is why logic, ethics and aesthetics always go together.

Ethics and Economics

Economics is one of the most important of the youngest social sciences. It is undoubtedly an indispensable part of political philosophy. According to one definition, economics is a study of human activity with regard to wealth. In other words, this science regards wealth as the end of life. Therefore its scope consists in solving the problems of production, distribution and consumption. Production of wealth stands for the production of those goods which are valued with reference to the wants of man. These goods satisfy the particular wants, e.g. hunger. Thus we find that economics is concerned with the general wants or the ends of human beings. On the contrary, ethics is concerned with the ultimate end of human life. Thus economic values are merely means, whereas moral value is intrinsic and an end in itself, which is why economics is regarded as secondary compared to ethics. The economic values of food, clothing and shelter are secondary because all these are the means of attaining the ultimate good of life. In the relation between ethics and economics the latter depends upon the former. It is necessary for students of economics to know the moral ideals of the society or the nation for whom economic standards are being propounded.

The relation between ethics and economics has been overlooked, and this misunderstanding has been encouraged by the idea that wealth is an end in itself. This mistaken notion has been one cause, or perhaps an effect of our commercialized civilization. Even the most civilized countries have sacrificed human life for the greed of wealth. We often read in the newspapers that some Western countries destroy millions of tons of food in order to maintain the price-level. Such measures may be desirable from the point of view of economics, but as long as there is hunger and starvation in various countries of the world, such an act can never be regarded as moral. We should never forget that wealth is meant for man and not man for wealth. Man does not live to eat, but he eats to live. Mere satisfaction of sensual desires cannot make a man happy. It is from this point of view that Mill remarked, 'It is better to be a Socrates dissatisfied than to be a pig satisfied'. This ideology can become popular only when economics is based on ethics, and when wealth is regarded only as a means and not as an end in itself. Fortunately the notions of economics are undergoing change. An Indian economist, Dr Mehta, has pointed out that the aim of economics is not to increase the wants of society, but rather to reduce them. In fact, this ideal is the expression of the time-honoured virtues of self-sacrifice and non-possession. Mahatma Gandhi also laid down the ideal of minimizing wants as the best economic formula. The economic point of view of Mahatma Gandhi is undoubtedly based on ethics, and, widely shared, this point of view could save the world from armed conflicts in the future, as James suggested in his *Varieties of Religious Experience*. Acharya Vinoba Bhave is engaged in promoting social well-being by basing his 'Bhoodan Yagya' on the same ideal. If the West can learn anything from India, it is the virtue of non-possession. The feeling of non-possession alone may save the world from Communism. Communism regards food and clothing as the ultimate wants of man and uses violence to bring about economic equality. On the other hand, capitalism declares that economic competition is the birthright of man and thus neglects human values. But the virtue of non-possession inspires man to be generous and encourages the satisfaction of social wants, thus bringing about equality without resorting to violent methods. Thus an economic philosophy based on ethics is capable of bringing about a compromise between Communism on the one hand and capitalism on the other.

Ethics and Political Science

Political science has also a very intimate relation to ethics. Political science came into prominence before the time of Socrates and Plato. Even before Socrates the inhabitants of Athens were given training in becoming good citizens. The aim of virtue was to become an ideal citizen. Aristotle was right when he said that 'Man is a social animal.' Therefore while laying down the duties of man, one cannot neglect society. The ideal laid down for the individual ought to correspond to the requirements of the society of which the individual is an integral part. In ancient times politics was considered the science of society. Aristotle laid such a great emphasis on the social aspect of man that he regarded ethics as part of political science.

At present we cannot say that ethics is a part of political science, because the modern definition of political science does not make it the broad subject it was in Aristotle's time. But there is no doubt that philosophy is the foundation of political science. Locke, Rousseau and Karl Marx are the chief propounders of modern political science. These men emphasized 'equality, liberty, and fraternity' in order to maintain the social organization, and this emphasis was inspired by moral ideals. These very notions are the foundation of political thought today. Thus from the theoretical point of view political science depends upon ethics.

From the practical point of view also it is necessary for political science to depend upon ethics if it is to lead to the well-being of human society. Nowadays politics is considered undesirable because immorality and injustice have dominated it. No doubt immorality has influenced modern politics to a large extent, and politics has been severely criticized for this reason, but this does not mean that politics can never be based on morality or virtue. There are numerous examples in history which show that a politics based on truth is ultimately victorious. Ashoka the Great based his politics on non-violence and was able to establish an empire without war. In our own time Indians were able to put an end to the long-standing and deep-rooted British imperialism by following the politics based on truth and non-violence under the leadership of Mahatma Gandhi. This fact proves the possible success of ethical politics. According to the Indian point of view, politics implies the path of righteousness. A well-known Sanskrit poet has referred to the qualities of a politician in the following verses:

Nindantu nītinipuṇāh yadi vā stuvantu
Lakṣmih samāviṣatuh, gachatu vā yatheṣtam;
Adyaiva maraṇamastu yugāntare vā,
Nyāyāt pathah padamn napravicalanti dhīrāh.

That is, persons who are adept in politics may praise or blame; wealth may come or go; death may come today or later; but courageous persons do not budge an inch from the path of righteousness.

The two World Wars in the first half of the twentieth century have compelled man to establish organizations for maintaining world peace. No international organization can foster international understanding unless it inspires the moral tendencies of man. Some thinkers consider one world government to be the only solution to world problems and the establishment of world peace. But it should be remembered that world government can be established only when the moral nature of man is awakened. The relation of politics to ethics is such that we cannot create morality with the aid of politics. There is no doubt that, 'Acts of Parliament cannot make men moral and that true morality rises from within.' In other words, ethics cannot be based on politics, but politics must be founded on ethics.

Ethics and Metaphysics

So far we have been studying the relations between ethics and various sciences. In the beginning we pointed out that ethics has a philosophical background. On the basis of that background and the above discussion it becomes evident that ethics is more a philosophy than a science. Our preliminary analysis of ethics will not be complete unless we explain the relation of ethics to metaphysics and religion. It is more necessary to explain the relation of ethics to metaphysics than to religion, because ethics is based on metaphysics, whereas it does not entirely depend upon religion. Many ethical problems are in fact metaphysical problems, and hence it is necessary to clarify the relation between ethics and metaphysics. In order to do this it appears necessary to throw some light on the nature of metaphysics.

The main business of metaphysics is to propound the nature of ultimate reality. Numerous metaphysical theories have been put forward by various philosophers from very early times in East and West. All these theories have tried to establish the widest points of view about the nature of the ultimate reality of the universe. But it is a pity that no philosopher has been able to establish a metaphysical theory that is universally accepted. The main problems of metaphysics are:

(1) Is matter the ultimate reality of the universe?
(2) Is spirit the ultimate reality of the universe?
(3) Does the soul continue to live after physical death?
(4) Is the will of man free?
(5) Does God exist?

Of these, the problems of the existence of God, of the freedom of will, and of the immortality of soul are three problems that have the most direct relation to ethics. That is why Kant regarded them as the presuppositions of ethics. He pointed out that morality is an 'ought' which implies a 'can'. We cannot expect a man to be moral without a free will. According to Kant when we say that such and such person ought to behave in such a manner, it is implied that that person has freedom so to behave.

Similarly Kant says that we get pleasure and pain as the fruits of our action. To get the fruit of all our action, then, it is necessary to believe in the immortality of soul. The consequences of our action are so far-reaching that it is not possible to experience all of them in one lifetime. It is therefore evident that a man continues to live even after physical death. Hence the immortality of the soul appears to be the basis of ethics. This argument makes it quite clear that the relation of metaphysics to ethics is most intimate. Ethics is always based on metaphysical theories. When metaphysics propounds a particular viewpoint about the reality of the universe, that very viewpoint is generally adopted for the guidance of behaviour. For example, a materialistic metaphysics encourages a hedonistic ethics, and a spiritual metaphysics usually regards self-control as the guiding principle of life.

However, ethics and metaphysics have certain points of difference as well. Metaphysics is mainly theoretical, whereas ethics is concerned with practical life. Metaphysics tries to understand the reality of the external world, whereas ethics tries to establish values for human life. Metaphysics is a reflective theory, whereas ethics studies those values of life which are applicable to human behaviour. Almost every great philosophy begins with metaphysics and ends in ethics.

Ethics and Religion

The meaning of the word religion in this context is religious theory. All religions in spite of minor differences possess one common characteristic, namely, belief in a divine power as the guiding principle of the world in some way or other. In the West religion stands for the belief in the existence of God who is regarded as the controller of the universe. Thus when we discuss the relation between ethics and religion we have to decide how far the problem of the existence of God influences ethics. Is it necessary to believe in God to lead a moral life? Before explaining the relation of ethics to religion it is necessary to answer this question in some detail.

Some thinkers are of the opinion that belief in God is not only unnecessary for leading a moral life, but that such a belief may even hinder an ethical life. The notion of God as omnipresent, omnipotent and omniscient implies that He is the supreme controller of all the ends of the universe. If everything that happens in the universe is the will of God, if the actions of individuals are the expression of His volition and are inspired by God, then man cannot be held responsible for right and wrong and good and evil in his actions. If God is the sole creator of the universe, then no one can ever be immoral, nor can any action be considered unethical. Such a belief converts human will into the will of God. Thus the freedom of will is denied. In the absence of the freedom of will the word 'ought' becomes meaningless. If man is free to choose his action, then the notion of an omniscient, omnipotent and omnipresent God becomes imperfect and mutilated. Hence religion and ethics cannot go together.

However, we can simultaneously believe in the freedom of will and the existence of God. Even to assume that God knows the origin, the process and the end of the universe does not mean that man has no freedom to act in his individual capacity. The intelligence and conscience of man are the reflection of the invisible divinity of God, but the embodied man is capable of using his discretion and distinguishing between right and wrong, and good and evil. Man also prays to God to give him the power to use his discretion rightly; that is why the Upaniṣad reads, 'From unrighteousness lead me to righteousness.' However, this does not warrant our neglecting the human power of discrimination by having a blind faith in God, and thereby giving up all actions. In other words, it does not mean that we should indulge in immorality in the name of God. Persons who believe in such a notion shirk responsibility. Such an attitude is indicative of the demoniac tendency which leads an individual to indulge in immorality and to blame God for such indulgence. Such a viewpoint can be rightly called a lower pantheism.

On the contrary, it may be pointed out that a true religion and firm faith in God automatically lead an individual to follow the path of righteousness. All the great religions of the world consider truth, non-violence, social service, and the feeling of brotherhood as unavoidable virtues leading to God-realization. So-called upholders of religion, however, often conceal selfish motives under the pretext of religion and sometimes resort to nefarious practices. In 1947 hundreds of thousands of innocent people were mercilessly massacred in India by the activities of such impostors in the name of religious principles. Such religious attitudes and beliefs are the result of ignorance. Neither Hinduism, nor Islam, nor any other religion advocates hatred.

The main purpose of religion is God-realization, and God is considered the embodiment of justice. That is why purity of action, generosity and love are regarded as means of God-realization. A moral man can afford to be an atheist, but a truly religious person can never afford to be immoral. According to the Bhagavadgītā, stability of intellect is regarded as the means of attaining God. A man of stable intellect has self-control, neither praises nor blames others, is neither jealous of nor inimical towards others. Similarly, non-stealing, avoiding falsehood, etc., have been considered basic principles which must be adopted by a devotee of God even according to Christianity. In short, religion propounds morality as its basis. In the middle ages, however, it was declared that 'Philosophy is the handmaid of religion'. This indicates that not only ethics but the whole of philosophy was intimately related to religion. Even in the modern period religion has influenced philosophy and ethics greatly. Spinoza began with metaphysics and ended in ethics. His philosophy can be regarded as a religious philosophy. The philosophy of Kant, which is basically an ethical philosophy, shows a religious tinge, and is greatly influenced by the Christian notion of God. In fact, the history of Western philosophy proves that the relation of ethics and religion is very close.

The relation of ethics to religion is reciprocal. We cannot say that religion is based on ethics, or that ethics is based on religion. The reason is that ethics has a theoretical outlook, whereas religion has a practical aim. As we have already said, a person who has a knowledge of ethical principles may not apply those principles to his practical life. On the contrary, a truly religious or God-intoxicated person may not be a student of ethics, but his practical life must necessarily be moral. Thus the study of ethical principles may be of great help to a religious person, and if a student of ethics were to follow religion he could also benefit in enriching his theoretical knowledge of morality. Thus ethics and religion, in spite of being separate, are interrelated, interdependent and supplementary.

CHAPTER II

HISTORICAL BACKGROUND OF INDIAN ETHICS

We have so far been discussing the general nature of ethics, and our survey indicates that ethics has a very wide scope. It is closely related to various sciences and to philosophy, but its proper domain is the rightness and goodness of human behaviour. In the light of this discussion we have to evaluate Indian ethics and ultimately to point out its difference from Western Ethics. After noting special features of Indian ethics, we shall in this chapter provide a brief survey of the historical background of Indian ethics.

Indian ethics means the theory of good and evil and of right and wrong as found in the Indian philosophical literature, and as practised and preached by the great thinkers of India from the Vedic period of the present day. Hence in this work I intend to analyse the various ethical theories existing in the Vedas, Upaniṣads, the Bhagavadgītā, in the orthodox and the heterodox schools of Indian philosophy, and in the life and works of the contemporary ethico-political thinkers, like Rabindranath Tagore, Mahatma Gandhi, Dr Sarvepalli Radhakrishnan and Shri Jawaharlal Nehru.

Our method of approach will not be only explanatory, but also critical and comparative in order to give a proper setting for Indian ethics in the field of philosophy, and to arrive at some conclusions with regard to its contribution to the promotion of human culture. With this effort we hope we may help bring about a synthesis of oriental and occidental thought.

I have to add a word of caution for readers who may be labouring under an illusion that Indian philosophy is not ethical, because it has emphasized that its goal lies beyond logic and ethics. As we shall see later, transcendence in Indian ethics, far from being a handicap, is an asset to it, which makes up a deficiency inherent in Western ethics. Western ethics is through and through relative, and it ends, as it begins, with paradoxes and puzzles. It cannot overcome this defect because the relativity of Western ethics cannot take it beyond contradiction and conflict which are bound to arise as long as perfection is not regarded as a state attainable by an individual even in his lifetime. The claim of Indian ethics to rise above the antinomies of life cannot be understood by a student who is trained in Western logical analysis which declares metaphysics a nonsensical enterprise.

Although logical positivisim, which aims at the elimination of metaphysics, has been severely criticized even by Western thinkers, yet the occident is not prepared to believe that there is any possibility of realizing a metaphysical state having attained which an individual can actually transcend the contradictory experience of heat and cold, pleasure and pain, praise and blame, loss and gain, etc. It is only by resorting to spiritual discipline and a stern ethical attitude of mind that an individual realizes the truth of transcendence, and having once attained it he is capable of communicating it even through speech, though imperfectly. We shall return to this important point at the proper place. The point of mentioning it here is to suggest that in Indian philosophy metaphysics and ethics present an organic whole, a concrete reality, and not an abstract notion or a queer combination or a paradox. The ethical ideal is not merely a symbol but an actual state of existence realizable in this life. The only proof of such a truism lies in practising the ethical code and uniting the self with reality, which is the source as well as the goal of existence. Although Indian ethics did not exist as a separate subject, nevertheless, as already stated, the ethical aspect of Indian philosophy is as old as Vedic thought, and hence Indian ethics is historically older than Greek ethics. This remoteness of the subject is undoubtedly a handicap from the point of view of research. In the absence of any historical evidence, one has to depend upon inference and internal evidence with regard to the chronology of ethical practices. Another defect one has to face while studying the philosophical theories of India is the impersonal attitude of the propounders of these systems. In India the propounders of the great systems avoided coming into the limelight, and always preferred to expound their ideology anonymously, partly because of their sincerity of purpose, partly because they always tried to prove that all true philosophy (including their own) was drawn from the Vedas. In spite of these defects, I shall try to give a systematic account of the subject as far as possible, keeping in view the import of Indian culture and remaining as detached as possible in the matter of preferring one point of view to another.

Indian ethics, therefore, has its own special features which mark it off from Western ethics. Since the present work is, perhaps, the first of its kind, so far as the comprehensive nature of the subject is concerned, it appears necessary to refer to the special features of Indian ethics before proceeding to give its historical background. But before enumerating the distinctive features of Indian ethics as compared with the Western ethics, it is very important to clarify a misunderstanding about the general nature of Indian philosophy.

Western Conception of Indian Philosophy

One essential feature of Indian philosophy is the practical applicability of its ideals. At first sight, this argument may appear to be inconsistent, especially to those who think that Indian philosophy is out and out pessimistic, digressive, and altogether impractical in the modern age of scientific investigation, logical analysis and material progress. The Western conception of Indian philosophy and of the Indian people is that the former preaches dejection and renunciation, divorced from all development of personality, and that the latter, being otherworldly in their outlook, always live in the world of imagination devoid of all reality. Mrs Sinclair Stevenson, in the introductory chapter of her book, *The Heart of Jainism* declares, 'If, therefore, we would try reverently and sympathetically to grasp the inner meaning of an Indian faith, we must put aside all thought of the perfectly developed personality, which is our ideal and of the joy and the zest that come from progress made and powers exercised, and, turning our thoughts backward, face for a while another goal in which death not life is the prize, cessation not development the ideal.'[1]

Indian Ethical Ideal

It appears that Mrs Stevenson has made this statement with special reference to Jainism and has at the same time forgotten

[1] Mrs Sinclair Stevenson, *The Heart of Jainism*, introductory chapter, p. 1.

for a moment all the ethical values and the most practical Jaina ideals which are to be followed for the perfect development of personality. As regards the other schools of Indian philosophy, her statement is equally untenable and prejudiced. Perfection, progress and immortality, as opposed to imperfection, cessation and death, are the ideals of all the Schools of Indian philosophy. Indian philosophy does not look backward, as Mrs Stevenson believes. On the contrary, it is far-sighted, progressive, ever-developing, ever-evolving and giving rise to new ideas and new ideals which aim at the highest goal, the *summum bonum.* Wellbeing, not only of human beings but of all the living creatures is the cherished goal of all Indian philosophers. The following Sanskrit verse sums up the Indian ethical ideal.

Sarve bhavantu sukhinah sarve santu nirāmayah
Sarve bhadrāṇi paśyantu makashchit dukha bhāgabhavet.

'May all be at ease; may all be sinless; may all experience happiness; may none experience suffering.'

The starting-point of Indian philosophy is man, suffering man, who is to be rescued from endless torture, misery, disease, destruction, old age, and even death. In order to fulfil this mission, the devoted and sincere Indian sages and philosophers have from time immemorial to the present day shown the path to peace and progress of all humanity, not only by laying down the theoretical ideals, but by actually applying truths in their practical life; not by imagining or theorizing, but by realizing the reality. Personalities like Ṛshabha, Krishna, Mahāvīra, Buddha and Gandhi who have again and again demonstrated the practical application of the philosophical ideals, and who by their personal examples have proved that self-realization alone can lift fallen humanity to loftier heights, cannot be said to be opposed to 'all thought of the perfectly developed personality', as Mrs Stevenson would contend. On the contrary, the aim of all these heroes of spirituality was development, perfection and immortality for all. The standards laid down by them have been followed and are being followed practically by people even today. These great personalities were conscious of the fact that their teachings would be so followed by millions of commoners, as is evident from the following verse of the Gītā:

Yadyadācharāti śreṣṭhah tattadevetaro janāh;
Sa yatpramāṇam kurute lokastadanuvartate.[1]

'Whatever action is performed by the great, is imitated by the common people; whatever standard is set by him, is followed by them.'

A Humanistic Approach

The fundamental difference in the approach of Indian and Western philosophies to truth is that the latter's viewpoint is mainly theoretical and intellectual, whereas the former's viewpoint has been throughout practical and spiritual. (I may add a word of caution here that Indian spiritualism should not be confused with the supernaturalism of the West.) The chief instrument in both philosophies is reason, and the primary ideal to be achieved by both is the well-being of man. Dr P. T. Raju says, 'The Greeks were primarily interested in social questions, while the Indians were attracted by questions about the nature of inner spirit Ātman . . . But, whether philosophy is concerned primarily with man as the Ātman, or as essentially a social being, it is concerned with man all the same'.[2] In the same paper the author emphatically says that all philosophy whether spiritual or materialistic is based on human interest, though it would be erroneous to call philosophy humanistic. In his opinion the humanistic tendency of philosophy is natural and unavoidable, firstly, because philosophy has a human origin, a human purpose and human conclusions, and, secondly, because even if the propounder of a philosophy avoids human interest in his intellectual pursuit, humanistic interpretation is bound to follow. 'If the philosophy be materialistic it would be difficult to avoid the conclusion that man under the conditions which the material world offers, should try to have the least possible discomfort and unhappiness and make the best of the life here; and if the philosophy be spiritual, the conclusion that he should ultimately aim at spiritual realization and utilize his material existence therefor, is equally inevitable.'[3]

[1] Bhagavadgītā III, 21.

[2] Dr P. T. Raju, 'Humanistic Transformation', *Aryan Path*, June 1951, pp. 259.

[3] *Ibid.*, 259.

The above remarks are applicable to the vast panorama of Indian philosophy, from ancient to modern times, because all its schools and systems, in spite of apparent differences, possess the common characteristic of regarding philosophy as a mode of life, and not as a mere intellectual pursuit. 'Indian philosophy has its interest in the haunts of men, and not in supra-lunar solitudes. It takes its origin in life, and enters back into life after passing through the Schools. The Gītā and Upaniṣads are not remote from popular belief. They are the great literature of the country and at the same time vehicles of the great systems of thought. The Purāṇas contain the truth dressed up in myth and stories, to suit the weak understanding of the majority. The hard task of interesting the multitude in metaphysics is achieved in India.'[1] The whole of Indian philosophy is a pattern, a mosaic, a bunch of variegated flowers of various hues and aroma, ranging from the positivistic and materialistic Cārvāka system, through the non-absolutistic (Anekāntavāda) philosophy of Jainism, to the absolutism of the Vedānta, as a reaction to which contemporary Indian philosophy has emerged. It would be erroneous to regard all Indian philosophy as purely spiritualistic and monistic in the presence of the Cārvāka and the Jaina systems in its domain. Even ancient Indian philosophers could not neglect the social, the economic, and the emotional aspects of life. A careful study of ancient Indian history would reveal that this country was materially progressive and economically sound. Speaking of the prosperity of India in ancient times, Radhakrishanan says, 'She knew how to chisel stone, draw pictures, burnish gold and weave rich fabrics. She developed all arts, fine and industrial, which furnish the conditions of civilized existence. Her ships crossed the oceans and her wealth brimmed over to Judaea, Egypt and Rome. Her conceptions of man and society, morals and religion were remarkable for the time. We cannot reasonably say that the Indian people revelled in poetry and mythology, and spurned science and philosophy, though it is true that they were more intent on seeking the unity of things than emphasizing their sharpness and separation.'[2] It was, therefore, natural for the philosophers of that time to bring about a synthesis of the social and economic, the emotional and the spiritual life. The

[1] Radhakrishnan, *Indian Philosophy*, Vol. I, p. 25.

[2] *Ibid.*, p. 30.

four ideals, Artha (the economic), Kāma (the emotional), Dharma (the moral) and Mokṣa (the spiritual), are the keynotes of all the systems, each emphasizing one or more of these values. But all these values taken together would certainly lead to the all-round development of philosophy and to the evolution of healthy, holy, happy and harmonious society.

Task of the Scholar

Man being the centre of all philosophy, and reason being its chief instrument, the task of the student of philosophy who really wants to contribute something to genuine research lies in reviewing the ancient and the modern systems with a view to pointing out the humanistic tendencies in them, and also to find out how far each philosophy, each system, and each branch of a system, paves the way to the well-being of mankind. Only with such an unprejudiced and dispassionate attitude shall we be able to do justice to the Eastern as well as the Western philosophies, and at the same time discover facts and theories anew so as to base philosophy on more solid ground than ever before. We shall have to admit that such a critical attitude towards philosophy is due to inroads of Western philosophy into India, which should not be grudged and considered disastrous. The development of philosophy as a search for truth (Darśana) cannot be limited to one sect, one country, or one continent. Many Indian philosophers today have realized this fact. 'No culture, no country lives or has a right to live for itself. If it has any contribution to make towards the enrichment of the human spirit, it owes its contribution to the widest circle it can reach.'[1]

The meeting-point of East and West is evidently man. In the face of the facts already mentioned, it would be erroneous to believe that ancient Indian philosophy neglected man and the influence of environment on his behaviour. Had Indian philosophy not been interested in the well-being of humanity it would have been extinct long ago. But on the contrary we find that it has from the very dawn of civilization continued to develop and grow, and is still growing and developing, imbibing the new and modifying the old to every reasonable extent. In other words the very existence, evolution, and expansion of Indian philosophy is the proof of its humanistic approach and

[1] Radhakrishnan, *Eastern Religions and Western Thought*, p. viii.

critical method. The various schools of Indian philosophy have existed and developed side by side because they could fulfil some need of society. The Cārvāka system aims at material development and the tapping of all the material resources for the comfortable life of man here and now. Thus it lays stress on the emotional and economic aspects of life, though the advanced and cultured (Sushikshita) Cārvākas aimed at the moral uplift of man as well. Vātsyāyana, the author of Kāma Sūtra, says that the Cārvākas cultivated sixty-four fine arts to accomplish the pursuit of refined pleasures. The other systems of Indian philosophy, in spite of their zeal towards attaining spiritual perfection, never advocated destruction of material or lower elements, or renunciation of wordly pleasures altogether. On the contrary, the attainment of the highest goal (Mokṣa, balanced life) which aims neither at the suppression of desires nor at the unlicensed satisfaction of desires, but at the systematization of desires, is recognised as the cherished ideal.

Special Features of Indian Ethics

The foregoing discussion indicates that Indian ethics has some distinctive characteristics which mark it off from Western ethics. It would be erroneous to hold that Indian ethics is radically different from Western ethics but it would be equally erroneous to hold that they are in most respects identical. Yet although the ideal of most ethics is the supreme good of mankind the difference between Indian and Western ethics lies in the method of approach and the interpretation of the supreme good.

That this is so is due largely to the fact that ethical thinking in India developed under different sorts of environment and at quite a different period of history as compared with the development of moral philosophy in the West. We may, therefore, enumerate the following special features of Indian ethics in order to distinguish it from Western ethics and to have an insight into its nature.

(i) Remoteness in time;
(ii) Practicality;
(iii) A metaphysical basis; and
(iv) Absoluteness.

When we say that Indian ethics is remote in time we mean that it is the oldest moral philosophy in the history of civilization. Because of their appalling ignorance of Indian philosophy in general and Indian ethics in particular, Western scholars overlook this aspect of Indian ethics and regard Greek ethics as the oldest. It is now an admitted fact that the Vedas, which are the oldest literature available in the world, are the perennial source of Indian philosophy and ethics. As we shall see later, the ethics of the Vedas, which is the very root of the Hindu Śāstras and Mīmāṁsā, the most systematic Indian ethical philosophy, is in fact the main theme of Vedic thought. Not only do we find in the Ṛigvedic Mantras the idea of universal moral law, but also the emphasis on non-violence and the cosmological foundation of the Varṇa and Aśrama Dharmas, which are the rock and foundation of Indian ethics. Now Ṛigveda is undoubtedly older than the beginning of Greek thought.

The remoteness of Indian ethics is a mixed blessing. It is responsible for the ambiguity of certain theories which are held to be based on the oldest Vedic literature. There is no definite evidence to ascertain the chronology of the various systems of Indian philosophy. It is very difficult to determine which of the systems, orthodox or heterodox, is prior and which of them is posterior, as all the systems—Jaina, Buddha, Nyăya, Vaiśesika, Sāṁkhya, Yoga, Mīmāṁsā and Vedānta—interpenetrate one another. Consequently, even internal evidence, which should be the sole guide in the absence of historical records, is of little help in this matter. In spite of relentless efforts of research scholars in the field of Indian chronology of ancient times, the only date that can be claimed to have been settled in 'the first one thousand years of it, for example, is that of the birth of Buddha, which occurred in 487 BC'.[1] This difficulty leads to various misunderstandings with regard to the priority of various philosophical and ethical viewpoints.

On the other hand, this remoteness has been responsible for making Indian ethics so well-established in the practical life of its followers that certain forms of behaviour persist even today as unshakable attitudes. In spite of the passage of thousands of years the fundamentals of Indian ethics are embodied in the day-to-day life of the followers of almost every school of Indian philosophy, thus confirming the endurance of ethical ideals in this country.

This continuity of Indian ethics is undoubtedly due to the

[1] M. Hiriyanna, *Outlines of Indian Philosophy*, p. 13.

practical outlook of Indian philosophy in general and of Indian ethics in particular. This feature of Indian ethics distinguishes it sharply from Western ethics which, being an integral part of Western philosophy, has an intellectual approach to moral problems. Two main theories of ethics that have appeared again and again in the history of Western philosophy are those of rationalism and hedonism taking 'reason' and 'pleasure' as the ends of human life respectively. Almost every ethical thinker has raised objections to either of the theories and has supported the one while rejecting the other. The ethical philosophy of the occident is a commentary upon these two theories with a thorough analysis of the idea of value or good.

On the other hand Indian ethics, instead of analysing the nature of good, lays down practical means of attaining a life of perfection here and now. It is not indifferent to the idea of good, but in place of explaining the nature of good, it gives us practical guidance toward attaining and realizing good, in our life. Indian ethics propounds the four Puruṣārthas or the ends of human life, which are the means as well as the ends, our duties as well as our goal of self-realization. The Puruṣārthas have no meaning apart from their practical application. Similarly Varṇāśrama Dharmas, or the duties of the individual and of the four chief classes of society, are out-and-out practical rules of the ethico-social organization of human beings. Even in the ascetic ethics of Jainism, the rules of conduct have been practically followed by the Jainas for thousands of years and are adhered to by them today. Kantian ethics exists only in the books of the West. Such, too, is the case with the utilitarianism of Mill. Thus Indian ethics is the actual application of moral ideals, whereas Western ethics is a mere discussion of ethical problems.

The third and the most important special feature of Indian ethics is its strong and deep metaphysical foundation. Although some systems of Western philosophy also present this feature, yet the indispensability of the metaphysical basis of Indian ethics has its own importance. The ethics of the Bhagavadgītā, which is regarded as the most practical and universal moral ideal, also indicates the metaphysical nature of Indian ethics. It regards God as the eternal infinite self-caused principle. While propounding this universal imperishable basic principle, the author of the Gītā says:

Avināśi tu tadviddhi yena sarvamidam tatam
Vināśamavyayasyasya na kaścit kartumarhati.[1]

'Consider that principle to be imperishable on the basis of which this entire universe exists, because no one is capable of destroying the imperishable one.'

Arjuna is made to understand that the universal principle, which pervades living as well as non-living existence, is not affected by the transitory changes of time, space, and causality, which are relative and not absolute. It is self-caused, self-abiding, immortal and immutable. It does not behoove Arjuna to be afraid of the death of his kith and kin in the field of battle and to consider himself the killer, since 'The imperishable spiritual reality has numberless perishable bodies; one who considers it to be a killer, and the one who considers it to have been killed, both are ignorant, since neither it kills, nor is it killed by anything'.[2] He is therefore asked to rise above pleasure and pain, loss and gain, and to engage himself in the battle of righteousness. The metaphysical background of the Bhagavadgītā is the foundation of its ethics.

The metaphysical background of Indian ethics makes it an ethico-metaphysical theory, a synthesis of theory and practice, of intellectual understanding and self-realization. The highest goal of Indian ethics is the attainment of Mokṣa, which means perfection not in the theoretical sense but in the practical sense of rising above all the contradictions of pleasure and pain, praise and blame, heat and cold, loss and gain, and even of right and wrong, and of good and evil. Indian ethics points out that the spiritual aspect of human nature is the very divinity; it is eternality, perfection, infinite existence, infinite consciousness, and infinite bliss. Thus Indian ethics is an absolute ethics. Spiritual perfection is responsible for this absolute nature of Indian ethics. On the contrary, Western ethics being devoid of Eastern ethics' metaphysical basis and religion, ends, as it begins, with the relativity of moral life. Thus Indian ethics is most cosmopolitan as well as absolutistic, because it is through and through spiritualistic.

Although Hegelian metaphysics influenced Western ethics

[1] Bhagavadgītā, II, 17.
[2] *Ibid.*, II, 18–19.

yet no feasible theory of the absolute as the *summum bonum* has ever been propounded by Western thinkers with the exception of Josiah Royce. The perfectionism of Green and the self-realization theory of Bradley are imperfect intellectual attempts at absolute ethics. The concept of the absolute in Indian philosophy, being based on the immanence as well as on the transcendence of the ultimate reality, is not merely an intellectual achievement of the philosophic mind, but a possible state of existence attainable by man through spiritual discipline. Only after the attainment of such a state the relative nature of morality is transcended. The transcendence of Indian ethics is a special feature which does not deny the relativity of morality, but explains it as a lower stage which has to be crossed ultimately by the seeker of truth.

A brief historical survey of Indian philosophy would confirm the transcendental but practical nature of the ethics propounded in India. The beginning of Indian ethics dates back to 2000 BC, the time when the Aryan race is reported to have migrated from Central Asia to the land of the five rivers in India. Some scholars even hold that 'The foundation of Hindu ethics was laid before the Aryan race reached India'.[1] A study of Indo-European mythology indicates that the concept of beneficent gods, as opposed to the demoniac powers (Asuras), was present before the migration of the Aryan race from Central Asia. Zoroastrianism, which was the creed of the Aryans who migrated to India shared this belief with the Iranians while they were settled in Central Asia. The proof of this statement lies in the various Purāṇas in which the history of the conflict between gods and demons is narrated in detail. The term 'Deva' (God) stands for the beneficent manifestation of the power of God, and the term 'Asura' (demon) stands for a person possessing a destructive nature. That the Vedic gods are not persons but the names of various natural entities will be discussed by us in the sequel.

However it is important to note here that the imperfect personification of the Vedic gods is not a handicap but an advantage, because it proves that 'Devatā' stands for an entity and not for any supernatural person. That is the reason the gods of the Vedas are regarded as the guardians of the eternal moral order. The concept of the divine and demoniac qualities in the

[1] B. W. Hopkins, *Ethics of India*, p. 1.

16th discourse of the Bhagavadgītā further supports our contention of the moral nature of the notion of the Vedic pantheon —'there are two types of beings created in the world, the divine and demoniac'.[1]

While describing the qualities of the divine persons the Bhagavadgītā mentions the virtues of non-violence, truth, freedom from anger, renunciation, tranquility, aversion to fault-finding, compassion to living beings, freedom from greed, gentleness, modesty, steadfastness, forgiveness, purity, freedom from malice; and excessive pride, anger, harshness, and ignorance. It is further asserted that precisely these divine and demoniac qualities are responsible for the formation of good and bad characters. Commenting upon this notion of the Bhagvadgītā Dr Radhakrishnan writes: 'In Indian religious symbolism, the distinction between the Devas, the shining ones, and the Asuras, the titans, the children of darkness, is an ancient one. Rāmāyana represents a similar conflict between the representatives of high culture and those of brutal egoism. Mahābhārata tells us of the struggle between the Pāṇḍavas who were devotees of Karma, of law and justice, and the Kauravas, who were lovers of power. Historical mankind remains remarkably true to the type . . . Some men are divinely good, some are diabolically false, and some are damnably indifferent.' We shall refer again to this point as we proceed. We may add here that when the distinction between gods and demons is referred to in the Vedas, it is always held that the former are good and the latter evil. This notion of good and evil is indicative of the ethical element in the early Vedic literature.

Moreover, lexicographic analysis of the Vedic terms, 'Ṛiju', which means straight, and 'Vrijana', which means crooked, and comparison with the English equivalents 'right', and 'wrong' is worth mentioning in this context. There is no doubt that the terms right and wrong which are derived from the same roots as the above mentioned Vedic terms are ethical terms, and bear the same connotation as the Vedic terms. This fact proves that the moral distinction between right and wrong was clear to the Vedic sages. E. W. Hopkins supports this argument with reference to the Ṛigvedic evidence in the following manner:

'Ṛigveda contains a large number of passages illustrating this

[1] Bhagavadgītā, XVI, 6.

distinction of right and wrong, as straight and crooked; but one in particular may be cited here because of its poetic beauty. It describes the rapid succession of the phenomena of sun-rise, the sudden change from darkness to brightness, the rush of the dawn light (not slow but swift in India), and the ascent of the sun God, who from above looks down upon the straight and crooked ways (good and bad activities) of man.'[1]

The hymn that gives this description is as follows:

> The turbid darkness vanished, bright sky shone,
> Upward light of Dawn, the heavenly, hastened,
> Unto his fields on high the Sun ascended,
> The ways of mortal straight and crooked seeing.[2]

Since Agni (fire God) is the representative of the Sun according to the Vedas, he is regarded as the most reliable witness of the matrimonial alliance. That is why at the marriage ceremony the bride and the bridegroom have to take the vows of faithfulness to each other in the presence of Agni. The above mentioned evidence amply proves that the ethical concepts of Indian philosophy are at least as old as the Ṛigveda.

Not only do we find the origin of Varṇa Dharmas, or the duties of the four major divisions of mankind, in the Vedas, but the concepts of non-violence and universal love are also found in the Vedic literature. Most scholars have overemphasized the ritualistic and sacrificial aspects of the Vedas, thereby neglecting the fact that the Vedas also lay down the maxim, 'Māhiṁsyāt sarv̄abhūtāni', that is, 'Do not kill any living being'. Although Jainism and Buddhism, whose basic ethical concept is non-violence, are supposed to be heterodox systems which reject the authority of the Vedas, yet they cannot be said to be absolutely independent of the Vedic and Upaniṣadic thought and philosophy. In this sense the germs of every system, whether orthodox or heterodox, are to be found in the Vedas and the Upaniṣads, hence from an historical point of view the origin of Indian ethics can be placed between 2000 BC and 1500 BC.

[1] E. W. Hopkins, *Ethics of India*, pp. 3–4.
[2] S. Radhakrishnan, *Bhagavadgītā*, p. 334.

Having discussed the ethical background of Indian philosophy with reference to the Vedic period, it appears desirable to refer to the tendencies of the pre-Buddhistic period of Indian history of philosophy before closing this chapter.

The pre-Buddhistic period of Indian philosophy was a transitional period during which various seeds of harmony as well as discord, of unity as well as diversity, spiritualism as well as materialism, orthodoxy as well as revolt against the authority of the Vedas, had been sown. The Vedic theological and ritualistic philosophy that had dominated the practical life of the common people had begun to be doubted even from the Upaniṣadic period, though the majority doubtless continued to follow it. The yearning for self-knowledge, Atma Jnana, the burden of the Upaniṣadic philosophy, was to rid the human soul of all the sufferings and tortures to which it was subjected. The sacrifice was reinterpreted and the principle of self-restraint leading to self-denial was advocated as the means of Mokṣa instead of offering oblations of animals to fire. Though the ritual persisted in modified form, eschewing animal sacrifice, a revolt against orthodoxy had been brewing in the social, religious and the philosophical fields. Commenting upon the philosophical revolution in the pre-Buddhistic period, B. M. Barua remarks, 'Some of the right-minded philosophers, with their later successors, were all ranged against the Vedic theologians, the Brahman priests. All of them agreed in viewing Vedic study in the light of not-knowledge (Avidyā), in estimating the four Vedas and the Vedic sciences as the lower knowledge, in teaching that the self (Ātman) was not obtainable by the study of the Veda, in holding that the three Vedas were subject to the three qualities (Guṇas), in questioning the divine origin of the Vedas and all efficiency of the sacrifices, funeral oblations, or the gifts to the priesthood enjoined in the Vedas, and in stoutly maintaining that the observance of moral precepts and the contemplation, knowledge, and realization of the nature of Brahman were far superior to the performance of Vedic sacrifices, and the acquisition of Vedic learning.'[1] The transition from the theological and the ritual period to the Sūtra period was no doubt gradual, but actual and practical, since in the period under consideration there existed various orders of teachers, both ortho-

[1] B. M. Barua, *A History of Pre-Buddhistic Indian Philosophy* (University of Calcutta), p. 193.

dox as well as unorthodox, representing different schools of thought, like those of Āsuri, Pippalāda, Bhārdvāja, Naciketas, Pūrṇa Kāśyapa, Kakuḍa Kātyāyana, Ajitakeṣakamblin, and others.[1] It was an age of free thinking, critical analysis, philosophic rumblings and a spirit of restlessness and dissatisfaction, with a yearning for Mokṣa through the purifying power of penance and asceticism.

It must be noted that the controversies existed prior to Mahāvīra and the Buddha, and that the antagonism between the two lines of thought (the path of sacrifice, Yajña, and that of renunciation) as it existed at the time was not surcharged with a strong caste bias, and a sharp cleavage between the Brahmanas on the one hand and the Kṣatriyas on the other, to the extent of mutual hatred and jealousy between the two upper castes of the Hindus, as some scholars of Jainism try to prove. The Kṣatriyas dominated the society in the eastern countries, whereas the Brahmanas were supreme in the western countries. This fact is no doubt based on evidence from the Brahmanic literature. But it does not prove that the two castes were so much opposed that one should lead a crusade against the other. On the contrary, the acknowledged leader of this philosophic revolt, which aimed at sweeping away sacrificial ritualism and animal sacrifice, was a Brahmana of the eastern country, Yainavalkya. The conflict was not between caste and caste, or between the spiritual community and the ruling class, but between opinion and opinion, between one type of philosophy and another, practised and followed by the adherents of different teachers. The conflict of ideologies and systems cannot be denied, but the alleged caste war between Brahamanas and Kṣatriyas as the cause of the 'revolt of the critical fair-minded Kṣatriya against the clever unscrupulous Brahman, who disallowed to all others the privilege of entering on the fourth order of the Sanyasins and claimed exclusive control of the sacrifices', is open to objection. In fact, the Brahmins never claimed a monopoly of the fourth order of Sanyasin. Even the Kṣatriyas and the Vaisyas could adopt the order of Sanyasin. Dr Radhakrishnan remarks:

'Were the exclusiveness of the Brahmins the cause of revolt, it should have been led not by the Kṣatriyas, who were as good or as bad as the Brahamins in this respect, but by the other classes.

[1] *A History of Pre-Buddhistic Indian Philosophy*, 'A', Part III.

It (Jainism) is an expression of the general ferment of thought which prevailed at the beginning of the epic period, and we need not invent any anti-Brahmin prejudice for an explanation of its rise. When different views of life and doctrines professed by different people come into touch with each other, there is bound to be an interpretation of thoughts, giving rise to an extraordinary development of feeling and belief, and Jainism is one manifestation of this mental unrest.'[1]

Jainism was no doubt only 'one manifestation' of the mental and the spiritual unrest alluded to in the beginning of this section. The orthodox as well as the unorthodox schools of Āsuri, Pippalāda, Bhārdvāja, Ajitakeṣkambalin, *et al.*, referred to in this section including the Cārvāka, Jaina, Baudha, the six orthodox systems and even the Bhagavadgītā, were no less revolutionary and different from the Vedic religion than Jainism, especially with reference to the idea of God as the creator, and their attitude towards animal sacrifice. The Bhagavadgītā advocates knowledge and freedom from worldly attachment for the attainment of perfection (instead of Vedic sacrifice, which is considered inferior to Ātma Jñāna, or self-knowledge) through self-control or meditation on God. The word 'sacrifice' is interpreted anew in the Bhagavadgītā and various forms of sacrifices other than the offering of oblations to fire are mentioned in the fourth discourse of this immortal book. The worship of various gods with flowers, etc., is one form of sacrifice; another sacrifice consists in offering the objects of sense to the fire of self-control; and still another sacrifice consists in burning the sensual desires in the fire of one's existence in God, enkindled by true knowledge. Different names are given to different ways of attaining perfection through different types of sacrifices. The twenty-eighth verse of the fourth discourse of the Bhagavadgītā runs as follows:

'Some people perform material sacrifices by spending their wealth in social service with their mind devoted to God; others in like manner, perform the penance sacrifice by following their own Dharma (duty); others perform yoga sacrifice by following the eightfold path; and still other aspirants, by following the great vows like non-violence, etc., by uttering the name of God

[1] S. Radhakrishnan, *Indian Philosophy*, Vol. I, p. 293.

and by studying the science that shows the path to God, perform the sacrifice of knowledge (Jñāna Yajña).'[1]

Thus it is evident from internal evidence that several schools and systems of philosophical thought, ethics and religion had arisen, all aspiring to attain spiritual perfection. Thus even from the Upaniṣadic period, of which the Gītā is the embodiment, tendencies different from the existing Vedic theology had been let loose, and by the time of the Buddhistic period the atmosphere had of course become 'ripe for revolt', as Mrs Stevenson also contends. But this revolt, as I have already pointed out, was many-sided, evisaged by the lingual, social, religious and philosophical transformation of the time.

This much historical background will help us understand the development of the ethical philosophies of India. A study of the ethical views of the various Indian schools of philosophy will confirm our contention that the entire philosophical tradition of our country has been uniform and harmonious, in spite of the apparent diversity which vanishes the moment we recognize that both non-dualism and pluralism have been accepted by the Vedas. This acceptance of the spiritual oneness and the physical manyness of the universe is what I have called the ethico-metaphysical nature of Indian philosophy.

[1] Bhagavadgītā, IV, 28.

CHAPTER III

THE ETHICS OF THE VEDAS

The Vedas are the oldest philosophical literature in the world and have been the perennial source of Indian thought and culture from 2000 BC to the present day. Vedic literature is usually divided into the following four parts:

(*a*) The Mantras or hymns,
(*b*) The Brāhmaṇas,
(*c*) The Āraṇyakas and
(*d*) The Upaniṣads.

(*a*) The Mantras or hymns are the oldest aspect of Vedic literature and have been classified into the four major collections or Saṁghitas known as (i) the Ṛigveda Saṁghita, (ii) the Yajurveda Saṁghita, (iii) the Sāmaveda Saṁghita, and (iv) the Atharva Veda Saṁghita. These Saṁghitas cover a very wide field, ranging from the social problems of marriage, love, and gambling to metaphysical theories of creation. But most of the hymns are addressed to gods who on a close examination turn out to be the names of various entities or the powers of one supreme God. This supreme ruler of the universe again is not a person, but a central reality, the master of creation that resides in the very core of everything that exists.

(*b*) The Brāhmaṇa literature explains the various rituals and also analyses the various terms used in the hymns. Unfortunately, the Brāhmaṇic literature has been neglected by scholars so far. In fact, however, the Brāhmaṇas are a link between the hymns and the Upaniṣadic philosophy. In the absence of a systematic study of the Brāhmaṇas the apparent conflict between the ritualistic philosophy of the Vedas and the 'Ātma Vidyā' of the Upaniṣads, which places knowledge above action, can never be overcome.

(*c*) and (*d*) The Araṇyakas and the Upaniṣads resemble each other in their aim and method. They are an attempt to explain the invisible basis of the visible universe. We shall have occasion to point out how the Upaniṣads expound the notions of Brahman and Ātman, which are ultimately identified, to arrive at the final notion of an Absolute, which transcends all contradictions and which is the efficient as well as the material cause of the cosmos.

For our present purpose we are concerned only with the ethical aspect of the hymns, which have up to now been considered the prayers of the Ārayans for wordly prosperity and protection from calamities. An impartial analysis of the Vedic hymns would reveal that the concept of Godhead in the Vedic literature presents a two-fold ethical theory, which accepts duty (Karma) and devotion (Bhakti) as the ideals to be followed by man for success in this life, and for bliss hereafter. Before we explain this two-fold ethical theory it is essential here to point out that our analysis of the ethical aspect of the Vedas will be mainly based on the Ṛigvedic hymns. Ṛigveda has been acknowledged to be the oldest collection and the basis of all the other three Vedas.

The concept of God (Deva) in the Vedas is very peculiar, and cannot be compared with any similar concept in any other religion or mythology. It should always be remembered that the Vedic gods are not the gods of mythology, and that they do not represent a polytheistic creed in any sense. They are the numerous manifestations of the central reality, termed the truth of truths (Satyasya Satyam), and the centre of centres (Kendrasya Kendram). This Vedic truth, the basic principle of the cosmos, is referred to as Ṛitam, or righteousness.

The exact equivalent of the Vedic term 'ṛitam' in Latin is *rectus*, from which the words 'right' and 'straight' are derived. Thus a Vedic god is regarded as good not only because he is benevolent and not harmful to men, but also because he is the upholder of Ṛita or Ṛitam, righteousness. Ṛitam represents the basic truth, harmony, system or eternal moral order of the entire universe. That which is universally true is Ṛitam and that which is the opposite or false is termed Anṛitam. It has been the firm belief of the Indian sages that ultimately truth is victorious because it is the basic principle. The Sanskrit quotation imprinted on our national emblem is 'Satyaṁ eva Jayate'. In fact it is a part of the whole statement, 'Satyaṁ eva jayate nānṛitam', i.e. Truth alone is victorious and not falsehood.

As we shall see during the course of our discussion of the ethical theories of Indian thinkers, the concept of truth, which has been derived from Ṛita and is the basis of moral harmony, is the supreme concept acknowledged by all the schools of Indian philosophy and by all the pioneers of Indian religion and ethics.

Before we proceed with our analysis of the Vedic hymns it is most important to note here that the concept of the basic moral truth in Indian philosophy and particularly in the Vedic philosophy is different from the Chinese concept of Tao propounded by Lao-Tze. Although Ṛita represents the harmony of the world and the regularity of nature that can be seen in the rotation and revolution of planets, yet it also stands for the regular conduct of men in their practical life. Lao-Tze's concept of Tao represents only an indifferent cosmic power. But the concept of Ṛita propounds the existence of an intelligent basic principle that regulates the cosmos as well as the life of individuals. Commenting upon this dissimilarity between the concept of Tao and that of Ṛita, E. W. Hopkins has remarked: 'It (Ṛitam) is not, like the Chinese Tao, a cosmic power, but it is the order instituted by the wise spirit as regulator of the world.'[1]

The concept of Ṛita has great ethico-metaphysical significance. It represents the sublime moral order, which is inviolable. The inviolability of Ṛita makes it superior to gods and cosmic ethics on the one hand, and individual human beings on the other, because Ṛita works throughout the cosmos inevitably and justly. This fact implies that even in the case of individual's actions Ṛita, the eternal moral law, is responsible for the apportionment of reward and punishment. Although Vedic literature does not propound the doctrine of Karman in a clear-cut fashion, yet it can be said that the notion of Ṛita anticipates the doctrine of Karman.

The divine order is designated as Vrata in the Vedic literature. This word literally means vow. The use of the term indicates that the concept of Ṛita, the moral law, is both metaphysical and ethical. With reference to gods it is metaphysical; with reference to human beings it is purely ethical. It is mentioned in the Ṛigveda that the gods have the power to judge the merits of thoughts, speech and actions of individuals internally, and that they alone give them reward or punishment according to their deeds.

Moreover, even Ṛigveda enlists bad intention, swearing,

[1] E. W. Hopkins, *Ethics of India*, p. 3.

falsehood, gambling debt, egoistic enjoyment, cruelty, adultery, theft and injury to life as vicious and sinful acts. It may be pointed out that these vicious tendencies have been referred to as demoniac qualities in the Bhagavadgītā. Thus the germs of the ethics of the Bhagavadgītā can be clearly seen in the Vedic thought. This is further proved by the fact that Ṛigveda as well as Atharva Veda mention honesty, rectitude, fellow-feeling, charity, non-violence, truthfulness, modesty, agreeable speech, Brahmacarya (celibacy), religious conviction, and purity of heart as the important virtues that are praiseworthy. These very virtues are mentioned in the Bhagavadgītā as divine qualities. Thus the Vedic philosophy lays emphasis on right conduct as the means of the development of the personality of the individual. Hence in a way the ethics of the Vedas is the ethics of right action.

On the other hand, a thorough study of the nature of the gods and their relation with human beings as depicted in the Vedas paves the way for the path of devotion (Bhakti Mārga). The Vedic gods have an intimate relation of love with human beings. Every individual has the right to be loved by the gods and also to love the gods in return. Although there is the element of fear of gods as well present in the Vedas, yet the fear is divine fear or reverential awe, and the affectionate relation of individuals with the gods has been expressed with reference to various similies. The gods love human beings, and human beings are referred to as desirous of loving gods (Deva Kāma). The god Agni has been referred to as one of the most affectionate gods who loves human beings as a father loves his son or as an elder brother loves his younger brother. Agni has been called a father, brother, and even a son. Even the battle-god Indra is regarded as an affectionate god. These very tendencies are responsible for the path of devotion (Bhakti Mārga) which appears in its full bloom in the Bhagavadgītā.

Vedic ethics is not merely religious, although it is inspired by the gods who are the representatives of the divine power of God. It is quite evident from the study of the Vedas that the early Aryans did recognize the family as a unit and did enjoin upon every member of the family to do his duty conscientiously. The members of a family, particularly husband and wife, ought to have mutual respect and love, according to the ethics of the Vedas. The sons and daughters in the same manner must have respect for parents and ought to obey their orders. The members of the family must be polite and respectful to each other. The wife's status was held to be very high, and a woman was often allowed to choose her husband. It may be mentioned, however, that polygamy was thought moral and polyandry immoral in Vedic times.

The existence of four major divisions (Varnas) of society, viz. (i) the Brāhmaṇa, the priestly class; (ii) the Kṣatriya, the ruling class, (iii) the Vaiśya, the professional class; and (iv) the Sūdra, the labouring class, is clearly indicated in Vedic literature. As we shall see later, there are Vedic hymns referring to the origin of the four Varṇas and these hymns prove the metaphysical and social nature of the four major classes.

Meanwhile it is essential to point out that the Vedic literature contains evidence of the similarity of the constitution of the individual to that of society and of the cosmos. If it is true that the microcosm is an exemplar of macrocosm, the constituents of the individual and of society, which is the totality of the individuals, must ultimately be the same as those of the universe. The development of modern science and its latest discoveries have strengthened this belief of Indian philosophy. The ancient Indian sages, the propounders of the unique Vedic knowledge, arrived at the conclusion of the unity of the basic reality through intuition or constant meditation. But the results achieved by them and expressed in the Vedic hymns are being corroborated by physics, astronomy and astrophysics even today. It is necessary here to refer to the metaphysical basis of the Vedic philosophy because ethics is just one branch of philosophy and it is very intimately associated with metaphysics. No philosophy can ever be regarded as logically complete unless its metaphysics, psychology and ethics are interrelated and consistent as a harmonious system. Our contention is that Vedic philosophy and its ethics, as well as its psychology, logically follows from its metaphysics.

Unfortunately, in spite of the fact that the Vedas are accepted as the perennial source of all the systems of Indian philosophy almost all scholars who have written on Indian philosophy in English have either omitted or overlooked the Brāhmaṇic aspect of the Vedas. Most of the works deal with the Mantras and with the Upaniṣads without reference to the explanations of the Vedic hymns given in the Brāhmaṇic literature. The Brāhmaṇas stand between the hymns and the Upaniṣads, and without referring to them it is impossible to link the development of Indian philosophy from the Vedas to the Upaniṣads. That is why the trend of scholars of Indian philosophy has been to forward a theory that the Upaniṣads are diametrically opposed to the Vedas, and that the Atma-Vidyā of the Upaniṣads, though a sublimation of the sacrificial cult of the ritualistic philosophy, is a sort of a revolt against Vedic thought. Such a blunder has been committed from the time of Max Müller to the present because the missing links found in the Brāhmaṇic literature have not been paid heed to.

If we examine the Vedic hymns critically with reference to their interpretation in the Brāhmaṇa books, we shall come to the conclusion that the Vedas present a monistic metaphysics from the inception of Vedic philosophy, and the Upaniṣads, the climax of Vedic thought, also present a monistic metaphysics. One of the oldest Sūktas of the Vedas, the Nāsadīya Sūkta, presents the idea that the Vedic Riṣis believed that prior to the creation of the universe there was one Absolute Reality, which was beyond all contradictions of existence and non-existence, light and darkness, and of time, space and cause. The Puruṣa Sūkta of the Ṛigveda also points to the organic nature of the universe, which is a cosmic person from whom all things, including human beings, arose. The Upaniṣads propound the notion of Brahman exactly along the same lines as indicated in the Vedas. The Vedavidyā is transformed into the Atmāvidyā. But the scholars of Indian philosophy, in their zeal to prove that Indian philosophy is an evolution, have made every possible attempt to establish that Vedic thought first began with nature-worship, which is a sort of polytheism, accommodating Agni, Sūrya, Mitra, etc.; then turned into henotheism, which raises every individual god to the status of supreme God; and, last of all, became monistic after passing through monotheism. Such a distorted view, which has gained popularity, can only be corrected if we try to understand the implications of the notion of gods in the Vedic pantheon from the Indian and Brāhmaṇic point of view. Unless we do so, we cannot account for the discrepancy of polytheism with monism, which is the root as well as the fruit of the Vedic philosophy.

In fact there is no polytheism or henotheism in the Vedas. The Brāhmaṇic literature shows that the various gods are nothing but the names of the various processes referred to as various entities and represented by various heavenly bodies. It is worthwhile quoting the Vedic theory of creation, which is known as the Prājāpatyabalsā Pañcaparvā Viśvavidyā, or the five-membered theory of the universe, based on the nature of Prājāpati as the central reality or the stem of the creative branch (universe). Before the theory is explained, it is necessary here to clarify the notion of Prajāpati, the lord of creation. Prajāpati is the central invisible reality which is the cause of the visible creation of the entire universe. It has been referred to as the truth of truths (Satyasya Satyaṁ) and as the centre of centres (Kendrasya Kendraiṁ) in the Brāhmaṇas. The following definition of Prajāpati given in the Vedic literature is most explicit:

Prajāpatiścarati garbhe antarājayamāno bahudhā vijāyate;
Tasya yonim paripaśyanti dhirāh tasmin hatusthu bhuvānani-viśvā.

That is, 'Prajāpati remains in the centre of all things; it is unborn; but it manifests itself in the multifarious universe; the wise know the secret of this reality, because all the orders of the (visible) universe are built on it'.

This invisible reality is all pervasive and is present in every manifestation in the form of the physical, biological and psychological universe. The universe, the expression of the one central reality, is therefore organic and dynamic. This dynamism is visible in the earth, in the planets, in the solar systems, in the galaxies and in the infinite universe as well as in man, who is cosmos in miniature. Now the five-membered theory of creation referred to above holds that there are various dynamic manifestations of the Prajāpati like earth, moon, sun, Parameṣṭhi (the galactic centre), and Svayambhu Prajāpati, the centre of the numberless universes, of which our universe is just a branch. The earth (Pṛtithvi) revolves around the sun in its orbit as Krāntivṛitta (the path of revolution). It is worth noting here that the word Vṛitta, from which has been derived the word vṛitti, which means a tendency, shows the dynamic nature of the Vedic terminology. The moon (Candra) revolves around the earth on its orbit, called the Dakṣavṛitta. The sun with all its planets revolves around its centre of gravitation called Parameṣṭhi. The orbit in which it revolves has been designated Āyatavṛitta. Thus numberless solar systems are revolving around Parameṣṭhi, the galactic centre. The Parameṣṭhis are also numberless and are revolving around Svayambhu Prajāpati, the Universal Centre, on their orbits. The orbit of the Parameṣṭhi of our universe is called Āndavṛitta. What astonishes us here is that the discoveries of modern science support this theory propounded thousands of years ago without the aid of instruments of any kind. I am prompted here to quote Sir James Jeans, whose statement is a corroboration of the Vedic theory explained above. In the concluding chapter of his book, *Physics and Philosophy*, Jeans says: 'We now know that the sun can no more be said to be at rest, in any absolute sense, than the earth; it is one of the thousands of millions of stars, which together form the galactic system. And even this centre of the galactic system cannot be said to be at rest. For millions of galactic systems can be seen in the sky, all pretty much like our own and all in motion relative to our own galaxy and to one another.'[1] If the philosophers of science support the Vedic theory of the five-membered universe with references to the latest discoveries of science, there is no wonder that the nature of man, and the constituents of society as an organic whole, will also be accepted as the corollary of the said theory of creation.

The main purpose of citing the Vedic theory of creation is to prove the consistency between the psychology and the ethics based on it. Vedic psychology explains the nature of man and society along the same lines. Man, the miniature of the universe, is regarded as an integrated whole of the four aspects viz.: (1) body, (2) mind, (3) intellect and (4) Soul. Body (Śarīra) corresponds to the earth element, and is known as pārthiva, or earthly. Mind (Manah) represents the moon element, and is known as lunar product, or Cāndra. Similarly, intellect, or Buddhi, is regarded as the product of solar (sauri) energy, and hence represents the sun element. Soul (Ātman) is a combination of two aspects known as Mahān Ātman and Avyaya Puruṣa. Mahān Ātman, or the great self, which stands for the potentiality of all the traits (inherited from seven ancestors and capable of being transmitted to seven succeeding generations) corresponds to Parameṣṭhi, the galactic centre, also designated as Viṣṇu, the light of lights (Jyotiṣāṁ Jyotih). Avyaya Puruṣa,

[1] 'Man and the Universe', *The Philosophers of Science*, p. 374.

or the invisible soul, is the highest spiritual potentiality, corresponding to Svyambhu Prajāpati and representing the highest reality or the supreme power.

The social psychology of the Vedas therefore divides society into four classes: (1) Śūdras, (2) Vaiśyas, (3) Kṣatriyas and (4) Brāhmaṇas. It must be remembered here that these classes are not at all based on birth or any economic or religious distinction. Śūdra is one whose personality is predominantly inclined towards bodily development, and who is more capable of doing physical labour than of mental, intellectual, or spiritual effort. Here the class (Varṇa) signifies the psychological tendency and the vocational choice based on that tendency. Śūdras therefore form the body of the social organism. Similarly the Vaiśyas, who are more inclined to undertake mental work than the other three kinds of pursuit, form the mind of society. Kṣatriyas, who are predominantly intellectual, form the intellect of society (which is why many Rajput families claim to be the descendants of the solar family, Sūrya Varṁśa). The Brāhmaṇas, who are predominantly spiritual in their outlook and behaviour, and whose main business is to study and propagate spiritual science, form the soul of the social organism. Thus the cosmos, society and the individual is a trinity, based on the five-sectional theory of creation. The fourth and fifth sections of the cosmos are reduced to one in the case of society and the individual, both of which are visible living entities and are positive manifestations of the dynamic cosmos as mentioned above. This classification has been responsible for the four-valued ethical theory propounded by ethical thinkers. These four values or ends of life are known as Puruṣārthas, ideals for man. An analysis of these ideals or values is most convincing and indicative of the consistency of the Vedic philosophy. The four Puruṣārthas are (1) Artha, or wealth, (2) Kāma, or satisfaction of desires, (3) Dharma, or moral duty, and (4) Mokṣa, or spiritual perfection or liberation. Artha is primarily meant for the development of the body, and in the case of society it is the aim of the labour class to produce wealth and thereby make the economic aspect of the society sound. The Kāma, or the satisfaction of desires, is necessary for the balanced development of mind, and in the case of society, artists do aim at the emotional and the aesthetic development of the society as a whole. The third value, Dharma, inspires and develops the intellect of the individual, and at the same time gives impetus to the administrative class of the society, which alone is the authority to administer and protect the moral duty. Mokṣa, or spiritual liberation, is the highest goal for man, who is potentially infinite soul and whose infinitude is inspired by this supreme good. Without the concept of Mokṣa as the goal of human life the ecclesiastical class would be extinct in the world.

The four ends of life on the one hand correspond to the four aspects of individual and society (viz. body, mind, intellect and soul), and on the other to an elaborate fourfold scheme of life known as Āśrama Dharmas, or four stages of life, which express the ethico-social organization of society, as well as a balanced ethico-social conduct for the individual. This scheme of life brings about a synthesis between the material and the spiritual development on the one hand, and, between the individual and social well-being on the other.

Let us explain the significance of the four stages of life in the light of the fourfold system of ethical values, corresponding to the fourfold personality of man and the fourfold division of human society, reflecting the Vedic theory of creation. The first stage of life, Brahmacarya Āśrama, which continues up to twenty-five years, is meant for the acquisition of learning, which is necessary for becoming worthy of earning wealth. During this stage the individual has to remain celibate, for celibacy is necessary for the maintenance of bodily health. Unless a man is healthy and learned he cannot earn wealth. Thus the first stage of life is to be devoted to education, in the natural surroundings in the hermitage of a guru or a university, for the purpose of realizing economic value, or Artha, without which entry into the next order of life, i.e. Gṛihastha, is not possible.

The Gṛihastha Āśrama, or the order of the householder, is regarded as the most important because it is at this stage that the individual enters into the first unit of society, i.e., the family, and the responsibility of supporting his wife and children falls on him. As a husband and a father he must experience love and utilize the wealth he earns for the fulfilment of his desires as well as those of his family members. The major part of the householder's life is devoted to the enjoyment and fulfilment of desires, or Kāma, the second value in the order that we have adopted. It goes without saying that the ultimate aim of all the four ends of life being spiritual perfection through an ethical code of conduct, wealth must be earned righteously and enjoyment ought to be according to the behests of Dharma, or moral duty. Adherence to morality or Dharma is a preparation for the third stage of life, which follows Gṛihastha, whose duration is between twenty-five years to fifty years.

The Vānaprastha Āśrama, or order of the anchorite, starts at the age of fifty years and continues to the age of seventy-five years. At this stage the individual does not altogether retire from social or family life, although he entrusts the entire responsibility of the household management to his heirs. He devotes his time to the study of the holy scriptures and meditation, yet he is accompanied by his wife in his mission. He does not only study ethics, but also practises it fully. He is consulted by the members of his family, and continues to give them guidance in worldly matters in accordance with the Dharma. This stage of life therefore is mainly devoted to the inculcation of the third Purusārtha, i.e. Dharma, or moral duty.

When the individual has attained the mature age of seventy-five years, when he has fully enjoyed wealth and affection with his kith and kin and has also practised and preached moral duty, wisdom dawns upon him, and he is inspired to go in search of the ultimate Reality by renouncing worldly life altogether. This is the stage of renunciation, or Sanyāsa, having attained which the individual devotes his entire time to learning the scriptures, discussing the nature of the ultimate Reality and meditating on it with a view to become one with it. In other words, Sanyāsa Āśrama is that stage of life devoted entirely to the attainment of Mokṣa, the supreme good, the *summum bonum*.

This brief survey of the four ends of life, the four Varnas or classes of society and the four stages of life or the Āśramas, with the corresponding duties of the classes and of the individual, proves beyond all doubt that the Vedic philosophy presents us an integrated scheme of life. This practical philosophy is based on the metaphysical notion of the central reality as Prajāpati, and is at the same time pragmatic, because it leads to the all-round development of the individual as well as of society.

Thus we find that the Vedic philosophy presents us a dynamic view of the universe, and hence a dynamic activism and morally evolutionary view of life. Although Vedic activism and ethical evolutionism were adopted by some schools and partially or totally overlooked by other schools of Indian philosophy, it can be said without exaggeration that Vedic philosophy, and particularly its ethical thought, is through and through consistent with the dynamism of the Vedas. The Upaniṣads, which are the integral posterior part of the Vedic literature and are at the same time the very rock and foundation of the classical schools of Indian philosophy, continue to uphold the same ideals of life as propounded by the Vedas, and re-affirm that Mokṣa is the supreme good of life. Their entire burden is to explain the nature of Mokṣa through discussions and dialectic, and they ultimately arrive at the conclusion that the individual and the absolute are identical. Moreover, man being a combination of the finite and the infinite, the limited and the unlimited, can attain the unity by following a strict code of ethical and spiritual discipline.

Although the Upaniṣads are a part and parcel of the Veda and present the continuity of Vedic philosophy, it is desirable to deal with Upaniṣadic ethics separately for two reasons. The first is that they are the utterances of the sages who had retired from active, social and political life, and are therefore more inclined towards the spiritual development of the personality than towards the physical, mental and intellectual development of it. The second reason is that they present to us such a metaphysical basis of ethics, which through a continuance of Vedic thought, gives a new inspiration to thinkers in the various schools of Indian philosophy. These two reasons, however, do not undermine the ethical importance of the Upaniṣadic philosophy. Spiritual reflection leads the Upaniṣads to arrive at the conclusion that Ātman is Brahman, the individual is the Absolute. This fact enhances the dignity of man and makes him the highest reality. But that perfect reality is the spiritual potentiality of man, which can be actualized by the adoption of a philosophical mode of life, whether that mode is logical and analytical like that of Nyāya and Vaiśeṣika, or evolutional like that of Sāṁkhya and Yoga, or activistic like that of Mīmāṁsā, or intellectual like that of the Advaita Vedānta. It is therefore necessary to discuss at length the ethical aspects of the Upaniṣads, which connect Vedic philosophy on the one hand and the traditional orthodox and heterodox schools of Indian philosophy on the other.

The Development of Varṇa Vyavastha

Before discussing Upaniṣadic ethics it is desirable first to give a brief survey of the development of the caste system, the ethico-social structure of the Hindus, which has been responsible for the preservation of the Indian culture, as well as of social evils which in due course of time began to sap the very life of India. Such an analysis is essential because the renaissance of Indian culture in the contemporary period would not be properly understood and appreciated by the reader without it. We have seen that the introduction of the caste system in the beginning was not in the least motivated by any economic, sentimental, or religious considerations, as many scholars have wrongly held. The division of society into four classes was the assertion of the cosmic division of the universe and the psychological constituents of the individual. However, the organization could not be effected without laying down the duties and functions of the various castes. Hence the cosmic and social basis of the caste system was further supplemented by its psychological and ethical bases. As time passed and the institution of castes was practised century after century and millennium after millennium, various traditions and anti-social conventions crept into it, with the result that custom and heredity predominated over the spirit and the ethical significance of the caste system.

In order therefore, to give a brief but systematic description of the Varṇa Vyavasthā, it is desirable to throw light on the following three aspects of it:

1. Metaphysical
2. Ethico-psychological, and
3. Traditional.

We have already dealt with the metaphysical aspects of the caste system in this chapter. However, it is of interest to note that besides the cosmological background of the caste system already given, the Puruṣa Sūkta of Ṛigveda mentions an apt analogy of the cosmic person, while describing the origin of the Varṇa Vyavasthā. It is mentioned that the Brāhmaṇa class forms the head of the cosmic person, the Kṣatriyas form the arms and the chest, the Vaiśyas form its body, and the Śūdras constitute its legs. What is noteworthy here is the point that society has been recognized as one organic whole and the division has never been taken in the physical sense either in the

Vedas or in the Upaniṣads or in the Bhagavadgītā. Racial segregation, or so-called 'purity of blood', was not at all the underlying motive of the caste system. Even when the practical utility of the caste system was emphasized it was only for the sake of the successful conduct of social and national life that different duties and functions were allotted to different classes. The differentiation was on the practical and the empirical level, and not at all on the spiritual or transcendental level. The following verse of the Bhagvadgītā reminds us that the classification of society was not at all real or spiritual, but only empirical and expedient:

Vidyā vinayasampanne brāhmaṇe gavi, hastini;
Śuni caiva śvapāke ca paṇḍitāh samadarśinah.[1]

That is, 'The wise look with equal eye on a Brāhmana endowed with learning and humility, a cow, an elephant, a dog and an outcaste'. The basic notion of unity in diversity has never been overlooked in Indian philosophy. Diversity of behaviour or conduct between a Brāhmaṇa and an outcaste who cooks a dog for his meal, and the diversity of species between a cow, an elephant and a dog cannot undermine the basic unity of spirit. Regarding the acceptance of the 'unity in diversity', so far as the caste system is concerned, wherever the differentiation of duties has been mentioned it is based on psychological and never on spiritual grounds. The constant reminder of spiritual oneness, in spite of the pragmatic differentiation, was thought necessary by the sages. That is why, for example, four national festivals were introduced for the whole society, and every caste participated jointly in all these festivals.

A clarification seems necessary in this context. Indian culture recognizes four national functions:

1. Rakṣābandhana (the tying of a sacred thread around the wrist)
2. Vijayadaśamī (the tenth day of victory)
3. Deepāvalī (the festival of lights)
4. Holī (the festival of colours).

The festival of Rakṣābandhana is celebrated by tying a sacred thread around the wrist of every person, irrespective of caste

[1] Bhagavadgītā, V, 18.

and creed among the Hindus throughout the length and breadth of the Indian continent. This festival has a spiritual significance. The tying of the thread indicates the spiritual binding of its wearer to sacrifice his personal interests, his family interests and his communal or caste interests for the realization of the well-being of the nation, which according to the Indian viewpoint means the whole human race. This festival reminds us that every individual is a Brāhmaṇa to the core, and that a true Brāhmaṇa is one who always works for universal well being.

The second national festival, Vijayadaśamī, or Dasehra, as it is popularly known, consists in celebrating the victory of Rāma, the champion of righteousness, over Rāvaṇa, the leader of demons or evildoers. All the castes celebrate their victory of righteousness with equal fervour so as to be reminded of their moral duty of sacrificing everything for the victory of good over evil. Every individual on that day assumes the role of a Kṣatriya, or protector of righteousness.

The third festival, Deepāvalī, or the festival of lights, is celebrated with a view to awaken the sense of beauty and art of decoration and illumination. Since a Vaiśya is one who has artistic skill and aesthetic sense and since every individual possesses that tendency, this festival reminds everyone of the bond of unity amongst the members of all the castes. Everyone, whether a Brāhmaṇa, or a Kṣtriya, or a Śūdra, assumes the role of a Vaisya on that day, thereby reviving the sense of 'unity in diversity'.

The fourth national festival, Holī, is the festival of sprinkling colour, playing pranks, and merrymaking. Every individual, whether Brāhmana or Kṣatriya or Vaiśya, assumes the role of a Śūdra on that day, by mixing with the members of all the castes, by smearing them with colours, and by being smeared with colours by them. Everyone is in a mood of humour, and no one minds the loss of self-respect by being laughed at on his cartoon-like appearance on account of the paint and colour on his body. The idea is that everyone assumes the same physical form, and the physical equality so created reminds us that we have the same spiritual unity underlying the body. The difference between a Śūdra and a Brāhmaṇa, or a Vaiśya and a Kṣatriya, is therefore not real but temporary, and that difference is cast off even physically on the day of the Holī festival.

Since all the castes participate in all these festivals jointly, these national celebrations are the constant reminder of the organic nature of the caste system and of spiritual unity in physical diversity. But, most unfortunately, the bulk of Indians have lost sight of the significance of these festivals and celebrate them blindly. A reorientation therefore is essential in this direction to maintain solidarity and spiritual awakening throughout India.

The allotment of different ethical duties to the members of the different castes has been made entirely on the basis of natural inclination. The forty-first verse of the Bhagavadgītā says 'The duties of the Brāhmaṇas, Kṣatriyas, Vaiśyas, and also of the Śūdras are clearly divided, O Scorcher of Foes, according to the dispositions born of their own nature (Svabhāva)'.[1] The ethical duties of Brāhmaṇa arising out of his bent of mind are serenity, self-control, austerity, purity, tolerance, uprightness, knowledge (Jñāna), scientific attitude (Vijñāna) and faith. Similarly, the ethical duties of a Kṣatriya, based on his psychological nature, are, heroism, boldness, not fleeing the battlefield, generosity and lordliness (Īśvarabhāva). In like manner the psychological inclination of the Vaiśyas calls for ethical duties of agriculture, cattle rearing, trade, engineering, etc. The ethical duties of Śūdras in accordance with their psychological aptitude are those of physical labour, obedience and maximum production of wealth for the nation. Again it is to be regretted that the spirit of these distinctions has been lost sight of, and artificial barriers have been created between various castes.

The traditional aspect of the caste system has predominated and has brought in its wake the social evils of heredity, segregation and untouchability. The Hindu community is today divided into numberless sub-castes and water-tight compartments, with the result that inter-caste marriages and co-dining between different castes are taboo. People do not know that even Manu, the great law-giver of the Hindus, declared that every human being is a born Śūdra. These social evils bespeak the appalling ignorance of the real import of the caste system, and prevent the recognition and acceptance of underlying spiritual unity. Unless that spirit is awakened and the intuitive knowledge of the oneness of Brahman (Jñāna) is synthesized

[1] Bhagavadgītā, XVIII, 41.

with the empirical knowledge (Vijñāna) of the plurality of the physical world, these artificial barriers between man and man cannot be smashed. That is why the explanation of the ethical implications of the Upaniṣadīc philosophy is essential to a proper understanding of Vedic ethics. We shall, therefore, proceed with the ethics of the Upaniṣads in the ensuing chapter.

CHAPTER IV

THE ETHICS OF THE UPANIṢADS

We have seen that the ethics of the Vedas is the fourfold scheme of life, with the four Puruṣārthas or ends of life, the four Varnas or social divisions, and the four Āśramas or stages of life incumbent upon each and every individual. The Upaniṣadic period of Indian philosophy was the most creative period, particularly from the point of view of the spiritual growth of man. The Vedas had already pointed out that the aim of all the ethical and social principles was the attainment of spiritual perfection. Even the knowledge of the external world in the form of various theories of the universe led to the conclusion that the central reality, Prajāpati, was the sole cause of creation, and as such this alone could be the ultimate end of the process of the universe and also of human life. The Upaniṣads elaborate this view of the Vedas.

We have stated elsewhere that the special feature of Indian ethics is its inseparability from and dependence on metaphysics. The ethics of the Upaniṣads confirms this view and proves that the goal of ethics is also metaphysical. If once it is established that the individual self or Ātman is ultimately identical with the universal self (Brahman), it goes without saying that the aim of life is not self interest in the sense of seeking satisfaction of individual desires, but self-realization, which lifts the aspirant from the lower level of renunciation to the heights where he rises above all contradictions, and hence above narrowmindedness and selfishness. The person who has attained Brahmānubhava, the true experience of the universal self, must constantly be devoted to the well-being not only of human beings but of all the living creatures. The Bhagvadgītā, which is rightly regarded as the quintessence of the Upaniṣads, has remarked that 'Ātmavat sarvabhūteṣu yo paśyati sa pasyati,' i.e. 'A person who considers all living creatures equal to his own self is the seer.' Coleridge, the well-known English poet, has said in the same strain:

He prayeth well who loveth well
Both man and bird and beast.

This tendency of the Upaniṣads towards universal love proves that the Upaniṣadic philosophy is far from being individualistic. It is ethically universalistic as it is metaphysically cosmic. This tendency has been responsible for the adoption of non-violence as the highest virtue by almost all the ethical schools of Indian philosophy, especially by Jainism and Buddhism. Thus we find in the Upaniṣads the germs of all those ethical doctrines propounded later by orthodox as well as heterodox systems. The doctrine of Karma is envisaged in the Upaniṣads. Similarly the Upaniṣads reveal the three paths of knowledge, action and devotion which are later on elaborated in the Bhagavadgītā. The extreme asceticism of the Jaina system and the pessimism of the Buddhist school owe their development to the Upaniṣadic attitude of indifference towards sensual pleasures with a view to attaining spiritual realization. But, as we shall see later, the Upaniṣads do not advocate asceticism at the cost of ethics and humanism. On the contrary, they harmonize the Vedic philosophy of active life, based on the Varnāśrama-dharmas, with the life of the spirit, having attained which a man though now beyond good and evil is spontaneously engaged in the well-being of all. Upaniṣadic ethics is on the one hand concerned with the ethical doctrines of the Vedas, which it transmutes into spiritual form, and on the other it becomes the source of inspiration for the various schools of Indian philosophy so far as ethical life is concerned. How far the Upaniṣadic thought has influenced the ethics of the classical schools is evident when we study the ethics of those schools. In the present chapter we are mainly concerned with the ethical implications of the Upaniṣads, their relation with the Vedic ethics, and the importance of ethical life so far as the attainment of Mokṣa, spiritual perfection, is concerned. It should not be forgotten that it is only in the Upaniṣads that the concept of Mokṣa is made explicit, and it is this concept of the *summum bonum* which makes Indian ethics unique.

It would not be an exaggeration to say that in this sense the Upaniṣads occupy the supreme position in Indian ethics. Although the Vedas do lay down the four ideals of life, yet they are not very clear about the attainment of Ātmajñāna, which is the key to Mokṣa. That is why when Nārada goes to Sanat Kumāra to learn the secret of the soul, and when he is asked as to why in spite of his learning the Vedas, which exhaust all knowledge, he is keen to learn more, Nārada replies that all his knowledge concerns the cosmos and not the self. Unless he knows the self all his cosmic knowledge would be meaningless. Since the Upaniṣads expound the knowledge of the self, and since this knowledge is the highest knowledge (Parāvidyā), as contrasted with the lower knowledge (Aparāvidyā) of the Vedas, it is quite evident that this supreme knowledge alone can propound the supreme goal of life. This fact, however, does not in the least undermine the importance of the Vedic knowledge, whose sole purpose was to explain the manifestations of the unmanifested central reality. It only points out that the central reality is capable of being realized and thoroughly understood only when man, who is the highest reality, comes to know his own inner self.

Thus in the Vedas where the gods are regarded as the protectors of Ṛita, the universal moral principle underlying the cosmos, we find that the inspiration to follow the ethical code of conduct is derived from the outside world. But in the Upaniṣads the desire to be ethical is an inner desire, and is therefore more spontaneous than the adoption of the rules laid down in the Vedic ritual. The Vedas point out that 'the fear of the law is the beginning of wisdom', whereas the Upaniṣads hold that morality is an inner growth. The aim of both the outer laws as well as the internal purity is undoubtedly the same, namely, the integrated development of the personality of man and the attainment of the state of Mokṣa. That is why the Upaniṣads do not contradict the authority of the Vedas, nor do they repudiate the Varna Dharmas or the Āśrama Dharmas. But they give a real meaning to the caste system by pointing out that all the social and ethical rules are made for man, and that they are subsidiary to his well-being, i.e. Mokṣa.

Varṇa Vyavastha

This liberal attitude of the Upaniṣads clearly indicates that up to that time rigidity had not crept into the caste system, and that the highest quality required for entering into the quest of the ultimate reality was adherence to truth. The Chāndogya

Upaniṣad illustrates how true Brahmanhood is not based on birth but on adherence to truth:

Satyakāma, the son of Jābāla addressed his mother and said, 'I wish to become a Brahmacārin, Mother, of what family am I?'

She said to him: 'I do not know, my child, of what family thou art. In my youth, when I had to move about much as a servant, I conceived thee. So I do not know of what family thou art. I am Jābāla by name. Thou art Satyakāma. Say that thou art Satyakāma Jābāla.'

He, going to Gautama, the son of Haridrumat, said to him, 'I wish to become a Brahmacārin with thee, sire. May I come to you?'

He said to him: 'Of what family art thou my friend?'

He replied, 'I do not know, sire, of what family I am. I asked my mother, and she answered "In my youth, when I had to move about much as a servant, I conceived thee. I do not know of what family thou art. I am Jābāla by name, thou art Satyakāma.' I am therefore Satyakāma Jābāla, sire.'

He said to him 'No one but a true Brahmin would thus speak out. Go and fetch fuel. I shall initiate thee. Thou hast not swerved from the truth.'[1]

The Upaniṣadic period therefore was an age of communal freedom, and a premium was set on learning and spiritual acumen rather than on birth. Even Kṣatriyas like Sanat Kumāra could teach Ātmavidyā to a Brahmin like Nārada. As I have already mentioned Upaniṣadic ethics was not concerned with external influence on the mind of man but with the inner growth of morality. That is why in the matter of ethics caste bars and sex distinctions were overlooked. Commenting upon the internality of the Upaniṣadic ethics, Radhakrishnan has remarked: 'Laws and regulations are necessary for those men who do not naturally conform to the dictates of conscience. But for those who have risen above their selfish egos morality becomes the very condition of their being, and law is fulfilled in love.'[2] Here the caste system and the duties of the various classes are subordinated to the highest duty of striving to identify the self with Brahman. The caste system is not given

[1] Chāndogya Upaniṣad, 4.1.4. Cited in Radhakrishnan, *Indian Philosophy*, Vol. I, pp. 222–3.

[2] *Ibid.*, p. 228.

up, nor is it regarded unavoidable, but it is given a proper place in the scheme of spiritual life.

Āśrama Dharmas

The case is similar with the four orders or the Āśramas of life, which regulate the conduct of the individual. The story of Satyakāma Jabālā shows that it was incumbent upon every individual to adopt the first stage of life, that is, Brahmacarya, and to join some hermitage for acquiring knowledge as a Brahmacārin. Since Brahmacarya Āśrama is a preparatory stage, the next stage of life, that is, the householder's level, is presumed to be a very important stage. But while advocating the adoption of Gṛihastha, it is pointed out that the ultimate aim of married life, as that of the whole life, is spiritual realization. The Taittirīya Upaniṣad points out that the chaste life of Brahmacarya is a preparatory stage for the adoption of married life, which is 'a religious sacrament, a form of divine service'. Without the presence of a wife no religious ceremony was considered to be complete in the Upaniṣadic period. The spirit of self-sacrifice for the interest of the family ultimately leads to detachment from worldly pleasures and concentration on God-realization. The experience of human love at the level of Gṛihastha is preparation for Divine Love. The purpose of all the rules of conduct for the individual, and even of the Puruṣārthas, or the four chief values of life, according to the Upaniṣads, is the identification of the Ātman, or the self, with Brahman. But it should be remembered that the Sanyāsa Āśrama, which is the last stage of life, and which is devoted to self-realization, could not be adopted without passing through the other three stages, and, particularly, the householder's stage of life. There is no doubt that the last stage of life is the stage of pure renunciation and detachment from worldly life. But renunciation is possible only when a person has enjoyed worldly life, and when he has discharged his duties sincerely as a householder, and as an ideal member of the society. It is only when a man has gained the knowledge of Ātman after passing through the stage of an anchorite that he longs to renounce possessions and enters into the order of a Sanyāsin, or a recluse. The Upaniṣads regard the Sanyāsa Āśrama as the highest stage of life because they believe the other three stages of life to be subsidiary stages of preparation. Thus the emphasis on Sānyasa Āśrama in the Upaniṣads is indicative of the recognition of the other three stages of life, i.e. Brahmacarya, Gṛihastha, and Vānaprastha.

The Four Puruṣārthas

Since the supreme good accepted by the Upaniṣads is self-realization, the oneness of the individual self (Ātman) with the universal self, Brahman, it is quite evident that the three Puruṣārthas, i.e. Artha (wealth), Kāma (the fulfilment of desires), and Dharma (duty), have been thought of as means to the attainment of Mokṣa. This, however, does not mean that the Upaniṣadic thinkers ever neglected wealth and the satisfaction of desires. The recognition of the Gṛihastha Āśrama by the Upaniṣads clearly indicates the acceptance of other Puruṣārthas than Mokṣa. But wealth was never accepted as an end in itself. On the contrary, the Upaniṣads point out that wealth, an instrumental and hence a lower value, cannot give complete satisfaction to human desires. Kaṭhaupaniṣad says 'No man can be made happy by wealth. . . . The hereafter never rises before the eyes of the careless youth, befooled by the delusion of wealth. "This is the world," he thinks, "there is no other." Thus he falls again and again into the power of death.'[1]

Wealth is thus thought of only as a means to the attainment of Mokṣa. Wealth becomes evil only when it is misused on account of lack of wisdom. The Upaniṣads repeatedly point out that everything that is desired is desired for the sake of the self. Even the objects of the world need not be regarded as evil by a wise man. A person who possesses a right vision declares with the Upaniṣads, 'Tato me sriyamāvah': 'Hence bring wealth to me.' Commenting upon the desire for wealth as one of the commands of the Upaniṣads, Radhakrishnan remarks: 'And Śamkara points out that wealth is an evil to the unregenerate, but not to the man of wisdom. Things of the world seemingly undivine are a perpetual challenge to the spiritual soul. He has to combat their independence and turn them into the expressions of the Divine. He does all work in this spirit of detachment.'[2]

Detached pursuit of God does not consist in giving up the

[1] Kaṭhaupaniṣad, I, 2.6.

[2] Radhakrishnan, *op. cit.*, Vol. I, p. 217.

world or giving up desires. On the contrary, it stands for the highest desire of the highest goal, which is either God-realization or self-realization. The concept of duty or Dharma in the Upaniṣads is not negative but out and out positive. It does not command us to give up or renounce the world, but rather to engage in the worldly strife, always aiming at the spiritual goal and subordinating all other desires to the strongest desire, or love for God. Thus Kāma, or desire, here is divinized, because even the Lord himself desired in the beginning to become the world. The Upaniṣad says, 'He desired, "Let me be many"'. Discretion consists in giving up false desires and entertaining true desires, which help us in developing the self. Dr Radhakrishnan has commented upon the Upaniṣadic notion of Kāma as follows: 'Kāma, which we are asked to renounce, is not desire as such, but only the animal desire, lust, the impulsive craving of the brute man. Freedom from Kāma is enjoined, but this is not blank passivity.'

The above aspect of the Upaniṣadic notion of desire is the longing of the aspirant for union with God. This very divine passion is converted into the path of devotion, or Bhaktimārga, in the Bhagavadgītā. This union is the identification of the self with the Brahman, which is the keynote of the Upaniṣadic philosophy.

The goal is attainable not only by a strong desire. Purification of heart and virtuous life are also the prerequisites of an aspirant, or a Jigyāsu. The Mundaka Upaniṣad advocates the development of 'soul force' by resorting to spiritual or ethical discipline. Chāndogya Upaniṣad mentions that the inculcation of the five virtues of self-renunciation (Tapas), charity or philanthropy (Dāna), right conduct (Ārjavam), non-violence (Ahiṁsā) and adherence to truth (Satya Vacanam) are the necessary virtues to be practised by an aspirant. Thus Dharma, or virtue, has a very prominent place in the ethics of the Upaniṣads. To sum up, we may say that Artha, Kāma, and Dharma are instrumental values, but at the same time essential methods for the attainment of Mokṣa.

The ethics of the Upaniṣads foreshadows the ethics of the Bhagavadgītā, which we shall discuss in the sequel. There is no doubt that the Upaniṣads implicitly contain the three fold path of knowledge, action and devotion, where knowledge stands for the knowledge of the Ultimate Reality, action stands for self-control, and devotion represents Brahma Jigyāsā, or passion for Brahman. The metaphysical background of the Upaniṣadic philosophy is non-dualistic reality. Its goal is self-realization, and the means of attaining it are reason, renunciation and devotion. Thus Upaniṣadic ethics is not only universalistic, but cosmic and anti-individualistic. It would therefore be desirable to throw some more light on its goal and the means of attaining it.

According to the Upaniṣads man is regarded as the highest reality, because of all the creatures of the world it is he who is self-conscious and most anxious to become infinite. In spite of finitude and imperfection man feels a great urge to attain infinity and perfection. This keen desire to go from the limited to the unlimited, from the mortal to the immortal, and from the relative to the absolute state of existence is indicative of the fact that man's real self is not the individual self but the universal self. The innermost nature of man is not contradictory, relative and pluralistic existence, but it is non-contradictory, absolute and non-dualistic reality. In other words, man is potentially God, and the aim of all ethics is to convert this potentiality into an activity, manhood into Divinity, and relativity into Absoluteness. This is what is meant by self-realization as the goal of the Upaniṣadic ethics. In order to achieve this goal man has to rise from the level of selfishness to that of self-sacrifice and self-devotion, from narrow sensual satisfaction to the state of equipoise and equilibrium, and from personal, individualized and egoistic attachment to the impersonal, universalized and absolute transcendence.

This very state of existence has been referred to as the state of Sthitaprajñā in the Bhagavadgītā, and that of Jīvanmukti in the Jaina, Bauddha, Sāṁkhya, and Yoga systems. The Upaniṣads, however, point out that once a person attains this level of existence he automatically eschews fear, hatred, jealousy and enmity. If a person comes to identify his personal self with the individual self or Brahman, which is immanent in the whole cosmos; if once a person comes to realize that he is one with the whole universe, organic as well as inorganic, sentient as well as insentient, and conscious as well as unconscious, then how can he hate, fear or envy? If he hates anybody, should he hate himself? If he is afraid of anybody, should he be afraid of his own self? If he is jealous of anybody, should he be jealous of his own self? When this stage is attained by knowledge the path adopted for self-realization is called Jñānamārga, and the person who attains self-realization is called Jñāna Yogin.

But Jñānamarga, the path of knowledge, is not the sole gateway to self-realization. The Upaniṣads also advocate the path of action, which enjoins upon the aspirant to control his senses and to subordinate the sensual self to the rational or the intellectual self. Ātman, the real self, has been compared to the occupant of a chariot. The Kaṭhaupaniṣad, says 'Know the self or Ātman as the Lord, who sits in the chariot called the body, Buddhi or intelligence is the charioteer, mind is the reins, the senses are the horses, and the objects are the roads. The self, the senses, and the mind combined, the intelligent call the enjoyer. But he who has no understanding . . . his senses run riot like the vicious horses of a charioteer. He who has understanding and is strong-minded, his senses are well controlled, like the good horses of a charioteer. He who is without understanding, who is thoughtless and impure never reaches the immortal immaterial state, but enters into the round of births. But he who has understanding and he who is thoughtful and pure reaches the state from which there is no return'.[1]

This quotation from the Upaniṣads points out on the one hand the necessity of true knowledge as well as purity of character, and on the other, explains the nature of Mokṣa, which means freedom from the transmigration of the soul. The activism of the Upaniṣads is evident from the very acceptance of the rules of conduct which were prescribed for the pupil and were followed by him after he left the hermitage and entered the order of a householder. The necessity of self-control and ethical discipline was emphasized when the pupil departed from his teacher. Taittirīya Upaniṣad says, 'Having taught the Veda, a teacher further instructs a pupil:— "Speak the truth (Satyam Vada), practice virtue (Dharman Cara) . . ." One should not be negligent of truth. One should not be negligent of virtue. One should not be negligent of welfare. One should not be negligent of prosperity.'[2] The caution of the teacher to the pupil not to neglect truth, virtue, or welfare proves that Upaniṣadic ethics did pay attention to social and moral well-being both of the individual and society. The honour and respect to the teacher

[1] Kaṭhaupaniṣad, quoted in Radhakrishnan, *op. cit.*, p. 211.
[2] Taittirīya Upaniṣad, 1.

and the parents was also enjoined upon the seeker of truth in the Upaniṣadic period. Thus morality consisted in service to others, self-control, and decent behaviour both at home as well as abroad.

As already pointed out, this ethical and active aspect of the Upaniṣadic code of conduct was subsidiary to, and the means of, the attainment of the highest state of infinite existence, infinite consciousness and infinite bliss (Saccidānanda). The Upaniṣads clearly state that self-control and detachment from sensual desires are the means toward identifying the individual self (Ātman) with Brahman. The Brihadāranyaka Upaniṣad, while describing the self of the unreleased and the released after death, says, 'Now the man who does not desire—he who is without desire, who is freed from desire, whose desire is satisfied, whose desire is the self—his life (Prana) does not depart. Being very Brahman, he goes to Brahman.'[1] The tendency of Indian philosophy to go beyond logic and ethics, which needless to say does not mean an anti-logical and anti-ethical tendency, proves the practical application of ideals to life, of theory to practice, of science to religion, and of metaphysics to ethics. In theory Mokṣa is an ideal, but in practice it is an actual state of existence experienced by an individual in this life. In theory, right and wrong and good and evil are ideals, and discrimination between them is the essential instrument for attaining the highest state of Mokṣa, but once the aspirant attains the actual state of Jīvanmukti, they become meaningless and pale into insignificance. Thus ethics and metaphysics, science and religion, and logic and mysticism merge into one whole spiritual experience, having attained which the aspirant promotes morality without being actively engaged in its propagation. He brings about the well-being of each and every person who comes into contact with him without making any voluntary effort on his part. Wherever he goes he sheds a divine light and causes 'the will and the kingdom of God prevail'.

Hence the ideal of self-realization as the attainment of Mokṣa is the ideal of God-realization. When man subjects himself to spiritual discipline his finite powers of knowing, feeling and willing are converted into infinite knowledge, infinite love, and infinite power, and man becomes God. But so long as he is

[1] Radhakrishnan and C. A. Moore (eds), *A Source Book of Indian Philosophy*, p. 87.

imperfect, so long as he is limited and finite, his longing to merge into the ultimate reality urges him to follow the path of knowledge, action and devotion to attain self-realization in the sense expressed above. It is this urge which brings about a synthesis between knowledge and action, and between reason and will. Thus the urge to become Divine is the strongest and most important, because it is the means as well as the end of perfection. The universal tendency of mysticism and self-surrender to God is nothing but the spiritual unrest in the bosom of man to transcend empirical limitations and to breathe, live, and have his being in God. This is called Brahma-jijñāsa, the cosmic wonderment in the Upaniṣads and the Vedanta, and is the first prerequisite of an aspirant.

Commenting upon this aspect of human nature, Dr Radhakrishnan remarks, 'Man is in anguish when he is separated from God, and nothing else than union with God can satisfy his heart's hunger.' The Upaniṣads emphasize the union of the individual self with Brahman because such a union alone gives satisfaction to the restless soul. The Kaṭhaupaniṣad says:

> The childish go after outward pleasures,
> They walk into the net of widespread death.
> But the wise knowing immortality
> Seek not the stable among things, which are unstable here.[1]

Worldly pleasures and sensual enjoyments pale into insignificance only when the highest bliss of the union with God is aimed at. Neither Saṁnyāsa, or renunciation of the worldly life, nor Karmayoga, or giving up the personal motive of gain, is possible unless the aim of God-realization is constantly kept before the mind. As we shall see later the path of devotion or God-realization is the only solution to the degeneration of Niśkāma Karmayoga into a philosophy of inactivity and motivelessness. The Upaniṣads contain the germs of the path of devotion because the central subject of the Upaniṣads is the existence of the all-pervasive spiritual reality of Brahman. The Kaṭhaupaniṣad supports this view of ours in the following manner:

[1] Kaṭhaupaniṣad, VI, p. 2.

The inner self of all things, the one controller,
Who makes his one form manifold:
The wise who perceive him as standing in one-self,
They, and no others, have external happiness.[1]

Eternal bliss cannot be experienced at any stage lower than that of God-realization. This is the keynote of the Upaniṣads, the keynote of the Vedas and the key-note of Indian philosophy. This fact is proved in the ethics of the Bhagavadgītā, which is foreshadowed in the Upaniṣads. We shall deal with the ethics of the Bhagavadgītā not in their historical chronology but later because it is the quintessence of the Indian ethics and presents to us a theory of life acceptable to persons of different faiths and temperaments. But before I close this chapter, I would like once more to point out that the central doctrine of the Upaniṣads is undoubtedly the elaboration of the central principle of Prajāpati of the Vedas. That is why the ethics of the Upaniṣads is not different from the Vedic ethics in kind, though it may be held to differ somewhat in quality. The spirit of both the Vedas and the Upaniṣads is the same, though the intensity and the emphasis is different.

The quotation from the Kaṭhaupaniṣad given above is merely the repetition of the notion of the central reality, Prajāpati, which has been referred to in the Vedas, as the truth of truths and the centre of centres (Satyasya Satyam, Kendrasya Kendram). While defining Prajāpati the Vedic seers have said that it is the unmanifested cause of the manifested and the manifold world. The same fact has been expressed in the Kaṭhaupaniṣad. Not only this, but the Vedic notion of the creation, which explains that the earth, the moon, the sun and the solar systems, are revolving around Prajāpati and are thus dependent upon Prajāpati, the sole generator of the universe, has been explicitly referred to by the Isa Upaniṣad in the following manner:

'O' Nourisher, the sole seer; O' controller, O' sun, offspring of Prajāpati, spread forth thy rays.'

While dealing with the nature of the Varṇa Dharmas concerning the social self and the four Puruṣārthas (meant both for the

[1] Radhakrishnan & Moore, *op. cit.*, p. 12.

individual as well as for the society), we have already demonstrated the interrelation of the individual self, social self, and the cosmic self clearly. It is necessary to remember here that man is the miniature cosmic self having body, mind, intellect and soul; the cosmos is the external universal self having earth, moon, sun, Paramesthi (the galactic centre) and Prajāpati (the centre of all the universes); and the social self is constituted by the Śūdras representing the body of society, Vaiśayas representing the mind of society, Kṣatriyas representing the intellect of society, and the Brāhmaṇas representing the soul of society. Corresponding to this trinity of the individual, society, and the cosmos, each of which is reduced to four aspects, are the four ends of life, viz.:—Artha, or wealth, for the development of body, Kāma, or the fulfilment of desires, for the development of mind, Dharma, or morality, for the development of the intellect, and finally Mokṣa, or spiritual perfection, for the development of the soul. Thus this ethico-metaphysical system is present clearly in the Ṛigvedic philosophy and it is also reflected in the Upaniṣads, which emphasize the oneness of the universe and hence entail the same non-dual reality as the goal of the cosmos, of society, and of the individual. The all pervasive spiritual substance is the ground; it is also the means and the goal of ethics in the Vedas as well as in the Upaniṣads. This immanence is expressed in the Īsa Upaniṣad as follows:

> By the Lord (Īśa) enveloped must this all be—
> Whatever moving thing there is in the moving world
> With this renounced, thou mayest enjoy;
> Covet not the wealth of anyone at all.

Īśa, or God, is here equivalent to the immanent Brahman, which itself is the unmoved mover and the uncaused cause of all that exists, moves and has its being in Brahman. Unless and until the immanence is recognized and the supremacy of the ultimate reality accepted, the desire to renounce the transitory objects of the world and the spirit of self-sacrifice, which are the necessary conditions of self-realization, can never be inculcated in the mind of a person. Firm faith in the divine power, which amounts to conviction, strengthens the willpower of man and facilitates self-control. That is why the Upaniṣadic statement above first refers to the immanence of God and then advocates the attitude of detachment in the midst of enjoyment, exhorting the individual to eschew covetousness. This attitude of renunciation in action, which is not renunciation of action, again becomes the means of realizing God or Brahman, knowledge of which in the beginning was the cause of detachment. Metaphysics and ethics, and religion and morality, are so intermixed and inter-related in Indian philosophy, that they are inseparable and inter-dependent. The entire Indian thought right from the early Vedic period, down to the latest classical systems and theological philosophies like Śaivism, Śāktaism and Vaisnavism are the expression of an ethico-metaphysical attitude of the Indian sages and philosophers.

The analysis of the ethical tendencies in the Upaniṣads given above has indicated that the Upaniṣadic ethics, which is basically Vedic, provides us with the background on which the ethics of the Bhagavadgītā and that of the classical systems of Indian philosophy is subsequently established. Not only do the ethics of the orthodox and the heterodox systems of Indian philosophy draw their inspiration from the Upaniṣads, but even their metaphysics, which is the basis of every system of Indian ethics, is ultimately derived from and based on Upaniṣadic metaphysics. Each and every system of Indian philosophy except the materialistic Cārvāka system, recognizes Mokṣa as the supreme ethico-metaphysical goal of life.

Before I proceed with the exposition of the ethics of the various schools of Indian philosophy, it would be desirable to explain at some length to what extent the orthodox and the heterodox systems are related to the Upaniṣadic thought. I will deal with the ethics of the Bhagavadgītā at a later stage, thereby resorting to a chronological departure from the presentation of Indian ethics to the reader. The purpose of this is to point out how the classical schools indirectly accept the basic concepts of the Upaniṣadic thought, whereas the Bhagavadgītā is the direct continuation of Upaniṣadic ethics. The ethics of the Bhagavadgītā appeals to everyone irrespective of his scholastic point of view, and that is why Bhagavadgītā presents a synthetic philosophy of life which accommodates all opinions.

I will not be able to show the relation of the orthodox and the heterodox systems to the Upaniṣads in detail for want of space in this work. The Pança Kośa theory of the self, or the theory of the five sheaths of the self, is worth mentioning in this connexion. The individual self consists of the bodily self, or the Annamaya Kośa; the biological self, or Prāṇamayakośa; the psychological or mental self, known as the Manomayakośa; the intellectual or rational self, known as Vijñānamayakośa; and the spiritual or the blissful self called the Anandmayakośa. This theory is explained in detail in the Taittirīya Upaniṣad. The first sheath of the person consists of the essence of food and is constituted by the various parts of our body like head, sides, legs, trunk, etc. The bodily self is known as the Annamaya Kośa, or the sheath constituted by the essence of food, because it is food that makes the body grow. We shall see later that the Cārvāka system takes only this sheath of the self to be the real self and does not go beyond it. Although it recognizes the presence of the consciousness, it holds that with the death of the body consciousness disappears forever.

The second sheath of the self is the biological self. It is called the Prānamayakośa or the self consisting of breath because 'breath is the life of beings', according to the Taittīrīya Upaniṣad. According to the Upaniṣads the biological self or the astral body continues to exist after the annihilation of the body. The biological self therefore is subtler than the bodily self and is the controller of the body. The Cārvāka thinkers do not recognize its existence and hence their ethics is concerned only with the satisfaction of sensual desires. All the other schools of Indian philosophy believe in the continuity of the biological self, and therefore advocate self-control, or the control of the bodily self, to keep the biological self intact.

The third sheath of the self is consciousness or mind, which remains within the biological and the bodily self. Even mind or consciousness is not the final stage of the individual's personality. That is why the satisfaction of desires through Kāma is not regarded as the ultimate end by any school of Indian philosophy except the Cārvāka school. Consciousness does make an animal superior to plants and non-living matter, yet it is not the highest level of human personality. Mind must be brought under control in order to rise above it and to reach the next stage of self-consciousness.

The fourth sheath of the self is the sheath consisting of understanding or intellect. It remains within the mental, biological and the bodily self and is subtler than all these. Therefore it controls all our actions. The Upaniṣad says:

> Understanding directs the sacrifice;
> And deeds also it directs.
> 'Tis understanding that all the gods
> Do worship as Brahman, as chief.

Since intellect is nearest Brahman or the spiritual self, its development leads to the realization of the spiritual self, which is the last and the highest level of the individual self. That is why all the schools of Indian philosophy lay emphasis on the understanding of the nature of the ultimate reality. The concept of Sthitaprajña, or the person having a stable intellect, is accepted by every school except the Cārvāka school in some form or other. We shall see later that this concept has a great ethical significance.

The final sheath—the highest stage of the individual self—is the stage which consists of bliss. It is within the intellectual, mental, biological and the physical self, and is therefore the subtlest of all. It corresponds to the Prajāpati, the centre of centres and the truth of truths. The realization of the spiritual or the blissful self leads to God-realization, or Brahmānubhava, having attained which the individual rises above all contradictions and antinomies. The two stages of self-realization, Mokṣa, i.e. the Jīvānmukti, or the liberation attained while living, and the Vidhehamukti, or the final release after the physical death, have been recognized by Nyāya, Vaiśesika, Sāṁkhya, Yoga, Mīmāmsā, Vedañta, Jainism, Buddhism and even by the Bhagavadgītā. Thus Upaniṣadic thought is the very rock and foundation of the metaphysical as well as the ethical concepts of all the systems of Indian philosophy.

CHAPTER V

THE HEDONISTIC ETHICS OF THE CĀRVĀKA SYSTEM

Cārvāka is the materialistic system of Indian philosophy. Chronologically its treatment must be given the first place even though this school appears as a note of discord in the symphony of Indian philosophy. On account of the tendency of this school toward gross materialism, atheism, individualistic hedonism, and radical selfishness, it has become an object of ridicule. However, this fact should not prompt us to overlook the ethical contribution of the Cārvāka school to the development of Indian thought. On the contrary, this protestant ideology and radical empiricism has been responsible for strengthening the logical aspect of all other systems of Indian philosophy. If we were to compare the history of Western philosophy and Indian philosophy it would not be an exaggeration to point out that the Cārvāka movement has the same place in Indian philosophy as Sophism had in the Greek Enlightenment in Western philosophy.

Before we discuss the ethical concepts of the Cārvāka school it is helpful to refer to the points of similarity and difference between the Sophist movement of the West and the Cārvāka philosophy. This comparison will assist our understanding of the ethical theory of the Cārvākas, which has been called egoistic hedonism. Ethical hedonism is purely Western, having its origin in Greece. All the other systems of Indian philosophy, orthodox or heterodox, are out and out spiritualistic in metaphysics and rationalistic in ethics.

Cārvāka is the single example in Indian classical philosophy advocating the blind satisfaction of desires as the ideal of life. This attitude is the outcome of the materialistic metaphysics of the Cārvāka school. The materialism of the Cārvākas is in turn the result of the total rejection of any other source of valid knowledge than perception. There is little doubt that this revolutionary spirit and hatred for spiritualism were caused by the prevailing dogmatism of the post-Upaniṣadic period in India.

Perhaps the subtle philosophy of Brahman and Ātman, which required intellectual acumen and considerable mental effort to be grasped, disgusted the man in the street. Like Protagoras of Greece the Cārvākas raised a strong voice against metaphysics, emphasizing that nothing should be regarded as real unless it was perceivable by the senses. It is here that this movement resembles the Sophist revolt before Socrates in Greece.

It is significant that the Cārvāka movement, which aimed at bringing down philosophy, particularly ethics, from heaven to earth, has many similarities to the movement of the Greek enlightenment of the sixth and the fifth century BC. This was a century when Greece as well as India experienced an intellectual upheaval. It was during this period that in the West 'men meditated upon the manners and customs of their times, upon the social and political institutions, upon the religious ideas and practices, upon the origin, nature and behaviour of the gods.'[1] This spirit was responsible for the type of scepticism practised by the Sophists who pointed out the discrepancies and contradictions in prevalent metaphysical concepts. Similarly the Indian Sophists raised their voice against Upaniṣadic metaphysical concepts of Brahman and Ātman, pointing out that the universe was not the result of spiritual Brahman but a combination of physical elements, and that the soul or self was nothing but the bodily self composed of the physical elements. Like the Sophists of Greece, the Cārvākas in their zealous adherence to gross positivism and crude humanism repudiated universal inferential knowledge and universal ethics, thereby making 'man the measure of all things'. The Greek Sophists declared that the individual was a law unto himself in matters of knowledge, and that there was no objective truth, but only subjective opinion. Similarly the Cārvākas emphasized that inference could not be accepted as a valid source of knowledge because it was based on Vyapti, or the universal relation between two terms or events, which amounted to objective truth. They held that only seeing was believing, agreeing with the Sophistic view that all knowledge was only subjective, direct experience. The result of this scepticism in Greece was a negative approach to the existing philosophy, and the declaration that no preceding philosophy was true. The Cārvākas also repudiated Vedic thought, rejected religion, derided metaphysics, and declared:

[1] Frank Thilly, *A History of Philosophy*, Second Indian edition, p. 53.

'There is no heaven, no final liberation, nor any soul in another world.

'Nor do the actions of the four castes, orders, etc., produce any real effect.

'The Agnihotra, the three Vedas, the ascetic's three staves, and smearing one's self with ashes, were made by nature as the livelihood of those destitute of knowledge and manliness.'

Even from the ethical point of view we find a striking similarity between the Sophists and the Cārvākas. Just as the Sophists reject objective value and preach individualism in the matters of moral choice, similarly the Cārvākas preach an egoistic theory of seeking pleasure as the highest moral ideal, agreeing with the Sophists that morality is a private matter and that even dishonesty can be justified if it helps an individual to enjoy life. As we shall see later, Cārvāka ethics aims at the blind satisfaction of individual's desires, and maximum material enjoyment by fair means or foul.

Another similarity between the two movements is the result or after-effect of this shortsighted but revolutionary philosophy of life. The criticism of knowledge on the part of the Sophists in Greece made it necessary for the more serious thinkers to undertake a profound study of human knowledge and to lay down a strong foundation of logic and epistemology. In the words of Frank Thilly, 'The Sophists forced philosophy to examine the thinking process itself, and opened the way for a theory of knowledge. In employing all sorts of logical fallacies and sophisms, they made necessary a study of the correct laws of thought and hastened the birth of logic.' Similarly Cārvāka scepticism was accepted as a challenge by all the other schools who began to propound systematic logic and theory of knowledge as the necessary foundation of their philosophy. Just as Socrates in Greece opened the way for a systematic logic after the Sophists, similarly Gautama laid down the firm foundation of Indian logic soon after the Cārvāka system, propounding the Nyāya system which, according to Theos Bernard, 'is the science of logical proof and furnishes a correct method of philosophical enquiry into the objects and subjects of human knowledge. . . . Vātsyāyana, the classic commentator on Nyāya Śutra, defines it as a "Critical examination of the objects of knowledge by means of the canons of logical proof." The Nyāya is also called Tarkavidyā, "Science of reasoning," or Vadavidyā, "Science of discussion".'[1]

Just as the Sophists inspired thinkers like Socrates, Plato and Aristotle to preach logic, morality and metaphysics to the people of Greece, similarly the scepticism and narrow humanism taught by the Cārvākas inspired sages and thinkers like Gautama, Mahāvīra, the Buddha, and Kapila to preach logic, non-violence, universal love, and realistic evolutionary metaphysics to the people in India by propounding the schools of Nyāya, Jainism, Buddhism and Sāmkhya. Cārvāka therefore, has great historical significance so far as Indian philosophy is concerned. Since its ethics is the logical outcome of metaphysical notions it is desirable here to explain the metaphysics of the Cārvākas at some length in this chapter. Our main sources for the study of Cārvāka metaphysics and ethics are Sarvadaraśanasaṁgraha of Madhavācārya, and Sarvasiddhantasārasaṁgraha of Śaṁkarācāryā. This study shall aid us in appreciating the ethical philosophy of the other Indian systems dealt with in the sequel.

Cārvāka metaphysics accepts gross matter as the only reality and the visible empirical world as the only existent world. From the Upaniṣadic point of view, this system does not go beyond Annamaya Kośa, the physical layer of the self. It is noteworthy that this attitude of the Cārvāka school is due to the fact that it rejects inference and testimony and accepts only perception (Pramāna) as the valid source of knowledge. Since soul, God and even ether cannot be experienced with the naked eye, their existence is denied by Cārvāka. This school is also known as Lokāyata school for two reasons. First, it believes in this world (i.e. Loka) only, and rejects the other world (Paraloka). Second, its ethical doctrine being based on the enjoyment of pleasures, appealed to laymen, and hence the system came to be known as Lokāyata. The subtle and intellectually keen reflective and logical concepts of the Upaniṣadic philosophy were beyond the ken of the man in the street. These are some of the reasons people were attracted towards the superficial philosophy of materialism. A character in the Sanskrit play, entitled "Prabodha Candrodaya," sums up the Cārvāka philosophy as follows:

[1] Theos Bernard, *Hindu Philosophy*, p. 20.

'The Śāstra, whose doctrines are obvious to all, and which is founded on the evidence of senses, which admits only the elements of earth, water, fire and air, which maintains that sustenance and love are the objects of human existence; which asserts that matter possesses intelligence; which denies the existence of separate spirits and affirms that death is blessedness was written by Vācaspati (Bṛhaspati).'[1]

We shall first refer to the Cārvāka theory of the world and then take up its notions about self and God. According to the Upaniṣads and all other schools of Indian philosophy, the material universe is composed of five elements, ether, air, fire, water, and earth. The Cārvāka school rejects ether, because it cannot be perceived directly through senses. If it is held that ether can be inferred from the quality of sound, the Cārvāka would retort that inference is not a source of valid knowledge. If nothing invisible can ever be accepted, the law of Karman must also be rejected. The rejection of ether, therefore, ultimately leads the Cārvākas to reject anything else that cannot be perceived, whatever logical reasons might prove its existence. That is why they do not believe in righteous action, which is supposed to lead to the acquisition of Puṇya, or virtue, in the next birth.

The acceptance of the four elements, earth, water, fire and air, as the sole bases of the creation of the living and the non-living world is responsible for reducing consciousness, intelligence or soul to a by-product or an accident of the physical body. Madhavācārya, summing up the view of Cārvāka, says:[2]

'In this school there are four elements, earth, water, fire and air; and from these four elements alone is intelligence produced. Just like the intoxicating power from Kiṇwa, etc., since, "I am fat" "I am lean", these mixed together abide in the same subject, and since fatness, etc., reside only in the body, it alone is the soul and no other.'

When the existence of soul is metaphysically denied, and when physical death is regarded as the total annihilation of the human personality, scepticism about the future and lack of

[1] 'Prabodha Candrodaya', quoted in *A Source Book of Indian Philosophy* by Radhakrishnan and Moore, p. 247.

[2] Sarvadaraśanasaṁgraha (Trans. Cowell), p. 5.

faith and conviction in moral values are bound to ensue. The Cārvākas advocated raw Epicureanism and regarded immediate sensual pleasure and satisfaction of biological needs as the goal to be aimed at. This nihilistic metaphysics is clearly expressed in the oft-quoted verse of the Cārvāka system which runs as follows:

Yāvadjīveta sukhaṁ jīveta ṛṇam kṛtvā ghṛtaṁ pīveta.
Bhasmibhūtasya dehasya punarāgamanaṁ kutah.

'While life remains let a man live happily, let him feed on ghee even though he runs in debt; when once the body becomes ashes how can it ever return again?'

Cārvākas base their hedonism on nihilism and advocate a 'fast' life even at the risk of incurring debt, because they believe that after physical death there is no continued existence of human personality in any form whatever. Consciousness is regarded as the emergent evolute of the four elements. In other words, though the four elements, earth, water, fire and air are themselves non-living and unconscious, yet their combination can give rise to a new element of life and consciousness, just as the combination of lime and betel nut, neither of which is red, can give rise to red when chewed together. Śaṁkarācāryā, while expressing this aspect of Cārvāka metaphysics in Sarvasiddhāntasaṁgraha, says:

'The soul is but the body characterized by the attributes signified in the expressions, "I am stout," "I am youthful," "I am grown up," "I am old," etc. . . . The consciousness found in the modifications of non-intelligent elements is produced in the manner of the red colour out of the combination of betel areca nut and lime.'[1]

Similarly the existence of God and thereby the possibility of Mokṣa and the transmigration of souls is rejected by the Cārvāka school. God, being an invisible entity is no part of this system. This view of the Cārvākas is expressed by Madhavācārya in the following manner:

'Hence it follows that there is no other hell than mundane

[1] Śaṁkarācāryā, Sarvasiddhāntasaṁgraha, p. 7.

pain produced by purely mundane causes such as thorns, etc.; the only supreme being is the earthly monarch, whose existence is proved by all the world's eyesight; and the only liberation is the dissolution of the body.'[1]

This conception is responsible for the rejection of Mokṣa, which is non-existent for the Cārvākas. If it is argued that the postulate of God is required to explain the functioning of the causes in the world the Cārvākas retort that there is nothing behind nature, beyond nature, or other than nature. The Cārvākas follow a theory of naturalism with regard to the events of the physical world, and thereby reject the need of any supernatural cause or God as the final cause of the world. It has therefore been said:

> The fire is hot, the water is cold, refreshing cool the breeze of morn.
> From their own nature was it born.[2]

The Cārvākas strongly object to the theory of existence of another world or the world of God, and dub all those who believe in the world of Śiva, or hell, and heaven as stupid impostors. This negativistic attitude towards spiritualism is at the root of the extreme egoistic hedonism of the Cārvāka ethics. God is not required either as the cause of the world, or as the moral judge to apportion virtue and happiness, as Kant's moral argument for the existence of God holds. This atheism added fuel to the fire of the strong passion of the Cārvākas to seek pleasure as the only goal of life.

With this metaphysical background we can proceed with the ethical view of the Cārvākas. At first it should be pointed out that the Cārvāka system accepts only the first two Puruṣārthas, or the ends of life, Artha (wealth) and Kāma (satisfaction of desires). Thus positively the Cārvāka ethics advocates wealth and the emotional value of the satisfaction of desires, whereas negatively it rejects and repudiates moral and spiritual values of Dharma and Mokṣa respectively. The positive aspect of Cārvāka ethics is undoubtedly a hedonism, and the negative aspect amounts to atheism and anti-socialism. We shall there-

[1] Sarvadaraśanasaṁgraha, p. 4.
[2] *Ibid.*, p. 10.

fore attempt critically to consider Cārvāka hedonism first, and then deal with its atheism and anti-social attitude.

However, before discussing the nature of Cārvāka hedonism, it is desirable to explain hedonism in general, and the Western notion of hedonism in particular. The word hedonism literally means a doctrine of pleasure. It stands for that theory or group of theories of conduct which regard pleasure as the goal of human desire and action. We may distinguish between two major types of hedonism, viz. (1) psychological hedonism and (2) ethical hedonism. According to psychological hedonism, it is held that pleasure is naturally and factually the end at which we aim. Ethical hedonism on the other hand propounds that the aim or the selected goal of all our desires and actions 'ought to be' pleasure and nothing else. It is quite evident that if psychological hedonism is rejected on factual grounds, ethical hedonism is not adversely affected, because a man can hold that wisdom lies in seeking pleasure, although hedonism is not a psychological fact.

Ethical hedonism, which holds that pleasure ought to be recognized as the ideal to be realized, is further divided into (1) egoistic hedonism and (2) altruistic or universalistic hedonism. Egoistic hedonism regards the individual's own pleasure to be the moral end, whereas universalistic hedonism considers the pleasure or the happiness of all to be the ideal. There are two more varieties of hedonism in Western ethics: (1) a hedonism which admits present pleasure to be the end and (2) a hedonism which prefers future pleasures to present ones. If we were to glance at the history of Western ethics we shall find that all these varieties of hedonism existed at different times.

Cyrenaic hedonism, which was the oldest egoistic hedonism, was established around 435 BC. It was a purely quantitative hedonism, which advocated the pursuit of the most intense pleasures, whether physical or spiritual, as the highest good. It was a sort of crude hedonism which was also pessimistic, because it admitted the presence of pain, and considered a man who could attain painless state as very fortunate. Epicureanism was the next hedonistic school of ethics, established by Epicurus (306 to 270 BC). It is regarded as a refined version of the cyrenaic school of hedonism. This theory was based on psychological hedonism and it advocated pleasure as the goal, because seeking pleasure and avoiding pain were regarded by Epicurus as the natural instincts of man. However this school advocated that mental pleasures 'ought to be' preferred to physical or sensual pleasures. Although Epicurus himself extolled the virtues of justice, courage and temperance, he considered these virtues as the best means of leading a life of pleasure. Later on Epicureanism mistakenly came to be known as the philosophy of indulgence in pleasures, and was supposed to have provided the slogan, 'Eat, drink, and be merry for tomorrow we die.'

Modern hedonism is universalistic or utilitarian. It believes that the 'greatest happiness of the greatest number' is the highest ethical ideal. Bentham, Sidgwick, and Mill are the three main supporters of modern Utilitarianism. Bentham and Mill have based ethical hedonism on psychological hedonism. Sidgwick tries to reconcile hedonism and rationalism by laying emphasis on the role of conscience in following the principle of justice while choosing pleasures. We are not concerned with the details of Western hedonism here. The above remarks are by way of introduction and should be of help to the reader to understand the hedonism of Cārvāka ethics.

As we have already stated, Vedic ethics had advocated four Puruṣārthas or the ends of life for the integrated development of the individual as well as that of society. At the time Cārvāka came into existence, many heretic and revolutionary schools of philosophy led by such figures as Āsuri Pippālada, Pūrṇa-Kāśyapa, Kakuḍa Katyāyana and Ajīta Keśa Kambalin were flourishing, and all of them opposed the traditional Vedic philosophy in one way or another. But Cārvāka was the first and the only system in India to advocate hedonistic ethics. Since the Cārvāka system is the oldest in the classical philosophy, and since the concept of Mokṣa was not presented systematically at that time, the Cārvākas levelled their criticism against the notions of Mokṣa and the other-worldly life as preached in the Vedas.

We have also pointed out how the Cārvākas rejected the Agnihotra, sacrifice, etc., thereby condemning all the injunctions of Dharma. They proclaimed that the Vedas contained doctrines invented by the cunning priests to dupe simple and credulous people. The ceremonies performed for the benefit of the dead, according to the Cārvākas, were invented by the Brahmans to earn their livelihood. Hence they ridiculed all rites, ceremonies, and sacrifices. They argued that giving away food to the Brahmans in the Śrādha ceremony with a view to supplying dead persons was a foolish practice. If the food offered to the Brāhmaṇas could reach dead ancestors, then why should one carry food while proceeding on a journey? The following quotation from Sarvadarśanasaṁgraha is worth mentioning here:

'If the Śrādha produces gratification to beings who are dead, then here too, in the case of travellers when they start, it is needless to give provisions for the journey. If beings in heaven are gratified by our offering the Śrādha here, then why not give the food down below to those, who are standing on the house top?'

Such statements reject the notion of Dharma, or spiritual duty. The rejection of heaven and liberation has already been pointed out. Thus neither the spiritual value of Mokṣa, nor Dharma, the means of attaining Mokṣa, is accepted by the Cārvākas.

Sacrifice is mocked at, and it is suggested that if killing a beast in a sacrifice is justified (because the sacrificed beast goes to heaven) then why do the Brāhmaṇas not kill their old parents to expedite their arrival in heaven? The sacrifices, the performance of rites and prayers, etc., are rejected straightway. In like manner duty towards parents with a view to accumulating merit is repudiated. Moreover the acceptance of Artha and Kāma or satisfaction of sensual desires, does not enjoin the duty of giving wealth to the needy and comfort to persons who are suffering. Thus even the acceptance of economic and emotional values is based on the selfish view of the Cārvākas. An individual should aim only at his own pleasure at the cost of morality, social service and religion. This negativistic and selfish attitude is responsible for the propagation of the egoistic hedonism of the Cārvākas.

Cārvāka ethics, then, is purely hedonistic, because it openly advocates the fulfilment of desires and the search for pleasure as the only ideals to be followed in life. The positivistic aspect of the Cārvāka ethics is the acceptance of wealth and the satisfaction of desires as the two most important ideals. Wealth is subordinated to Kāma, the enjoyment of pleasure, the primary goal of life. Wealth is the means of sensual enjoyment, and the accumulation of wealth by fair or foul means is recommended as moral for each and every individual. Mere enjoyment is considered the sole purpose of life and even an unscrupulous pursuit of pleasures is regarded as a satisfactory behaviour. Śaṁkara refers to this attitude of the Cārvākas in his work:

'The enjoyment of heaven lies in eating delicious food, keeping company of young women, using fine clothes, perfumes, garlands, sandal paste, etc. The pain of hell lies in the troubles that arise from enemies, weapons, diseases; while liberation (Mokṣa) is death which is the cessation of life force. . . . Chastity and other such ordinances are laid down by clever weaklings. Gifts of gold and land, the pleasure of invitations to dinner, are devised by indignant people with stomachs lean with hunger.'[1]

This philosophy of pleasure is undoubtedly a shortsighted view of life, but it should be remembered that this radical hedonism was the strong reaction to an ascetic view of life prevalent at that time. In the beginning the Cārvākas might have advocated a fast life. But later on it appears that they did make an attempt to refine their views with regard to the nature of the pleasure to be sought, and also with regard to the means to be adopted for such a satisfaction. Sarvasiddhāntasaṁgraha, while explaining the tenets of the Cārvākas, says, 'The wise should enjoy the pleasures of this world through the proper visible means of agriculture, keeping cattle, trade and political administration.'[2] If the right means for seeking pleasure are advocated, the theory may be acceptable even to educated people. But this attitude of the Cārvākas seems to be an afterthought. It may be that after being severely criticized by the other schools for their thirst for sensual pleasures without paying heed to social duties, the Cārvākas might have revised and presented their theory in a more acceptable form. Whatever might have been the motive of justifying the Cārvāka ethics, it goes without saying that it is hedonistic.

In subordinating wealth to pleasure seeking, and in advocating a comfortable life, the Cārvākas offer arguments in support of their view. They admit that in the world pleasures are mixed with pains and our life is not a bed of roses. But they argue that the presence of pain and suffering does not mean that one

[1] Sarvasiddhāntasaṁgraha, pp. 9, 10, 12.
[2] *Ibid.*, p. 15.

should be foolish enough not to enjoy whatever pleasure one can grab in this struggle for existence. Wisdom consists in eliminating pains as far as possible, and making hay while the sun shines. The world is an opportunity for the individual and the wisest man makes a virtue of necessity by spending the precious moments of his life in merrymaking by hook or by crook. Resorting to penances for some future hope of liberation is most foolish according to Cārvāka: 'The wise therefore ought not to take pains in behalf of [liberation]; it is only the fool who wears himself out by penances, fasts, etc.'[1] Negatively Cārvāka ethics denounces asceticism and postively it preaches the pursuit of pleasure and the avoidance of pains as far as possible.

The arguments offered to prove the satisfaction of seeking pleasure in spite of the presence of pains are based on observation of the behaviour of the common man in his daily life. Enjoyment produced by sensual pleasures is regarded as the only end of human life in spite of the presence of pain in the world, because it has been held that 'It is our wisdom to enjoy the pure pleasures as far as we can, and to avoid the pain, which inevitably accompanies: just as the man, who desires fish takes the fish with its scales and bones and having taken as many as he wants, desists; or just as the man who desires rice, takes the rice, straw and all, and having taken as much as he wants, desists.'[2] It is further held that no one should reject pleasure through fear of pain because psychologically we are inclined towards pleasure and disinclined towards pain. Such behaviour is regarded as instinctive and congenital in man. Many examples from daily life are put forward to prove this. It is pointed out that nobody gives up sowing rice, simply because there is the fear of the crop being eaten by animals, and nobody stops cooking food simply because beggars are expected to pester us for a share of the meals. If a person were to reject pleasure on account of the fear of the presence of some obstacles he would be a fool. This view of the Cārvākas is expressed in the following manner in Sarvadarśanasaṁgraha:

'The pleasure which arises in men from contact with sensible objects is to be relinquished as accompanied by pain—such is the reasoning of fools; the berries of the paddy, rich with the

[1] Sarvasiddhāntasaṁgraha, p. 11.
[2] *Ibid.*, p. 3.

finest white grains—what man, seeking his true interest, would fling away because covered with husk and dust?'[1]

Before we attempt a critical analysis of Cārvāka hedonism it is essential to point out that the Cārvākas are emphatic on the point that future pleasure should not be preferred to the pleasure of the moment. They say that a bird in the hand is worth two in the bush. It is desirable to prefer a present pleasure to the future one, even if the latter appears to be better and stronger than the former. The sceptical attitude of the Cārvākas is perhaps a cause of this limitation. They say, 'Better a pigeon today than a peacock tomorrow.' It may also be that momentary pleasures were preferred to remote ones because the Cārvākas strongly opposed penance, sacrifice, etc., since such acts held promise for the future.

This brief survey of Cārvāka hedonism with the general background of the Western notion of hedonistic ethics shows that the ethical theory of the Cārvākas is undoubtedly based on the choice of pleasure as the ideal of life. Since the Cārvākas believe that hedonistic behaviour is congenital and instinctive, it is evident that their ethical hedonism is based on psychological hedonism. It was almost bound to follow this course because the Cārvākas did not probe human nature very deeply and believed only in the common man's perception as the only valid source of knowledge.

But at the same time the Cārvākas try to defend ethical hedonism by forwarding some crude arguments. Examples no one rejects (concerning the rice and chaff, fish and bones) are offered only to convince the layman. The exhortation for the pursuit of pleasures is further intensified by saying that those who reject pleasure because of the presence of pains are fools, thereby indicating that ethical hedonism is logical. Even if one were to disregard the fact that we are always inclined towards pleasure, he would be a fool to do so. Wisdom lies in adopting pleasures and eschewing pains. Thus Cārvāka hedonism is not merely based on psychological evidence, but also tries to be an independent ethical theory.

If we were to apply the criterion of Western hedonism to Cārvāka ethics we shall have to say that it is not utilitarian or universalistic. Western hedonism advocates the greatest happi-

[1] Sarvadarśanasaṁgraha, p. 4.

ness of the greatest number. But Cārvāka hedonism harps only on the satisfaction of sensual desires by the individual, even if he has to incur debt. Cārvāka hedonism is grossly egoistic—nay even selfish. This very narrow-minded attitude is visible with regard to the conflict between present pleasure and remote pleasure. The pleasure of the moment is regarded as the sole purpose of man's behaviour. If the Cārvākas had admitted the utilitarian view of the greatest happiness of the greatest number, they might have abandoned their whole theory, because it would lead to the recognition of Dharma, or social duty. The Cārvākas are consistent in their shortsightedness, and therefore they do not advocate social well-being. That is the reason it is sometimes remarked that Cārvāka ethics is a lower type of hedonism. Before we discuss how far this remark is justified we ought to examine the Cārvāka ethics dispassionately. We should not forget that the modification with regard to the means of seeking pleasure in the Cārvāka school indicates that it was not a stark sensualism and a grossly selfish philosophy of life.

It is quite correct to say that for the Cārvāka system pleasure is the highest good and that to sacrifice the present to future is unjustified. The past and the future being dead and doubtful respectively, the present alone is regarded as the possession of the individuals. These facts lead us to the conclusion that Cārvāka hedonism was an extreme form and that sensual pleasure was the only end of life. But at the same time it is noteworthy that later on the Cārvākas leaned towards social well-being and even towards spiritualism. The later Cārvākas believed that consciousness was a quality of the mind and that the mind could control volition as well as other organs. The Cārvākas began to admire the higher level of spiritual pleasures and preferred the pleasures of intellect to those of the body. The learned Cārvākas, the Suśikṣita Cārvākas, practised sixty-four fine arts. This proves, however, that after all Cārvāka was not a lower type of hedonism. The cultivation of the fine arts itself indicates the cultural tastes of the ancient Indian materialists.

If we were to measure Cārvāka hedonism from the point of view of the collective pleasure of the society, again we shall have to admit that it lacks the utilitarian touch which we find in the Western hedonism of Mill, Bentham and Sidgwick. There is no doubt that the conflict between the pleasure of the individual and that of society, between individual rights and social obligations, and between egoism and altruism has been a constant puzzle for Western hedonists and philosophers, and that they have not been able to offer any satisfactory solution to this knotty problem. But the Utilitarian school of Mill, democratic philosophy, and lately Marxist Communism in the West emphasize the general good. The Cārvāka ethics, being grossly individualistic, at least in the beginning, neglects and even derides social service and declares that social organizations like the caste system are of no avail. The main trouble with the Cārvāka philosophy is its narrow sceptical attitude, which makes it commonplace and shortsighted.

The charge of selfishness against Cārvāka ethics cannot be refuted easily. But although the narrow egocentric and individualistic attitude of Cārvāka hedonism indicates the absence of foresight, universal love, and social obligation among the followers of Indian materialism, yet the fact should not mislead us to conclude that Indian philosophy was ever devoid of the concept of social well-being and universal brotherhood. On the contrary, as we have seen, the Vedas propound an ethico-social system, in which the interests of the individual and those of society are reconciled and made interdependent. Similarly the concept of non-violence in the heretic schools of Jainism and Buddhism implies love for all living beings. The Bhagavadgītā also exhorts the individual to give up selfish motives and to work for the well-being of the world by resigning all actions to God (Jagat hitāya Kriṣnāya). Even Cārvāka ethics shows some recognition of social obligations. We have mentioned above that the Cārvākas advocate the enjoyment of pleasure 'through the proper visible means of agriculture, keeping cattle, trade, political administration'.

This statement should be measured in connection with the social and ethical environment at the time of the Cārvākas. The professions of agriculture and business indicate the presence of the Vaiśya community, and the reference to political administration is clearly indicative of the presence of the Kṣatriyas class which was devoted to the promotion of Dharma. Since the Cārvākas were radically opposed to the Vedas, and since they dubbed Brāhmans selfish and cunning people, they thought it unwise to mention the profession of teaching and preaching philosophy as a means of attaining happiness. Whatever might have prevented the Cārvākas to avoid reference to social obligations leading to the prosperity of the classes rather than that of individuals, the admission of enjoyment by discharging one's duties as a member of some professional group or the other does indicate that their hedonism was not a lower type of hedonism, and, as such, it was not absolutely blind to social well-being.

There is evidence to show that at a later stage the Cārvākas became less radical, and were inclined not only to admit Dharma as one of the ends of life, but also identified the self with the sense organs, with the principle of life, and even with mind, thereby attempting to propound a broader view of the self. The doctrines of Dehātmavāda, which identified the soul or the self with the physical body, and which was the sole cause of the egocentric attitude of the Cārvākas, lost its vogue. At least it was no longer advocated in the same form it had in its beginning. Mentioning this change in the development of the Cārvāka school one writer says:

'The first view, or the doctrine of the identification of self with the sense organs, is based on the facts that consciousness and bodily movements follow from the initiation of the sense, and that the judgments expressed in "I am blind," showing the identity of the self with the sense organs, are universally accepted as valid. Still opposed by the spiritualists it [Cārvāka] maintains that vital principle itself is really the source of intelligence, as the senses depend for existence and operation on it. When this view was attacked its sponsors came to maintain that consciousness is a quality of the mind.'[1]

This fact shows how gradually the Cārvāka philosophy tried to give up its rigidity and attempted to rise from love of the material, and the biological concepts of the self, to the mental concept (Manomayakośa) of it, as propounded in the Upaniṣads. My contention is that all the schools of Indian philosophy, whether heterodox or orthodox, derive their main concepts from the Upaniṣadic and the Vedic philosophy, which is the rock and foundation of Indian thought and culture. The different schools have undoubtedly based their tenets, particularly their metaphysical notions, on the Upaniṣadic philosophy, and have in fact given different interpretations of the nature of ultimate reality. The differences have mainly arisen because of the emphasis of

[1] D. Shastri, *A Short History of Indian Materialism*, pp. 38–9.

the schools on one or other Kośas, or 'layers' of human personality, the fact being that man is not one or two, but all the five Kośas, the physical, or Annamaya; the biological, or Prāṇamaya; the psychological, or Manomaya; the intellectual, or Vijñāmaya; and the spiritual, or Amandamaya Kośas, all in one.

The order in which physical, biological, psychological, intellectual and spiritual aspects of human personality are mentioned, has a special significance. The physical body is controlled by the biological self, the biological aspect is controlled by the psychological, the psychological by the intellectual, and the intellectual self is controlled by the spiritual self, the core and centre of all the outer sheaths or layers of personality. The Cārvākas commit the mistake of stopping at the physical level and refusing to acknowledge the deeper and the more subtle layers of personality, thereby reducing man to a machine. It appears that the later Cārvākas realized this mistake, and made an attempt to reach as far as the mental self. Even this progress is half way. In man mind and intellect co-exist. But this does not mean that intellect is merely a quality of mind. According to the Upaniṣads intellect is a higher reality and is subtler than mind, which is under the control of intellect. That is why, according to the Bhagavadgītā, the quintessence of Indian metaphysics and ethics, the best way to realize the self is to make the intellect stable. The concept of the Sthitaprajña, which we shall explain elsewhere, is an original contribution to philosophy and ethics. Intellect has always been regarded nearest the spiritual self, and without a stable intellect it is not possible for anyone to accomplish self-realization.

Moreover, the road to the development of spirit, which ultimately rises above discursive thought, lies through the intellect. Dharma is regarded as the goal, the motive, as well as the end of the intellect. When Socrates said that 'virtue is a kind of knowledge', what he meant was that it depended upon intellect, and that it also led to the development of intellect. The greatest thinkers in the East as well as in the West have therefore laid emphasis on the intellectual development of personality, which automatically leads to the integrated growth of the body, the biological self and the mind, on the one hand, and the knowledge, or, rather, the realization of the soul, on the other.

Thus the intellect, which brings about a liaison between the material world of living and non-living, conscious and unconscious beings on the one hand, and the spiritual world on the other, has great importance in the ethical life of man. The Cārvākas commit a grave error by neglecting this aspect of human personality and by declaring it as a mere quality of the consciousness or mind, which again is dependent on life and body. This mistaken notion has been responsible for the degeneration of Cārvāka ethics into a sort of lower type of hedonism, although the presence of those who advocated intellectual pleasures in the fold of the Cārvākas does indicate that not all the followers of this school were brutish in their outlook.

For this reason the Cārvāka system fails to grasp the spiritual aspect of man and the universe on the one hand, and the need of a disciplined moral life on the other. This system of philosophy has always been severely criticized by all the systems of Indian philosophy because of this very deficiency and the absence of any depth of understanding. The Lokāyata school consequently remains a view of the layman who cannot and perhaps does not want to go beyond sense perception and the reality of the gross physical body.

Luckily for us, the mistakes of this system have led the Indian seers to base philosophy and ethics on stronger grounds, and to be analytic both with regard to the knowledge of ultimate reality and the ethical aspect of human life. The first and the foremost school among the orthodox systems which emphasized the need of logical analysis was the Nyāya school.

CHAPTER VI

THE ETHICS OF JAINISM

Historically Jainism is undoubtedly older than Buddhism. It is well known that the Jaina philosophy accepts and advocates non-violence as the highest ideal of life, and as the means of attaining Mokṣa, or liberation. For these reasons Jainism may be regarded as the oldest philosophy based on non-violence. The Jainas hold that their religion and philosophy are even older than Vedic thought. There is no doubt that Vardhmāna Mahāvīra cannot be regarded as the founder of the Jaina religion, for he was only a reformer or rejuvenator of Jainism. It is a fact that the Jaina Tīrthaṅkara Pārśvanātha was a historical person who lived at least 250 years prior to Mahāvīra, and that the parents of Mahāvīra were the followers of Pārśvanātha. Mahāvīra systematized the Jaina philosophy and established ethical principles based on non-violence that are being followed by Jaina ascetics and laity to this day. Jaina ethics is very strict and based on hard moral principles. But before we explain Jaina ethics, it appears necessary to explain why Jainism lays ever greater emphasis on strict adherence to its ethical code.

Ascetic Attitude of Jainism

We should remember that Jainism adopts the path of renunciation and opposes the Vedic path of prosperity which considers active social life desirable. The hymns recited by the ancient Āryans were, in fact, the praises of various gods, exhorting these divine beings to make them prosperous and successful in worldly life. But gradually the Vedic thinkers also realized that Mokṣa could not be attained without the spirit of self-sacrifice. As a result of this, the fourfold scheme of Āśramas, viz. Brahmacarya, Gṛhastha, Vānaprastha and Saṁnyāsa Āśrama, was devised. We have previously explained this fourfold scheme. Similarly the Vedic thinkers accepted the four values of life, the Puruṣārthas, viz.: Artha, Kāma, Dharma and Mokṣa. According to the Vedic point of view Mokṣa can be attained gradually, although it is necessary for the aspirant to adopt renunciation, or Sanyāsa, before attaining the final goal. The first three Āśramas are preparatory stages for the stage of Sanyāsa, the stage of self-realization. At the Brahmacarya level, it is necessary for a person to spend his time and energy to acquire learning, for in this manner he can gain the ability and efficiency to earn wealth and therefore to enjoy married life later on. After the enjoyment of life for twenty-five years, it is necessary to engage in religious and moral pursuits for the next twenty-five years in the Vanaprastha stage. During this stage of life an individual follows Dharma and also preaches it, thereby engaging social well-being. The last twenty-five years, the stage of Saṁnyāsa, are devoted to the attainment of self-realization, or Jīvanmukti, which ultimately leads to the final release, or Videhamukti.

Thus, the Vedic philosophy or Brāhmaṇic philosophy believes in a gradual march towards renunciation and the detached life. This scheme of life was no doubt attractive and comprehensive. But the thinkers of that time, particularly the supporters of Jainism, realized that there were two main obstacles to the execution of this plan. The first obstacle was that when once a person accustoms himself to worldly life, it becomes very difficult for him to renounce and relinquish carnal desire and the desire for sensual objects. Desire is insatiable and can never be completely fulfilled. The Uttarādhyāyana Sūtra expresses this view as follows:

'And if somebody should give the whole earth to one man, it would not be enough; so difficult it is to satisfy anybody. The more you get, the more you want; your desires increase with your means. Though two Māshās would do to supply your wants, still you would scarcely think ten million sufficient.'[1]

Secondly, this gradual march toward the life of detachment presupposes living one hundred years. Life is most uncertain; it may be snapped off like a thread at any moment, and having once missed the opportunity of working for one's spiritual uplift, one may have to wait for ages to be reborn as man. This is the reason Mahāvīra says, 'As the fallow leaf of the tree falls to the ground when its days are gone, even so the life of a man (will come to its close); Gautama, be careful all the while! As a dew-drop dangling on the top of a blade of Kuśa-grass lasts but

[1] S.B.E. XLV, Uttarādhyāyana Sūtra IX, 16, 17. p. 34.

a short time, even so the life of men; Gautama, be careful all the while!'[1] The realization of the uncertainty of life and the fact that death is a necessary end has often led thinkers and philosophers to advocate detachment from active worldly life. Tennyson talks about such retirement for similar reasons in his poem, 'Lotus Eaters':

> Death is the end of life;
> Ah! why should life all labour be?

Whereas Tennyson appears to plead for rest and peace here and now—which amounts to leisure and inactivity—Mahāvīra preaches the stoppage of all Karmas and the annihilation of Karmic matter through active and severe austerities in order to attain the state of Nirjarā, pure consciousness, equipoise and beatitude (Jīvanmukti) here, and Nirvāna hereafter. Sometimes the poets also feel that only right and just conduct can help a man to live after physical death. But in all such cases the uncertainty of life and the unavoidability of death are incentives to such a philosophy. Two stanzas from James Shirley's poem, 'Death, the Leveller' are the best examples:

> Glories of our blood and state
> Are shadows not substantial things;
> There is no armour against fate;
> Death lays his icy hand on kings;
> Sceptre and crown
> Must tumble down,
> And into the dust be equal made
> With poor crooked scythe and spade.
>
> The garlands wither on your brow,
> Then boast no more your mighty deeds;
> Upon death's purple altar now
> See where the victor victim bleeds;
> Your heads must come,
> To the cold tomb;
> Only the actions of the just
> Smell sweet and blossom in the dust.

It was the sight of suffering and death which actuated the Buddha to renounce the world and to search for truth. The case

[1] S.B.E. XLV, Uttarādhyāyana Sūtra, X, 1–2, pp. 41–2.

was similar with Aśoka the Great, whose name shines in the history of the world as an apostle of love and peace. Kant's unique doctrine of the categorical imperative, which makes morality unconditional and universal for mankind and leads to the discovery of the jewel of goodwill, is the result of his contemplation on sufferings and miseries to which mankind is subjected. The case was similar with Mahāvīra. Strong diseases require strong remedies; even so the sufferings, disease, fear, famine, death and destruction which caused untold miseries could be stopped or prevented only by attaining Nirvāna, freedom from rebirth and transmigration. This strong feeling made Mahāvīra advocate an abrupt renunciation and the strictest possible ascetic life for the aspirant. Consequently he laid the foundation of a very elaborate moral code for ascetics, aiming at complete detachment, mental, physical and actual (pertaining to 'action') from worldly affairs. Not only was it essential for the ascetic or nun to adopt non-violence; but also neither to do violence nor be instrumental in doing any kind of violence in any way. Similarly an ascetic is required not only to be true, but also to avoid telling lies and being instrumental in any falsehood or lie mentally, bodily and by action. In like manner the vow of non-stealing demands an ascetic neither to steal nor to be party to stealing directly or indirectly. The great vow of Brahṁacarya demands of an ascetic to avoid all sexual intercourse and to avoid being instrumental in such acts. The fifth vow of non-possession similarly demands that an ascetic neither possess any property nor give consent to be a cause for the possession of property by any individual. The Jaina Sūtras are very particular in emphasizing strict observance of these vows in spirit as well as in letter. The comprehensive instructions issued to the ascetics and nuns might appear to be trifling for a layman, but they are of vital importance to a Sādhu or a Sādhvī, who sacrifices everything for the sake of attaining his or her cherished goal—liberation.

Such a strict moral code and ethical discipline is demanded by Jainism, because it considers Mokṣa the final goal of life. Before we discuss in detail the ethical theory of Jainism, it appears necessary to throw some light on the inseparable relation between ethics and metaphysics once again. We are prompted to do so here because Jainism is essentially an ethico-metaphysical system. Without metaphysics not only does ethics become impracticable, but it also turns out to be illogical and absolutely ineffective. A truly ethical man must essentially be a philosopher, and a true philosopher is not one who only knows the truth, but one who applies philosophical conclusions to his practical life. Will Durant quotes Thoreau: 'To be a philosopher . . . is not merely to think subtle thoughts, nor even to found a school, but so to love wisdom as to live according to its dictates a life of simplicity, independence, magnanimity and trust.'[1] Heraclitus, the earliest propounder of ethics in the West, based his theory of morality on his metaphysics. He regarded the cosmic process to be in accordance with 'the fixed measure' or law. He held this law to be rational and permanent, in the midst of all change and contradiction. Consequently he advocated that human life should be guided by this very rational and spiritual principle, which is also present in man. According to him 'to be ethical is to live a rational life, to obey the dictates of reason, which is the same for all, the same for the whole world . . . Morality means respect for law, self-discipline, control of passion; it is to govern oneself by rational principles'.[2]

If we consider the history of Western philosophy, we shall come to the conclusion that every philosophical system, like the Spinozistic system, begins with metaphysics and ends in ethics. As far as the schools of Indian philosophy are concerned, we can say that all the orthodox and heterodox systems, including the Cārvāka school, in spite of having the same ethical purpose, the well-being of man, differ from each other for metaphysical reasons. The atheistic Cārvāka system also bases its ethics on its metaphysical notions. It is a pity that we have not enough evidence to prove that the Cārvāka system was fully developed and organized. Even so we find references to Cārvāka epistemology, Cārvāka metaphysics, and Cārvāka ethics in other schools of Indian philosophy. All the other schools have refuted the Cārvāka notions, and only in this context have the Cārvāka principles been quoted. Therefore the evidence we have about the Cārvāka philosophy only proves that its epistemology, metaphysics and ethics were negativistic.

Indians are by their very nature metaphysicians; no school or system without metaphysics, or with an unsound or weak meta-

[1] Will Durant, *The Story of Philosophy*, p. 26.
[2] F. Thilly, *History of Philosophy*, p. 23.

physics, can flourish long in the land of spiritualism and sages, whose very sagacity and greatness lay in unveiling the metaphysical mystery through *Darśana*, or direct perception of the ultimate reality. This is the explanation of the rise and fall of numerous systems in the history of Indian philosophy. This fact also explains the contradiction in the history of Indian culture pertaining to the disappearance of the world renowned and most ethical religion, Buddhism, from the land of its birth. Buddha's finest ethics, the simplest eightfold moral code, though based on the spiritual concept of non-violence, could not attract the masses and classes of this country because it lacked metaphysical appeal. This does not mean that Buddhism had no metaphysics. The fact is that its metaphysics was not convincing to the Indian mind, which cannot rest content with a partial view of reality and agnosticism with regard to the nature of ultimate principles. Thus in India only such systems have survived the tide of time which have a sound and convincing metaphysical background. This very fact has also been responsible for the dynamic and evolutionary character of Indian ethics. The history of philosophical theory and practice in India proves that an ethics without metaphysics is blind, as metaphysics without ethics would be empty.

All the schools and sects of Jainism, in spite of the differences of opinion with regard to ethics and the forms of worship of the Tirthankaras, agree that true knowledge of the fundamental truths as enunciated by Mahāvīra is absolutely necessary for attaining Mokṣa. According to Jainism the sole cause of the bondage of the soul is ignorance about the ultimate truths or categories. Hence to attain a thorough knowledge of Jaina ethics it is necessary to throw light on Jaina metaphysics. The categories of Jaina metaphysics are nine in number. They are, (1) Jīva (living beings), (2) Ajīva (matter), (3) Punya (merit), (4) Pāpa (demerit), (5) Āśrava (the inflow of Karma), (5) Saṁvara (self-control), (7) Bandha (bondage), (8) Nirjarā (beatitude), and (9) Mokṣa (liberation). Jainism explains these categories thoroughly, so that we may know how the soul is caught up in the vicious circle of births and deaths and how it can get liberation. It is important to note that according to Jainism, Jīva and Ajīva, or soul and matter, are the two chief categories, and that all the other categories are the varieties of these two. In other words Jīva and Ajīva are the two basic realities, and

Puṁya, Pāpa, etc. are their conditions or modifications, e.g., Jīva, Āśrava, Saṁvara, Nirjarā and Mokṣa are the five spiritual categories, and Ajīva, Punya, Pāpa and Bandha are the material categories.

Jīva (*Soul*)

Jīva is regarded as a conscious entity, and its chief characteristics are knowledge (Jñāna) and perception (Darśana). Jīva possesses five kinds of knowledge, viz.: (1) Mati, (2) Śruti, (3) Avadhi, (4) Manah Paryāya and (5) Kevala. The four types of perception (Darśana) are (1) Chakasu (visual), (2) Achaksu (non-visual), (3) Avadhi (physical recognition), and (4) Kevala (omniscience). Knowledge as well as perception in all these forms are inherent in the Jīva. But because of the mingling of the Jīva with the Karmic matter, true knowledge and true perception are hidden, and it is therefore necessary for the Jīva to shake off its Karman in order to attain its beatific state (Jīvanmukti). The ultimate end is to attain Kevala Jñāna (omniscient knowledge) and Kevala Darśana (omniscient perception). This is possible only when the Jīva is absolutely absolved of the Karman (effects of action conserved in the soul) which has settled down on it through the Āśrava. The Jīva in all stages, from earth bodies (Prithvikāya), water bodies (Apakāya), fire bodies (Tejaskāya), air bodies (Vayukāya) and vegetable bodies (Vanaspatikāya), to human bodies and gods, are bound by Karman and are worldly Jīvas. Only the liberated Jīvas are free from Karman which may be defined as the subtle matter (Pudgala) accumulated and transformed by righteous and unrighteous activities of the soul.

Ajīva (*Non-Soul*)

According to Jaina philosophy there are five Ajīvas or non-soul substances, viz.: (1) Dharma (motion), (2) Adharma (rest), (3) Pudgala (matter), (4) Ākāśa (space), and (5) Kāla (time). Dharma and Adharma have special significance in Jainism. Here Dharma does not stand for virtue or religious belief. It is instead the basic principle of motion. Dharma is that substance which helps motion in a particular manner. It makes the subtlest matter and the subtlest motion possible. In like manner,

Adharma is that substance, which specially helps the stability of objects. In other words, motion is the characteristic of Dharma, and stability that of Adharma. Pudgala is pure material substance. It possesses the qualities of form, taste, smell, etc., but it can neither be analysed nor synthesized. It is atomic, but possesses form; therefore Pudgala has been referred to as that which possesses form (Rūpi). Its minutest form is the atom, and the entire universe is its gross manifestation. Length, breadth, subtlety, grossness, lightness, heaviness, bondage and separation form light and darkness, and sun and shade are all material elements. Bondage of the soul means its repletion with Karmic Pudgala, and Nirjarā means the annihilation of the Karma Pudgala. The explanation of this aspect of matter is necessary, because the aim of Jaina ethics is to destroy the Karmic matter. The aim of adopting stringent ascetic rules and of practising right knowledge, right perception and right character (Samyak Jñāna, Samyak Darśana and Samyak Caritra) is freedom from Karmic matter. Jainism considers space (Akāśa) as all-pervasive substance. There are two divisions of Akāśa, viz. Lokākāśa (the space encompassing the world) and Alokākāśa (the space beyond the world). Lokākāśa is that part of space in which Dharma, Adharma, Pudgala and Kala are present. Alokākāśa is that (empty) substance, which is beyond Lokākāśa, and in which the above mentioned five substances do not exist. Alokākāśa is beyond the soul, which is the subject. There is no motion or stability possible in the Alokākāśa because of the absence of Dharma and Adharma.

Jainism regards time (Kāla) as a substance, which is the basis of the transformation of matter and soul. We should remember that Dharma, Adharma, Pudgala and Jīva are present in the Lokākāśa part of space. Matter and Jīva are influenced by motion and rest, and they also influence each other. Matter is the cause of the bondage of the soul, and the Jīva tries to attain Nirjarā, or liberation in life, by getting rid of Pudgala. While making this attempt the Jīva has to undergo many transformations. The matter also undergoes many transformations in becoming gross from its subtle form. This transformation of matter and soul, which is the cause of their evolution, is based on the category of time. This explanation of Jīva and Ajīva takes the world as an evolutionary process in which space, time, matter and soul are the four material causes, and Dharma and

Adharma are the efficient causes. In this way the world-view of Jaina philosophy is analogous to the Western notion of evolution.

Puṇya

Ordinarily Puṇya is understood to be good action. In Jaina philosophy this definition of Puṇya is accepted. But there are two aspects of Puṇya. From the conative point of view Puṇya is that good action which is performed by the Jīva. But when by good action we mean Karmic matter, which is accumulated by the Jīva and the fruit of which is experienced in the next incarnation, then we are referring to the material or the Pudgalic aspect of Puṇya. That is, Puṇya is a tendency as well as a potentiality. Here tendency means activity and potentiality stands for Karmic matter. Actions which lead to good potentialities are called Puṅyas. According to Jainism there are the following nine types of Puṇya:

(1) Anna Puṇya (the virtue of food);
(2) Pāna Puṇya (the virtue of water);
(3) Vastra Puṇya (the virtue of cloth);
(4) Layana Puṇya (the virtue of lending the house);
(5) Śayana Puṇya (the virtue of supplying beds);
(6) Mana Puṇya (the virtue of controlling mind);
(7) Śarīra Puṇya (the virtue of controlling body);
(8) Vacana Puṇya (the virtue of controlling speech);
(9) Namaskāra Puṇya (the virtue of salutation).

Anna Puṇya or the virtue of food, means supplying food to a hungry and poor person worthy of receiving it. In like manner, Pāna Puṇya means the virtue of quenching the thirst of a person by supplying water. Vastra Puṇya means giving cloth to those who are in need of clothes to cover their bodies. Although according to Jainism the charity of food, water and clothing can be extended to any worthy person, yet these virtues, if practised with reference to the Jaina ascetics, are all the more effective. The virtues of Layana and Śayana mean respectively providing residential accommodation and beds to the ascetics. Mana Puṇya, Śarīra Puṇya and Vacana Puṇya stand for control over mind, body and speech, in order to avoid every kind of violence to others and to exhort them to be moral and ethical.

The Namaskāra Puṇya means saluting or bowing down to the ascetic.

Pāpa (*Vice or Demerit*)

According to Jainism Pāpa means being influenced by attachment and jealousy instead of rationality, and performing evil deeds under that influence. It is the rebellion of man's meaner nature against his virtuous tendencies and inherent goodness. Therefore Pāpa is regarded as the manifestation of the individual's ignorance and immorality in his voluntary actions. The following eighteen demerits or vicious acts are recognized by Jainism:

(1) Prāṇavadha or Jīva Hiṁsa Pāpa, 'crushing out the organic energies of an organic soul';

(2) Asatya or Mṛiṣāvāda Pāpa, untruthfulness;

(3) Adattādāna Pāpa, stealing, directly or indirectly;

(4) Abrahmacarya Pāpa, or unchastity, indulgence in sexual intercourse mentally or physically;

(5) Parigraha Pāpa, which consists in over-attachment to one's belongings; covetousness;

(6) Krodha Pāpa, or anger;

(7) Mānā Pāpa, or egoism;

(8) Māyā Pāpa, hypocrisy;

(9) Lābha Pāpa, greed or avarice;

(10) Rāga or Āsakti Pāpa, personal attachment;

(11) Dveśa Pāpa, ill will or hatred towards anything;

(12) Kleśa Pāpa, quarrelsomeness;

(13) Abhyākhyana Pāpa, spreading false rumours or scandals in order to lower someone's prestige;

(14) Paiśūnya, tale-telling;

(15) Paraparivāda Pāpa, talking ill of others or emphasizing the badness of others;

(16) Rati Arati Pāpa, attraction towards sensual and emotional life, and distraction from discipline or self-control;

(17) Māyā Mṛiṣa Pāpa, resorting to improper or sinful acts under the pretext of propriety and virtue;

(18) Mithyā Darśanaśalya Pāpa, taking an unreal thing to be real, even when one is capable of discriminating between real and unreal.

Bandha, or bondage, means the mingling of the Karmic matter with the soul, like the mingling of water with milk. The relation of the soul with the Karmic matter is thought, however, to be without any beginning. This relation is not endless. The individual can break up this relation and attain the beatific stage. The Uttarādhyāyana Sūtra mentions that a houseless monk destroys the four remnants of Karman which even a Kevalin [a released soul] possesses because his character which makes him unshakeable 'like the king of the mountain'. It is further said that after that 'he obtains perfection, enlightenment, deliverance and final beatitude, and puts an end to all misery'.[1]

There are four kinds of bondage according to Jainism: (1) Prākṛiti Bandha, natural bondage, (2) Sthiti Bandha, stable bondage, (3) Anubhāga Bandha, the bondage indicating intensity, and (4) Pradeśa Bandha, mingled bondage.

Āśrava is that quality of the soul which attracts Karman towards it. It takes this name because it is that tendency of the soul which attracts good as well as bad Karmic matter towards the soul and thus leads to bondage. Āśrava means the inward flow of Karman in the soul. P. C. Nahar gives the following definition of Āśrava:

'Āśrava is the influx of the Karma particles into the soul, or it may be said to be the acquirement by the soul of the fine Karma matter from without.'[2] Āśrava is usually divided into the following two classes:

(1) Bhāva Āśrava, or internal flow;
(2) Dravya Āśrava, or material flow.

Bhāva Āśrava is that mental state or transformation that makes the Jīva as attractive and dynamic as a magnet to make it capable of attracting Karmic matter. Material influx, or Dravya Āśrava, stands for that Karmic matter which is attracted and accumulated by the Jīva.

There is another classification of the Āśrava. From this point of view Āśravas are compared to those inlets of a tank through which the water flows. These types of Āśravas are as follows:

1. Mithyātva, or ignorance (of reality);

[1] S.B.E., XLV, Uttarādhyāyana Sūtra XXIX, A.
[2] P. C. Nahar, *An Epitome of Jainism*, p. 526.

2. Avirati, or attachment;
3. Kaṣāya, or propension;
4. Pramāda, or negligence;
5. Yoga, or the functional activity of mind, speech and body.

Mithyātva means wrong notions about the nature of the ultimate reality. Avirati indicates disinclination towards renunciation. Pramāda means lethargy towards right conduct. Kaṣāya means the intense arousal and influence of attachment and hatred. Yoga stands for the activities of the body, mind and speech, which bring about the union between the soul and the Karmic matter. Yoga is further subdivided into (1) Śubha Yoga, or auspicious activity and (2) Aśubha Yoga, or inauspicious activity. Auspicious activity brings about auspicious bondage, or Puṇya Bandha, and inauspicious activity leads to inauspicious bondage, or Papa Bandha. Śubha Yoga, which brings about the accumulation of merit and which leads to the bondage of the soul with auspicious Karmic matter, takes the soul towards the beatific state. There are many long lists of Āśravas in Jaina philosophy but all such schedules can be reduced to the above-mentioned classes.

Saṁvara

Āśrava, or the influx of Karmic matter, is regarded as the cause of bondage, although the Āśrava leading to auspicious union does bring about the beatific state. Because the sole purpose of Jaina philosophy is to set one completely free from bondage, to attain liberation, from the point of view of Jainism the most important category is that which brings about the complete annihilation of the Karmas. This very important category is designated Saṁvara. Since Āśrava conceals the real nature and the freedom and the divinity of the soul, therefore Saṁvara is that category which is directly opposed to Āśrava, and which reveals the real nature of the soul by reviving its beatific state. The inflow of Karmic matter or Āśrava is prevented by Saṁvara. Saṁvara thus means the adoption of those principles of life and penance which free the soul from Āśravas and destroy the new bondage of Karma. The following five Saṁvaras have been accepted as the most important:

1. Amithyatva, or rightmindedness or full faith in the basic reality;
2. Virati, or non-attachment;
3. Akaṣāya, or freedom from indulgence;
4. Apramāda, or carefulness;
5. Ayoga, or freedom from physical, mental and verbal activities which bring about bondage.

These five principles of self-control are further sub-divided into sub-classes so that ultimately fifty-seven rules of conduct are accepted as binding upon the aspirant. Their sole purpose is to stop the influx of the Karmic matter.

Nirjarā (*Beatific State*)

Nirjarā or beatitude signifies that state of the soul in which the influx of Karmic matter is altogether stopped and man attains liberation in this life. Nirjarā is that state having attained which the soul partially frees itself from all the Karmas and yet it continues to reside in the physical body. In order to clarify this notion, three illustrations are presented:

1. Just as the stagnant water of the tank is let out through the outlets, in the same manner when the water in the form of Karmas is let out of the soul, through spiritual discipline, the person attains Nirjarā, or the beatific state.
2. Just as the rubbish is swept out of the house by the broom, similarly when the soul is freed from the rubbish in the form of Karmic matter by following righteousness, a person attains Nirjarā.
3. Just as the water collected in the boat is thrown out with the hands, similarly when the soul throws out the water in the form of Karmic matter, a person attains Nirjarā.

Mokṣa (*Liberation*)

Mokṣa is complete liberation of the soul from Karmic matter. We have already stated that the four kinds of bondage unite the soul with Karmic matter. Although we have explained the nature of bondage above, it is necessary to clarify the notion of bondage, or Bandha, by referring to the following three illustrations, which will throw light on the nature of liberation:

1. Just as the sesame and the oil are intermingled, one with the other, similarly the soul and Karma are intermingled one with the other through bondage.

2. Just as milk and the butter are intermingled one with the other, in the same manner soul and the Karmas are mingled one into the other through bondage.

3. Just as mineral and the earth are merged into each other, similarly the Jīva and the Karma are merged into each other through bondage.

Since the state of liberation means complete freedom of the soul from all kinds of Karmas, the following three illustrations clarify the notion of Mokṣa, or liberation:

1. Just as the oil is pressed out of the sesame by the oil press, similarly when the soul is weaned out of the Karmic matter by means of self-control or penance then man attains Mokṣa.

2. Just as butter is churned out of milk by means of the churn, similarly when the soul is separated from the Karmic matter by means of penance and self-control a person attains Mokṣa.

3. Just as the mineral is separated from the earth by means of fire, similarly when a person separates the soul from the Karmic matter by means of penance or self-control he attains Mokṣa.

Asceticism or Renunciation in Jaina Ethics

The special feature of Jaina ethics is its severely stringent character, because its goal is Mokṣa, which means the acquisition of infinite knowledge, infinite perception, infinite power and infinite bliss. The attainment of such a unique state cannot be accomplished without eschewing selfishness completely. According to the Jaina point of view, only an ascetic can follow the strict code of conduct because he gives up all wordly ties. In fact almost all schools of Indian philosophy accept principles of renunciation as a means of attaining the highest state. Detachment from all worldly objects is generally considered necessary for self-realization. Such longing, such yearning for renunciation is inspired by the intense desire of the soul to become infinite. This ascetic attitude expands the soul, frees the individual from narrow selfish desires, and leads him to adopt a life in which love and sympathy for all human beings predominate.

Asceticism means service and self-sacrifice. Service and self-devotion cannot be adopted by a weakling; on the contrary, only the brave and courageous soul can follow such a path. To a layman the life of renunciation might appear incomplete; but this so-called incomplete life is actually a life of perfection. The life of simplicity and truth is the highest life. Such a life was adopted by the great Chinese philosopher, Lao-Tze, who wrote that a simple life is a life of plainness, in which profit is discarded, cleverness abandoned, selfishness minimized and desires reduced. It is the life of 'perfection', which seems to be incomplete, of 'fullness which seems to be empty', of 'absolute straightness, which seems to be crooked', of 'skill, which seems to be clumsy', and of 'eloquence which seems to stutter'. It is the life of 'producing and rearing things, without taking possession of them', of 'doing work, but not taking pride in it', and of 'ruling over things, but not dominating them'. It is the life which is 'as pointed as a spear, but does not pierce, as acute as a knife, but does not cut, as straight as an unbent line, but does not extend, and as bright as light, but does not dazzle'.[1]

It is this paradoxical nature of the ascetic life which cannot be easily understood by scholars who do not try to go deep into its spirit. The purpose of the life of an ascetic is the uplifting of humanity, and the ideal he adopts is the ideal of the attainment of full life. Such a goal is positive existence, not annihilation. There is no doubt that the ascetic scorns the so-called comforts of life, yet he aims at happiness. He seems disgusted with, or at least indifferent to everything around him, yet he is most concerned with the realization of the ultimate reality. Indian philosophy can be best understood with reference to the four noble truths of the Buddha, which we shall explain in the sequel, but which may briefly be stated as follows: (1) There is suffering in the world; (2) there is a cause of suffering; (3) there can be an end to this suffering, and (4) there is a way to attain it.

Jainism is often called Śramanism, for Jains believe that only an ascetic can attain Mokṣa by following absolute non-violence. Although it propounds moral principles even for householders, Jaina ethics is predominantly the ethics of asceticism. The ethics laid down for householders is called the Anuvratās, or atomic vows. Before explaining the nature of the Mahāvratās,

[1] Lao-Tze, quoted in C. Moore (Ed.), *Philosophy East and West*, 1946, pp. 34–5.

or great vows, and the Anuvratās, or atomic vows, it is necessary to explain that Jaina ethics considers Mokṣa to be the only end of life, or Purusārtha.

According to Jainism Mokṣa is not merely an abstract ideal that commands men to end their desires, nor does it advocate unlicensed satisfaction of desires like Western hedonism. Mokṣa brings about infinite knowledge, infinite bliss, infinite intuition and infinite power, thereby leading to perfection and the automatic satisfaction of all desires. Such eternal and universal self-realization accommodates the rational form of Kantian ethics and the material content of happiness envisaged by hedonism. Mokṣa is no doubt a rational and conceptual notion, and from the ordinary point of view it cannot be said to be materialistic. At the same time, the realization of Mokṣa, which means self-realization, unites the soul with the universal self, and this universal self-realization brings about a synthesis of reason and happiness.

A perfect moral theory is in need of such a metaphysical concept, which in spite of being an ideal must be capable of being actually experienced, and which in spite of being subjective must be universal. Although Kant emphasized the internality of virtue, he accepted the presupposition of an external God in order to make his ethical theory complete. Kant accepts a universal point of view as the ideal, and says that we should never use man either in our own person, or in that of others as a means but always as an end in himself. He makes an attempt to establish the kingdom of ends, although his purposivism is vague. Although Kant held that virtue and happiness are both combined to give us complete good, he never made clear how these two could be synthesized. In order to solve this knotty problem he accepts the notion of such an omniscient and ominipotent God who should award happiness to every individual in proportion to his virtue. It is really strange that Kant, who is the upholder of the kingdom of ends, and who emphasizes that man has intrinsic value, himself introduces God through the back door to bring about a reconciliation between morality and happiness, thereby reducing God to an instrument for the satisfaction of human needs. Kant in spite of declaring man as an end in himself could not give a consistent theory of morality because he was unaware of the theory of self-realization. He was unaware of the concept of Mokṣa.

Some Western ethical theories consider morality to be relative and a contradiction. According to Bradley, 'Morality does involve a contradiction. It does tell you to realize that which can never be realized and which, if realized, does efface itself as such. No one ever was or could be perfectly moral; and if he were, he would be moral no longer; where there is no imperfection, there is no ought. The ought is a self-contradiction.'[1] Since the notion of Mokṣa is foreign to Western scholars, they are not aware of the fact that the contradiction of morality can be transcended and that one can attain a level at which one rises above reason and intellect. Kant did establish a transcendental metaphysics but he could not present a transcendental ethics. That is why he had to take refuge in theism and to accept the concept of an external and personal God. Jainism is not satisfied with the contradiction and imperfection of man. According to it man by his very nature is above contradiction and implies perfection. The aim of his life is to actualize the potential perfection by adopting moral and spiritual discipline. Man is not a 'contradiction'. We should not accept a morality which is a contradiction. Bradley himself wrote that 'Man is something more than contradiction.' What I wish to emphasize is that this 'something more' is the spiritual potentiality which makes a man capable of experiencing perfection and harmony, or of attaining Mokṣa. The antimonies of right and wrong, good and bad, reason and happiness and individual and social well-being can be overcome by accepting the ethico-metaphysical notion of Mokṣa. In this way Jainism considers Mokṣa to be the only moral ideal. Let us study Jaina ethics keeping in view this ideal.

Ascetic Ethics

As we have already stated, according to Jainism non-violence is the highest virtue. It lays down the five great vows or the principles of morality: (1) non-violence (Atiṁsā), (2) truth (Satya), (3) non-stealing (Asteya), (4) celibacy (Brahṁacarya), and (5) non-possession (Aparigraha). Jaina philosophy considers these five principles to be basic rules of the conduct for ascetics. Non-violence means refraining from all injury and violence, whether such violence pertains to the subtlest invisible living beings or to animals or to human beings. Violence does not mean causing

[1] F. H. Bradley, *Ethical Studies*, p. 134.

only physical injury, but it also includes mental and verbal injury. When a Jaina ascetic adopts non-violence, he tries his best to follow it absolutely and not to cause injury to any living being, physically, mentally and verbally. Thus non-violence requires three principles which are called the three Guptis. In other words, following the principles of non-violence through mind, word and deed implies three Guptis, the Guptis of mental non-violence, verbal non-violence and physical non-violence. Other Mahāvratas must also be adopted with reference to these three Guptis or implied rules. We should remember that the foundation of all the great vows is the great vow of non-violence. All other moral rules are accepted only to maintain this great vow of non-violence. Speaking truth is necessary because by telling lies against somebody we cause at least mental injury to him. A person would not be able to follow non-violence by neglecting truth. By telling lies we commit verbal violence and injure the feelings of another person. In like manner stealing somebody's property, violating the third great vow, amounts to violence. A person whose property is stolen is mentally injured. Therefore, non-stealing as well is based on non-violence. Hence it is evident that even Brahṁacarya is based on non-violence. Non-possession means not to possess surplus property. A person who hoards wealth deprives poor and hungry persons of their wants. Surplus wealth could be used to provide food and clothing to the needy. Thus adopting the principle of non-possession means following a non-violent way of life.

The conduct of ascetics must be absolutely non-violent. Therefore all the Jaina ascetics must adopt the following five Samitis, or co-rules, besides the five great vows and the three implied rules, or Guptis:

1. Iryā Samiti, or caution in avoiding injury to living beings while walking.
2. Bhāṣā Samiti, or control over speech to avoid verbal injury.
3. Eṣaṇā Samiti, or careful checking of food to assure that whatever food or drink has been given to him was not specially prepared for him.
4. Ādāna Nikṣepaṇā Samiti, or using necessary articles cautiously to avoid injury to subtle lives.

5. Parithāpāṇikā Samiti, or disbursing or throwing away unnecessary articles with care and caution.

These five Samitis aid the ascetic in following the path of non-violence and they also show that the life of an ascetic must be exemplary under all circumstances. This strictness of the ascetic code is very important, because it aims at eschewing both attachment and hatred. An ascetic can never attain Mokṣa until and unless he rises above the worldly antinomies and practises absolute non-violence. Ordinarily, non-violence means protecting the lives of animals, which is why most Jaina householders, or Śrāvakas, feed birds and nurse wounded birds and animals. Thus non-violence is regarded as equivalent to compassion. But the Terāpaṅthī sect of the Jaina Śvetāmbara school gives a strange definition of non-violence and distinguishes it from the protection of life. This definition must be dispassionately analysed since non-violence is the supreme end of morality in Jainism. So far as the ethical code of ascetics is concerned, the explanation of non-violence from the absolutistic point of view has special significance.

The explanation of absolute non-violence is undoubtedly beyond the understanding of the common man. According to the viewpoint of absolute non-violence, there is no difference between avoidable and unavoidable violence. Thus violence is violence under all circumstances whatever. If we once accept the existence of 'subtle' lives, there is no reason that the violence to infinite subtle lives should not be regarded as immoral from the spiritual point of view, even if such a violence aims at the protection of human lives. Perhaps an intelligent person cannot adopt absolute non-violence, because he cannot maintain his own life without killing subtle lives. But from the metaphysical point of view it would be equally erroneous to regard such 'relative violence' to be 'non-violence'. The Terāpaṅthīs hold that if a man is obliged by circumstances to practise relative is violence, and if this course is supposed conducive to Mokṣa, a serious error occurs. They are of the opinion that there is a difference between spiritual life and practical life. Man should admit that he is weak and that he cannot at all times follow the spiritual morality. Absolute non-violence, according to which violence to subtle as well as to gross life is equally immoral, can become the ideal only for the ascetic. This concept of non-violence, according to the Terāpaṅtha, does not accept the difference between compassion to human beings and to subtle lives, though it recognizes the weakness of ordinary men who make the distinction.

Surely it is impractical to expect man to adopt absolute non-violence. Mahatma Gandhi expressed a similar view. In his words, 'Absolute or complete non-violence means freedom from every ill will against all kinds of living beings and therefore it encompasses the wild and poisonous animals other than human beings as well.'[1] In another place Gandhi says:

'Non-violence is a very extensive term. Man cannot live without external violence. He continues to commit some sort of violence willy-nilly while eating, drinking, sitting and standing. One who tries one's best to get rid of such violence, whose mind is full of compassion and who does not desire the destruction of non-violence, the self-control and tender-heartedness of such a man, will continually be on the increase. But there is no doubt that no living being can be absolutely free from external violence.'[2]

Having considered absolute non-violence impossible, Gandhi did advocate relative violence for the common man. He made clear in his speeches and writings that his non-violence is a peculiar non-violence. For example, he does not think compassion shown to man-eating wild animals is non-violence. Yet the Terāpaṅthi ascetics presume that it is unavoidable for an unattached ascetic to follow absolute non-violence. Therefore they do not consider the protection of life to be non-violence from the spiritual point of view. They hold that from a practical point of view the protection of life can be regarded as praiseworthy, but it cannot be accepted as a moral duty from the spiritual or transcendental point of view. The present leader of this sect, Ācārya Tulsi, has defined compassion in the following manner: 'Compassion means the protection of one's own soul, as well as that of others from unrighteousness. From a practical point of view the protection of life also can be regarded as compassion.'[3]

We can say that when ordinary compassion is compared with

[1] M. K. Gandhi, quoted in Acarya Bhikshu Aura. Swami Nag Raj, *Mahatma Gandhi*, p. 6.

[2] M. K. Gandhi, *Buddha Aura Ahimsa*, p. 175.

[3] Ācārya Tulsi, *Jaina Siddhānta Dipika*, p. 107.

spiritual compassion it falls short of non-violence. Thus a person who protects the lives of others under the inspiration of compassion can be praised. But if compassion instead of Mokṣa is taken to be the motive, then such an action would be immoral from the spiritual point of view. The protection of life under the motive of compassion can be executed by adopting many means other than non-violence, e.g. the life of a goat can be protected by paying money to the butcher. In such a situation compassion cannot be regarded conducive to Mokṣa, because an ascetic can neither possess money himself nor can he pay money to others. If instead of paying money he can change the heart of the butcher by preaching non-violence, then such an action, being motivated by the protection of the soul, would become spiritual duty, although incidentally it would also lead to the protection of life. This proves that the protection of the soul is superior to the protection of life only from the spiritual and transcendental point of view.

It should be remembered here that so far as the conduct of an ascetic is concerned, indifference towards the protection of life may be accepted as right to some extent. Since the ascetic aspires for Mokṣa, he has to rise above good and evil and to be absolutely free from love and hatred towards living beings. Good as well as bad actions are considered to be the cause of bondage in Jainism. 'Demeritorious and meritorious Karmas can be compared with iron and gold fetters respectively, to get liberation one must be free from both. It is necessary that attachment should be given up, and one should absorb himself in his pure self, otherwise all penance and religious practices are fruitless.'[1] But the Terāpaṅthīs overemphasize this indifference and consider the protection of life 'merely' as practical compassion. There is no doubt that we can support the metaphysical aspect of Jainism by declaring the protection of life to be secondary. But by calling that duty 'merely' practical, and by transferring that responsibility to the householders, the Terāpaṅthīs overdo spiritual indifference. They forget that an ascetic can remain unattached even when he is protecting life, and in this manner the protection of life, like the protection of the soul, can be transformed into spiritual compassion. Particularly it is not necessary for an ascetic to be influenced by love and hate while protecting living beings. One can remain free from love, hatred,

[1] Shri A. N. Upadhye, *Pravacana Sāra*, Introduction, p. 47.

jealousy, fear, etc., while following the spiritual principle protecting life.

Such an ideal is found in the concept of Sthitaprajña as expounded in the Bhagavadgītā. An ascetic has to experience pleasure and pain because these experiences are the fruits of his past actions. But the difference between him and the householder is that whereas the latter is in a state of imbalance, influenced by emotion, the former remains calm and quiet, being balanced in his intellect. He is neither attached to nor is he displeased with anyone, and he behaves equally towards good and evil in a detached manner. This ideal of the Bhagavadgītā is similar to the ideal of the Jaina ascetic. In the words of Kundakundācārya, 'In the case of an Ajñānin, the function of Karman leads to further bondage, while the Jñānin feels spiritually light when the Karman gives its fruit.' The ascetic who is free from emotions while protecting living beings, who adopts a transcendental attitude, can never be a victim to attachment, nor can his actions lead to bondage.

The concept of Sthitaprajña is not opposed to the Jaina view of non-violence. The concept of a Jñānin, or wise person, propounded by Kundakundācārya is analogous to the concept of Sthitaprajña. He agrees that the wise person should remain contented and stable in his own self. This self-contentedness is the cause of his bliss. He must be unattached in order to attain self-realization. Supporting this view the Ācārya says, 'Attachment ... causes a great danger to self-realization, even though one has mastered all the sacred texts. One should absorb one-self in his-self, which is an embodiment of knowledge, and thus be satisfied; that is excellent happiness.'[1] This notion of the wise man is exactly the same as that of the Sthitaprajña. According to the Bhagvadgītā a person who renounces his desires and remains satisfied within his own self is a man of stable intellect. The ideal of Sthitaprajña was propounded by the great yogin, Krishna, to make Arjuna understand the possibility of remaining unattached while performing the soldier's duty on the battlefield. If a soldier performs his duty without attachment his action does not lead to bondage. In like manner a Jaina ascetic or aspirant while protecting life can remain balanced and thus remain free from the influence of the Karmic matter. Of course there is a difference between the duties of an ascetic and

[1] *Pravacana Sāra*, Introduction, p. 46.

those of a warrior. But the aim of the Jaina principles which guide the conduct of an ascetic, and the aim of the principles of the Bhagavadgītā which guide a warrior are the same. According to the Bhagavadgītā an aspirant while performing his duty in the battlefield without attachment can attain Mokṣa like an ascetic. But a Jaina ascetic or aspirant performs his duty in the spiritual field just like a warrior, and remains indifferent towards material results because of his detachment. His aim is also liberation. If the duty of protecting one's nation (performed by a warrior with a spiritual attitude) can be helpful for the attainment of Mokṣa, then the duty of the protection of life (performed indifferently by the ascetic, who is the votary of non-violence) must be recognized as a spiritual duty. The Terāpaṅthījainas, while over-emphasizing the need of detachment, forget that the protection of life, like the protection of the soul, can also be undertaken without any expectation of the result.

Just as it is necessary not to over-emphasize the protection of life lest the aspirant may forget the supreme good of Mokṣa, similarly it is necessary not to over-emphasize the protection of the soul lest he overlook the protection of life, which is the noble means of attaining Mokṣa. If neglect of the spiritual aspect can bring about the mistake of regarding the protection of life as an intrinsic good, then the tendency of not accepting protection of life as the means of Mokṣa can also generate hatred towards the protection of life in the mind of the aspirant. If attachment towards living beings is the cause of the bondage, then hatred towards them also is such a cause. As a matter of fact both viewpoints are supplementary to each other. Jaina philosophy propounds the protection of the soul as well as the protection of life. The protection of the soul lays emphasis on the metaphysical aspect of Jainism, while the protection of life magnifies the importance of the ethical aspect. Hence the protection of life as well as that of the soul have equal importance for the ascetic, and the synthesis of these two proves that Jainism is an ethico-metaphysical system.

Ethics for Householders

Although Jainism does not consider it necessary for the aspirant to pass through the stages of a householder and of an anchorite

(Vānaprastha), and instead advocates the direct adoption of an ascetic life with a view to attaining Mokṣa, it holds that a householder can lead the life of renunciation and prepare for asceticism partially by following the five great vows. All the schools and sects of Jainism agree that it is necessary for the householders, or Sravakas, to follow the Anuvratas, or atomic vows, to practise the life of renunciation. It is important to note that the adoption of the Anuvratas is in fact the training for ascetic life. Anuvrata means the minutest part, or atom, of the great vow (Mahāvrata). In other words, Anuvrata is a simple principle based on the great vows. For example, a householder adopts the following six atomic vows, thus partly applying the great vow of non-violence:

(1) I will not kill innocent moving animals voluntarily;
(2) I will not commit suicide;
(3) I will not commit abortion;
(4) I will neither join an organization or party whose aim is violence and destruction, nor will I participate in such activities.
(5) I will not consider any individual as an untouchable;
(6) I will not behave cruelly towards anyone.

In the same manner the following Anuvratas can be derived from the great vow of truth:

(1) Not using false weights and measures while selling and buying things.
(2) Not passing false judgments intentionally.
(3) Neither filing a false suit against anybody, nor giving false evidence in court.
(4) Not giving out anyone's secret out of selfishness and jealousy.
(5) Not refusing to return anything kept with a person as a deposit.
(6) Not indulging in any kind of forgery.

One can follow the following Anuvratas, based on the great vow of non-stealing:

(1) Not taking anything belonging to others with a view to stealing it.
(2) Neither intentionally purchasing stolen goods nor aiding a thief in stealing.

(3) Not dealing in the goods prohibited by law.
(4) Not resorting to nefarious practices in business.
(5) Not misappropriating the property or money belonging to a trust or an organization in the capacity of an office-holder of such an organization.

The following Anuvratas are based on the great vow of celibacy:

(1) Neither committing adultery nor prostitution.
(2) Not indulging in any kind of unnatural sexual intercourse.
(3) Restraining from sexual intercourse for at least twenty days in a month.
(4) Observing celibacy at least up to eighteen years.
(5) Not marrying after the age of forty-five years.

The following Anuvratas may be adopted to follow the fifth great vow of non-possession:

(1) Not possessing anything more than one's normal quota.
(2) Not accepting bribes and presents.
(3) Neither offering nor accepting money for securing or giving votes.
(4) Not prolonging the treatment of a patient out of greed.
(5) Not demanding any amount of money in the matters of betrothal and marriage.

These atomic vows are apparently negative principles, yet even so their adoption can solve various moral and social problems. They may lead to self-purification and self-realization on the one hand, and build a strong character based on non-violence, justice and courage on the other.

A study of the above-mentioned moral principles of Jainism indicates that this philosophy represents the practical application of an ideal to life. This systematic moral discipline raises a person from the common level and makes him capable of knowing and practising truth through a highly moral and spiritual course of conduct. Jainism has been said to be based on the three principles of right belief, right knowledge and right conduct. This three-fold code is known as Ratna-trayī, or the three jewels. First of all, right belief or right conviction is postulated because without it right knowledge is not possible, nor can one follow right conduct without conviction. Right knowledge means the knowledge of the nine categories of Jainism with which we have already dealt. Right conduct consists in adopting those truths in life, which are accepted to be real and consistent. Since Jainism recognizes bondage and regards the great vows as the sole means of attaining liberation from bondage, the adoption of these great vows or of the atomic vows in life is regarded as right conduct.

This discussion clearly indicates that non-violence is the supreme duty, and that non-violence appears to be a negativistic concept. But when this great ideal is practically followed in life it proves to be something more than a negative standard. We have already stated that the adoption of absolute non-violence in life is not only difficult, but impossible for practical reasons. Hence the path of non-violence is not simple, but very arduous and complicated. While defining non-violence Mahatma Gandhi remarked again and again that this path is not meant for a coward or a weakling but for the brave and courageous. We shall discuss the non-violence of Mahatma Gandhi in the sequel. It will suffice here to say that Jainism is a system that has adopted the path of non-violence for ages and is still applying this ideal to practical life in the contemporary age. Non-violence does not only mean avoiding injury to other persons, but it also implies active service of others. Although Jainism lays emphasis on the practice of the principles of non-violence in all individual matters, it is evident that its ultimate goal is the well-being of humanity and social progress.

Today the world is divided into the opposing camps of capitalism and communism. Perhaps the way out of the conflict between capitalism and communism is the adoption of what I may call spiritual communism, which is the natural outcome of the path of non-violence propounded by Jainism. In fact the bloodless revolution brought about by Vinoba Bhave in the form of Bhūdāna Yajña is entirely based on the principles of non-violence and non-possession. Nor is it improper here to mention that the non-violent path which Mahatma Gandhi adopted in the struggle for independence, and which was strictly followed by millions of our countrymen at the risk of their lives, was clear proof of the success of the practical application of the atomic vows in politics. We shall return to this point at the proper place. It is sufficient to note here that moral strength is more forceful than physical power.

CHAPTER VII

THE ETHICS OF BUDDHISM

Chronologically Buddhistic philosophy comes second in the history of Indian thought, although Jainism and Buddhism are almost contemporary as classical systems. There are a number of similarities between these two schools of Indian philosophy, particularly with regard to their ethical concepts. Both systems are opposed to the Vedic cult of sacrifice to the extent that they repudiate the idea not only of killing animals, but also the notion of material prosperity, which was supposed to result from animal sacrifice. The Vedas advocated wealth and pleasure (Artha and Kāma) as two of the four ends of life. Jainism and Buddhism laid emphasis only on Dharma (moral duty) and Mokṣa (liberation) at the price of economic and emotional values. Both Jainism and Buddhism strike a pessimistic note, and both advocate strict adherence to non-violence (Ahiṁsā). Both give special importance to the ascetic order and are therefore known as Srāmanic systems, as opposed to the six Brāhmaṇic systems.

It is due to the various points of resemblance between these two cults of non-violence that one system is sometimes confused with the other. But it should be remembered that the main resemblance is their emphasis on the virtue of non-violence. So far as aiming to attain Mokṣa is concerned, it may be said that the two systems agree with each other, but at the same time they are diametrically opposed with regard to the nature of Mokṣa and the means of attaining it. Although both believe in non-violence as the royal road to Mokṣa, yet whereas the Jaina system believes that the attainment of Mokṣa brings about infinite knowledge, infinite power and infinite bliss to the individual soul, the Baudha system believes that Mokṣa means the total annihilation of the self. This difference of the nature of the *summum bonum* between the two systems is responsible for the different ethical ideals and moral principles adopted by both these schools.

Another difference between the two systems is that Jainism

advocates penance as the means of self-realization, whereas Buddhism does not believe in self-mortification. Thus Buddhistic ethics is more humanistic and more compassionate than the rigorous ethics of Jainism. The ethics of Buddhism is the ethics of right life, both theoretically as well as practically. Even so it is strange that Buddhism died out from the land of its birth, whereas Jainism survived the tide of time. To my mind this accident in the history of Indian philosophy is mainly due to the fact that Buddha was silent about the metaphysical aspect of philosophy, whereas Jainism paid heed to the metaphysical foundation of ethics. The Indian mind is fundamentally metaphysical, and a system which lacks the metaphysical background or shows itself indifferent to metaphysics is almost universally denounced in the land of spiritualism and sages, who advocated the identity of the individual soul with the universal truth or the cosmos as the prerequisite of self-realization.

We shall see that in early Buddhism, or Pali Buddhism, there is very little metaphysics because the Buddha was so urgently engrossed with the problem of the removal of human suffering that he purposely did not delve into metaphysical problems. This however does not mean that the Buddha had no grasp of the ultimate reality. On the contrary, it shows his extreme pragmatic view of the ideal of philosophy. He knew much more than he preached, but he realized that the need of the hour was not an emphasis on metaphysical discussions, which might even end in confusion, but the spiritual, and the ethical regeneration of mankind. The following quotation from Hiriyanna's *Outlines of Indian Philosophy* is worth mentioning here:

'Buddha taught only what is necessary for overcoming evil, whose prevalence is, according to him, the chief characteristic of life.'[1]

The Buddha himself explained this pragmatic attitude to his disciples. Once the Buddha was sitting under the shade of a Siṁsupa tree and at that moment he took a few leaves of the tree in his fist and put them before his disciples, asking them whether those leaves exhausted all the leaves of the tree. Receiving a negative answer from his disciples, he remarked:

[1] M. Hiriyanna, *Outlines of Indian Philosophy*, p. 137.

'As surely do I know more than what I have told you . . . And, wherefore, my disciples, have I not told you that? Because, my disciples, it brings you no profit, it does not conduce to progress in holiness, because it does not lead to the turning from the earthly, to the subjection of all desires, to the cessation of the transitory, to peace, to knowledge, to illumination, to Nirvāna! Therefore have I not declared it unto you.'[1]

The fact that the Buddha renounced the world when his heart was overwhelmed at the sight of suffering, pain, disease and death itself goes to prove that his main concern was the redemption of suffering humanity. He is reported to have said he would be prepared to shift the sufferings of all the living beings of the world to him if it could help to relieve them of their pain. The Buddha's gospel is the gospel of love, which advocates 'gentleness, serenity, compassion through liberation from selfish craving', as its fundamental teachings. The Buddha was constrained to sidetrack metaphysical issues for if he hadn't he probably would not have succeeded in his mission, relieving the sufferings of fallen mankind. This however should not lead us to conclude that Buddhism has no metaphysics at all. On the contrary, the righteous path of the Buddhistic ethics is based on metaphysical assumptions. Before we give a brief survey of the metaphysical aspects of Buddhistic ethics, however, it appears necessary here to remark that although the Buddha neglected metaphysics in his keen desire to attend to the more urgent needs of his time, this fact led to the misinterpretation of the Buddhistic philosophy by his followers, who ultimately propounded a nihilistic metaphysics. The Buddha did believe in various metaphysical concepts of the Upaniṣads and took many spiritual terms and principles for granted. The immortality of soul, the doctrine of Karman, and the concept of Mokṣa, which are certainly basic concepts in Buddhism, clearly indicate the great influence of Upaniṣadic thought on the philosophy of the Gautama, the Buddha, the 'enlightened one'.

Nevertheless he purposely ignored and avoided discussion of metaphysical problems like the eternality of the universe, the immortality of soul, and the relation of body and mind, etc., because in his opinion such discussions did not have any immediate practical value. The immediate need was to recognize evil

[1] *Outlines of Indian Philosophy*, p. 137.

and adopt ways of removing or abolishing it so that humanity might attain Nirvāna or freedom from pain and sorrow. In early Buddhism this fact is illustrated in a dialogue between the Buddha and his disciple Malunkyaputta, in which the latter resolves not to follow the Buddhistic religion until the Blessed one explains to him whether the world is eternal or non-eternal, whether the world is finite or infinite, whether the soul and the body are identical or separate, or whether the saint lives after death or perishes forever. While answering this query of Malunkyaputta the Buddha points out that in initiating his pupils to the path of piety or Dharma, he never assured them he would explain such metaphysical subtleties to them if they followed his faith. Secondly, he emphasizes that indulgence in such discussions is as inessential and beside the point as it would be unimportant for a wounded person to inquire about the caste, creed and complexion of the man who wounded him before allowing the surgeon to remove the arrow from his body.

That is, suffering humanity could not be redeemed by discussion of abstract and complicated metaphysical problems, the solutions to which cannot be easily given, and indifference to which would not stand in the way of attaining Nirvāna. The Buddha, while answering the questions of Malunkyaputta, therefore says, 'The religious life, Malunkyaputta, does not depend on the dogma that the world is eternal, nor does the religious life, Malunkyaputta, depend on the dogma that the world is not eternal. Whether the dogma obtains, Malunkyaputta, that the world is eternal, or that the world is not eternal, there still remain birth, old age, death, sorrow, lamentation, misery, grief and despair, for the extinction of which in the present life I am prescribing'.[1]

Thus had the Buddha clearly stated that the *summum bonum* lay in the attainment of a state of liberation which alone could put an end to all suffering. Whatever was necessary to be explained to attain Mokṣa, Buddha explained in his teachings. It is summed up by the Buddha himself in the following passage:

'And what, Malunkyaputta, have I explained? Misery, Malunkyaputta, have I explained . . . the cessation of misery have I explained . . . And why, Malunkyaputta, have I explained this?

[1] E. A. Burtt, *The Teachings of the Compassionate Buddha*, Mentor Series, p. 35.

Because, Malunkyaputta, this does profit, has to do with the fundamentals of religion, and tends to aversion, absence of passion, cessation, quiescence, knowledge, supreme wisdom and Nirvāna; therefore have I explained it.'[1]

The Buddha was led to adopt this attitude because his heart was full of love for mankind, nay, for all living creatures, and his sole purpose of dedicating his life to the propagation of truth was to provide for a permanent cure for worldly ills. The Buddha therefore was moral above all, and could tolerate no hindrance in the way of prescribing for a righteous life and a cure for sick souls and bodies, even if it meant scepticism with regard to metaphysics, God and soul, etc.

We are not concerned here with the philosophical justification or the propriety of the elimination of metaphysics on the part of the Buddha. But it would not be out of place to mention that the relation of ethics and metaphysics is such that the segregation of the two is not possible. The human mind cannot rest content with a sceptic or agnostic attitude. It cannot shut itself up in isolation from the whole of reality and attempt to lead an ideal life, without at the same time deciding whether the purpose of life tallies with the purpose of the universe or not. The Buddha himself accepted the law of Karma and the possibility of Mokṣa, both of which are metaphysical concepts. If he had pushed the inquiry into Mokṣa further, he would have arrived at a theory of the universe not contradictory to the attainment of liberation. The doctrine of Karman again reminds us of the universal ethical principle which is at the root of the world and its evolution. The silence of the Buddha in these matters, though pragmatic, was responsible for the nihilistic attitude adopted by later Buddhism, and which was ultimately responsible for the extinction of Buddhism from the land of its birth. However, it should not be forgotten that the transitoriness of the world, or the metaphysical concept of constant flux as the sole reality, is the starting point in the Buddhistic philosophy, and the cause of the establishment of ethical idealism, which is the quintessence of Buddhism. The four 'noble truths', the Ārya Satyas, the rock and foundation of Buddhism, ought to be mentioned before we enter into the detailed study of the Buddhistic ethics. The first noble truth is the existence of suffering in

[1] *The Teachings of the Compassionate Buddha*, p. 36.

the world; the second, that the suffering has a cause; the third, that suffering can be got rid of; and the fourth, that there is a way to accomplish this aim. The presence of suffering is evident from the painful nature of birth, decay, disease, death, and even from relation with unpleasant objects. The cause of suffering is the attachment of the mind to worldly objects or desires. A chain of causes of suffering is explained in Buddhism. We shall refer to this chain in the sequel. If the chain of causes of suffering is broken, one can get rid of it immediately. The way to break this chain lies in a life based on righteousness, or Dharma.

The life of righteousness is the key to Buddhistic ethics and it is this aspect of Buddhism which has been responsible for its popularity both in India and in other countries. Discontent with worldly life, which prompts us to lead a life of detachment as commanded by the Buddha, should not, however, be misunderstood as a merely pessimistic note. Yet the ethics of the Buddha is the result of the transitory nature and the painful ending of so-called worldly pleasures, because they are based on attachment. Before we discuss the four noble truths in detail in order to explain the ethics of righteousness, let us clarify the point that the spiritual disquietude of Buddhism is in fact based on insight into the cause of human suffering, born of ignorance, or Avidyā. This fact is well illustrated in the story of the Buddha and his brother Nanda, a ruling prince.

Nanda possessed a charming personality and was regarded as the most handsome man in the world. He had a queen, Sundarī, who was the prettiest woman of her time. They were deeply in love with one another and would seldom separate from each other. Once it happened that both of them were together in the private apartment of the palace and were lost to the world when Lord Buddha, who once belonged to the royal family, came to the royal palace to beg alms. The Buddha had attained enlightenment and had been acknowledged as a world teacher. But as ill-luck would have it none of the servants of King Nanda noticed the arrival of Tathāgata (Buddha). So he waited at the door of the palace for some time and afterwards started to return to his āshrama. At the time of returning he was noticed by a bold maidservant, who mustered courage to enter the private apartment of the king and inform him that the great spiritual teacher had come to beg alms at the royal door and that he had returned unattended, without being offered a seat, or words or alms, as if he had returned from a desolate forest. Nanda, being full of great regard for the Buddha, was disturbed on hearing these facts from the maidservant. He immediately asked leave of Sundari to pay homage to Tathāgata. She gave permission on the condition that he would come back before the sandal paste on her body went dry. Nanda hurried towards the āshrama of the Buddha and soon reached there. He bowed to the teacher and apologized for his negligence. The Buddha ordered him to stay in the āshrama and meditate for some time as penalty for his carelessness. Although Nanda made sincere efforts he could not forget the beauty of his wife and was distracted in his meditation. The Buddha called him near and asked, 'Perhaps you are disturbed by the thoughts of your beautiful wife and you are feeling her absence strongly. Is it true?' Nanda replied in the affirmative. The story tells us that the Buddha told Nanda to close his eyes, and both of them began to rise. After some time the Buddha asked him to open his eyes. They had reached the height of a dry and desolate mountain. Nanda saw an ugly old one-eyed monkey, sitting on the dry branch of an old lonely tree on the mountain. The Buddha said to Nanda, 'Look at this she-monkey. Does she look beautiful in comparison to your wife?' Nanda replied 'Respected master! not to speak of the comparison, I cannot fathom even the contrast between the charm of Sundarī and the ugliness of this she-monkey.' The Buddha again asked him to close his eyes and they began to soar higher upwards. After some time they reached the garden of Indra, inhabited by beautiful heavenly damsels whose loveliness and divine charm dazzled the eyes of the mortal Nanda. When he was asked by the Buddha to compare the beauty of those heavenly figures with that of Sundarī Nanda said, 'Venerated master, the contrast between the beauty of these fairies and Sundarī is as unfathomable as it was in the previous case between Sundarī and the she-monkey.' After that they returned to the hermitage and the Buddha suggested Nanda meditate without being disturbed if he desired the company of heavenly damsels. With this object in view, Nanda succeeded in concentrating his mind and forgot everything about Sundarī.

Now Nanda was able to concentrate his mind for several days, after which the Buddha called him again and asked, 'Does the thought of Sundarī disturb you even now?' Nanda answered,

'Reverend master! I am so much absorbed in meditation that I cannot think of Sundarī, even for a moment.' The Buddha asked again, 'Is it not due to the fact that you are aspiring for the company of the beautiful heavenly damsels and the pleasures and enjoyments of the garden of Indra?' Nanda confessed it was so, and the Buddha continued, 'You will undoubtedly attain all pleasures contemplated by you as the fruit of your meditation and righteous life. But will you not have as much attachment for these heavenly pleasures, as you had recently for the pleasures of your palace and for the beauty of your wife? When the store of your merits is exhausted, you will have to bid a farewell to the heavenly damsels of Indra's garden, and you must imagine the intensity of the torture and the pangs of separation you will have to undergo at that time.' Nanda began to shudder at the very thought of it, and the Buddha said, 'Therefore, if you want to have permanent pleasure, eternal enjoyment and peace, you must continue to meditate on the Supreme Truth without any expectation and attachment.'

The transitory nature of sensual enjoyments and worldly pleasures, and the antinomies of the alternating experiences of pleasure and pain, joy and sorrow, struck the imagination of the enlightened Buddha, who advocated a detached attitude to worldly life. The aim of the ethics of Buddhism is the highest stage of the Bodhisattva. The Bodhisattva is one who must give up egoism altogether and rise above anger, hatred and error to gain the virtues of conviction, compassion, benevolence and disinterestedness. We shall refer to the ideal of the Bodhisattva at the end of the chapter. It will suffice here to say that the crux of Buddhistic ethics is that spiritual perfection, which consists in a harmonious life, alone can lead the aspirant to rise above the antinomies of pleasure and pain, heat and cold, joy and sorrow, and loss and gain. In this respect Buddhism agrees with the concept of the Sthitaprajña, or stable intellect, of the Bhagavadgītā, which is a unique ethical ideal, and which makes Indian ethics superior to and more practical than western ethics, which, in the absence of such an ethico-metaphysical notion, ends in contradictions, and reduces ethical values to a state of relativity. We shall return to this point in the proper place. The purpose of referring to it here is that Buddhism is at one with the orthodox as well as the heterodox schools of Indian philosophy in the assertion that there is no possibility of attaining Mokṣa unless a person has first reached the empirical state of equilibrium and equipoise, Jivanmukti, or liberation from flesh and blood.

This fact must always be borne in mind for the moment we overlook it we are bound to misconstrue Indian philosophy and Indian ethics as pessimistic and merely eschatological, and hence futile and imaginary. Even Buddhism, which starts with the dismal note of the presence of suffering, and the flux and transitoriness of the physical and mental world, is not negativistic in its ultimate analysis. Dr Radhakrishnan has rightly remarked that

'The Buddha does not want a suppression of emotion and desires, but asks for the cultivation of true love for all creation. This glowing emotion must fill the whole universe and result in an overflow of goodwill. The adoption of universal love, tenderness and compassion, has been advocated in the well-known Buddhistic work, Majjhima Nikāya, which reads as follows: "Our mind shall not waver, no vile speech will we utter, we will abide tender and compassionate; loving in heart, void of secret malice; and we will be ever suffusing such a one with the rays of our loving thoughts, and from him forthgoing we will be suffusing the whole world with thought of love, far-reaching, grown great and beyond measure, void of ill-will and bitterness".'[1]

It is due to the prejudicial viewpoint of Indian ethics adopted by some, perhaps most, western scholars that Indian morality is identified with asceticism, other-worldliness, and withdrawal from social responsibilities. It should not be forgotten that almost all the schools of Indian philosophy advocated a mean between the extremes of unlicensed indulgence in worldly pleasures and complete renunciation of social life. With this much general background of Buddhistic ethics we can now explain the ethical nature of the four noble truths of the Buddha.

The four noble truths, which emphasize the existence, the cause, and the method of extinction of evil, respectively correspond to and represent the three characteristics of the Buddhistic philosophy: (1) Pessimism, (2) Positivism, (3) Pragmatism.

[1] S. Radhakrishnan, *Indian Philosophy*, Vol. I, p. 433.

In order to have an insight into the ethical significance of the four noble truths, it appears necessary to throw some light on these three characteristics of the Buddhistic school.

We have already mentioned that Buddhism emphasizes the transitoriness and worthlessness of worldly pleasures. In this respect it is opposed to the Pravṛitti Mārga, or the path of attachment and desire for worldly pleasures and prosperity. Here Buddhism overemphasizes the dark side of life. Dr Radhakrishnan believes that the pessimism of the Buddhistic religion is due to the fact that every religion exaggerates the suffering of life, for the aim of religion is redemption from sin and suffering. But this view does not seem to do justice to Buddhism. We should not forget that the Buddha had resolved to dedicate his life to removing the suffering of all human beings because his heart was touched on seeing disease, old age and death. It was due to the tenderness of his heart and his keen observation that he drew the attention of all towards pain. Nor should we forget that reference to pain and suffering in Buddhistic philosophy is made only to awaken slumbering humanity to work its way out of suffering to reach bliss and to shun transitoriness to witness permanence. Referring to the pessimism of Buddhism Hiriyanna has rightly said, 'When we describe Buddha's teaching as pessimistic it must not be taken to be a creed of despair. It does not indeed promise joy on earth or in a world to come as some other doctrines do. But it admits the possibility of attaining peace here and now, whereby man instead of being the victim of misery will become its victor.'[1] The very fact that the Buddha recognizes 'ill and the ending of ill' proves that its pessimism is only initial and not final. It does not teach us how evil is avoided but rather tells how to face evil and how to overcome it. Thus, this philosophy instead of being escapism is the philosophy of courage and perseverance, effort and labour to move towards eternal bliss and happiness from transitory pleasure and suffering.

The positivistic character of Buddhism is indicated in its reaction to the traditional beliefs of Buddha's times. He repudiated the authority of the Vedas and rituals. He turned the attention of the people towards the hard facts of life to work out their salvation from suffering and pain. He believed in that reality which could positively be known. We shall see how the

[1] M. Hiriyanna, *Outlines of Indian Philosophy*, p. 136.

positivistic attitude towards life makes the philosophy of the Buddha a coherent logical system which appeals to intellect and which helps the individual to conquer the sole cause of suffering. Dwelling upon the positivistic aspect of the philosophy of the Buddha, M. Hiriyanna has said that although positivistic doctrines were unknown at the time, Buddha recognized nothing beyond the sphere of perception and reason. 'Such a view is also supported by the predominantly rationalistic lines on which . . . the teaching developed in later times.'[1] Even Buddha's concept of Nirvāna is a positivistic concept. According to him Nirvāna is not a state of extinction, but that of liberation, inner-peace, power, intuition of truth, the bliss of the identification of the self with the ultimate reality, and love for all living beings in the universe.

Similarly Buddha's thought is through and through pragmatic, informing us of only that which is essential for the attainment of liberation, and eliminating everything else, whether metaphysical or ethical, held by other schools of thought existing in his time. I have already referred to his pragmatic attitude by quoting the dialogue between him and his pupils in which he gives the example of the leaves of the Śiṁsupa tree. He avoids discussions on the existence of God, the immortality of the soul, and the permanence and impermanence of the world because he believes such discussions do not help the emancipation of the soul from suffering, and that following the law of Karma and turning away from desire are sufficient to lead an individual to illumination or liberation. It has been rightly asserted that 'Deliverance from pain and evil was his only concern and he neither found time nor need to unveil metaphysical subtleties. He was thus eminently practical in his teachings.'[2]

The Buddha's pragmatism is also evident in his preference for the middle course. He avoided extreme views about the way of life. He advocated neither the life of sensual indulgence nor that of rigorous asceticism. In his very first sermon at Benares just after his enlightenment he said:

'These two extremes, monks, are not to be practised by one who has gone forth from the world. What are the two? That conjoined with the passions and luxury, low, vulgar, common,

[1] *Outlines of Indian Philosophy*, p. 137.
[2] *Ibid.*, p. 137.

ignoble and useless; and that conjoined with self-torture, painful, ignoble and useless. Avoiding these two extremes the Tathāgata has gained the enlightenment of the middle path, which produces insight and knowledge and tends to calm, to higher knowledge, enlightenment, Nirvāna.'[1]

This reconciliation between the Pravritti, or the path of luxurious life, and Nivṛitti Mārga, or that of renunciation, agrees with the ethics of the Bhagavadgītā on the one hand, and corresponds to the Aristotle's concept of virtue on the other. The Bhagavadgītā propounds the middle course of the Niskāma Karma Yoga, which enjoins an aspirant neither to give up action, nor to be attached to it, but to perform it without any expectation of reward. Thus it advocates neither the renunciation of action, nor attachment to it, but a change of attitude, which prompts the aspirant to adopt renunciation in action. Similarly, according to Aristotle, virtue is a golden mean between two extremes, e.g., courage is a golden mean between the two extremes of cowardice and foolhardiness. Thus the Buddha was constrained to adopt the middle course which was most pragmatic for his purpose of preaching Dharma or virtue, which alone could bring about redemption from sin and suffering.

Existence of Suffering

The middle path that the Buddha laid down was the eightfold path of righteousness. But this path is in fact the fourth noble truth, which he unfolded in his first sermon at Bernares as a result of his search for truth for several years. The first noble truth is the presence of suffering or pain: 'Birth is painful, old age is painful, sickness is painful, death is painful, sorrow, lamentation, dejection, and despair are painful. Contact with unpleasant things is painful, not getting one's wishes is painful.'[2] The purpose of expounding this noble truth was to call attention to the imperfection and transitoriness of human existence. This pessimism, as we have already stated, is a special kind of pessimism which does not stop short of the existence of suffering or evil but goes beyond it to remedy it. Thus the first noble truth reveals the pessimistic characteristic of the Buddhistic ethics.

[1] E. A. Burtt, *The Teachings of the Compassionate Buddha*, p. 29.
[2] *Ibid.*, p. 30.

The Cause of Suffering

Even while expounding the truth of the existence of evil, the Buddha laid emphasis on the origin of suffering. He pointed out that ignorance was the cause of human suffering. There are twelve links in the chain of the causes of suffering according to the Buddha: (1) Ignorance (Avidyā); (2) action (Saṁskāra); (3) consciousness (Vijñāna); (4) 'name' and 'form' (Namārūpa); (5) the six-fields of the five sense organs and the mind (Śaḍāyatana); (6) contact between the senses and the objects (Sparśa); (7) sensation (Vedanā); (8) desire (Tṛiṣnā); (9) clinging to existence (Upādāna); (10) being (Bhava); rebirth (Jatī); and (12) old-age and death (Jarāmaraṇa), which is actual suffering. This chain of causes is held to have the above-mentioned twelve links in the serial order given so that ignorance gives rise to action, or Saṁskāra, which means the bondage of the soul to the world, which gives rise to consciousness. Consciousness is the cause of the 'name' and 'form' of the individual. It is necessary to explain the words 'name' and 'form'. Nāma does not stand for name in the usual sense but for the psychic factors which constitute the aggregate of the mental experience of an individual without any self, which is usually supposed to 'hold' or 'contain' the mental processes. As we pointed out earlier, for the Buddhistic psychologist there is no ego or self, but the aggregate, or Samghāta, of psychical processes. Similarly, Rūpa here stands for the physical body, which again is an aggregate of physical constituents. The name and form, or Nāmarūpa, therefore, means the psycho-physical organism, which is the result of the previous link of consciousness, and is itself the cause of the next link in the chain, namely, six fields of sense organs and mind, together with the objects of senses and of mind. These six fields are responsible for the contact of the sense organs with the objects, thereby giving rise to sensation, which, in turn, leads to desire. Desire causes us to cling to existence, which itself leads to being, or Bhava. Being brings about the cycle of births and deaths, during which the individual experiences pain or suffering.

The Removal of Suffering

The twelve links of the chain are so intimately connected that the last link, that is, suffering and pain, is said to be the direct result of ignorance. Commenting on the cause of suffering in the Buddhistic ethics Radhakrishnan writes: 'Ignorance is the main cause out of which false desire springs. When knowledge is attained, suffering is at an end. Ignorance and false desire are the theoretical and the practical sides of the one fact.'[1] It is therefore evident that suffering, which is due to the above mentioned chain of causes, can be removed once the chain is broken. Hence the Buddha expounded the third noble truth according to which he declared that the cessation of suffering is also a fact. The desire to live (Bhava) is the sole cause of suffering and egoism, and this is all due to ignorance; the cessation of suffering is not possible as long as the desire to live continues. If the craving for passion, existence, birth, rebirth and pleasure is the cause of evil, the removal of evil can occur through the cessation of craving. Hence while expounding the third noble truth, the Buddha declared, 'Now this, monks, is the noble truth of the cessation of pain, the cessation without a remainder of craving, the abandonment, forsaking, release, non-attachment'.[2] Here Buddhism agrees with the Jaina view according to which bondage is due to the inflow of Karma, i.e. desire or attachment, and release or liberation is possible only through detachment. The only difference between Jainism and Buddhism is that whereas the former advocates a rigorous asceticism as the means of the cessation of suffering, the latter lays down the eightfold path of righteous life. The Buddha, however, proves the cessation of suffering on the ground of his theory of causation and hence appeals to reason or logic. The cessation of pain according to him, is implied in the admission of the cause of pain. This is the reason the Buddha proceeds with the fourth noble truth of the way to bring about the liberation, or Nirvāna.

The Path to Liberation

The knowledge of the four noble truths came to the Buddha not automatically, but after he had practised a life of righteousness. According to Buddhism, as according to all other schools of Indian philosophy, mere theoretical knowledge is not enough for the attainment of perfection. The ethical life means the practice of virtue, not only a nodding acquaintance with it. The

[1] S. Radhakrishnan, *Indian Philosophy*, Vol. I, p. 367.
[2] E. A. Burtt, *op. cit.*, p. 30.

Buddha works out the details of the ethical life and lays down the eight-fold path for the guidance of the aspirant. In the Benares sermon, the Buddha declared, 'Now this, monks, is the noble truth of the way that leads to the cessation of pain: this is the noble eight-fold way; namely right views, right intention, right speech, right action, right livelihood, right effort, right mindedness, right concentration'.[1] It is necessary to explain the eight types of right conduct of life in some detail.

Right Views: The Buddha realized that as long as the aspirant entertained false notions he was not on the way to release. Thought and action, theory and practice, and belief and behaviour are interrelated and interdependent. Unless we entertain right views, we cannot get rid of egoistic feelings, and hence our action would be such as to strengthen the bondage of the soul, which would not enable us to snap the chain of the causes of suffering. Right knowledge alone can remove the ignorance which is the root cause of the suffering of the individual soul. Hence right views or right knowledge is the first prerequisite of the spiritual aspirant.

Right Intention: The second prerequisite is right intention or right aspiration. Right aspiration is not possible without right views which is why right intention is given second place in the eight-fold path of righteousness. Socrates was right in regarding virtue as knowledge. No one can be moral by accident. But Aristotle emphasized that virtue was a kind of habit. He was emphasizing the second aspect of moral action, that is, right intention. It is quite true that the virtuous man is one who actually practises virtue, not one who merely knows it. But the intention to be righteous would not be in the mind of the individual unless he knew what righteousness meant. The Buddha meant by right intention the aspiration for renunciation. It is only the intention or longing for renunciation that generates in man love for all living creatures, for then only does he rise above his individual self and give up the idea of separateness. Right intention prompts the aspirant to work for the whole human race. Buddhistic ethics is altruistic through and through. The Mahāyāna school of Buddhism, which developed later, emphasized this aspect of the righteous life and required every aspirant to declare, 'I must bear the burden of all creatures'. The prerequisite of right intention makes Buddhistic ethics socialistic

[1] E. A. Burtt, *op. cit.*, p. 30.

and universalistic, and indicates clearly that Indian ethics cannot be construed as individualistic and pessimistic, as many western scholars have wrongly throught.

Right Speech: After right intention, Buddhistic ethics ranks right speech, for speech reflects the character of the individual. Moreover, Buddhism puts a premium on non-violence, which means non-injury to all living beings. This is not possible unless the aspirant controls his speech as well as action. Injury does not mean only physical injury, it also means mental disturbance. It is a fact that words are sometimes more harmful than swords. Speech is the expression of the intention of the speaker, and the person to whom it is addressed is bound to be affected pleasantly or unpleasantly by it. Even Jainism is very particular about the restraint on speech and holds the injury done by speech as evil as that done by physical means. Moreover, right speech requires an individual to restrain himself from falsehood, backbiting, curt language and frivolous talk. Mahatma Gandhi was very particular about right speech, and he emphasized that one should neither talk about nor call attention to the faults of others. In the modern age of democracy and constitutional life speech is perhaps the chief means of expression of the intentions and commitments of a community, state or nation. Thus right speech is a mandate which holds as good today as it did at the time when the Buddha preached his eight-fold path of righteousness.

Right Action: Right knowledge, right intention and right speech would have no significance, especially no moral significance, if they are not followed by right action. In fact, right action, which according to Buddhism means unselfish action, is the outcome of right knowledge, right intention, and right speech. Simply uttering holy mantras, or hymns, and performing ritual ceremonies, cannot make a person moral. For this reason the Buddha raised his voice against the rituals. Bathing in the holy river of the Ganges cannot cleanse the heart of a man and make him moral unless he gives up telling lies, killing living beings, and taking away the wealth of others. Similarly, mere laws and statutes cannot make people moral unless they are actually followed. It is in this sense that the futility of legislation is brought out by the saying that 'Acts of parliament cannot make men moral; true morality arises from within'. International organizations like the League of Nations and the

United Nations Organization are bound to fail as long as their resolutions remain pious resolutions, without being practically followed by member nations. Right action, therefore, is the chief criterion of morality in the case of the individual as well as in the case of a nation or a community. Thus social well-being depends entirely upon the practice of righteousness or the fostering of right action. In short, our thought, speech and action must correspond to one another in order to bring about a harmonious development of the individual and of society.

Right Livelihood or Right Living: The imperative of right action, which means the application of right thinking, right motive and right words to conduct, leads to right living or the right conduct of life in every sphere—domestic, social, national and international. Freedom from vice, from deception, from lying and misleading people for self-aggrandizement, in short, building a pure character, or Śīla, is enjoined by the Buddha as the most essential prerequisite of an aspirant. Every action, every movement of the aspirant must be the reflection of his righteous character. Whether one is a politician, a preacher, a businessman, an administrator, a teacher, a student, a man or a woman, purity of character, or subjective purification, is a necessary condition if he desires to attain liberation while performing his duty as an ideal member of his profession or occupation. Character is the sum total of our habits of willing, thinking, and feeling. Hence the next three mandates of the Buddha are right effort, right mindedness (or thought), and right concentration. As we shall see, right effort means the habit of thinking rightly, and right concentration means the habit of concentrating our feelings rightly. Thus Śīla, or right livelihood, means the transmutation or sublimation of the character of the individual. It is the conversion of the whole personality from the gross and ignoble life of indulgence to the pure and noble life of the saint, or Bodhisattva, who attains freedom from suffering in this life, and who goes on working for the freedom of others as long as he lives in the bodily-self.

Right Effort: By right effort here is meant maintaining emotional equilibrium, to form the habit of always choosing the right path and expelling evil ideas from the mind. The following five methods are advocated for right effort:—(1) Attention to good ideas; (2) Facing the danger that will result from the practice of the bad idea; (3) turning attention from the bad idea;

(4) analysing the antecedents of the bad idea to counteract the temptation; and (5) causing the mind to remain away from the bad idea through bodily effort. When a person's attention is drawn towards a good idea, his interest in it automatically increases, and he forms the habit of choosing the good and rejecting the evil. Similarly, when a person comes face to face with the bad consequences of an evil resolution and thereby realizes the harm that he would do to the individual or to society, he is prompted to form the habit of right effort. Turning the attention away from the bad idea is the negative check on the mind, and it thereby helps the individual to develop the habit of choosing the right. Analysis of the antecedents of a bad idea reveals its futility, and closer examination of evil leads to Vairāgya, or detachment. Many a time persons who lead lives of sensual indulgence and are habitual rogues suddenly turn ascetics, because during their indulgence in evil they happen to analyse its antecedents and are thus suddenly enlightened. Bodily effort to get away from the evil through hard life also aids the individual to form the habit of choosing the right path. Right effort, therefore, paves the way for the attainment of true knowledge, enlightenment, or Nirvāna.

Right Mindedness or Right Thought: Right mindedness stands for the habitual exercise of reason to control the emotions of fear and anger, joy and sorrow, which bring about mental disturbance. Right thought, which means the constant intellectual effort to ponder over the noble truths, or Prajñā, again corresponds to the notion of the Sthitaprajñā of the Bhagavadgītā. It should be recalled here that intellectual effort does not stand for mere understanding but for intuitive experience. The Buddha was very particular that each and every aspirant should experience the truth himself, with his own effort, without depending on the grace of any God or that of a Guru, or preceptor. Right thought includes right experience of the truth through the intellectual effort of the aspirant. The Buddha declared that his followers should not borrow his views, but should accept them only when they have themselves realized them. The Buddha says, 'Then, monks, what you have just said is only what you yourselves have recognized, what you yourselves have comprehended, you yourselves have understood'.[1] The purpose of cultivating right thought is to get enlightenment directly by

[1] Majjhimanikāya, 38th Discourse.

controlling the emotion, because without the reign of reason over passion no spiritual progress is possible. The Buddha had gained spiritual insight through right thought and he expected others to do so themselves. In short, mental equilibrium is impossible without mental culture or right thought, and no liberation is possible without balance of mind or equipoise.

Right Concentration: Last but not least is the method of right concentration, meditation (Dhyāna). Concentration ultimately leads the aspirant to attain tranquillity of Samādhi. The following four stages of concentration are admitted in the Buddhistic ethics: The first stage brings joy and delight, generated from a life of seclusion, insight and reflection. At this stage the aspirant contemplates truths and has a keen desire to know them. He must concentrate without indulging in sensual enjoyments. The second stage of Dhyāna is marked by internal joy and calmness the aspirant experiences while concentrating his mind. At this stage there is no conscious reflection as there is in the case of the first stage. At the third stage, all passions and biased views totally disappear, and there is no keen desire to live (Ātmamoha). At the fourth level of Dhyāna, the aspirant reaches the climax of meditation where he rises above worry and joy, experiences perfect peace, and is self-possessed. Concentration is thus the gradual effort of the aspirant to rise to the highest stage of existence where he frees himself from egotism and merges himself with the universal truth. This gradual march towards universality, according to the Buddha, could be facilitated by constantly cherishing the four sublime moods, or Brahmavihāras, viz. friendliness or love (Maitrī), compassion or mercy (Karuṇā), cheerfulness (Muditā), and impartiality (Upekṣā). Besides the cultivation of the above mentioned qualities as essential conditions of the attainment of the highest stage of meditation, Buddhism also advocates physical and hygienic rules for discipline. The body must be brought under control, hence psychological exercises of detachment from the external world are advocated. In Buddhism Dhyāna does not mean reverie, but rather an exercise which withdraws the powers of mind from the external world and leads to the realization of the calmness of the highest order. The ultimate aim of meditation is to eradicate desire and to attain Nirvāna, in which the aspirant rises above all existence. It is worth while quoting M. Poussin here to clarify the meditative stage as advocated by the Buddha: 'The mind once concentrated and strengthened by exercise with the clay disc, or any other exercise of the same kind, is successfully to abandon its content and its categories. The ecstatic starts from a state of contemplating, coupled with reasoning and reflection, and he abandons desire, sin, distraction, discursiveness, joy, hedonic feeling: he goes beyond any notion of matter, of contact, of difference; through meditation on void space, knowledge without object, contemplation of nothingness, he passes into the stage where there is neither consciousness or unconsciousness, and finally he realizes the actual disappearance of feeling and notion.'[1] This description of the highest state of Samādhi should not be misunderstood as a blankness of mind. It is instead a state of a fullness, where all the powers of mind having been withdrawn from outside are concentrated inside in such a manner as to bring about self-realization or spiritual perfection, having attained which all contradictions are transcended. We wish to explain this fact further and throw more light on the nature of Nirvāna, which is incorrectly understood as a state of non-existence.

The Nature of Nirvāna

Like all the other schools of Indian philosophy Buddhism is a doctrine which aims at the cessation of all pain through constant endeavour, spiritual discipline, and righteous living, culminating in the transformation of the finite and limited individual self into the infinite and unlimited eternal existence. It is this perfect state of existence which is called Nirvāna in the Buddhistic philosophy, and which, being above all contradictions and relativities, is an absolute but positive state, and not at all a pure negation. The Buddhist concept of Sūnya, or Sūnyatā, has a special significance because the 'void', which is the literal meaning of this word, indicates the indescribability of the experience of the aspirant when he reaches this absolute state. This concept was arrived at not merely by intellectual analysis or by a process of elimination. On the contrary, after following spiritual discipline for a long time, Buddha first experienced it and later preached that each and every individual could attain the blissful state. He who purposely evaded metaphysical discussions to avoid abstraction and to lead aspirants directly to

[1] M. Poussin, *The Way to Nirvāna*, p. 164.

Mokṣa could not have propounded a concept which might turn out to be a mere intellectual abstraction. The inexpressibility of the ultimate Reality which is realized in the state of Nirvāna should not be misunderstood as nothingness in the sense of non-existence. According to the Mahāyāna school, the Buddha is reported to have said,

'All the Buddhas and all sentient beings are nothing but universal mind, besides which nothing exists. This mind which has always existed is unborn and indestructible. It is neither green, nor yellow, and has neither form nor appearance. It does not belong to the categories of things, which exist or do not exist, nor can it be reckoned as being new or old. It is neither long nor short, big nor small, but transcends all limits, names, speech, and every method of treating it concretely . . . It is like the boundless void which cannot be fathomed or measured.'[1]

Nirvāna is the mystic experience of the holy existence; a spiritual state or divine stage (Brāhmīsthiti) having attained which the individual does not return to physical existence, as on the contrary the Christian notion of mystic or holy experience and the Bhagavadgītā's concept of the Sthitaprajña depict. Otto, in his well-known work, *Idea of the Holy*, calls this indescribable aspect of the religious experience the *mysterium*, which having no parallel in the empirical world of experience is just a symbol because it is 'wholly other' and hence a sort of 'nothingness' or void. The Upaniṣadic notion of Brahman as transcendental existence, into which the individual soul or Ātman is merged at the attainment of Mokṣa has simply been reasserted by the Buddha in propounding the concept of Nirvāna. What the Buddha added was that this indescribable state of Mokṣa was in fact experienced by him and could be experienced by each and every individual. Thus the ethics of the Buddhistic philosophy is not at all different from that of the Upaniṣads so far as the ethico-metaphysical concept of Mokṣa is concerned. This concept of Mokṣa, the special feature of Indian ethics, makes it superior to Western ethics and brings about a reconciliation of the contending relative theories of rationalism and hedonism and hence resolving a conflict which has not been resolved in Western ethics.

[1] E. A. Burtt, *op. cit.*, p. 195.

What we wish to emphasize here is that, according to Buddhism, Nirvāna is the unity of the individual self with the universal self, and that this unity is actually experienced by the aspirant who, having attained that state in this life, in consequence begins to love all living creatures. He merges himself into the original source of existence. To quote the Buddhistic canon again, 'Our original Buddha nature is all truth, nothing which can be apprehended. It is void, omniprescient, silent, pure; it is glorious and mysterious peacefulness, and that is all which can be said.'[1] Buddhahood is the last stage attainable in this life and is therefore the state of perfection, brilliance, enlightenment, freedom, Nirvāna.

We have outlined the eight-fold path above and we have shown that this path in fact explains the eight stages of the development of the individual soul towards the universal self. However, the Mahāyāna school of Buddhism, which is a later growth, mentions ten stages, or Bhūmis, for the attainment of Nirvāna. The first stage is the Pramudītabhūmi, or the stage of joyfulness, which is generated because the intellect rises above the common-sense level. The aspirant, or Bodhisattva, at this stage undertakes resolutions which help him in following the spiritual path. For example, he takes the vow not to accept final release until every thing that exists in the universe has attained Nirvāna. This indicates that the Bodhisattva has dispelled ignorance and has attained purity of heart. At the second stage the aspirant comes to recognize the transitoriness of all things, and thereby becomes compassionate and pure-hearted. This stage is called Vimalā. The third stage of the Bodhisattva is known as Prabhākarī, or the shining stage, at which the aspirant practises patience and forbearance and banishes anger, hatred and illusion. At the same time he inculcates belief, benevolence, mercy and non-attachment. At the fourth stage the aspirant gives up egoism, engages himself in righteous action, and becomes virtuous. This stage is called Arcismatibhūmi, or the brilliant stage. At the fifth stage, known as Sudūrjayābhūmi, which is dominated by concentration and meditation (Samādhi), the Bodhisattva becomes unconquerable because most of his time is spent in meditation. At the sixth stage, termed Abhmuktibhūmi, or the stage of 'turning toward [Mokṣa]', he comes to understand the basic principles of Nairāt-

[1] E. A. Burtt, *op. cit.*, p. 197.

myavāda, or non-substantiality and dependent origination (Prātītyasamutpāda). It may be added here that the principle of dependent origination is the basis of the third noble truth, because it indicates that the process of becoming is not an absolute necessity, and that if one link of the chain of the causes and effects is broken, the whole process can be stopped because of the dependence of the effect on the cause.

Even at the sixth stage the aspirant is not completely detached. He yet craves to become Buddha, the awakened. The next stage is called Dūraṅgamabhūmi, at which he is devoted to the attainment of right knowledge to achieve his object of universal salvation. The seventh stage is that stage at which the aspirant becomes immovable (Acala), because he is now firmly bent upon not attaching himself to any object whatsoever. At the eighth stage the Bodhisattva sees all things rooted in Tathata, i.e. all things in their reality. Even at this level the aspirant is actively engaged in preaching Dharma to society. The ninth stage is designated Sādhumatibhūmi, or the stage of the good persons. At this stage the aspirant is completely detached in his actions, but he continues to work for the well-being of humanity without any selfish motive whatsoever. This in fact is the last stage of a Bodhisattva, because at the next stage he becomes a Tathāgata or the Buddha, the enlightened. The ninth stage is indicative of the altruistic aspect of the Buddhistic ethics, which though spiritual in its essence is not selfish in its aim and disproves the charge of being individualistic. This gradual march towards Nirvāna is in fact the systematic development of the individual to a state of universality and is therefore a humanistic ethical growth of his personality. Buddhism, particularly the Mahāyāna school, believes that not only monks, but all men can become Bodhisattvas irrespective of caste, creed and sex.

CHAPTER VIII

THE ETHICS OF NYĀYA AND VAIŚEṢIKA

Introductory:

So far we have been discussing the ethical views of the heterodox or Nāstika systems—the systems which declare themselves as staunch opponents of the traditional philosophy of the Vedas and the universalistic and purely spiritualistic monism of the Upaniṣads, which in their view have very little scope for a practical ethics for laymen. The heterodox systems of Jainism, Buddhism and the Cārvāka are regarded as non-believer systems, or Nāstika schools, not because they deny God but because they deny the authority of the Vedas and disown the Upaniṣadic philosophy. But all the three agree that the primary aim of all philosophy is freedom from pain or the well-being of humanity, which consists in the cessation of all pain and suffering.

These schools challenged the traditional philosophy, attacked the traditional institutions, spurned the ritualist mode of life, particularly that involving animal sacrifice, and also denied the existence of God either as the cause of the universe, or as the moral governor and the judge of human conduct. Two of these schools, Jainism and Buddhism, however, continued to believe in the transmigration of souls and the supremacy of the law of Karman, thereby supporting and postulating the immortality of soul, and the possibility of its liberation through a spiritual discipline or self-control. But the third school, Cārvāka, rejected the existence of a soul apart from the body, ridiculed the promise of happiness after physical death, and advocated enjoyment of sensual pleasures even at the cost of social well-being, thereby reducing ethics to the pursuit of egoistic satisfaction of the desires of the individual. Jainism advocated ascetism as the only means of attaining Mokṣa and preferred the sudden renunciation on the part of the aspirant to the systematic and gradual growth towards Sanyāsa by regarding the stage of the householder as an unavoidable step towards self-realization, since the divine love of God was impossible without the experience of human love on the part of the aspirant. This attitude was indicative of the revolutionary spirit which could not tolerate any restrictions put upon the prerogative of man to attain spiritual perfection, even if such restrictions aimed at a systematic march towards the final goal of liberation. The Buddhistic school also reasserted the dignity of man, and threw overboard the supremacy of God. Buddhism brought down philosophy from heaven to earth, and showed the futility of abstruse metaphysical discussions which obstructed the pragmatic result of attaining of Nirvāna. Nirvāna was possible through simple living and high thinking. One did not need to resort to self-mortification, which in being accepted by the revolutionary school of Jainism, was indicative of a check on the free and spontaneous spiritual growth of man towards the divine level of Bodhisattva and that of the Buddha, the enlightened soul.

These theories and counter-theories, charges and counter-charges with regard to the means of attainment and the nature of Mokṣa among the heterodox schools mentioned above had a healthy effect on the orthodox schools, which had accepted the authority of the Vedas and Upaniṣads as sole guides to ultimate reality and the purpose of human life. The sages, who depended on the intuitive method, and had taken for granted that their theories concerning the universe and ethics would be accepted by lay followers blindly, were awakened from their dogmatic slumber. Scepticism and doubt about the truth and practicability of the established theories and ideals compelled the Brahmaṇic thinkers to re-assess them and to subject them to analysis and rigorous logical examination. The result was that the acceptance of the authority of the Vedas was not to be based on blind faith, but on rational conviction. Intuition was to be strengthened by reason, and introspection by objective observation, so that the ideals instead of being abstract notions might be converted into empirical and practicable principles of concrete life. The critical spirit of the age, therefore, was responsible for the critical systematization of the traditional thought of the Vedas, by thought fundamentally based on criteria of consistency and validity of knowledge and reflection. The sages came to realize that faith must be grounded on scientific knowledge, and ethics on logic. This led to the formulation of the two important Schools of Indian philosophy, Vaiseśika and Nyāya, the first being interested in the analysis of the physical universe, and the latter in the discovery of valid sources of knowledge. The former gave a scientific foundation to religion, and the latter led to the building of an immense logical structure for ethical ideals to make them convincing and practicable. But both schools unequivocally declared that their sole purpose was the attainment of the highest goal, the supreme good of Mokṣa, or liberation, which was an ethico-metaphysical goal, and which could not be refuted even by the heterodox schools, like Buddhism and Jainism, because this end alone could bring about the well-being of man, the dignity and the supremacy of whom had been declared by the Vedas and the Upaniṣads and also by the heterodox systems. Both these systems gave a more realistic emphasis to Indian philosophy and paved the way for certain humanistic tendencies in it. Hence from our point of view the ethics of these two systems cannot be overlooked, even if they resemble that of the Vedas and Upaniṣads, on the one hand, and also to Jaina and the Baudha notion of happiness as the supreme good of life, on the other.

Although chronologically the Vaiseśika system is considered older than the Nyāya school, yet it is desirable here to refer to the Nyāya viewpoint first, and the Vaiśesika ethical view later. It is not out of place to mention that although these two systems developed independently and were propounded by two different thinkers, yet by the tenth century they came to be synthesized. The difference between the two systems must not, however, be overlooked. Nyāya, which literally means a judgment, lays emphasis on argumentation and the method of true knowledge. It is analytic in its approach and makes a constant effort to find out causes, as a result of which Nyāya is also known as Hetuvidyā, or the 'science of causes'. This analytic tendency leads it to accept a pluralistic nature of reality. But, usually, the metaphysical notions of Nyāya are neglected by scholars and its formal or logical aspect is given prominence. We should not forget that Nyāya is a pluralistic theory of reality, although it is Vaiśesika which emphasizes the Viśea, which means difference, and which has a clear foundation of pluralistic realism. The metaphysics of Vaiśesika is more marked, but both Nyāya and Vaiśesika combined present a method and the result arrived at by that method, respectively. The method is logical and the result is pluralism. Nyāya is the scientific attitude which favours realism, and Vaiśesika is the practical result of the analytic method which entails pluralism. Both the schools are interdependent and complementary to each other. Both are therefore realistic in attitude and pluralistic in result. Nyāya and Vaiśesika therefore present us a whole, and, as such, the study of their ethics can be attempted in one chapter. But for the convenience of readers we shall deal with Nyāya ethics first and Vaiśesika ethics last.

I. Nyāya Ethics

The Nyāya system states categorically that knowledge of truth is the means for the attainment of the highest bliss, or Mokṣa; but it gives a negative definition of the state of liberation by stating that it stands for the absolute abolition of pain. The aim of Nyāya is clearly mentioned in the very first aphorism (Sūtra) of Gautama, or Aksapāda, who says 'Proof, that which is to be proved, etc.,—from the knowledge of the truth as to these things, there is the attainment of final bliss'.[1] Nyāya is thought necessary for the purpose of becoming one with ultimate reality for it is the only science whose business is to employ reasoning in order to understand the nature of the material world, human experience and soul. Without the application of reasoning or analysis, no one can understand the import of our complex material reality, and without real knowledge none can ever be either moral or holy. Logic is therefore the basis of all science and also (particularly) of the science of soul (Atmajñāna) which in turn is held to be Parāvidyā, or supreme knowledge. Madhava Ācārya points out the indispensability of the science of logic by saying that 'This science of reasoning (Anvīksikī), divided into the different categories, "proof", etc., the lamp of all sciences, the means of aiding all actions, the ultimate appeal of all religious duties, is well proved in the declarations of science'.[2] The Nyāya declared long ago that 'logic is the science of all the sciences' and the 'art of all the arts'. As the basis of science and knowledge it must necessarily be the background of ethics, which is a science of morality. Moreover, Nyāya philosophy agrees with Socrates who said that 'Virtue is a kind of knowledge' and that none could be moral by accident. If ignorance of

[1] Madhava Ācārya, *Sarvadarśanasaṁgrah*, p. 161.
[2] *Ibid.*, p. 161.

the nature of truth is the cause of the bondage of the soul, the Nyāya system is justified in holding that the only remedy of the suffering born of such ignorance is freedom from false knowledge and the attainment of true knowledge. Thus the Nyāya system, by propounding the valid sources of true knowledge, leads to Mokṣa because it strikes at the very root of suffering, the individual's ignorance with regard to real knowledge.

But before we discuss the nature of liberation according to the Nyāya system, it appears necessary to make clear whether the final release from suffering as envisaged in the Nyāya takes place immediately after the attainment of true knowledge, or whether there is a gradual release. Nyāya favours the latter view, and holds that 'Pain, birth, activity, faults, false notions: on the successive annihilation of these in turn there is the annihilation of the one next before it'.[1] In other words, knowledge destroys false notions, false notions destroy faults, faults destroy activity, which in turn, stops births and deaths, and the annihilation of births and deaths brings about the destruction of pain. This attitude of the Nyāya resembles the Buddhistic notion of liberation by breaking the link of the chain of causes which is responsible for suffering. In order to make it clearer, it appears to be necessary to quote *Sarvadarśanasaṁgraha*: 'False notions are: the thinking, the body, etc. [which are not the soul] to be the soul; "faults" are: a desire for those things, which seem agreeable to the soul, and a dislike for those things which seem disagreeable to the soul'.[2] It is further pointed out that by the natural reaction of different faults one becomes covetous, and covetousness is nothing short of stupidity. Similarly, anger and the performance of forbidden acts, like injury, theft, etc., are the result of the faults which are responsible for the bondage of the soul. It is therefore enjoined that in order to attain liberation one must avoid false notions which are the cause of the faults of body, mind and speech—like violence, falsehood, malevolence, etc. If one does not avoid them, one accrues demerit, and this demerit leads to the birth of the soul in a low family. If a person resorts to laudable actions of body, mind and speech (giving alms, protecting other living beings, truthfulness, upright counsel, chaste thinking, etc.) these rightful activities produce merit in the soul and lead to its birth in a

[1] Madhava Ācārya, *Sarvadarśanasaṁgrah*, p. 165.
[2] *Ibid.*, p. 165.

high family. But in both cases activity is responsible for continuous births and deaths, which ultimately bring about suffering.

Nyāya, like Jainism and Buddhism, holds desire the sole cause of suffering, whether that suffering is due to merit or demerit accrued by the Jīva, or soul. But it does not agree with Jainism in its view that activity should be stopped altogether. On the other hand meritorious activity is regarded as the cause of liberation, because it is due to the force of good deeds that the individual comes across a great teacher who imparts true knowledge to him. True knowledge abolishes ignorance, which is the root cause of faulty activities, and prompts the individual to meditate on the truth of the Vedas, of logic, of trade and agriculture, and to meditate on the doctrine of piety, or Dharma. This meditation reveals knowledge of truth, which gives him the right view of the things as they are, and the right view dispels false notions or ignorance; the abolition of false notions brings about the cessation of activity; the cessation of activity leads to the cessation of birth; and 'with the cessation of birth comes the entire abolition of "pain", and this absolute abolition is final bliss'.[1]

It is necessary here to point out that the acceptance of the eternal truth of the Vedas prompted by the abolition of ignorance is the most important factor in Nyāya ethics. Western scholars, who have called Indian philosophy pessimistic, antisocial, and anti-ethical have always misunderstood the meaning of Mokṣa, which is defined as the cessation of all suffering by the cessation of births and deaths. They allege that all the systems of Indian philosophy, by aiming at the cessation of births and deaths, are negativistic, and imply cessation of or abolition of, instead of the development of personality, which is the goal of all ethics. If freedom from all desires is necessary for the attainment of Mokṣa, it would mean that Nyāya, like Buddhism and Jainism, is negativistic and aims at the stoppage of activity through asceticism and abandonment of worldly life.

This allegation turns out to be baseless in the face of the fact that according to Nyāya true knowledge leads the individual to meditate on the truth of the Vedas. As we have already seen, the Vedas regard man as an integrated whole of body, mind, intellect and soul and they advocate a complete development of

[1] Madhava Ācārya, *Sarvadarśanasaṁgrah*, p. 165.

the personality of the individual by his adopting Artha (wealth), Kama (love), Dharma (morality) and Mokṣa (liberation) as the four ends of life without sacrificing any one of them for the others. The Vedas urge us to bring about harmony between the individual, society, and the cosmos, and they want us to follow a gradual march towards perfection through the intellectual or the ethical development of the individual and society. Hence any system which accepts the truth of the Vedas, and thereby accepts the systematic development of the individual and society by recognizing the Varna Dharmas (social duties) and the Āśrama Dharmas (the ethico-spiritual duties), must be accepted as a progressive system and not as pessimistic or retrogressive system. It should not be forgotten that nowhere does Nyāya exhort an individual to give up worldly life and to retire to the forest, thereby transgressing his Vārnāśrama Dharmas. None of the orthodox systems advocates a sudden renunciation, or Sanyāsa, as the Jaina and the Buddha systems sometimes do. But even in Jainism and Buddhism, society consists of two parts (the Śramanas, or the ascetics, and the Śrāvakas, or laymen), and neither of them can exist apart from the other. Both these heterodox systems, as we have seen, advocate the virtues of love, compassion, truth and non-violence. These virtues are indispensable for a sublime ethical life. The acceptance of Jīvanmukti, or liberation in this life, again refutes the charge of other-worldliness and pessimism against the orthodox and the heterodox systems of Indian philosophy.

Nyāya, like all the spiritualistic systems, aims at a full life and not at a one-sided development of personality. The cessation of activity does not mean inactivity. When a person attains true knowledge and reaches the stage of a Jīvanmukta (liberated while living), his faulty activities come to an end and he is freed from bondage, the sole cause of human suffering. Even the Buddhistic notion of Śūnya does not hint at nothingness in the sense of emptiness or non-existence. It will be helpful to explain the significance of the ascetic attitude adopted even by Jainism and Buddhism before we conclude the section of Nyāya ethics in this chapter.

We have to be very clear concerning the *summum bonum* of Mokṣa to understand the significance of the adoption of asceticism in Indian philosophy. Asceticism is a spiritual discipline, the means to attain the goal of liberation, which as the highest state of existence cannot be defined in intellectual terms. It can only be experienced, like the experience of seeing yellow or green. Any attempt to reduce it to definite intellectual concepts like our concepts of material things would be self-destructive, because material things are relative and the state of Mokṣa is absolute. Hence the only way to understand and to communicate the state of Mokṣa is to give an approximation to it through symbols; but in doing so we have to maintain its uniqueness and dissimilarity to all relative objects. For this reason a negative explanation of Mokṣa is usually favoured, and it is maintained that Mokṣa means the cessation of pain.

Although Mokṣa is the highest bliss it would be an error to say that it is happiness in the sense of being a pleasant experience, because every pleasant experience is ultimately the cause of pain and suffering. Nyāya accepts Mokṣa as the cessation of all pain, not in the sense of annihilation of the soul or the removal of obstacles, but in the sense that this blissful state is incomparable and unique, and the absence of pain is only its symbol. Mokṣa is a holy state, a spiritual existence, or what Otto has called the experience of feeling the presence of the *numinos*, which though capable of being communicated in rational terms or symbols by way of analogy, is so unique that in spite of its resemblance to the relative experiences of art, music, poetry and sublime love, is 'wholly other'.

Like all the other systems of Indian philosophy Nyāya endorses the Upaniṣadic view of liberation as spiritual perfection and at the same time advocates a gradual ascent of the individual from the state of a householder to that of the recluse. That alone proves that Nyāya ethics is a synthesis of asceticism and worldly life, of activism, love and social service.

Nyāya's emphasis on the validity of knowledge and its logical exposition of the theory of reality was an answer to the scepticism generated by the Cārvāka system, and it was partially adopted by Buddhism and Jainism. We have already seen that if we go deep into the spirit of the apparently pessimistic system of Jainism and Buddhism, we are bound to conclude that they have a humanistic value of their own. Nyāya being a continuation of the Vedic philosophy, particularly in its ethical theory and practice, could not break loose from the Vedic trend of preferring a path to the development of an integrated personality. Writers who wrongly suppose that Nyāya strikes a pessimistic note forget that the study of the Vedas is regarded by this system as the most important step towards spiritual development. My contention is that this is a most significant factor to be taken into consideration in presenting a dispassionate estimate of Nyāya ethics as also of the ethics of the other orthodox schools of Indian philosophy.

The manner in which we have surveyed the ethics of Vedas indicates clearly that right from the period of the Ṛig Veda the Indian mind emphasizes the organic unity of man and the universe, and that man is regarded as the highest reality. It is necessary here to dilate upon this humanistic and cosmopolitan outlook of Vedic ethics. We have seen how the Vedic theory of the universe, the oldest scientific theory of creation in the world, holds that the various manifestations of the cosmos are based on one invisible central reality, and that man is the replica of that very cosmos, which is again reflected in the four-fold division of society. Now in spite of recognizing the invisible central reality of Prajāpati as the all-pervading God, and in spite of accepting the various 'elements' of sun, moon, etc., as the essential constituents of the universe by giving them the divine names of Indra, Mitra, Varuna, etc., none of these awe-inspiring and luminous realities are ever supposed superior to man, because all are uniquely manifested in man.

This fact is illustrated in the Mahābhārata with reference to an episode in an assembly of sages called to discuss philosophical problems. During the course of discussion someone raised the question, 'What is the most superior reality? Is it Prajāpati or the invisible spiritual self (Avyaya Puruṣa)? Is it the various gods without whose existence creation would have been impossible? Are the great sages who have given us the revealed knowledge of the Vedas most superior? Are the demons or the malicious forces of nature the topmost reality?' The questions were dealt with in the same order. It was first asserted that Prajāpati ought to be regarded as the most superior reality. But when this view was put forward silence prevailed in the assembly indicating that the answer was incorrect. One by one, when all the suggestions pointing out that gods, the sages and the demons were most superior were rejected by the assembly, the great sage, Vyasa, who was presiding over the congregation, said with great poise and confidence, 'Guhiyataraṁ brahman idam bravīmi, na hi mānusāt sreṣṭhataram nu kincit'. That is,

'I am going to reveal the most secret doctrine to you now. There is nothing superior to man in the universe.'

This superiority of man is tacitly accepted by all systems of Indian philosophy, orthodox and heterodox. The orthodox systems, however, being direct descendants of the Vedic philosophy, cannot afford to deviate from this view. For this reason, in spite of the severe criticism proffered by the orthodox systems while examining the validity of various philosophical doctrines, they all regard the study of the Vedas as the preparation for the attainment of Mokṣa. We have already pointed out that metaphysics as well as ethics centre around man whether as the cosmic person or as the social organism or as an individual human being. The acceptance of the Vedic scriptures as one of the valid sources of knowledge reaffirms the faith of the orthodox systems in humanism. Human well-being is the goal of Indian philosophy, whether it is to be attained through the logical exposition of Nyāya, through the atomic analysis of the material world on the part of the Vaiśesika system, through the acceptance of the evolutionary nature of the universe, ending in the emancipation of the self from the material Prakriti, through the spiritual discipline of the Yoga, through the Karma Kānda, the activistic view of the Mimāṁsā, or, lastly, through the saving knowledge of Brahman as advocated by the Vedānta. As we proceed further, we shall confirm the view that the orthodox systems of philosophy particularly advocate a gradual approach of the individual towards spiritual perfection through intellect and moral duty. Perfection is not merely a concept, as western ethical thinkers believe; on the contrary, it is an actual state of existence attainable in this life. Nyāya particularly emphasizes that the cessation of pain does not amount to the cessation of existence, because for it the soul is something beyond cognition.

It would be needless to repeat that reference to the transcendental nature of the state of liberation in each and every school of Indian philosophy strengthens our contention that the ethical views of all the orthodox and heterodox systems, with the exception of the Cārvāka school alone, are uniform so far as the ultimate goal of life is concerned. This uniformity is undoubtedly due to the acceptance of the underlying spiritual reality, which is the invisible central unifying basis of the visible extended and diversified physical world. In order to realize the inner self, which will make the individual rise above the relative experience of pleasure and pain and attain unity with the cosmos, one has not to give up activity or desire, but has only to get rid of narrowmindedness and the sense of separateness. Commenting upon this aspect of Nyāya ethics, Dr Radhakrishnan has remarked:

'The Naiyāyika asks us to suppress all sense of separateness . . . Those who are saved in this life go on performing work as long as they are in body, and this work does not bind them. So long as we cling to individuality, and accumulate virtue to become Indra or Brahmā, we are bound to the circuit, for even the states of Indra and Brahmā have an end. The highest good consists in freedom from all sense of separateness.'[1]

My point is that it is only with reference to the supreme good that Nyāya, like all other systems, agrees that the spiritual reality in man is the highest reality.

An Indra or a Brahmā indicates one manifestation of the central reality, and each manifestation comes to its end. The other manifestations of the Avyaya Puruṣa, or cosmic spiritual self, though more powerful and more lasting than man's biological existence, are inferior to its human manifestation, for it is only in man that longing for liberation fructifies through moral effort. Although Mokṣa means a state beyond right and wrong and good and evil, its attainment is possible only through right and good, the application of which in public life takes place in human existence and not in the divine existence like that of Indra-Brahmā. For this reason Nyāya advocates virtuous acts as means for the attainment of Mokṣa. The performance of virtues leads to the discrimination of the soul and body, and this discrimination leads to true knowledge, the attainment of which brings about the annihilation of the sense of separateness and hence that of suffering.

II. Vaiśesika Ethics

The Vaiśesika system seems to be predominantly interested in the analytical exposition of the Padārthas, or objects of thought, like substance (Dravya), quality (Guna), action

[1] S. Radhakrishnan, *Indian Philosophy*, Vol II, p. 163.

(Karma), generality (Sāmānya), particularity (Viśeṣa) and inherence (Samavāya) which it takes to be final categories, and the knowledge of which leads to the highest union of the individual with the ultimate reality (Yoga). The fact that the aim of this analysis is the attainment of Mokṣa, and the fact that the opening sentence of the Vaiśesika Sutra reads, 'Now, therefore, we shall explain duty', go to prove the ethical significance of this system. In the Sarvadarśanasaṁgraha, Mādhavācārya, while commenting on the Vaiśesika system of Kaṇāda, emphasizes the ethical aspect of this philosophical theory by saying, 'Who so wishes to escape the reality of pain, which is established by the consciousness of every soul through its being felt to be essentially contrary to every rational being, and wishes therefore to know the means of such escape,—learns that the knowledge of Supreme Being is the true means thereof . . . Now the knowledge of the supreme is to be gained by hearing (Sravaṇa), thought (Manana), and reflection (Dhyāna) . . . Here thought depends on inference, and inference depends on the knowledge of the Vyāpti (universal proposition), and the knowledge of the Vyāpti follows from the right understanding of the categories.'[1] Thought or inferential knowledge is thus the means to the final goal of Mokṣa. The categories mentioned above provide the metaphysical background of the Vaiśesika system. This school, therefore, like all the other orthodox schools of Indian philosophy, is ethico-metaphysical in its outlook, and subordinates knowledge to action, reason to meditation, and empirical experience to spiritual perfection. Nihśreyasa, or spiritual good, is regarded as the good or the Dharma, or morality. The Vaiśesika system gives us a two-fold aim of duty or Dharma, worldly prosperity (Abhyudaya) and spiritual perfection (Nihśreyasa). The attainment of worldly good is possible through the performance of ceremonial duties, and spiritual realization, or self-realization, is possible through spiritual intuition, or Tattvajñāna.

Thus the ethics of Vaiśeṣika, though absolute in the sense that it aims at Mokṣa, is at the same time relative because it does not neglect material prosperity which is attainable by the performance of Dharma. It holds that the actions issuing from desire and aversion (Icchā-dvesa-pūrvaka) are voluntary actions based on pleasure and pain, and that ceremonial duties

[1] Madhavācarya, *Sarvadarśana Saitgraha*, p. 145.

can bring about material prosperity. In other words, Vaiśesika ethics gives place to hedonism in ethical life. But at the same time it prompts the aspirant to rise above this lower ethical level and to regard Nihśreyasa as the highest good. Radhakrishnan refers to this ethical aspect of Vaiśesika as follows:

'The highest kind of pleasure, according to Praśatapāda, is the pleasure of the wise, which is independent of all such agencies as the remembrance of the object, desire, reflection, and is due to true knowledge, peacefulness of mind, contentment, and the peculiar character of their virtues.'[1]

The relativity of the well-being of society and social institutions is not sacrificed for the sake of spiritual well-being. On the contrary social duty is regarded as a means to the attainment of Nihśreyasa, spiritual perfection. The way to the transcendental state of liberation is through relative duty (Dharma). Thus, after all, spiritual perfection is not opposed to material life, and is therefore to be attained through the worldly ethical behaviour of the individual.

Vaiśeṣika's classification of duties is remarkable and requires a special reference in this chapter. There are two categories of duties: (1) universal duties, which ought to be obeyed by every person irrespective of caste and creed, and (2) particular duties, enjoined upon individuals, with reference to their particular station of life, i.e. the Varṇa and Āśrama to which a person belongs.

Let us first explain the universal duties, which are regarded categorical for all individuals. These are thirteen in number in the following order:

(1) Śraddhā, or conviction; (2) Ahiṁsā, or non-violence; (3) Bhutahitatva, or kindness to all living creatures; (4) Satyavacana, or truthfulness; (5) Asteya, or non-stealing; (6) Brahmacarya, or chastity; (7) Anupadhā-bhāvaśuddhi, or mental purity; (8) Krodha-varjana, or freedom from anger; (9) Abhisecana, or physical purity; (10) Śucidravya sevana, or using purifying materials; (11) Viśistadevata-bhakti, or devotion to the deity; (12) Upavāsa, or fasting; and (13) Apramāda, or alertness in performing one's duties. These duties require a brief elabora-

[1] Radhakrishnan, *op. cit.*, Vol. II, p. 222.

tion for when adhered to altogether they lead to the integrated development of the personality, making an individual fit for attaining Mokṣa.

Conviction or faith is given first place in the list of obligations because Indian philosophy, unlike Western philosophy, starts with a firm conviction opposed to doubt and fickle-mindedness. It should never be forgotten that a philosophy which aims at practical results instead of mere theoretical discussions cannot afford to be sceptical and pessimistic in its outlook. Western philosophers tend toward a sceptical attitude and affirm that philosophy, a child of wonder, begins in doubt. That is why many great systems of Western philosophy end as they begin, in doubt and despondency, uncertainty and confusion, divorcing theory from practice and science from faith. On the contrary, in India faith or conviction is the rock and foundation of philosophy, a prerequisite of intellectual pursuit and a necessary condition of the highest knowledge. The Bhagavadgītā remarks:

Śraddhāvāna labhate jñānaṁ saṁśayātmā vinaśyati

'A man with firm faith (alone) attains true knowledge, a sceptic perishes.' Faith gives courage, and the courageous man alone can go ahead with the search for truth, hazarding everything that he possesses. However, Śraddhā here should not be taken to be blind faith or superstition. It is conviction in truth and reason, which requires an aspirant to be religiously devoted to the pursuit of true knowledge. It stands for a strong passion for self-realization, or for becoming one with the ultimate reality, the knowledge of which does not consist merely in cognition of partial facts, but in intuiting the universal element invisibly present in all phenomena.

Next place is given to non-violence, regarded as the highest virtue (Paramo Dharma) in man. After an aspirant has firmly set himself on the path of righteousness he must adhere to the most universal humanistic duty of avoiding injury to all living creatures mentally, verbally, and physically (Mansā, Vacasā, Karmaṇā). Non-violence though apparently negativistic has an important positive implication of entertaining love not only for human beings but for all living creatures. The Bhagavadgītā also holds that a person who treats all living creatures as he would treat himself should be regarded a philosopher.

The third universal duty, kindness to all living creatures, is purposely regarded an essential obligation because it brings out the positive implication of the obligation of non-violence. Thus, according to Vaiśeṣika ethics, as according to Jaina and Baudha ethics, it is not only the well-being of man but the well-being of all the living beings that should be regarded as the *summum bonum*. This duty makes Vaśeṣika more catholic and more compassionate than Western ethics, which tends to neglect man's duty towards sentient beings other than men. Although many compassionate persons in the west have organized societies whose aim is to prevent cruelty to animals and preserve wild life by propagating vegetarianism, yet no ethical system propounded by Western thinkers except Albert Schweitzer's has accepted compassion to all living creatures as a universal obligation. This duty of Vaiśeṣika ethics reveals a true Indian spirit of morality and catholicism.

Truthfulness occupies the fourth place in the hierarchy of the universal obligations propounded by the Vaiśeṣika system, because the practice of this virtue is limited to human relations and human problems. In this sense truthfulness is less universal than compassion to living beings and non-violence. It is held that truth must be adhered to under all circumstances in word and deed. The word, Satya Vacana, literally means truthfulness in speech or words. But the Indian ethical tradition is that keeping one's word is preferable to death. The great Indian poet, Tulsī, refers to this ethical tradition in the following manner: 'The tradition of the great family of Raghu [the family in which the great personality, Rama, was born] is that one should embrace death rather than falsify one's word.' It is in keeping with this attitude of remaining true to one's word that truthfulness of speech is propounded as a universal duty in the Vaiśeṣika system.

The fifth duty of non-stealing, which consists in refraining from misappropriation of the property of others, is a corollary of the fourth duty of truthfulness and is hence given next place. We have already mentioned this obligation in Jaina ethics as one of the five great vows. It is needless to repeat the implications of this universal obligation here. It is sufficient to remark that non-stealing is the duty which emphasizes that 'Honesty is the best policy' in all walks of life. Thus the obligation, though apparently negativistic, has a positive implication.

Chastity or continence is the sixth universal obligation, and it requires the maintenance of purity in matters of sex. It would be wrong to translate the word Brahmacarya here as celibacy. In Jaina ethics, Brahmacarya, as the fourth great vow of the ascetics, means complete abstinence from sexual relations and marital life. But in the present context it stands for a restricted sexual satisfaction, which means confining one's sex relation to one's spouse. The Vaiśeṣika system believes in the adoption of Gṛahastha Aśrama, the stage of the householder, in which the individual has to be faithful in marital love. Whereas Jainism believes that giving up matrimonial life is the means to the attainment of Mokṣa, the Aśrama Dharmas of the Veda hold that Mokṣa is not possible unless one has enjoyed married life. Thus chastity means a restricted and sublime satisfaction of carnal desire. This obligation is necessary both from the point of view of social harmony and that of family happiness. Marriage in India has always been regarded as sanctified, and not a mere partnership or friendship. The universal duty of continence encumbent both upon husband and wife brings about harmony and emotional balance in marital life. The ancient Indian sages realized the necessity of sexual morality, but they also realized that the suppression of the sex instinct would be dangerous to mental and social health. It is in this context that the universal duty of chastity in sexual matters should be interpreted and understood.

The seventh general duty of purity of mind, or rather of good intentions, is purely an ethical duty and requires an individual to be motivated always by goodwill. All the systems of Indian philosophy agree that a mental act is equivalent to a physical act, at least from the moral and spiritual point of view. Intending to commit an immoral act amounts to its physical committal and brings about a Karmic bondage of the soul to the world. For this reason purity of mind is necessary to attain freedom from suffering. As is evident from the general trend of Indian ethics, purity of mind is possible through spiritual discipline and self-control. The six universal duties preceding mental purity involve a discipline that leads to self-purification which is the pre-condition of spiritual bliss. Ātma-Śuddhi, or self-purification, is enjoined as the goal of a Yogin in the Bhagavadgītā. A person of stable intellect who has risen above emotional conflicts attains self-purification.

This fact leads us to the eighth universal duty of angerlessness. The Vaiśeṣika ethics states that it is the duty of all individuals to renounce anger, for the pugnacious behaviour of man is highly emotional and leads to infatuation which blinds reason and discretion, thereby bringing about the loss of memory and the destruction of intellect—virtually the total annihilation of human personality. Of all the disturbing emotions which distract mind from meditation on the supreme reality anger is regarded as the most harmful. Indulgence in anger makes a person deviate from all seven universal duties explained above. An angry person, having forgotten his status as an ethical individual in the surge of acute emotional disturbance, is bound to lose conviction, commit violence, neglect human kindness, transgress truthfulness, pay no heed to honesty, and violate sexual morality. Anger disturbs the peace of mind in letting loose the above mentioned chain of six evils, and hence it becomes the cause of the violation of the first seven universal duties.

The next two general obligations concern bodily purity and enjoin upon every individual a clean life. 'Cleanliness is next to godliness' is the proverb, and godliness may be attained by regular bathing and using purifying substances, like sandal incense, etc. Hence the ninth duty consists of physical purity by resorting to washing and bathing, and the tenth duty is that of using purifying materials.

The eleventh universal obligation, devotion to the deity, might appear to be uncalled for to modern man, who considers the existence of gods and deities a mere superstition. But the fact remains that gods in Indian philosophy, as already indicated in our previous chapter, are only manifestations of the Supreme Reality. Hence devotion to any particular deity is in fact devotion to the Supreme God, whose grace brings about Mokṣa. In the Bhagavadgītā, Shri Krishṇa having himself become Brahman, says:

Ye yathā mām prapadyante
Tāna tathaiva bhajāmyahaṁ.

That is, 'I appear before my devotees in the manner in which they remember me'. Thus devotion to deity here stands for devotion to God, for such a passion for the Divine Being is always conducive to moral life.

The twelfth general obligation consists in observing fasts. It has been held by all schools of Indian philosophy, and particularly by the Bhagavadgītā, that observing fasts brings about purity of thought and action. A person who remains without food is not overcome by sensual desires. For this reason the ascetic school of Jainism lays great emphasis on observing fasts. Jainism regards fasting as the sole means of the attainment of Mokṣa and recommends fasting unto death as the gateway to Nirvāna. Occasional fasting has also been approved from the hygienic point of view. Fasting helps bring about bodily health and mental balance.

The above mentioned twelve duties, being categorical and obligatory on every normal individual, are further strengthened by the thirteenth universal imperative of Apramāda, or alertness in performing one's moral duties. Negligence of duties is regarded as a heinous crime, and it is emphasized that one should prefer death to the transgression or negligence of one's duty. The entire teaching of the Bhagavadgītā is nothing but a reminder of alertness in performing one's duty in life.

The particular duties accepted by the Vaiśeṣika system are those of Varṇa Dharmas (morality of the caste system), and they represent the duties allotted to every individual according to his natural inclination and also according to the order of life (Āśrama) to which the individual belongs at the time he is called upon to perform his duty. The recognition of the unavoidability of the stage of a householder, during which the aspirant experiences love and affection with his kith and kin, proves that the ethics of the Vaiśeṣika system does not repudiate the idea of enjoying human life during one's gradual march towards perfection. Thus the ethics of the Vaiśeṣika system brings about a synthesis between the Nivritti Mārga, the path of renunciation or self-sacrifice, on the one hand, and that of indulgence in sensual pleasures, or Pravṛitti Mārga, on the other. Vaiśeṣika therefore tries to bring about a harmony between worldly prosperity and social well-being and moral development and spiritual well-being. That the spiritual ideal is the attainment of Mokṣa requires no further explanation.

The performance of one's duties, universal as well as particular, is the means to the ideal of perfection or self-realization as already explained. It is further necessary to point out that Vaiśeṣika system believes in a gradual liberation, Karma Muktī.

The individual soul, which passes through numberless incarnations, accumulates Dharma merit and this Dharma means the power or quality which resides in the soul and is destroyed when the individual has reaped its fruit. Similarly Adharma, or demerit, which is the accumulation of a bad quality due to bad deeds, continues to exist in the individual in his various incarnations. Dharma and Adharma are designated Adṛsta by the Vaiśeṣika. Bondage is nothing but union with Adṛsta, or the invisible power of Karma residing in the soul. The performance of good deeds and adherence to one's duties leads the individual progressively towards final liberation. But Dharma and Adharma are discernible through selfless insight into the truth of things. Vaiśeṣika clearly points out that the true nature of Ātman is above all particular differences, and the knowledge of the spiritual universality in man alone dispels ignorance. Dr Radhakrishnan, dwelling on this aspect of the Vaiśeṣika ethics, remarks:

'Activity motivated by the feelings of separate self-existence is based on the ignorance of the truth of things. When we realize that the objects which look so attractive and repulsive are only temporary compounds of atoms, they cease to have power over us. Similarly when we realize the true nature of ātman, which is distinct from this or that form of its existence, we shall know that all souls are alike.'[1]

This exposition of the ethics of the Vaiśeṣika system is in keeping with our thesis that Indian ethics is the quest of the absolute, and that its aim is the identification of the individual self with the universal self with no neglect of social progress and material advancement. What Vaiśeṣika points out is that the particularity of the objects of the world proves the relative worth of the mundane life, although Ātman is above such relativity and transitoriness.

The very fact that Vaiśeṣika repeats the social obligations of Varṇa and the individual obligations of Āśrama, which determine the station and duties of the individual, is indicative of the fact that it repudiates pessimism and abhors asceticism. Indian ethics, particularly the ethics of the orthodox schools, is not otherworldly though it is absolute. It is not abstract,

[1] Radhakrishnan, *op. cit.*, Vol. II, p. 232.

though it is spiritual, not speculative though reflective, and not superstitious though theistic. It is humanistic as well as universalistic, rationalistic as well as empirical, formal as well as material, logical as well as psychological, and secular as well as ecclesiastical in the sense that it overcomes contradictions both in theory and in practice.

This synthetic nature of Indian ethics, towards which the Vaiśeṣika ethics has made its special contribution, will become more and more explicit as we proceed with the ethical views of the other orthodox systems. We have so far referred to the logical and the pluralistic aspects of the absolute nature of Indian ethics with reference to Nyāya and Vaiśeṣika, both of which though different in their approach have the same goal before them, for they represent the same synthetic point of view of life and believe in the integrated development of the individual and of society. We shall now proceed with the ethics of Sāṁkya and Yoga, which respectively expound the evolutionary and the disciplinary aspects of the absolutistic ethics of Indian philosophy. As a matter of fact, both these systems hold to the same metaphysics and aim at the same supreme good. The only difference between them is their emphasis on two different aspects of the same reality. Let us therefore close this chapter with the remark that Nyāya and Vaiśeṣika, with their emphasis on the methodological and the analytical aspects of the ultimate reality, lead us to question what sort of ethics Indian philosophy would recommend if the logical approach and the analytical attitude towards the nature of the universe bring us to the conclusion that the world is a result of a universal evolution of the two ultimate categories, Puruṣa, or self, and Prakṛiti, or primal matter. The answer is given by Sāṁkhya and Yoga.

CHAPTER IX

THE ETHICS OF SĀṀKHYA AND YOGA

Sāṁkhya and Yoga are the two most original systems of Indian philosophy, but at the same time they cannot be said to be heterodox because both of them recognize the authority of the Vedas. Sāṁkhya, though spiritualistic, does not touch the problem of God, and Yoga accepts the existence of God, not as a Creator, but as the benevolent guide of the aspirant towards Mokṣa. Both accept a dualistic metaphysics and regard the visible world as an evolution of Puruṣa, the self, and Prakṛiti, the not-self, or matter. Both hold that liberation (Kaivalya) consists in eradication of the pure conscious, intelligent and subjective Puruṣa from the unconscious, changing, and unintelligent Prakṛiti. The difference between the systems is that whereas Sāṁkhya lays emphasis on the theoretical aspect, Yoga gives practical guidance for the attainment of Mokṣa or Kaivalya. Yoga differs from Sāṁkhya also in its belief in the existence of God for practical reasons. Thus we shall find that the ethics of the Sāṁkhya is mainly a theory, whereas that of the Yoga is a practical application. We shall therefore deal with their ethics separately.

The Ethics of Sāṁkhya

To understand the ethical doctrine of Sāṁkhya it is essential to give a brief account of the metaphysics of this system since the concept of Mokṣa, which is the *summum bonum* for this school, is an ethico-metaphysical concept. Ethics is the means for the attainment of Mokṣa, and Mokṣa is the basic metaphysical notion of all Indian systems, therefore it is not possible to overlook the metaphysics of Sāṁkhya if we want to have insight into the moral philosophy involved in that system. The peculiarity of Sāṁkhya lies in the fact that by accepting the existence of two ultimate realities, it is metaphysically relative and realistic, but its ethics is ultimately pluralistic and idealistic.

The metaphysics of Sāṁkhya is summed up in the acceptance of the two basic principles of self or spirit (Puruṣa) and matter or not-self (Prakṛiti), the mutual co-operation and contact of which brings about the evolution of the entire world of objects, including physical bodies composed of subtle substances, sense organs, mind, ego, and intellect or reason. Prakṛiti is the all-pervasive physical and material cause of the cosmos and as such is unintelligent, unconscious, non-living, though an active and evolutionary principle. Since all the objects of the world exhibit experiences of pleasure, pain, and indifference, the ultimate constituents (Guṇas) of Prakṛiti, which is the uncaused ultimate cause of the material world, are Sattva, or manifestation, Rajas, or activity, Tamas, or non-activity. The Puruṣa, on the other hand, stands for the principle of pure consciousness. It is the self, the experiencer, the enjoyer and the seer. It is always the subject and never the object, and its existence is proved by the presence of Prakṛiti, which, being the object of experience, is experienced, enjoyed and seen by the subject Puruṣa.

Prakṛiti has two states of existence, or two transformations which determine the evolution and the dissolution of the material universe. The three Guṇas, the constituents of Sattva, Rajas and Tamas, although contradictory to one another in functions and effects, co-operate with one another in order to bring about the evolution of the world of objects. Just as the wick, the oil, and the flame in spite of being opposed to one another co-operate to dispel darkness and to spread light, similarly the three Guṇas in spite of their antagonistic nature, co-operate with one another in the interest of the evolution of the objective world.

When Prakṛiti is in the state of dissolution, and when these Guṇas are separated from one another there is no material world, and there is no motion among the Guṇas. But when the Puruṣa comes near the Prakṛiti, the latter is stimulated and a motion is started first of all in the compartment of the Rajoguṇa. The activity in the Rajas leads to the activity of the other two Guṇas and thus the process of evolution starts. The contact of the Puruṣa and Prakṛiti is not like the ordinary contact of two physical objects. On the contrary, it is like the contact of the body and mind, or like the contact of a magnet with iron. Mere presence of the Puruṣa in the vicinity of (Sanniddhi Matra) Prakṛiti is enough to cause the evolution of the world.

The first evolute of Prakṛiti is called Mahat, or the great, which is the all-pervasive material cause of everything that exists in the spatiotemporal order of the universe. In individuals it is the basis of intelligence or intellect. Mahat therefore stands for the all-pervasive cosmic intellect. Buddhi, or intellect, is the psychological aspect of the Mahat in the individual. It is worth mentioning here that Buddhi is a material product which is predominantly Sāttvika, i.e. in it the principle of light and the brightness of knowledge and reason predominate. The intellect is like a mirror of the conscious Puruṣa which reflects the consciousness of Puruṣa to such an extent that it apparently becomes self-conscious, and therefore the cause of the knowledge of the objects of the world. The intellect being predominantly Sāttvika possesses the attributes of virtue (Dharma), knowledge (Jñāna), equanimity (Vairāgya) and lordship (Aiśvarya). It is also noteworthy here that Buddhi, in the case of the individual, and Mahat, in the case of the cosmos, being the first product of Puruṣa and Prakṛiti, is the basis of the other products which follow from and which are produced out of the cosmic intellect. Since it is the source of ego, mind, and senses it is evident that the control of intellect would automatically lead to the control of the mind and the senses. Intellect is very close to Puruṣa and it works directly for Puruṣa; it enables the latter to experience all existence and discriminate between itself and Prakṛiti. As a matter of fact Buddhi should be taken in the cosmic sense so far as the Samkhya theory of evolution is concerned, because it is mentioned that at the time of the emergence of Buddhi in the universe the ego, the mind, and the senses are not present. As such, intellect is the basis and the foundation of discursive knowledge, which enables an individual to distinguish between subject and object, and between the perceiving and the perceived.

Intellect in its turn gives rise to ego (Ahaṁkāra), the sense of self, or individualization. It is due to Ahaṁkāra that each Jiva or individual soul acquires a separate mental constitution. Here as well Sāṁkhya belives in the existence of a cosmic ego from which the individual subjects and objects are derived. The second product, Ahaṁkāra, as compared with intellect, is material and not cognitive. Whereas the intellect functions to give us knowledge of the external world, ego leads to the sense of self-love. But this sense binds the individual to the material

Prakṛiti, thereby obstructing the liberation of the Puruṣa from Prakṛiti. If the function of intellect is consciousness and knowledge, that of Ahaṁkāra is self-consciousness and self-knowledge, in the sense of the identification of Puruṣa with the acts of Prakṛiti. Buddhi which is a higher evolute and nearer the soul, alone can do away with this false notion. We shall see in the sequel that in the Bhagavadgītā the stability of intellect is regarded as the means to the attainment of Brāhmīsthiti, which amounts to Jīvanmukti, or liberation of the soul in this life.

It is noteworthy that though Ahaṁkāra is secondary as compared with the Buddhi, and is a principle of individualization, yet it individualizes not the universal consciousness but the impressions which we receive from the external world. When Ahaṁkāra is predominated by Sattva Guṇa, it is bound to lead the individual towards Mokṣa by prompting him to follow virtue and to curb vice. But Ahaṁkāra may also be predominated either by Rajas or by Tamas. When it is under the influence of the former it leads us to perform evil deeds, and when it is predominated by the latter we perform indifferent works. Thus even the notion of Ahaṁkāra is ethical in its essence.

On the metaphysical side, three types of Ahaṁkāras have been distinguished by Sāṁkhya, viz., Sāttvika, Rājasa, and Tāmasa, according to the predominance of Sattva-Guṇa, Rajoguṇa and Tamoguṇa respectively. The Sāttvika Ahaṁkāra gives rise to mind (Manas), the five sense organs (eye, ear, nose tongue, and skin) and the five organs of action (Karmesdriyas), viz.—the organs of speech, located in the mouth, hands, feet, anus, and sex organ. The Tāmasa Ahaṁkāra generates the five subtle elements (Tanmātras) of sound (Sabda Tanmātra), of touch (Sparśa Tanmātra), of colour (Rūpa Tanmātra), of taste (Rasa Tanmātra) and of smell (Gañdha Tanmātra). The subtle elements further give rise to Ākāśa, or ether, Vāyu, or air, Agni, or fire, Apa, or water, and Prithvi, or earth respectively, each of them possessing its distinctive quality of sound, touch, colour, taste and smell in the same order.

This theory of evolution, starting with the subtlest spiritual reality of Puruṣa and the subtlest material reality of Prakṛiti, explains how the subtle gradually changes into the gross, ultimately, the subtle reality is the potentiality which is actualized in grossness. But this evolution is not the goal at which the individual must aim. On the other hand, it is a regression and fall of spirit leading it to grossness and bondage. The wisest is he who understands the real nature of the spirit and gives up the notion of Ahaṁkāra, or egoism. The aspirant must ascend from the gross to the subtle nature of his personality and ultimately experience the effulgence of the spirit which is self-luminous. This is the ethical and the spiritual significance of the Sāṁkhya theory of evolution. If Nyāya and Vaiśeṣika aim at liberation through logic and physical analysis, giving proper place to rational and physical sciences in the philosophical order, Sāṁkhya aims at liberation through the understanding of the evolutionary process, thereby giving proper place to biological sciences in the same philosophical order. In India, philosophy has always been regarded as an intellectual attempt to synthesize the sciences and as an ethical effort to realize the highest reality or attain Mokṣa. Philosophy is not merely a speculation, nor is it indifferent to science and analysis. But along with its intellectual acumen and scientific analysis, it also pays equal attention to the practical aim of philosophic thinking, which is nothing short of spiritual-realization, having attained which the aspirant rises above all contradiction, thereby giving proper place to sciences, philosophy, and mysticism.

We should not forget that Sāṁkhya philosophy is a link between the pluralistic philosophy of Nyāya and Vaiśeṣika on the one hand, and the activistic philosophy of Mīmāṁsā and the monistic philosophy of the Advaita Vedanta on the other. Though its philosophical concepts are not final and are transcended by those of the Vedānta, yet they have their own practical value and ethical significance. Our purpose of studying Sāṁkhya in this volume is not to evaluate its metaphysics, but to bring out its ethical significance.

The purpose of giving a brief survey of the Sāṁkhya theory of evolution is to connect it with Sāṁkhya ethical theory. It is noteworthy that Sāṁkhya, like all the other systems of Indian philosophy, originates from the spiritual disquiet which prompts a thinking mind to confess the existence of the suffering which afflicts each and every living being. It would be erroneous to call Sāṁkhya pessimistic on this account because the system does not stop at the acceptance of evil. On the other hand it aims at striking at the very root of evil and the attainment of the liberation of the individual soul from every kind of suffering, mental, physical and social. Sāṁkhya recognizes three main classes of suffering or affliction, (1) Ādhyātmika, suffering aroused by the psycho-physical nature of man, (2) Adhibhautika, suffering issuing from the physical world, and (3) Ādhidavika, the suffering stemming from the invisible malevolent forces of the universe. In the first class are included pains or diseases due to bodily or mental disorders. The second class includes physical injuries caused by aggressive human beings, beasts and other physical objects like thorns, etc. The third type of pains, which have been interpreted by some as pains caused by supernatural agencies like ghosts and demons requires elaboration here. As a matter of fact Ādhidaivika means that which is predominated by the invisible power. In the Vedas, the word 'Devatā' does not stand for any ghost, demon, or even a god personified. On the other hand it indicates the Tattvas, or physical though invisible entities like heat, motion, etc. Now some invisible forces are benevolent and life-giving, while others are malevolent and harmful to life and health. Hence it would be in keeping with the Vedic terminology to translate the word Ādhidaivika as pains, not pains due to supernatural influences, but those caused by invisible physical agencies and planets. This interpretation is also given by Dr Radhakrishnan who writes, 'The second type is due to men, beasts and birds, while the third owes its existence to the influence of planets and elemental agencies'.[1]

Starting with the acceptance of suffering as a factual existence, Sāṁkhya also holds that psychologically each and every individual is inclined to get rid of suffering. The recognition of suffering need not be interpreted as pessimistic, particularly when it is clearly stated that human beings desire from the core of their heart to avoid every kind of pain, and that the aim of Sāṁkhya is liberation, 'the absolute and complete cessation of all pain without a possibility of return'.[2] What is interpreted as a pessimistic attitude is perhaps the idea that liberation brings about an annihilation of pains by freeing the individual from birth and rebirth. The words, 'Without the possibility of return', are objected to, and it is held by Western critics that Sāṁkhya, like all other systems of Indian philosophy, degrades worldly existence and hence does not believe in the dignity of man and the purpose of life.

[1] S. C. Chatterjee, *Introduction to Indian Philosophy*, p. 323.
[2] *Ibid.*

This charge of pessimism, however, is misconceived. We have already pointed out that man is the central point, interest, and subject of Indian philosophy, and that the aim of the Vedas, the Upaniṣads, and all the systems is the well-being of man, who is the miniature universe. When man is regarded as the highest reality and potential god, and when liberation is primarily Jivanmukti, it would be most unbecoming to hold Indian philosophy pessimistic. When Sāṁkhya points out that after the attainment of Mokṣa there is no return, what is meant is that having once attained the highest state of freedom from pain, the individual does not return to the lower stage of suffering and pain. Liberation having once been reached continues eternally. It is this eternality and infinitude of existence and bliss that is emphasized by referring to the stoppage of the process of transmigration. This aspect of Indian philosophy has been lost sight of, with the result that eternality has been misunderstood as non-existence, transcendence as negation, and immortality as the cessation of life. The goal of life cannot be death, nor can that of activity be inertia. When Sāṁkhya aims at the abolition of suffering and evil, and when it is asserted that 'It (Apavarga or Puruṣārtha) is the ultimate end or the *summum bonum* of our life', a pessimistic interpretation is not only uncalled for, but entirely unbecoming and grossly illogical.

Sāṁkhya observes that wants and desires have no limit, and as long as a person considers satiation of desires and the fulfilment of wants as the ideal, he strikes a wrong note. To eliminate pains by pursuing transitory pleasures with the idea of complete gratification is futile and frustrating. Hedonistic ethics is no ethics, either from the practical or the spiritual point of view. It is impractical because the fulfilment of all the desires of an individual, much less that of a society, is impossible and beyond the capacity of human beings in spite of marvellous progress in science and arts, and in spite of the command of virtually unlimited physical power that man wields today that proves his superiority. Even if this superiority is analysed, we shall have to admit that it is not due to his hedonistic tendency of satisfying animal desires, but rather that it is due to reason and discretion, which urges him to control passions and to channelize the feelings of pleasure and pain. Self-control and equanimity rather than satisfaction and appeasement of desires makes man a human being, a rational being, and an ethical person, rather than an animal, a brute and an instinctive creature without any knowledge of right and wrong and good and evil.

Sāṁkhya therefore rejects the Cārvāka theory of hedonism which exhorts every individual to seek pleasure and to avoid pain, and which does not bother about virtue and liberation. It agrees with the Cārvāka view that one cannot have an unmixed pleasure in the world. But whereas the Cārvāka philosophy deduces a hedonistic conclusion from this fact and advocates the satisfaction of desires as the ideal, Sāṁkhya ethics, recognizing the imperfection of human personality, confesses that as long as the soul resides in the imperfect body, pleasures are bound to be mixed up with pains. Moreover, sensual pleasures are transitory and hence their end is always painful. In order to put an end to all sufferings it is necessary to aim at the goal which can bring eternal bliss and beatitude. This is possible only when we accept Mokṣa as the *summum bonum*. Mokṣa is accepted by Sāṁkhya ethics as the state of existence which brings absolute freedom from all pain and suffering. The question arises as to how this goal should be achieved. We have already stated that no amount of material progress, whether of science or of technology, can ever help us to put an end to miseries once for all. Material advancement satisfies our material wants to a great extent, but the more we seek to satisfy transitory desires, the greater is our longing for them. No individual is ever fully satisfied by the appeasement of sensual desires. True happiness does not come from outside; it is not something that descends on an individual. On the contrary, it rises from within, generated from a mental attitude and an intellectual conviction. Hedonism, whether egoistic or altruistic, whether gross or rational, whether based on common sense or supported by science and technology, always remains imperfect and proves incapable of bringing lasting peace to the individual and to society.

For the knowledge on which we base our ethical theories is merely theoretical knowledge, the knowledge of the superficial surface of the material, biological and intellectual aspects of man and the universe. Sāṁkhya admits that knowledge alone can lead us to the final goal of ethics. But this knowledge does not concern the physical world only, it is more deeply and truly concerned with the spiritual basis of the material world. Again it must be clarified that knowledge of the material world, the development of science and technology, is not spurned by Indian philosophy in general and Sāṁkhya in particular. What is emphasized here is that whereas this theoretical knowledge has helped us in our practical life (so far as the material advancement of mankind is concerned) it has not enabled us to overcome imperfections and to reach nearer the final goal of complete cessation of suffering and pain. When knowledge of the ultimate reality, Tattva Jñāna, is advocated by Sāṁkhya as means to the attainment of liberation, it does not forbid us utilizing material amenities of life provided by science and technology. It merely demands an additional spiritual effort to experience the joy and the zest that material progress can provide by supplementing it with practical knowledge, the intuitive knowledge of the spiritual depths of man, which alone is the means for the attainment of liberation, without at the same time making an abstraction of man by cutting him off from the social and the material world.

Since ignorance of the real nature of Puruṣa, or self, is the sole cause of human suffering, the only way to attain eternal bliss or liberation is true knowledge. When an individual suffers because he becomes aware of the physical or mental pain, the awareness itself is illusory, because suffering in reality touches the Citta, or the inner organ, which is nearest the Puruṣa. The Puruṣa does not suffer in reality; the pain or suffering is simply reflected in Puruṣa through the Citta (mind). The self is always pure and chaste. Therefore, to believe that Puruṣa is bound would be a mistake. Nor is the bondage due to time, space, and Karma. On the other hand, it is simply an attitude of the Citta due to the conjunction of Puruṣa and Prakṛiti. But Puruṣa in its true nature is 'eternal and pure, enlightened and unconfined'.[1] It is due to the non-discrimination between the self and the not-self, between the spiritual and eternal Puruṣa, and the material and changing Prakṛiti that Puruṣa appears to suffer. When the Buddhi, which is more closely allied to the Puruṣa, gets the power of discrimination, it smashes the ignorance of the Jīva and arouses in him true saving knowledge, breaking off the shackles of bondage and making the soul shine forth in its pristine lustrous form. Misery comes to an end only after the destruction of Aviveka, or indiscrimination.

Though Puruṣa in its true nature is eternally free, nevertheless moral effort is necessary to arouse the true knowledge in the

[1] Radhakrishnan, *op. cit.*, p. 308.

intellect of the Jīva. This effort aims at the purification of the intellect necessary for the attainment of Mokṣa. Thus morality has an instrumental value but certainly the most important value in Sāṁkhya. In the words of Radhakrishnan,

'The supreme good, which the Jīva aims at and strives for, is to realize the perfection of Puruṣa. All ethical activity is for the fuller realization of the Puruṣa in us. . . . The ethical process is not the development of something new, but a rediscovery of what we have forgotten. Release is a return into one's true self and deliverance from a yoke to which the Jīva was subjected itself.'[1]

The freedom from bondage brought about by the knowledge arising through Yoga, or spiritual discipline, is in keeping with the general spirit of Indian philosophy and the ethico-metaphysical nature of the *summum bonum*, i.e. Mokṣa. It is this rediscovery and reawakening of the soul which arouses infinite potentialities of the soul and brings back to it man's spiritual powers, which transmutes man into superman and the bound soul into virtual God. As to what spiritual discipline facilitates the attainment of liberation, which at the first stage is attained in this life, and later after the physical annihilation of the body, will be discussed in detail in our next section, which deals with the ethical implications of the philosophy of the Yoga.

The Ethics of Yoga

The ethical significance of the Yoga system is evident from the very etymological sense of the word Yoga, which comes out of the Sanskrit root *yuj*, to unite, and is equivalent to the English word yoke. Since the attainment of Mokṣa, union with spiritual reality, is regarded as the supreme good of life by all the systems of Indian philosophy, the spiritual discipline of the Yoga, which leads to the attainment of spiritual liberation, is in fact the practical methodology which is accepted as the best means for self-realization by all the systems of Indian philosophy, whether orthodox or heterodox. Even Jainism and Buddhism give recognition to Yoga. Thanks to the unique genius of Patanjali, Indian philosophy discovered a technique for the

[1] Radhakrishnan, *op. cit.*, p. 309.

attainment of spiritual liberation of immense practical value. Yoga here stands for the union of the self with ultimate reality. Such a state of the self cannot be attained suddenly. The way to spiritual perfection is not very easy. One has to pass through various stages before reaching the final stage of Mokṣa.

The meaning of Yoga is not to be taken literally when it is used with reference to the stoppage of the transitory, relative and limited activities of body, mind and ego. It is to be understood as Cittavṛittinirodha, or the cessation of mental activities, having attained which, the real nature of the self or soul shines forth and the individual experiences the self-luminosity of the soul. But before describing the various stages through which one has to pass in reaching the highest state of Samādhi, or trance, it is necessary also to point out why the cessation of mental activities is considered as means to the attainment of liberation. Does it mean that Mokṣa is equivalent to the annihilation of the self? If so, then the charge of pessimism against Yoga would be justified. In order to answer the question, we shall have to refer briefly to the metaphysical and the psychological background of the Yoga system. On the face of it, the term Cittavṛittinirodha (the stoppage of the activities of mind) appears to be a negativistic. But this negation of the transitory stage is actually an affirmation of the highest, the abiding state of Samadhi, which is the result of the spiritual discipline advocated by Yoga. Yoga is a practical code of conduct which enables the seeker of truth not merely to have theoretical knowledge of the real, but also to realize it by becoming the real, by having the unitive experience of reality. Hence cessation of mental activity is at the same time the arousal of spiritual knowledge which is all-embracing and all-pervasive, the attainment of which leads to the acquisition of wonderful, still mysterious powers. The so-called stoppage of activities, in fact, makes the aspirant a dynamic source of all activities. The cessation of mental activities therefore should not be taken to be an inactivity or a state of coma. On the other hand it is the state of the highest activity, the highest motion and the highest consciousness attainable by man. The meaning of this will become clearer as we proceed with the metaphysical notions and psychological background of the Yoga.

Metaphysics of the Yoga

The Yoga system of Patanjali accepts Sāṁkhya metaphysics with a few alterations and additions. The evolution of the world is based on twenty-five principles already mentioned in the previous section. Although Yoga agrees with Sāṁkhya in asserting that the universe is eternal and evolutionary without the need of a creator, yet it accepts the existence of God, who is outside the evolutionary universe and who helps the spiritual Puruṣa to overcome the obstacles offered by the material Prakṛiti and Avidyā (illusion producing power). The individual Jivas or the Puruṣas attain liberation through the grace of God. Thus the notion of God as the redeemer and as the intelligent principle is the innovation of the Yoga, which turns the atheistic Sāṁkhya into theistic Sāṁkhya. Dwelling on the metaphysical aspect of the Prakṛiti, Radhakrishnan remarks, 'The yoga accounts for creation by the two agencies of God and avidyā. Through the force of the latter, the ever-evolving energy of Prakṛiti transforms itself into modifications as the mental and the material world, while God, though remaining outside the pale of Prakṛiti, removes the obstructions offered by the latter. . . . The individual in the yoga is not so much at the mercy of Prakṛiti as in the Sāṁkhya. He has greater freedom, and, with the help of God, he can effect his deliverance.'[1]

Like Sāṁkhya the Yoga system also accepts the presence of suffering and pain, the removal of which ought to be the aim of every individual. The cause of this suffering is ignorance of the true nature of things, leading to desire, activity, etc. But according to the Yoga system it is meaningless to inquire about the origin of ignorance, because it is co-existent with the world and the world is beginningless (Anādi). Ignorance, or Avidyā, which is present in every individual Citta, continues to be in them even during the dissolution of the world, when they return to Prakṛiti. When the individual Cittas are recreated at the beginning of evolution, this individual ignorance is again responsible for the appearance of suffering in the Citta of each individual soul. It is worth mentioning here that Citta according to Yoga means Mahat, the cosmic intellect, which is the first product of Prakṛiti. It has a wide meaning, and mind (Manas), self-consciousness or ego (Ahaṁkāra) are included within it. In

[1] S. Radhakrishnan, *op. cit.*, p. 343.

fact it stands for the individualized self with mental modifications of various kinds, depending upon the relative, preponderance of the three Guṇas. The objects are manifested in it through the mediacy of the senses, which are the products of Ahaṁkāra.

The Psychology of the Yoga

Here we enter into the psychology of the Yoga, which explains how the Citta, in which the consciousness of the Puruṣa is reflected, causes the impression that the self is the experiencer, when actually it is the Citta in which the experiences appear as modifications due to the activity of the three Guṇas. According to the Yoga, there are as many Cittas as there are Puruṣas. In fact, the Citta appears to be a shadow self, or Puruṣa, because it is connected with each and every Puruṣa. There are two modifications of the Citta, (1) Kāraṇa Citta and (2) Kārya Citta. Kāraṇa Citta is the all-pervasive (Vibhu) cause. Its pervasiveness is compared to that of space, Ākāśa. The causal Citta attaches itself to each and every Puruṣa separately and continues to be with it through various lives, contracting and expanding according to the body in which it resides. For example, while residing in an animal body, it is contracted and while dwelling in the human body it is comparatively expanded. The Citta as the all pervasive cause, or the Kāraṇa Citta, is originally unconscious, and it becomes conscious only by the reflection of the self in it. Kāraṇa Citta does not manifest the states of consciousness in it. It is only the Kārya Citta, the expanded or the contracted Citta, which manifests itself in the states of consciousness. In fact, the all-pervasive Kāraṇa Citta, which is always present with the Puruṣas during their transmigration, manifests itself as the Kārya Citta in every incarnation according to past Karmas. The purpose of the Yoga is to convert the Kārya Citta, or the limited Citta, to Kāraṇa Citta, which always remains all-pervading. This can be done only by the stoppage of all the manifestations of the Citta (Cittavrittinirodha) which are aroused due to the influence of Rajas and Tamas. When these activities are suppressed through the spiritual discipline of the Yoga, the yogin, having converted the Kārya Citta (the limited consciousness) to the Kāraṇa Citta (all-pervading consciousness), becomes omniscient.

Thus the Citta is on the one hand all-pervasive, conscious, and pure due to its proximity with the Puruṣa, and on the other hand it assumes the form of the object when the latter is reflected into it, because the Citta (Karya Citta) is very closely associated with the world. The Citta is the thinking substance, which brings about a liaison between the self, or the spiritual world of the Puruṣa, and the Prakṛiti, the material world of objects, although it is itself the first product of Prakṛiti. Its existence is primarily for the sake of Puruṣa, who rises above thinking, feeling and willing, which (Puruṣa) in fact is the sole and the invisible cause of the Citta itself, because the latter gets its consciousness through the reflection of the Puruṣa in it. Liberation is effected through the purification of the Citta.

During the bondage of the Puruṣa it happens that the modifications of Citta, or the cognitive mental states which actually belong to Citta, are appropriated by the self or Puruṣa. Although it is the Citta which undergoes the changes of the body and the mind, and although the self is above growth, decay, death and mental modifications, yet due to the close association of the Citta, the self wrongly takes itself to be the subject of all these changes. This association of the self with the Citta is in fact that of the reflection of the former in the latter. Just as a person takes the reflection of his own self to be his real self due to ignorance, similarly the self takes its reflection to be itself due to Avidyā. Just as the moon appears to be moving, when actually the clouds passing under it are moving, similarly the modifications of the Citta appear to be the modifications of the self to the self when it looks at them in the Citta, which is held before it like a mirror. That is why the self appears to be experiencing the five kinds of suffering or afflictions as follows: (a) Avidyā, or ignorance, which is responsible for taking not-self to be the self and the non-eternal to be the eternal; (b) Asmitā, identifying the self with the intellect or mind; (c) Rāga, or attachment to sensual pleasures; (d) Dveṣa, or the tendency to hate or avoid pains and their causes, and (e) Abhiniveṣa, which stands for the presence of the fear of death.

The Ethical Aspect of the Yoga

Since ignorance is the cause of the bondage of the self which wrongly identifies itself with the Citta, it is evident that discriminative knowledge (Viveka Jñāna) alone is the best means of attaining liberation. According to Yoga, this knowledge can be brought about by self-purification, by the conversion of the Kārya Citta into Kāraṇa Citta, and there is a quite practical way to achieve this self-purification. This practical method is the ethical discipline advocated by the Yoga system, and the adoption of it alone is responsible for the attainment of the knowledge of the ultimate reality. We have already stated that the ethical or the spiritual discipline of the Yoga has been accepted by almost all the schools of Indian philosophy. The Yoga system however makes a very elaborate study of it and points out that there are eight Aṅgas, or parts, of it. Therefore this methodology is known as Aṣṭāṅga Yoga, or the eightfold means of the Yoga. Since the ultimate aim of freedom from suffering, or the realization of the true nature of the self, is attainable through the discipline laid down in the eight-fold means of Yoga, and since this happens when the modifications of consciousness have been suppressed once and for all (Cittavṛittinirodha), it will be helpful first to return to the psychology of the Yoga and to explain briefly the various levels of consciousness, or the Cittabhūmis. This explanation will also incidentally lead us to the four kinds of Samādhi attainable at the last two levels of the mental life. The Yoga system recognizes the following five stages of consciousness, which differ from one another depending upon the relative predominance of Sattva, Rajas, and Tamas in different proportions:

(1) Restless state of mind (Ksipta Avasthā).
(2) Torpid state (Hūdhāvasthā).
(3) Distracted state (Vikṣiptāvasthā).
(4) Concentrated state (Ekāgrāvasthā).
(5) Controlled state (Niruddhāvasthā).

These different states of mind are mutually exclusive and cancel one another. Let us explain each one of them briefly and ascertain how the last two stages are conducive to the Yoga.

The first state of mind, the restless state, or the state of fickleness, is caused by the predominance of the elements of Rajas and Tamas. At this level the mind is especially inclined towards sensual pleasure and the attempt to gain power. Hence, this state of mind cannot lead to the cessation of the modifications of consciousness. The satisfaction of sensual desires and the longing for pleasures have no end. They are always on the increase and the resulting restlessness of mind never brings equilibrium. Our modern life of speed and indulgence is undoubtedly indicative of the restless state of the modern mind, which is responsible for the absence of mental peace not only among individuals but among so-called advanced nations.

The second level of the mental life, the torpid level, is aroused by excess of the element of Tamas. Since Tamas is heavy and dull, the mental level caused by it is naturally that of ignorance, vice, dullness and sleep. Under the influence of Mūdhāvasthā, or the torpid state of mind, a person cannot control his senses nor can he think of adopting Yoga to be liberated.

The third level of consciousness, the distracted or the Vikṣipta state, is also not conducive to the Yoga, although it is free from the element of Tamas and is influenced only by Rajas. The distracted state of mind manifests to us outside objects and also leads the individual towards virtue, knowledge, etc. At this stage the mind can concentrate itself on objects, but this concentration is temporary and not lasting because it is constantly interrupted. Even this stage of consciousness is not conducive to the Yoga and cannot control the mental modifications. The influence of Avidyā remains unaltered at the Vikṣipta stage of mind.

The fourth level of consciousness, the concentrated stage, or Ekārgrāvasthā, is predominated by the purer element of Sattva, which is light and transparent. There is no adverse effect of Tamas or Rajas in the mind at this level. The Citta is capable of concentrating itself on any object without distraction in such manner and for such time that the true nature of the object is revealed to the yogin. It should be remembered that when we translate the word Citta as mind it should not be understood to be the internal organ of sense, which is called Manas. On the other hand it stands for consciousness or Buddhi (intellect) as understood in the Sāṁkhya philosophy. The fourth level of mind or consciousness has the capability of meditation, which leads to the state of Samprājñāta Samādhi, i.e., meditation on gross or subtle objects. When the mind concentrates its attention on a gross physical object belonging to the outside world, the kind of trance that takes place in this state of consciousness is called Savitarka Samādhi. When, for example, a man concentrates his attention on the image of God, or on the moon, the Samādhi he attains would be the Savitarka Samādhi. This is in fact the first stage of Samādhi. The worship of the images of God in any form is therefore prescribed for every layman who wishes to rise to the higher levels of Samādhi.

It is noteworthy here that image worship, idolatry, was not resorted to in India as a result of ignorance about the oneness of God, as was the case in other parts of the world. Many Western scholars have wrongly accused Hinduism of idolatry, as if Indian religion was a pagan religion. Such an accusation is due to ignorance of the purpose of concentration on external objects, which is, in fact, training the mind for a still higher stage of Samādhi, the attainment of which leads ultimately to spiritual realization. Similarly, permitting individuals to worship the idol of any god is not indicative of a polytheistic tendency, as has been wrongly held by many scholars, Western as well as Indian. In the first place, we should not forget that all the gods or incarnations are various manifestations of the one and the same ultimate reality. Secondly, the aim of worshipping any and every idol is merely the preparation of the mind to proceed from concentration on any gross object to any subtle object, from the subtlest object to the ego, and from the ego to the self or spirit which converts the Samādhi into Asamprajñāta, or objectless concentration in which the self shines by its own light. When at the concentrated level, the Ekāgrāvastha of consciousness, a person concentrates on the subtle object like Tanmātras or the subtle elements, the Samādhi which so arises is called Savicāra Samādhi. When one concentrates one's mind on the subtler objects like the senses, the Samādhi so aroused is called Sānanda Samādhi, because it manifests the real nature of the senses, just as the Savikāra Samādhi manifests the real nature of the subtle elements or Tanmātras. When a man concentrates his attention on the ego, and the nature of the ego is revealed to him, the Samādhi which arises in such a concentration is called Sāsmita Samādhi. Since the Ekāgra level of the Citta gives rise to the four kinds of Samprajñāta Samādhi, and since this Samādhi is in fact a prelude to the Asaṁprajñāta Samadhi, which is Yoga *par excellence,* it is evident that the fourth level of mind is more conducive to the practice of the Yoga. However, the fourth level, though helpful to the yogin for concentration, cannot put an end to mental changes once for all. The meditation or Samādhi aroused during this level always has some gross or subtle objects as its target. It is only when the mind is absolutely free from mental modifications and is at the Niruddha level that the complete control of body, mind, senses and the ego is attained, and the yogin experiences calmness of mind. At the Niruddhāvasthā there is complete cessation of mental modifications, and the state of Samādhi aroused thereby is called Asamprajñāta Samādhi, in which nothing is known or thought by the mind. It should be remembered that the cessation of mental modifications, and the absence of any object or thought in the Asamprajñāta Samādhi, is in fact indicative of its positive aspect as the highest knowledge of the self, which cancels the relative knowledge of objects and other thoughts. In the words of Radhakrishnan, 'When the distinction is realized, the positive nature of spirit manifests itself. This manifestation of the nature of spirit on its own plane, above all confusion with Prakṛiti, is the highest form of Samādhi. In this superconscious Samādhi, the seer abides in himself. All possibility of confusion between the self and the activity of citta ceases. . . . When we strip the citta of its fluctuations, its workings cease, and it is reduced to a condition of absolute passivity. We then enter into silence, which is untouched by the ceaseless noise of the outer world.'[1]

It is quite evident that the stoppage of relative activities is not a mere negative occurrence, but a positive stage of human existence, the result of an unmanifested concentration of the mind. Although the modifications of the mind have ceased, yet the self shines by its own light. But the march towards the goal is an uphill task. The eight-fold means of the yoga system advocated by Patañjali are as follows:

(1) Yamas, or restraints.
(2) Niyamas, or the principles of the development of the personality.
(3) Āsana, or bodily postures.
(4) Prāṇāyāma, or breath-control.
(5) Pratyāhāra, or the withdrawal of the senses.
(6) Dhāraṇā, or attention.
(7) Dhyāna, or meditation.
(8) Samādhi, or concentration.

[1] S. Radhakrishnan, *op. cit.*, p. 362.

Let us now explain each of the above-mentioned means or the methods of Yoga in some detail.

Restraint (*Yama*)

The word Yama literally means control. That principle which requires an individual to control some activity or behaviour is called Yama. Almost every ethical code of every philosophy or religion is negative in its command because it indicates restraint or control, which means a check on some activity, without which moral behaviour is not possible. The Yoga system admits the following five Yamas or restraints:

(1) Non-violence, or Ahiṁsā;
(2) Truthfulness, or Satya;
(3) Non-stealing, or Asteya;
(4) Continence, or Brahmcarya and
(5) Non-possession, or Aparigraha.

The practice of non-violence requires that an aspirant should not cause injury to any living being through body, mind or speech. Although this command is negative and exhorts us to avoid mental, verbal or physical violence, it should not be forgotten that it implies universal love and brotherhood, which are equally important for the purification of mind. Non-violence is understood to be non-hatred (Vaira Tyāgah). As such, love and fellow-feeling are the necessary constituents of the observance of non-violence. Dr Radhakrishnan has explained this point in the following manner: 'Ahiṁsā is interpreted broadly as abstinence from malice towards all living creatures in every way and at all times. . . . The cultivation of friendliness, sympathy, cheerfulness and imperturbability with regard to things pleasant and painful, good and bad, produces serenity of mind (Cittaprasādanam).'[1] Yoga ethics demands that jealousy and hatred towards living creatures be eschewed. This respect for life is necessary for the aspirant of Mokṣa. The world today is in great need of such an interpretation of the Yama of non-violence. We shall see in the sequel how Mahatma Gandhi expounded his philosophy of universal love by basing ethics on non-violence as the highest virtue.

The second Yama, which is positive in its command because

[1] S. Radhakrishnan, *op. cit.*, p. 353.

it requires an aspirant to adhere to truthfulness, is in fact a restraint on indulgence in falsehood. It is noteworthy that this commandment is related to the first one. If we adhere to the principle of non-violence we shall have to give up falsehood, because if we are not truthful and thus deceive others we shall cause them mental injury. Thus the observance of non-violence implies the observance of truthfulness.

Non-stealing, which enjoins the yogin from appropriating the property of other persons for personal use, is indicative of respect for property. Apart from its importance for the purification of mind, this Yama has a great ethical significance in the modern world.

Continence or restraint from sexual intercourse is also of great importance, both from the spiritual and the ethical point of view. Spiritually the observance of celibacy purifies the yogin, conserves his energies, and makes him physically fit and mentally alert. Even a married person who takes up the path of the Yoga can practise continence by gradually reducing the frequency of sexual intercourse with his wife. From the economic and the social point of view the observance of continence would undoubtedly help to solve the problem of overpopulation by substituting self-control for birth control, thereby providing a natural remedy of the problem without causing any physical or mental harm to the observer and to his partner.

The fourth principle of restraint, non-possession or Aparigraha, means limiting one's wants and requirements, enjoining upon the yogin the ideal of 'simple living and high thinking'. The tendency of possession or acquisition is insatiable, and a wise man must always put limits on this instinct. Since the aim of Yoga is the suppression of mental modifications which stand in the way of understanding the infinite nature of the soul, or self (since avarice invariably leads to attachment, attachment to anger, anger to the delusion of understanding, delusion to the loss of memory, loss of memory to the destruction of intellect, and the destruction of intellect to the total annihilation of the individual), it is of utmost importance for a yogin to be vigilant in observing the principle of non-possession. From the social point of view this self-imposed limitation on one's requirements would ultimately lead to a classless society without distinctions of rich and poor, haves and have-notes, and of high and low. Such a socialism or communism would not be based on violence or external force. On the contrary, it would be a voluntary and spiritual communism without malice and hatred against anyone. Vinoba Bhave's Sarvodaya movement, and particularly his Bhūdāna Yajña, or the surrender-of-extra-agricultural-land-campaign (which is in fact based on the Gandhian philosophy of minimizing one's wants), is a step towards such a spiritual communism.

The Principles of Culture (Niyama)

The ascent towards spiritual realization is not only based on the restraints and restrictions enunciated in the five Yamas, but it is also marked by the cultivation of virtues. The Niyama, or the regular code of conduct enjoined upon the yogin to form good habits, leads to the integrated development of personality, infuses spiritual longing into the mind of the aspirants, and expedites his march towards Mokṣa. The following five Niyamas are accepted as basic principles for the conduct of the life of a yogin: (1) Śauca, (2) Santoṣa, (3) Tapas, (4) Svādhyāya, and (5) Iśvarapraṇidhāna.

(1) Śauca stands for bodily and mental purity, and consists in keeping the body clean in the cultivation of the virtues of love, brotherhood, compassion, meekness, and so on.

(2) Śantoṣa, or contentment, means not being overenthusiastic in pursuing the pleasures of the world and being satisfied with whatever one gets as a result of one's honest labours.

(3) Austerity, or Tapas, stands for the habit of forbearing the odds of life and the suffering caused by heat and cold, sun and rain, etc.

(4) Svādhyāya, or self-study, consists of the formation of the habit of devoting one's time regularly to the study of philosophy and holy scriptures, so as to be constantly reminded of the fact that the spiritual self is the real self.

(5) Complete self-surrender to and constant meditation on God, designated Iśvarapraṇidhāna in Yoga, is the most important principle of culture enjoined upon the spiritual aspirant.

All these principles, as already indicated, enhance the spiritual power of the yogin and lead him Mokṣaward. Cleanliness has spiritual as well as aesthetic value. The inclusion of purity of mind by the cultivation of benevolent habits, fellow-feeling, love and compassion has undoubtedly great ethical significance, especially in the modern age of economic culture, industrial competition and political rivalries, which have led to the disappearance of these virtues. The message of Indian ethics to the modern world is an insistence upon giving a premium to love and humanitarian feeling over self-aggrandizement and economic gain. The purpose of this message will become clearer especially when we deal with contemporary Indian ethics. It will suffice here to say that universal brotherhood and love for man are regarded as prerequisites for spiritual realization in the Yoga system, and it has been recognized that to love man is to love God. In like manner, contentment and forbearance have been universally recognized as ethical virtues. The detailed discussion of these need not detain us here. Self-surrender to God, which indicates the theistic aspect of the Yoga, is transformed into the path of devotion, which has had a brilliant record in the history of Indian ethics. We shall refer to it again at the proper place in the sequel.

Posture (*Āsana*)

This discipline of the Yoga is a special feature of this system. It advocates the adoption of various bodily postures conducive to bodily health, mental equilibrium, and spiritual development. The technique of adopting the various postures, like Padmāsana, or the lotus-like posture, Mayūrāsana or the peacock-like posture, and Sīrṣāsana, or the posture of head standing, etc., has both hygienic and spiritual value. Modern medicine has recognized its medical utility, and physiotherapy, which aims at curing some diseases by resorting to physical exercises, is gradually proving the scientific value of the Āsanas. Various Āsanas prescribed by the Yoga system ward off various physical diseases and keep the yogin hale, hearty, and full of energy and strength. 'A sound mind in a sound body' is essential for the aspirant because psychological balance is the prerequisite of concentration, or Samādhi, which is Yoga *par excellence*. Some Āsanas are easy while others are difficult to learn. Expert guidance is necessary in adopting the Āsanas. Many enthusiastic aspirants fall victim to physical diseases and deformities when they make attempts to adopt difficult Āsanas without proper guidance. However, Padmāsana, which is regarded as the best posture for meditation can be learned by everyone without difficulty. The Āsanas bring the nervous system under the control of the yogin.

Breath Control (*Prāṇāyāma*)

Breath-control, or Prāṇāyāma, is a technique of bringing the body and the mind under control and for entering into Samādhi, or deep concentration, for as much time as one intends. There are three steps in the technique of the regulation of respiration, viz.: (1) Pūraka, or gradual inhaling; (2) Kumbhaka, or checking the breath; and (3) Recaka, or exhaling the breath slowly. The best proportion of time to be allotted to the three steps is one, four, and two, respectively for inhaling, controlling, and exhaling the breath. For example, if one takes five seconds for inhaling, one should check it for twenty seconds and take ten seconds while exhaling. This proportion is kept while the yogin goes on increasing the time limit from seconds to minutes and from minutes to hours, and so on. The practice of breath-control must be under the guidance of a most experienced yogin. There is no doubt that one who can successfully control his breath gains physical and mental powers, and one's capacity for concentration increases. The yogin 'rolls up' the breath, withdrawing air from every part of his body and concentrating it in his forehead, thus experiencing an ineffable bliss when he undergoes the Asamprajñāta Samādhi. Before entering into the state of trance, the yogin makes a decision to remain in the state of Samādhi through breath-control for four minutes, four hours, or four days, or whatnot. It is noteworthy that though the yogin is insensitive to all external stimuli, and even though his heartbeat stops, the exhaling process starts automatically at the appointed time. As a matter of fact, the heart-beat or breathing does not stop. But the rhythm of the heart, like the rhythm of inhaling, controlling, and exhaling, increases its interval according to the proportion of the time which the yogin selects for the purpose of Samādhi. The report of a yogin who has undergone the process of Samādhi for hours tallies with the explanation that I have rendered above. Breath-control is also a fit subject-matter for research. We witness astounding feats of yogins who remain alive for months 'buried alive'. Disinterested research in this field is bound to throw important light on physiology and psychology besides illuminating the Yogic importance of the breath-control.

Withdrawal of Senses from Objects (*Pratyāhara*)

A layman draws himself into the vicious circle of longing for sensual objects by constantly striving to satisfy sensual desires and by giving unlicensed freedom to the play of senses. Such behaviour both diminishes his psycho-physical powers and renders him unfit to advance on the path of Yoga. Hence the withdrawal of the senses from their external objects or stimuli, and bringing them under the control of mind, is advocated by this system as the fifth means of the practice of the Yoga. It has been remarked that when the senses are introverted the mind is not distracted by external stimuli, and that the senses so controlled by mind add to its power of concentration. Thus the restraint of the senses helps the aspirant to progress towards the stage of Samādhi. This gradual march of the aspirant prepares him for the total stoppage of mental modifications, which does not abolish knowledge but makes his knowledge all-pervasive as a result of spiritual discipline, the five stages of which we have described above. These five steps are designated as outer means (Bahiraṅga Sādhanas) because of their aim of controlling the environment, or the effect of the environment, on the yogin through Yama, Niyama, Āsana, Prāṇāyāma and Pratyāhāra. These means, however, are not enough to put a full stop to mental modifications. They must be supplemented by the remaining three means of Yoga, viz., Dhāraṇā(attention), Dhyāna (contemplation) and Samādhi, or pure meditation or concentration, which are called the inner means of Yoga (Antaraṅga Sādhanas).

Attention (*Dhāraṇā*)

Literally, Dhāraṇā means holding the object of attention before the mind. It is the first step towards Samādhi. While adopting Dhāraṇā the aspirant fixes his mind on some external object, which may be either a solid object, like an image of a deity, or a part of his own body, like the tip of the nose, the navel, etc. Dhāraṇā is in fact a mental exercise which helps a yogin undertake the next two steps of Dhyāna and Samādhi without difficulty.

Contemplation (Dhyāna)

While attention is oscillating and short-lived, Dhyāna, or continuous contemplation, is the fixing of the mind on its object without a break. S. C. Chatterjee describes Dhyāna in the following manner: 'It is the steadfast contemplation of the object without any break or disturbance. . . . But by long continued meditation, the mind can develop the partial representation of the object into a full and live presentation of it. Thus the dhyāna reveals the reality of the contemplated object to the yogin's mind.'[1] This stage of Yoga, though revealing so far as knowledge of the external objects is concerned, is far from being the stoppage of mental activities.

The Trance (Samādhi)

The climax of concentration and the spiritual discipline of the Yoga is Samādhi. In the state of Samādhi the mind is not only absorbed in the object of its contemplation, but is completely lost so far as its modifications are concerned. When a yogin attains the state of Samādhi he does not have cognition of the act of awareness. It is at this stage that the yogin is capable of stopping all mental modifications and rising to the loftier heights of self-illumination. We have already described the nature of Samādhi.

A survey of the eight-fold means of Yoga proves the pragmatic value of the ethical and the spiritual discipline laid down by this system. Although the aim of Yoga is Cittavṛttinirodha, yet as I have said repeatedly this restraint is not something negative, but it leads to the positive stage of an all-pervasive knowledge attained by the yogin through arduous practice of the principles mentioned above. The practical utility of the practice of Yoga cannot be discussed, since its proof lies only in applying it to practical life. It will suffice here to say that the practice of Rājayoga or Pātañjala Yoga does not come into conflict with one's social, ethical and secular life. This will be evident when we discuss the ethics of Mīmāṁsā in the next chapter.

[1] S. C. Chatterjee, *Introduction to Indian Philosophy*, p. 352.

CHAPTER X

THE ACTIVISTIC ETHIC OF MĪMĀṀSĀ

The system of Mīmāṁsā occupies the most important place in Indian philosophy in general and in the orthodox or the Vedic philosophy in particular. It is essential to clarify at the very outset that the word 'orthodox' here does not signify conservative, but is used only to signify those systems of Indian philosophy which recognize the authority of the Vedas and which offer complete logical justification for the basic ideas propounded by the Vedic seers, the Ṛsis. Unfortunately the philosophy of Mīmāṁsā has not received the attention of contemporary scholars and the subject remains unexplored, especially from the point of view of the ethics implied in the system. Strangely enough, in spite of the comparative disregard of research scholars towards Mīmāṁsā, the practical life of Hindu society, its religious practices and its jurisprudence, have all along followed the injunctions of this system. Mīmāṁsā has propounded and explained those basic principles of life which have been followed and are being followed by millions upon millions of Indians. The aim of this chapter is to bring out the ethical significance of Mīmāṁsā without at the same time neglecting its metaphysical background, which unquestionably is the most important link between the pluralistic and dualistic systems, Nyāya Vaiśeṣika and Sāṁkhya Yoga on the one hand, and the monistic systems on the other.

The central theme of the philosophy of Mīmāṁsā is the adoption of Dharma or duty as enjoined in the Vedas, and the strict adherence to the performance of the rituals as enunciated in the Vedas. Such adherence leads the individual to Mokṣa as surely as the knowledge of Ultimate Reality does. The emphasis of the Mīmāṁsā on duty and activism was justified for two reasons. First, the Sūnyavāda (nihilism) of the Buddhistic philosophy and the extreme asceticism of the Jaina system endangered the social development of human life by neglecting material progress, thereby giving rise to a lop-sided view of life. Second, the over-emphasis on the speculative aspect of the Vedic philosophy, which had resulted in giving preference to knowledge of the self (Ātma Vidyā), or the unmanifested cause of the manifested universe, had led to the neglect of the scientific interpretation of the Vedic terms as enjoined in the Brāhmaṇas. Mokṣa is spiritual liberation, and the soul is the central reality in man; but the way to Mokṣa is not a sudden detachment from the world, but a gradual march towards it. Buddhism and Jainism in their zeal in attacking the Vedic ritual had forgotten that the scheme of Āśrama Dharmas, which aimed at the adoption of Sanyāsa, or detachment, after passing through the preparatory stages, was more scientific and pragmatic than that of sudden detachment favoured by the two heterodox systems. It is necessary to throw more light on these two reasons which led to the systematic enunciation of the Karma Mīmāṁsā, whose very name signifies its activistic trend, before entering into the discussion of its ethical aspect.

The Jaina ethics in its extreme form requires an individual to stop all Karmas and even to give up food and to court death by voluntary starvation. Though the underlying idea of attaining Nirjarā, or the beatific stage, is rising above the relativity of pleasure and pain, heat and cold and praise and blame, etc. by the aspirant, yet the fact remains that this highest state of existence is not the denial of the world, but the transcendence of it. Hence it is attainable only by a chosen few. But when a Jaina, attracted by the transcendental nature of Nirjarā, forgets that it is a positive evolution and not a negative repudiation, and when he begins to adopt a pessimistic attitude towards the material and social aspects of human personality, he strikes a false note. It is due to this misunderstanding that Jainism was later on split up into various schools and sects, all vying with one another in claiming the correct interpretation of their holy scriptures.

Similarly Buddhism, in spite of its ethical code of non-violence, love and righteousness, laid down that becoming an ascetic was most essential for a devout Buddhist. Not one, or two, or a few, but hundreds of thousands of persons courted asceticism and turned missionaries when Buddhism reached its climax in India. Such an emphasis on ecclesiastical order was a potential danger to secularism and humanism, and it could not be checked without a drastic measure or an antidote which might revive the conviction in action, and cure the escapist tendency and the pessimistic attitude. Renunciation does not mean turning one's back upon worldly life or shirking moral and social responsibility. If spiritual life is the life of fullness, if the attainment of Mokṣa means the actualization of the potential powers of man, renunciation as the means of spiritual perfection should not be opposed to material advancement, mental development and intellectual achievement of man. Over-emphasis on the other-worldly attitude and the extreme ascetic tendency of the Jaina and the Buddhist ecclesiastical orders prompted the sages of yore to reassert the faith in morality, to revive the ethico-social tendencies expressed in the Vedas and the Upaniṣads, and to bring home to the common man that true renunciation consisted not in giving up ardour for and zest of life, but in subordinating enjoyment to Dharma, sensuousness to the sense of duty and attachment to spiritual realization. The values of Artha (wealth), and Kāma (love) were neglected and even repudiated by Jainism and Buddhism. Hence Mīmāṁsā drew the attention of the spiritually anxious, but bodily negligent, mentally imbalanced and intellectually perverted extremist aspirants of those times to the fact that the integrated development of the individual and of society could be brought about only by synthesizing all the four values of Artha, Kāma, Dharma and Mokṣa. Since Dharma is the connecting link between the material and the spiritual aspects of human nature, the Mīmāṁsā system lays emphasis on this value more than on all the other three values, and bases all activity or Karma on duty, and it starts with an inquiry into the nature of activity from this point of view only.

The Mīmāṁsā system arose not only to counter-balance the extremist views of the heterodox schools of Jainism and Buddhism, but also to compensate for the negligence of the orthodox systems towards the ritualistic and the activistic aspect of the Vedic thought, which in spite of being the sole source of the idealistic and spiritualistic philosophy of the Upaniṣads also embodied the knowledge of the physically manifested universe of stars and planets, of man and society, and of the relation of human life to cosmic reality. The hymns of the Ṛigveda not only contained the germs of the notion of Brahman as the immanent and the transcendent reality, but they also explained the organic nature of the universe and its close relation to man, who was not only spiritually but also physically a miniature universe. The significance of this inseparable relation was enjoined in the ritualistic performances and the Vedic hymns, whose scientific and practical interpretation lay in the Brāhamaṇic literature.

The fact is that the activistic philosophy of Mīmāṁsā is neither opposed to the spiritualistic metaphysics of the Upaniṣads, nor to the ethico-metaphysical utterances of the Veda, which propounds both the unity of the cosmos and the diversity of the manifested universe. In order to explain the monistic, invisible, immortal, omnipresent, immanent and immutable basis, background and source of the pluralistic, visible, changeable, susceptible, mortal spatio-temporal and destructible world, and the mutual relation of oneness and many-ness, it is essential to understand the real import of the Vedic hymns and the Upaniṣadic statements with reference to the Brāhmaṇa Granthas. The failure of scholars to present such an interpretation has been responsible for misunderstandings with regard to the significance of the Karma-Mīmāṁsā, which is wrongly supposed to be antagonistic to the non-dualistic theory of the Vedāñta. It appears to be necessary to explain the two words 'science', 'Vijñāna', and 'knowledge', 'Jñāna' from the Indian point of view.[1]

At the very outset, I would like to make it clear that the word Jñāna in Sanskrit has a very wide connotation and its translation as 'knowledge' is undoubtedly a poor one. In English, knowledge is supposed to be inferior to science, which is regarded as systematic, methodical and exhaustive knowledge. But in Sanskrit the word Jñāna stands for the highest knowledge, the knowledge of the Supreme Reality, of the invisible unity, the indestructible, the immanent and the transcendent central truth of truths and the centre of centres, which is untouched, unaffected and unchanged by the dynamic, changeable, changing pluralistic and destructible physical

[1] This interpretation has been consistently and most logically presented by a great contemporary but little known oriental scholar and Mīmāṁsaka, the late Pandit Moti Lal Shastri. I base the discussion that follows on his views to clarify the inseparable link between Jñāna and Karma, which has so far been neglected by various scholars and which has resulted in the misconception that Mīmāṁsā has a lower status than that of the Vedānta.

universe, although this central reality is the cause of the manifested universe. In like manner, the word, Vijñāna, which is translated as 'science' in English, is used in Indian philosophy to signify that specialized knowledge, which is the knowledge of the change, the dynamism, the manifested universe with its manyness and manifold nature. The significance of the difference between Jñāna and Vijñāna will become clearer if we adopt the Indian method of defining and explaining the terms based on Brāhmaṇic literature. We shall see that this method is consistent, logical and most intelligible.

Incidentally, this method of approach would help us to understand that Indian and Western philosophy are not only complementary but essentially aim at the same goal with regard to the purpose of the philosophical inquiry, the well-being of man. This well-being, according to Mīmāṁsā, is spiritual as well as social and material. Spiritual well-being is termed Nihśreyasa, and socio-material advancement is designated Abhyudaya. Mīmāṁsā lays emphasis on material progress through scientific knowledge of the physical universe and is thus pragmatic and activistic. It draws the attention of the extremists, the so-called non-dualistic mystics. It points out that one should not overlook material differences between various aspects of the universe, nor those between individuals. Such differences are neglected by them under the false notion that everything is homogeneous, which indicates they do not understand the real meaning of non-dual reality. This methodology gives us an insight into the meaning of the oft-quoted characteristic of Indian philosophy, 'unity in diversity', identity in difference, and harmony in discord.

This method of philosophical inquiry partly consists in pointing out that the knowledge of the philosophical terms used in a discussion lies in appreciating their lexicographic derivations. This method particularly applies to almost all the philosophical terms used in Vedic literature, including the Upaniṣads and the six orthodox systems as they were propounded by their pioneers. For example, the Sanskrit word for 'heart' is 'Hṛidayam', which is derived from three Sanskrit letters, viz.: Hṛi, dā, and yam. The first letter, Hṛi, signifies one fact, the second letter, dā, stands for another fact, and the third, yam, implies still another fact. Hṛi itself comes from the root, Hṛi harane, which means the activity of 'taking in'; dā, which comes from dā avakhanḍane, implies 'giving out', 'pumping out' or returning; and yam stands for 'control' or stabilizing. Hṛi indicates that energy or power which takes in an element; the energy or the power which returns an element is called dā, and yam is the meeting point of the power of 'taking in' and 'giving out' an element. Thus, Hṛidayam is that organ which exhibits the threefold function of 'taking in', giving out, and controlling the functions of taking in and giving out. It is worth mentioning here that Hṛi, dā and yam respectively stand for the three transformations of motion, termed in Brāhmaṇic literature Āgati (inward motion), Gati (outward motion), and Sthiti (stability), which is the central point, at which the inward and the outward motions meet. The word Hṛidayam therefore has philosophical significance, as it stands for the threefold motion or energy, Hṛicchakti, or controlling power, which is connected with the entity termed Prajāpati in the Yajurveda, which is considered present in Hṛidaya or Sāntara, i.e., the centre of everything.

Every object that exists is regarded as a world in itself, and the origin and destruction of every object depends upon the central power (Hṛicchakti), which consists of the threefold function. The word Prājapati is used for the central power of the universe. Its literal meaning is 'master of creation'. The same universal centre of centres and the truth of truths (Kendrasya Kendram, Satyasya Satyam), when present in individual living or non-living objects, is designated Hṛicchakti, or the power residing in the heart, and when it is asserted that God resides in every heart what is meant is that this central power resides in the innermost recess of every object. This is the true interpretation of the Vedic term, Prajāpati, which has been incorrectly understood to be one of the attempts of the simple-minded Aryans to raise a (personal) god, Prajāpati, to the power of the supreme God, with a view to propound monotheism out of polytheism. This hackneyed interpretation of the Vedas given by Western scholars, which holds Vedic religion first to have been polytheism, then henotheism, and finally an attempt to become a monotheism stands exploded in the presence of these facts which are based on the evidence of the Vedic literature. These scholars, having neglected the interpretation of the hymns (the Brāhmaṇa Granthas), have wrongly construed Vedic religion as a representative of the universal tendency of anthropomorphism by calling it a polytheism or henotheism or even monotheism of a peculiar sort. It is crystal-clear from the conception of the Vedic word, Devatā (translated as god), that it does *not* stand for any person, but for a manifested power of the central reality. It is correct to hold that the central reality is construed in the Vedas as the invisible, indestructible, uncaused cause, and the unborn generator of the universe; but the manifest universe, which evolves in the form of various powers due to the three-fold dynamic function, resulting in constant motion, has always been regarded as visible, destructible, causal and evolutionary. The world is an activity, a motion (Gati), and no object, no individual living or non-living is regarded free from the three-fold motion of the spatio-temporal world. The three gods, Vishṇu, Shiva and Brahmā, who have been metaphorically regarded in the Puraṇas as the preserver, the destroyer, and the creator with a view to teaching metaphysics to the masses, are the three names indicating the three-fold function of the central reality, i.e. Prajāpati. The relation of these three functions of the three Devatās has been summed up by the late Pandit Moti Lal Shastri in the following manner:

'An object preserves its existence by taking in energy. That is why Vishṇu devatā, who represents the power of "taking in" has been designated as the preserver of the creation. Discharge or disintegration leads to the destruction of an object. That is why Indra or Rudra (Shiva), personifying the power of discharge (outward motion), has been accepted as the destroyer of the creation. In like manner, controlling factor, stability (Sthiti) or the conjunction of inward and outward motion (i.e. absorption and discharge of energy), leads to the creation of an object (however subtle or gross it may be), and, hence, Brahmā Devatā, personifying the controlling power, has been designated as the creator of the universe. Thus the three-fold power of inward motion (absorption), outward motion (discharge) and the conjunction of the two motions, which are not different from Vishṇu, Rudra and Brahmā, the natural dynamic forces, is the sole determining factor of everything that exists (in the manifested universe).'[1]

[1] Moti Lal Shastri, *Bhāratiya Dṛiṣṭi Se Vijñāna Śabda Kā Samanvaya*, p. 9.

Nor are these three powers separated or segregated from one another, but are understood further as three stages or states of the same power, designated the invisible nature (Avyakta Prakriti), and which is indestructible (Akṣara). This indestructible energy or power has also been named 'absolute' or 'ultimate motion' in Brāhmaṇa literature and even in the Bhagavadgītā. The three states or modes of motion, as we have already seen, are named Vishṇu, representing the motion from the circumference to the centre, Rudra or Shiva, representing the motion from centre to the circumference, and Brahmā, representing the meeting point of the two opposite motions. This explanation alone removes the ambiguity of the interpretations of the Vedic gods, which are clearly the names of dynamic forces and not at all theistic conceptions, as Max Müller and others have wrongly supposed, thus having thrust polytheism, henotheism, etc. on Vedic philosophy. The neglect of the scientific and the analytic approach of the Brāhmaṇas, the connecting link between the Vedic hymns and the Upaniṣadic utterances, has been responsible for the disjointed view of Vedic thought, which in reality presents to us both a monistic metaphysics and a pluralistic conception of the physical world, and which asserts that pluralism and monism, realism and idealism, and pragmatism and spiritualism, are not only compatible, but complementary counterparts of the same truth. It appears unavoidable to clarify this point at some length, with reference to the difference between 'knowledge', Jñāna, and 'science', Vijñāna, from an Indian point of view.

Following the same procedure let us first try to understand the import of the word Vijñāna, which is the synonym for the word 'science'. It is evident that the word is the compound of the two words, vi and Jñāna; the prefix indicates three adjectives, viz., Viśeṣa, or special; Vividha, or multifarious; and Viruddha, or antagonistic. Thus Vijñāna may either be taken to be special knowledge (Viśeṣa Jñānam, Vijñānam), or multifarious knowledge (Vividham Jñānam), or antagonistic knowledge (Viruddha Jñānam). It is quite evident that the word science, Vijñāna, does not and cannot be taken in the third sense of the term, because science as the meaning of the word Viruddha Jñāna, or antagonistic knowledge is impossible. 'Antagonistic knowledge' is in fact the cancelling of knowledge, knowledge which goes against our self-realization. Knowledge which is antagonistic to the real nature of things is in fact ignorance. The terms Viśeṣa (special) and Vividha (multifarious) both indicate that science according to the Vedic point of view is regarded as a special knowledge of the manifold world, because whereas universality signifies monism as its basis, speciality stands for the pluralistic nature of reality. It is only in this sense that the term science (Vijñāna) is used in the Vedas, as well as in the Bhagavadgītā, to distinguish it from knowledge (Jñāna), which is concerned with the most universal and cosmic knowledge of the Brahman, the immanent as well as the transcendent basis of the entire cosmos. If science or Vijñāna is relative knowledge, because it is concerned with the nature of the spatio-temporal world, then knowledge means the absolute knowledge of the basic reality on which the spatio-temporal structure of the universe is based. But the Vedas do not indicate that science as the knowledge of the manifoldness is opposed to Jñāna, the knowledge of oneness. Differentiation or manyness or division is regarded as real, so far as both the relative nature of the spatio-temporal world and also of the human individual as an integrated whole of body, mind, intellect and soul is concerned. But just as the soul is the invisible unitive principle of the human personality, similarly Brahman is the invisible unitive principle of the manifold physical universe.

Now someone may point out that the Kaṭhopaniṣad is opposed to the manifoldness of the universe as it says: 'Mrityoh sa mrityum-āpnoti ya iha nāneva paśyati', i.e. 'whosoever sees manyness in the world sees death and meets death'.[1] It is true that wherever the words manyness, differentiation and separateness have been used in the Upaniṣads they have been associated with death and disintegration. Wherever the words oneness, indifferentiation and inseparability have been used they have been associated with immortality. But the scholars have not noticed that when it is asserted that seeing manyness means death, the word, 'seeing' as used above has a special significance. Seeing implies the seer, which in the Vedas and the Upaniṣads stands for Ātman or soul. When soul is regarded as the seer, its function of seeing means the knowledge of the eternal, unchangeable, immanent and transcendent Brahman. It is clearly mentioned in the Upaniṣads that the soul can be seen only by adopting a proper method, which consists in hearing

[1] Kaṭhopaniṣad, I, 4, 11.

(Śravaṇa) from the preceptor, reflection (Manana) and meditation (Nididhyāsana). After these three stages one can see Brahman or Ātman. The word 'Paśyati', as used in the Kaṭhopaniṣad, indicates that manyness cannot be and should not be 'seen' or realized by adopting the threefold spiritual discipline, which leads to the perception of the soul. In the Bhagavadgītā as well, when the word Paśyati is used, it is always associated with the soul. Thus seeing means intuition, and whoever makes the manyness of the spatio-temporal world the object of intuition is adopting a wrong method. The manyness can only be perceived empirically, and the empirical or scientific seeing in the Vedic sense is associated with the pluralistic nature of the universe. What the Vedas point out is that change, evolution and development should not be repudiated or denied. The physical changes which are occurring every moment form the subject-matter of 'science', Vijñāna as propounded in the Vedas, and such changes represent constant motion. Hence the Vedas advocate activity and the Mīmāṁsā reasserts activism. But motion or activity requires a motionless and inactive ground for the motion to take place. Thus activity and motion are relative to stability and changelessness. Vijñāna, which is concerned with motion remains in need of Jñāna, which has the unchanging reality of Brahman as its subject-matter. Those who neglect the activistic aspect of the universe and only imagine that they are experiencing oneness with the universe dupe themselves and are bound to perish. Although Brahman is immortality and immutability, yet the sentimental, ignorant aspirant, who while living as a human being overlooks his spatio-temporal existence and neglects his real contact with the physical world of Devatas, the physical forces, is most impractical and unphilosophical, despite popular opinion to the contrary. The fact remains that plurality is not to be 'seen', but to be applied to the practical conduct of life, whereas the oneness has be 'seen', in the sense of being intuited, not in the sense of being imagined.

It is necessary to distinguish the two terms Darśana, seeing in the sense indicated above, and Varttana, behaving or engaging in activity, in order to support the view according to which Jñāna, knowledge, and Karma, action, and, hence Vedānta and Mīmāṁsā, are not only complementary but, as mentioned before, two aspects of the same reality. We shall have to clarify which aspect of the human personality and of the cosmic individual is concerned with the Jñāna, and which aspect is concerned with the Karma—which aspect is to be seen, and which aspect is to be applied to activity. As already indicated, Jñāna means insight, real contact with the unity (of the cosmos), which is indestructible and eternal, but which being absolute, is not affected by the pluralistic reality of the universe and which is therefore said to possess the transcendental characteristics of truth, knowledge, and infinity (Satyam, Jñānam, Anantam). In fact, truth, knowledge, and infinity are to be understood here as three synonymous terms. But at the same time these absolute terms expressing the absolute experience of the soul (Ātman) attained through spiritual discipline, also indicate that the unity of the reality is to be 'seen' in the sense of being intuited, whereas the diversity, which is relative to that unity, has to be applied to practical life. Whereas Darśana has been used in connexion with the unity of the cosmos, Varttana, practical application or behaving, has been used in connexion with the pluralistic existence of the physical world. When the Upaniṣad says that 'Whoever sees manyness, sees death', it implies that manyness is to be lived and not to be intuited. It is quite correct that Samvarttana, the same behaviour of every object and every individual (without thereby recognizing the real differences in the spatio-temporal world) would amount to death, just as Viṣamadarśana, or not having insight into the basic unity of the differentiated universe, would amount to death and self-destruction. In this sense the best course is the adoption of Viṣama Varttana, differentiation in behaviour (because behaviour is activity and differentiation) and that of Samadarśana, a unitive attitude of the self or Ātman with regard to the basic reality (because the self means identity in difference and stability in change). Thus the activity enjoined upon the individual by the Vedas, with its background of the unity of Prajāpati or Brahman, represents a demand to be realistic and pragmatic in our practical life and to be idealistic and spiritualistic with regard to our metaphysical notions, which are the basis of our ethics.

The above statement might confuse the reader and lead him to believe that perhaps the Vedas and the Mīmāmśa system advocate a dualistic and hence a hypocritical view of life. But such a conclusion would be hasty and ungrounded. Even from the philosophical point of view there is no antagonism between the oneness of the universe and its manyness, between the unity of the soul and the diverse behaviour of the individual so far as the physical, mental and intellectual aspects of his life are concerned. In fact knowledge (Jñāna) and science (Vijñāna) are the two attitudes towards the same organic reality, which presents unity in diversity and diversity in unity. This interrelation of the two attitudes has been expressed by Shri Moti Lal Shastri in the following manner:

'We are forced to arrive at this conclusion that science (Vijñāna) can be conveniently defined as the attempt to understand diversity by postulating unity or one reality. This very conclusion also implies the definition of knowledge (Jñāna). Knowledge may be conveniently defined as the attempt to understand the unity or one reality by postulating manyfoldness or diversity (of the universe). Scientific attitude consists in expounding diversity, by presuming unity and gnostic attitude consists in expounding unity by presuming diversity.'[1]

The Vedas recommend and adopt both the attitudes, i.e. scientific and gnostic, which for want of a proper translation of the Sanskrit word Jñānātmaka, may be termed 'intuitive'. The scientific and the intuitive attitude towards the organic nature of the cosmos aims at a synthetic metaphysics, a synthetic psychology, and a synthetic ethics. It is at once pragmatic as well as spiritualistic, realistic as well as idealistic, and pluralistic as well as monistic, thereby bringing about a merger of science and religion, and of metaphysics and ethics.

A further word about this synthesis of knowledge and action or metaphysics and ethics appears necessary in this connexion. The Vedas recognize a pluralistic universe with Svayambhu Prajāpati as the nucleus. This centre, as its name implies, is regarded as the self-existent reality; it is, in fact, the invisible central power around which numberless universes or galaxies are revolving. Every galaxy or universe has its own centre (Parameṣṭhi) around which numberless solar systems are revolving. Every solar system has a sun as its nucleus, around which the planets revolve, and the earth is one of the planets of our solar system. But the earth itself is the nucleus for the moon, which revolves round it. Similarly man, as the miniature universe, has Avyaya Puruṣa, or the invisible self, as the centre of his being, representing Svayambhu Prajapati. Mahān Ātma, or

[1] Moti Lal Shrasti, *op. cit.*, pp. 29–30, referring to Kaṭhopaniṣad, 1, 4, 11.

the great self, which stands for the hereditary self passed on to the individual by seven preceding generations and is transmitted to seven succeeding generations, represents Parameṣthi. The intellect or reason represents the sun; the mind or consciousness represents the moon, and the body represents the earth. In this organic system of the cosmos and of man, it is only Prajāpati or Brahman (in the case of the cosmos), and Avyaya Puruṣa, or the pure self (in the case of the individual), which is regarded transcendental, i.e. above the spatio-temporal order. This is the case because Prajāpati or Brahman, or its individual form of the Avyaya Puruṣa, is the very cause of the spatio-temporal order. The scientific theory of creation presented by the Vedas is undoubtedly the oldest in the world. When the Mīmāṁsaka asserts that the Vedas are Apauraṣeya, or impersonal, what is meant is that they deal with the eternal truths and that no individual opinion or view can falsify the eternal truth. Whether a sage of yore discerns the organic nature of man and the universe, or science arrives at this result after a continued research, the truth remains unaltered. The injunctions of the Vedas are to be admitted as duty for the sake of duty, because they are based on discoveries of eternal truths, and it would be impossible to explain to every individual their scientific significance and their intuitive import. Just as Vijñāna is not opposed to Jñāna but is necessary for practical life, which depends upon the recognition of the manyness and the relativity of the spatio-temporal order, similarly Karma, which is the very basis of the physico-mental and intellectual life of differentiation is not opposed to Jñāna or the knowledge of the unity of the self. But it should be remembered that just as the recognition of the basic unity is unavoidable for practical purposes of science, similarly the recognition of Viṣama Varttana, differentiated behaviour as enjoined by the adherence to the Vedic rituals, is considered unavoidable for the successful conduct of life. This pragmatic and realistic attitude towards life is the keynote of the ethical and the activistic philosophy of Mīmāṁsā.

The emphasis on adherence to duty for the sake of duty in Mīmāṁsā indicates that its sole purpose was to restore conviction in the conduct of life (Varttana) and to bring about a synthesis between the spiritual and the material aspects of human personality. Explaining the aim of Mīmāṁsā, Shri Moti Lal Shastri says 'Varttana (conduct) or dealing in life has been associated with the conative tendency, Acarana, or practical application or action (Karma). The conative tendency, involving the practical application of morality, depends upon the physical nature of the individual, which is a synthesis of intellect, mind, and body. The physical body combined with intellect, mind and the senses, the existence of which is self-evident, is regarded as the basis of Varttana. From the Indian point of view conduct means actual differentiated conduct (Viṣamavarttana) associated with the moral activity of man, the integrated whole of intellect, mind, senses and body with soul as the central reality. Man as the combination of intellect, mind, body and senses is the worldly or the spatio-temporal being; and the same man is a transcendental (Alaukika) being, because of the presence of soul as its central point. The spiritual self of man makes him the knower of unity (Samadarśana), and the same man, as the embodiment of intellect, mind, body and senses, practises differentiated conduct or behaviour'.[1]

This interpretation of the philosophy of Mīmāṁsā is undoubtedly more convincing and in keeping with the true spirit of the system. We have already dealt with the ethical philosophy of the Vedas and have seen how the individual and society are regarded as organic to each other and how the Varṇāśrama Dharmas lead to the ethico-social organization of the Hindus, keeping this ideal in tune with the nature of the cosmic unity. The Mīmāṁsā system, which enjoins upon every individual obedience of the injunctions of the Vedas, and which emphasizes that the rituals are to be adopted as a duty for the sake of duty, takes it for granted that the Varṇāśrama Dharmas are categorical for each and every individual. Because of the preponderance of the critical spirit, and especially because of the presence of the heretical tendency of putting a premium on asceticism and renunciation, it was but natural for the Mīmāṁsā to overemphasize the value of Dharma, or moral duty, and also to reassert the importance of the Vedic philosophy. This explains that while advocating adherence to Dharmas the Mīmāṁsā system maintains throughout that the Veda reveals Dharma. But besides advocating the adoption of Dharma in keeping with the Vedic injunctions, this system also explains why morality is essential even for secular advancement.

From the secular point of view Mīmāṁsā asserts that virtue

[1] *Ibid.*, p. 23.

is a conscious or semiconscious adjustment of conduct to interest. It draws our attention to the adoption of Artha and Kāma for the advancement of the secular life of the individual as well as of society, and the adoption of Dharma for the attainment of Mokṣa. The former two values have social well-being as the ideal and lead to Abhyudaya, or progress, and the latter two values, of which Mokṣa is the highest, aim at spiritual well-being as the ideal, culminating in Śreyasa, or eternal bliss. The fact is that social well-being is not the highest end, but is the means to the attainment of the highest value of Mokṣa. When Kumarila wants us to distinguish between Dharma and Mokṣa, enjoined upon us by the Veda, and Artha and Kama, which are learned by us in our worldly behaviour, what he tries to point out is that spiritual well-being and social well-being, Śreyasa and Abhyudaya, though distinguishable from each other, are interdependent.

Ordinary morality is not repudiated but given its proper place in Mīmāṁsā ethics, in comparison with spiritual morality or Dharma which leads to Mokṣa. Commenting upon this aspect of the Mīmāṁsā ethics M. Hiriyanna has remarked: 'Śabara says that charitable acts like providing water huts (prapā) though for the benefit of others and therefore good, are not yet Dharma. That is, the Mīmāṁsā judges conduct by a utilitarian standard; but it is not egoistic, and as is indicated by the very example given by Śabara, is based upon the realization of the social nature of man.'[1] The critics forget that when Mīmāṁsā names the obligatory acts like Yajña as Dharma, and the prohibited acts (Nisiddha Karmas) like gambling and killing as Adharma; and when the effects of both these acts are regarded as Apūrva, the invisible power of the conservation of the acts (Karmas), it is evident that spiritual and social well-being have been given equal status in the Mīmāṁsā ethics. If the Nitya Karma, or the obligatory acts of performing a Yajña (ascrifice), lead to Mokṣa, negligence towards the prohibited acts would hinder the spiritual progress of an individual. It is wrong to suppose that the fields of social morality and spiritual morality are bifurcated. At least in Indian philosophy in general, and in the Mīmāṁsā ethics in particular, they are inseparably linked. It is true that for the realization or the fulfilment of Artha, the economic value, and the Kāma, the emotional value (of satis-

[1] M. Hiriyanna, *Outlines of Indian Philosophy*, p. 326.

faction of desires), the individual is asked to seek guidance from the social sphere and common sense, and for the realization of Dharma, moral value, and Mokṣa, the highest spiritual value, he is asked to depend upon the guidance of the eternal knowledge of the Veda. But we should not forget that the Vedas advocate an integration of the individual, social and spiritual well-being, and emphasize the organic nature of the man and the universe, with the result that they propound the four Puruṣarthas. We have already indicated how the Varna Vyavasthā (the social organization) corresponds to the integrated development of the four sections of the society, viz; Śūdra, Vaiśya, Kṣatriya and Brāhmaṇa. Now it would be desirable to throw light on the integrated development of the four-fold scheme of values.

Artha (*Wealth*)

The importance of the economic aspect of human life has reached its climax in the contemporary age of economic culture and commercialized civilization when money is given a premium over life and economic interests supplant ethical duty. But the ancient Indian sages had included wealth as the most important instrumental value for individual and social development. The difference between the Western and the Indian concepts of Artha lies in the fact that whereas the West has considered wealth to be instrumental only for the satisfaction of sensual desires (Kāma), India has advanced the notion that it is equally essential for the attainment of Dharma, or morality, and hence for happiness here and bliss thereafter. The Brahmacarya Āśrama, which is relegated to the acquisition of learning, is, in fact, a preparatory stage for the attainment of efficiency to earn wealth. The following verse of Sanskrit indicates this aim of education and learning:

Vidyā dadāti vinayam,
Vinayam dadāti pātratām;
Pātrattvāt dhanamāpnoti,
Dhanāt dharmām tatah sukham.

'Learning gives modesty, modesty leads to worthiness; worthiness brings wealth; wealth leads to morality, and morality brings happiness.' India realized long ago that economic exploitation and an unequal distribution of wealth could lead to social decay and moral degeneration. It has been stated that 'a hungry man is prone to commit every kind of sin'. That is why it was enjoined upon every individual to aim at earning money in order to be successful in social, moral and even in spiritual life. The West has not paid attention to the moral and the spiritual utility of wealth as much as India has.

However, this does not mean that Indian philosophy neglects the physical development of human personality or looks only to the other-worldly and hence imaginary utility of wealth, thereby condemning the practical utility of economic value. On the other hand, wealth has been praised and desired for its pragmatic purposes and for the honour and facilities that it brings to a common man. It has been stated that wealth should be collected by every individual to gain social status and to overcome obstacles. A Sanskrit verse says:

Dhanairniskulīnāh kulīnāh bhavanti,
Dhanairāpadam mānavāh nistaranti;
Dhanebhyo paro, bāndhavo nāsti loke,
Dhanānyarjyadhvam dhanānyarjyadhvam.

'Wealth turns a man of a lower social status to that of a higher social status; people can overcome all obstacles by means of wealth; there is no kith and kin better than wealth; collect wealth, collect wealth.' There is no dearth of common-sense morality or lack of recognition of the utility of money among the Indians, as most of the Western scholars and philosophers are misled to imagine. On the contrary, laymen have been exhorted by Indian poets and writers to be serious, to make their economic position sound so as to be praised and propitiated in society. It would not be out of place to quote here one more Sanskrit verse to support this view. The verse says:

Yasyāsti vittam sa narah kulinah;
Sa panditah srutavāna guṇajnah;
Sa eva vaktah, sa ca darsānīyah,
Sarve guṇāh kāñcanāmāsrayanti.

'A person who has wealth is regarded as one belonging to a high family; he is considered to be wise, to be learned and the knower of virtues. He is considered to be an orator and a handsome person; in short, all the virtues attach themselves to gold (wealth).'

This, however, does not mean that wealth is desirable only as a means to become famous and highly placed. Rather, as we have already stated, the primary purpose of wealth is to develop the body, since a nutritious diet is possible only when a person's financial position is sound. The maintenance of the health of the body is most essential, because the body alone is the temple of God, and the vehicle of the mental, intellectual, and spiritual personality of man. Kalidāsa has said in his immortal work, *Kumārasambhava*, 'Śarīramādyam khalu dharmasādhanam,' i.e. 'The body is the primary basis of the performance of moral duty'. It is from this point of view that Mīmāṁsā, like the Vedas, accepts wealth or Artha as an instrumental value. The moment the instrumentality of the value of Artha is lost sight of and the moment it is pursued for its own sake, or only for the sake of sensual pleasures, one falls victim to the endless vicious circle of pleasures and pains and continuous births and deaths. It is true that wealth as one of the most important values, or Puruṣārthas, must not be neglected, but at the same time it is equally true that it is not an end in itself, not even the means of the satisfaction of body and mind, but also as the means of Dharma, or morality, which in turn leads to Mokṣa, or liberation, the *summum bonum*.

Kāma (*Love*)

The same is the case with the second Puruṣārtha of Kāma, love or emotional satisfaction. The very fact that this value has second importance in the ascending order, shows that it is related to the second level of human personality, that is, mind (Manas). We have purposely adopted this serial order of Artha, Kāma, Dharma, and Mokṣa (wealth, love, morality, and liberation), so as to move from gross reality to subtle, from subtle to subtler, and from subtler to the subtlest reality of the soul. We shall see that the Bhagavadgītā also, while explaining the nature of the soul starts with the gross body and ultimately comes to the conclusion that soul, Ātman, is subtler even than the intellect or the Buddhi. The acceptance of Kāma as one of the four basic values points out the dire necessity of the instinctive and the emotional urges of man, particularly the urge of sex, which has always been regarded as the strongest desire. The ancient Indian sages had recognized long ago that the suppression of the sex urge leads to mental imbalance, and hence to the destruction of personality. That is why the satisfaction of the sex urge through marriage has not only been preached but has been considered necessary for the integrated development of the individual and for the progress of society. It has been declared that a person who is not married is mentally deficient and does not deserve to be called normal. Manu has said that 'A man is half man as long as he is unmarried'.

In fact this is the reason the sex instinct or sex act has been divinized in Indian philosophy. Such an act, which leads to the creation of a new life, and particularly to that of a man's life, should be regarded as a sacred and sanctified act, as Radhakrishnan has also observed in his work, *Society and Religion*. Moreover Kāma, seen as the sacred sentiment of mutual attachment of man and woman, has its importance as a value of life further enhanced. Marital love, Dāmpatya-rati has a special significance and connotation in Indian philosophy in general and in Mīmāṁsā in particular. Love is the content of mind according to the Indian point of view, although in order to be aroused and ingrained in man it is aided by the intellect and even by the soul, particularly when the love is true and divine. A word of explanation appears necessary here to support the interpretation of Mīmāṁsā ethics towards which we have been led in this chapter.

If mind is the container, and if love is the liquid which it contains, there can be three possible kinds of waves produced in that liquid. When turbulence below makes the liquid move upward, the state so produced is called Śraddhā, or adoration, which means the love of a younger or inferior person towards an elder or superior person. Such is the love of the son or daughter towards his or her parent, or that of a pupil towards his preceptor, and so on. If the wind makes the wave move downward from above, the erotic state of mind so aroused would be called Vātsalya, or filial affection. Such is the love of parents towards their child, or of a preceptor towards his disciple or pupil. But if there is no upward or downward movement in the content of mind and the liquid remains at one level, the erotic state of mind so aroused would be termed Sneha, or mutual affection. Such is the love between two friends or persons of equal status. Now according to the Indian point of view marriage is not a partnership nor is it a contract between two friends. It is not a mere give and take of certain rights and privileges, or a mere recognition of the conjugal relation between husband and wife. On the contrary, it is considered a spiritual association of two souls which continues not for some years or even for one life, but life after life in various incarnations. Such is the belief of a common Hindu about the sanctity of marriage. Hence marital love, or Dāmpatyarati, can neither be adoration alone, nor filial affection alone, nor only mutual affection, but the combination and synthesis of all these three types of love. The love between husband and wife is sometimes adoration of the one for the other, sometimes filial affection, and sometimes mutual affection. During a long married life uninterrupted by any threat of divorce, on the mere excuse of dislike for certain physical features or some undesirable habits, husband and wife have to nurse each other lovingly when either of them is ill, and thereby express even filial affection to each other. Monogamous marriage is regarded as the ideal marriage in Hindu society, and Manu observes that the husband must also have the same adoration and devotion towards his wife as the latter has for him. The secret of the stability of married life among the Hindus lies in the fact that marital love, according to the Vedic rites and beliefs is not merely a mutual affection, but Dāmpatyarati, or deep domestic devotion, consisting of love and adoration, faith and conviction, and self-surrender and self-sacrifice on the part of both the husband and the wife.

The married couple symbolizes the eternal pair of Shiva and Shakti, or God and his creative power. Kāma experienced in married life, besides being conducive to the mental health of the individual, paves the way for divine love or devotion towards God. If God is love and love is God, then to love mankind is to love God. A person who has never experienced human love, who has never sacrificed his self-interest for the interest of his or her beloved partner of life, can never love God nor attain Mokṣa. It is in this sense that Kāma as one of the ends of life, besides being self-gratifying so far as the mental aspect of man's personality is concerned, is instrumental for the attainment of the supreme goal of human life, Mokṣa.

Dharma (*Moral Duty*)

It should always be remembered that if Artha and Kāma are primarily associated with the development of body and mind respectively, Dharma or moral duty is concerned with the intellectual development of the individual and also that of society. The concept of Dharma is the oldest in Indian philosophy as it originated in Vedic times in the form of Ṛita, the eternal moral order upheld by the gods. According to Mīmāṁsā, Dharma is not only the virtuous act, as enjoyed by the Vedas, but it also stands for the potentiality which stores the effects of the virtuous act and which is called Apūrva. Although Dharma as Apūrva has its own significance as one of the Kāmya Karmas, or optional actions, which store merit and aim at the attainment of Svarga, or heaven, the real meaning of Dharma is understood to be the disinterested duty of the individual to perform sacrifice, Yajña, etc., strictly according to the behests of the Vedas without aiming at any fruit, the attainment of heaven or the like. The Mīmāṁsā system enunciates the standard of 'duty for the sake of duty', so far as the notion of Dharma is concerned. This detached performance of duty should not be misunderstood as a blind faith of the Mīmāṁsā system in the authority of the Vedas, as most of the scholars of Indian philosophy and religion have wrongly construed it. We have sufficiently discussed and elaborated the real import of Vedic thought with reference to Brāhmaṇas and have come to the conclusion that the activism of Mīmāṁsā is not merely an overemphasis on the ritualistic aspect of the Veda, but rather a necessary practical aspect of Viṣam Varttana, differentiated conduct, which without the aim of the unitive knowledge of Brahman is not possible. Hence Dharma as 'duty for the sake of duty' is not an empty command like that of Kant's categorical imperative.

On the other hand it is quite evident from the context of the Vedic thought and culture that the adoption of Dharma means the acceptance of the pluralistic nature of the manifested world in the form of the forces, called the Devatās, keeping in view the aim of realizing the oneness of the universe through spiritual discipline. The Dharma must be adhered to if we want to conduct our life successfully, and if we want to adjust ourselves to the spatio-temporal world. Buddhi (intellect), which is the representative of the sun, the centre of our solar system, obliges us to accept the regulations of the spatio-temporal order, which is a real order. Thus Dharma is associated with intellect, which is its basis, the development of which is not possible without the adoption of Dharma. This very Dharma, the recognition of which reminds us of the dynamic and the pluralistic order of the universe, has been expounded in the Vedic Mantras and the Brāhmaṇas which explain to us the methodology of ritual, performing sacrifice, etc. The Dharma brings us into close contact with the forces of nature and helps us to keep physically healthy, mentally alert and intellectually moral. That is why Mīmāṁsā lays all its emphasis on the acceptance of the authority of the Vedas without any question or doubt about the efficacy of the rituals. Without the background of the import of the scientific aspect of the philosophy of the Vedas, as previously described to us, adherence to Dharma in accordance with the Vedic behests would certainly turn out to be orthodoxy, conservatism and blind faith. But with the recognition and appreciation of the scientific background of the Vedas 'duty for duty's sake' certainly is not motiveless, for it reveals that this ethical attitude, though categorically acceptable, has as its purpose the total development of the human personality, and that it ultimately leads to Mokṣa. Moreover, it is certain that the action performed as an unconditional obligatory duty has positive potency, which leads to the attainment of good results hereafter. Thus the categorical command of the Vedas is different from Kant's abstract notion of 'duty for duty's sake'.

Dharma or good action is not only dictated by the Vedas, but the Smṛiti (code of conduct) texts also mention Dharma. But the injunctions of Dharma contained in the Smṛiti may not be consistent. In the event of conflict between the Smṛiti and the Vedas, the view of the Vedas must be accepted as true and categorical, for reasons given by us in this connection. Though the Dharma of the highest order according to Mīmāṁsā must necessarily be deduced from the Veda, yet the guidance of the Smṛiti, as well as the examples set by good persons and good institutions, have also been regarded as the basis of duty by the Mīmāṁsakas. This fact proves the pragmatic nature of Dharma in the ethics of Mīmāṁsā. In fact the notion of Dharma presented by this system is the basic notion in the Hindu philosophy and is adhered to by millions of Hindus today. Commenting on the importance of the Mīmāṁsaka interpretation of Dharma Radhakrishnan remarks: 'The life of the Hindu is governed by the rules of the Vedas so that the Mīmāṁsā rules are very important for the interpretation of the Hindu law'.[1] Unfortunately the negligence of scholars with regard to the connecting link of the Brāhmaṇic literature between the Vedas and the Smṛitis has been responsible for various misunderstandings about the philosophy of Mīmāṁsā. In spite of this fact the truth remains that the Mīmāṁskā notion of Dharma reigns supreme in Indian philosophy and in the practical life of the Hindus.

Mokṣa (Liberation)

Like all the other schools of Indian philosophy, Mīmāṁsā accepts liberation or Apavarga as the supreme goal of human personality and hence the sole purpose of the ethical life. The historical and literary evidence clearly shows that the concept of Mokṣa or Apavarga as the ideal to be achieved was definitely accepted by Prabhākara as well as by Kumārila, the founders of the Prabhākara and Bhātta Schools of Mīmāṁsā, respectively. Some interpreters believe that according to Mīmāṁsā liberation is a negative state, which means the extinction of pleasures as well as pains. But according to other commentators, it is a positive state of existence, where the antinomy of Dharma and Adharma ceases to exist. However, both interpretations agree in accepting Mokṣa as complete freedom from pain. In other words, the transcendental nature of Mokṣa has been universally recognized by the followers of Mīmāṁsā. The relativity of pleasure and pain, of heat and cold and of right and wrong is transcended in Mokṣa. Worldly pleasures being transitory and relative, pale into insignificance when compared with the eternal, painless state of Mokṣa, where all the Karmas or actions must be exhausted. The desire for this absolute state of existence arises on account of the relative nature of pleasure and pain. Radhakrishnan has elaborated this point of view of Mīmāṁsā in the following words:

'The individual, feeling that in Saṁsāra pleasures are mixed up with pain, turns his attention to liberation. He tries to avoid the forbidden acts as well as the prescribed ones, which lead to some sort of happiness here or hereafter. He undergoes the necessary expiations for exhausting the previously accumulated karma,

[1] Radhakrishnan, *Indian Philosophy*, Vol. II, p. 418.

and gradually, by a true knowledge of the soul aided by contentment and self control, gets rid of his bodily existence.'[1]

This approach to Mokṣa, beginning with spiritual disquiet and discontentment with the relative nature of the worldly life, should not be supposed to be a pessimistic note or an escapist tendency. On the contrary, the Vedas advocate a gradual march towards Mokṣa with reference to the Varṇāsrama Dharmas, and Mīmāṁsā is firmly grounded on the injunctions of the Vedas. It is only when a person becomes Jiva-mukta due to 'true knowledge' (Sama darśana) of the soul that the relative nature of the spatio-temporal world is transcended, but not denied. Even after the attainment of true knowledge he has first to exhaust the previous Karmas, and in so doing he must continue to follow the laws of the spatio-temporal order. It should be remembered that the unity of the spiritual reality which is the goal does not abolish plurality at the level of Dharma, through which this ultimate unity has to be achieved. This plurality of the world, the Dharma aspect of human personality or intellect, cannot be denied or repudiated. On the other hand, it is through Dharma and intellect that the individual rises above relativity so as to achieve absoluteness.

The acceptance of the release or liberation, which means an unalloyed state of eternal existence after the soul gives up mortality (since the soul is the indestructible universal principle, as opposed to the destructible particular world of physical existence), shows that Mīmāṁsā, like the Vedas, propounds a pluralistic physics and monistic metaphysics, an activistic ethics and spiritualistic theory of liberation, and a secular philosophy and a pragmatic theism. Dharma exhorts an individual to adhere to the scientific attitude (Vijñāna); the concept of Mokṣa drives him to attain the natural form of the soul. Mokṣa is the complete cessation of the transitory and relative experiences of pleasure and pain which he can attain not merely by Vijñāna (scientific knowledge), but by Jñāna, the intuitive knowledge of the highest reality existing within his own self. It is this supreme knowledge, not the relative Karmas, which would lead an individual towards the final release.

Just as Jñāna (intuitive knowledge) and Vijñāna (science) are complementary and dependent upon each other, similarly the

[1] Radhakrishnan, *Indian Philosophy*, Vol. II, p. 423.

realization (Darśana) of the natural form of the soul and the practice of Dharma in all the varied spheres of life are complementary to each other. It is not merely theoretical knowledge that brings about liberation, but the practical and intuitive knowledge of the Ultimate Reality which is gained gradually by the practice of Dharma for the sake of Dharma, on the one hand, and the realization of the unity of the spirit, on the other. Dharma exhorts us to conform to the rituals and to perform our duties according to the Varṇa, or caste, and the Āśrama, or the stage of life which we have adopted due to our psychological tendency and special occupation, thereby recognizing the plural nature of the physical and the social order. Mokṣa as the highest goal inspires us to bury all physical and social differences, because the state of liberation can never be regarded as free from all pains and physical obstacles unless the attainment of Mokṣa makes a person rise above the contradictions and antimonies of pleasure and pain, heat and cold, joy and fear, etc. These differences, though practical, must be resolved at the Mokṣa level, which is the level of the infinite, eternal, universal, omnipotent existence of the self, free from all the Upādhis, or conditions that are responsible for differentiated experiences in the spatio-temporal world. Mīmāṁsā, therefore, does not repudiate knowledge of the underlying non-dualistic spiritual reality, or Brahman, nor does the Advaita (non-dualistic) view set aside Upāsanā and Karma activity. This fact will become clearer in the next chapter as we proceed to expound the ethics of the Vedānta.

CHAPTER XI

THE ETHICS OF THE ADVAITA VEDĀNTA

The six orthodox systems of Indian philosophy beginning with the analytical and pluralistic theories of Nyāya Vaiśeṣika, passing through the dualism of Sāṁkhya Yoga and the activistic pluralism of the Pūrva Mīmāṁsā, culminate in the non-dualistic theory of the Advaita Vedānta of Śaṁkarācārya, which presents the highest logical, speculative, intellectual and critical acumen ever exhibited by a philosopher in the world. The non-dualism of Śaṁkara is unquestionably one branch of the system of Vedānta, which includes the Viśiṣṭhādvaita, the qualified monism of Ramāṇuja and the other Vedāntic schools of Madhvācārya, Vallabhācārya, Nimbārkācārya, and so on. But we shall deal with the ethical aspect of the Advaita system of Śaṁkara here for special reasons. First, the non-dualism of Śaṁkara is the most logical and authoritative exposition of the philosophy of the Vedānta, which is the quintessence of the universal statements, or Mahāvākyas, of the Upaniṣads, as explained and synthesized in the Brahma Sūtra of Bādarāyaṇa, which is the seed and the source of the Vedānta system.

Second, there is a mistaken notion prevalent among some scholars that Uttaramīmāṁsā or Vedānta is directly opposed to Purvamīmāṁsā, because the former emphasizes the futility of Dharma as the means of the attainment of Mokṣa, and this notion has been supported with reference to quotations from Śaṁkara's Advaita Vedānta. Since we have pointed out in the last chapter that Purvamīmāṁsā (activism) is not opposed to Uttarmīmāṁsā (non-dualism), it is incumbent upon us to throw more light on this problem with reference to the non-dualistic ethics of Śaṁkara.

Third, Karma Kānda, the activistic aspect of the Vedic philosophy, is based on the acceptance of diversity, and the non-dualism of the Advaita Vedānta is the outcome of the acceptance of unity as the basic reality. If the Vedas expound 'unity in diversity', the essence of Indian ethics must also lie in this truth. It is possible to understand this by a thorough analysis of the non-dualistic ethics of Śaṁkara's Vedānta, soon after the study of the ethics of Karma Mīmāṁsā or Purvamīmāṁsā with its pluralistic background.

Lastly it should be pointed out that the schools of Vedānta other than Advaita virtually accept the ethical view of the Bhagavadgītā, so I have purposely devoted one chapter to the ethics of Bhagavadgītā after the discussion of the ethics of Saṁkara's Vedānta.

The Interdependence of Mīmāṁsā and Vedānta

It is universally agreed that Mīmāṁsā and Vedānta are the direct continuation of the Vedic philosophy of action and reflection, of ritualism (based on the Vijñāna, special knowledge) and self-realization (based on Jñāna, universal knowledge). Thus both systems are two parts of the one whole, two expositions and interpretations of the same thought and culture. As we have said and shall see again, the basic concept of Indian philosophy is Dharma, which is an ethico-metaphysical concept, and which ultimately aims at spiritual perfection (Mokṣa). But in order to avoid the misunderstanding according to which liberation is understood to be the repudiation of social, moral and practical life, it is essential to lay equal emphasis on the ethical as well as the spiritual or metaphysical aspects of Dharma. The ethical aspect of Dharma is embodied in the Mīmāṁsā, but this does not mean that Mīmāṁsā overlooks its spiritual value. On the contrary, to enhance the spiritual or metaphysical importance of Dharma, it emphasizes that the ethical aspect of Dharma also leads to liberation. Similarly when Vedānta, especially the Advaita Vedānta, lays emphasis on the spiritual aspect of Dharma and subordinates actions to knowledge of the Ultimate Reality, it does not spurn its ethical value. Śaṁkara himself was a most active personality and was not antagonistic to Karma Kānda. He admits that Karma (action) when performed without self interest leads to Ātma Śuddhi and to the well-being of humanity as a whole. We shall return to this point in the sequel. The purpose of mentioning this fact here is that knowledge of the Ultimate Reality is not opposed to action performed according to the behests of the Veda. On the contrary, the methodology advocated by Mīmāṁsā is equally useful for the aspirant of liberation. This importance of Mīmāṁsā has been nicely expressed by a well-known writer in the following manner:

'The main subject-matter of Pūrvamīmāṁsā, as also of Uttara Mīmāṁsā or Vedānta, is the same, i.e., the means of knowing Dharma, and through that, Truth. The Pūrvamīmāṁsā performs the preliminary function of establishing the conclusion that the Veda provides the only source from which the right knowledge of Dharma can be derived and of showing how to understand the exact meaning of the Vedic texts bearing upon such knowledge. The idea that it deals with the Karma Kānda is due to the fact that all the examples that the Pūrvamīmāṁsā uses for elucidating its methodology are taken from the ritualistic performances. . . . These performances also constitute the Dharma of man; indeed the ordinary man is more nearly concerned with these performances than with the far subtler methodology of meditation and the rest needed for the obtaining of Jñāna, pure knowledge of soul or self. But the methodology evolved by the Pūrvamīmāṁsā is as useful in the knowledge of rites and sacrifices as in that of the self.'[1]

We should not forget that the authority of the Veda is accepted both by Mīmāṁsā and Vedānta, and that the propounders of these systems did not aim at splitting Indian philosophy. Not only these two systems but all the orthodox systems of Indian philosophy present to us a harmonious whole. It would not be out of place here to mention that any sharp distinction between the various schools of Indian philosophy was not recognized by the ancient Indian thinkers. This fact shows that there is no conflict between the schools of Indian philosophy and much less so between the Mīmāṁsā and the Vedānta. Dwelling upon this fact Dr G. N. Jha writes:

'We thus see that in no work, except one, which provides a comprehensive view of our philosophical systems, do we find the name "Ṣaṭ—darṣana", "six systems", used in its definitely and specifically stereotyped connotation that has been attributed to it, as standing for the six systems known to us . . . The old

[1] G. N. Jha, *Śaṁkara Vedānta*, pp. 17–18.

division of Philosophy appears to have been into the two broad classes of "Nyāya" and "Mīmāṁsā", as mentioned by Yajña-valka:—Where the term "Nyāya" stands for Reasoning and "Mīmāṁsā" for Investigation, Deliberation.'[1]

It is evident from these remarks that all philosophy, whether orthodox or heterodox, whether Indian or Western, can be summed up in Reasoning and Investigation. Reasoning leads to the recognition of the oneness of the universe, and investigation brings us face to face with the plurality of the spatio-temporal world. At least in India, philosophy synthesizes science and metaphysics, morality and self-realization, and material progress and spiritual advancement. The opposition between Karma Mīmāṁsā and Vedānta, if there is any at present, is due neither to the aim and purpose of these systems nor due to Śaṁkara himself, but due to misunderstandings that crept into Indian philosophy by writers who succeeded Śamkarācārya. We have evidence to prove that earlier than Śaṁkara, Mīmāṁsā and Vedānta were considered complementary. A very important work entitled 'Brahma Siddhi', perhaps the oldest systematic exposition of the Vedānta, provides us with such evidence. A dispassionate study of this rare and little-known work of the great thinker Maṇḍana Miśra, who propounded Jñāna Karma Samuccayavāda, the theory of the synthesis of knowledge and action, proves that Vedānta does not repudiate the utility of rites and sactifices. We should not forget that the synthesis of knowledge and action has been expressed and advocated in Indian philosophy from the time of Manu, and that the sole purpose of the Vedic ideology, whether expressed in the Brāhmaṇas, Upaniṣads, or the Bhagavadgītā, is the synthesis of Jñāna and Karma, which accommodates both spiritualism and secularism.

Maṇḍana Miśra held that at first the aspirant realizes the true nature of the Ātman (self) through meditation of the Vedic utterances (Sabda), which are certain and indubitable. But this realization does not make the individual shake off all the illusory notions that have clung to him during various incarnations. In order to get rid of all the illusion-producing Karmas, mere knowledge from Śruti (Sravaṇa) is not enough, hence continued contemplation of the Ultimate Truth is advocated as the next

[1] G. N. Jha, *Śaṁkara Vedānta,* p. 10.

step. According to Maṇḍana Miśra, repeated contemplation (Manana) is aided by the repetition of the sacrifices performed in accordance with the injunctions of the Vedas. There is no doubt that the direct cause of true knowledge is contemplation, but the Vedānta also holds that the revelation of this knowledge is expedited by the performance of virtuous acts (Dharma), as explained in the Vedas. The sacrifices and charitable acts advocated in the Vedas are undoubtedly great aids. This view of Maṇḍana Miśra has been summed by Dr G. N. Jha in the following manner: 'Just as when a man has got to go from one place to another, though it is possible for him to reach the place on foot, yet for accomplishing the journey with greater ease, he has recourse to a conveyance; in the same manner though repeated contemplation itself may bring about the desired end of man, his course is made easier by the performance of such acts as sacrifices and charities. In this sense even a man who has attained Brahma—knowledge may be said to need certain other aids in the shape of Actions.'[1]

Thus hearing the sacred text of the Vedas from the preceptor (Sravana), repeated meditation aided by the performance of Dharma (Manan), and direct self-realization (Nididhyāsana) as explained by Maṇḍana Miśra, brings about the synthesis of the Pūrva Mīmāṁsā (or Karma Mīmāṁsā) and Uttara Mīmāṁsā or Jñāna Mīmāṁsā (Vedānta). The knowledge of Brahman which precedes self-realization requires action (performed in keeping with the moral ideal) to attain the state of self-realization. This ethical action, or 'duty for the sake of duty', is described and accepted by Śaṁkara as action performed without any mundane motive (Niṣkāma), and he holds that such disinterested action leads to self-purification (Ātma Śuddhi). This fact has been neglected by writers who have stressed only the apparent points of difference between Vedānta and Mīmāṁsā.

Moreover the acceptance of gradual liberation (Krama Mukti) which is universal in Indian philosophy, and has been described and explained in the Upaniṣads and in Mīmāṁsā, supports our contention of the interdependence of action and knowledge. Maṇḍana Miśra pointed out that the various paths suggested in the Upaniṣads for the attainment of self-realization indicate acceptance of the theory of the gradual march towards liberation. The highest state attained by the aspirant according

[1] G. N. Jha, *Śaṁkara Vedānta*, p. 28.

to the Upaniṣads is the region of Brahmā-Prajāpati, where he attains the highest knowledge of the pure self. The Upaniṣads also mention that a person who does not reach the highest region of Brahmā-Prajāpati but instead attains the regions of the 'Sun or the Moon',—what happens is, that while these regions continue to exist, the soul, having experienced the joys of these regions, returns to the earth where it is reborn. No so the man who reaches the region of Brahmā-Prajāpati.[1] It is noteworthy here that Maṇḍana Miśra appears to have in his mind the Vedic theory of the universe according to which, the earth, the moon, the sun, the galactic centre (Parameṣthī), and Svayaṁbhu Prajāpati, the cosmic centre, are regarded as ascending orders of the manifested universe based on the one Unmanifested Reality. We should not forget that the word used is 'Brahmā-Prajāpati', which is equivalent to Svayambhu Prajāpati, or self-manifested Prajāpati. When the soul returns from the lunar and the solar levels it performs virtuous actions (Dharma); later on it is able to ascend to the higher level of Parameṣthi and, last of all, to that of the Svayambhu Prajāpati. As we have already stated, the cosmic centre is the manifestation of the unmanifested Prajāpati, and the dissolution of the cosmic centre is yet possible. When the Upaniṣads state that the soul, having once attained Brahmā-Prajāpati, does not return, they mean that it remains in the state of self-realization as long as the manifested centre of the cosmos, i.e. Brahmā Prajāpati, is not dissolved. This view of ours is supported by Dr G. N. Jha who presents the idea of Maṇḍana Miśra with regard to the Upaniṣadic notion of 'not returning' in the following words: 'In this latter region the soul continues to remain until that region itself falls into dissolution. This is what is meant by the man's "not returning" to rebirth.'[2]

This interpretation is quite in keeping with the view that we have been trying to elucidate, and according to which there is no antagonism between Jñāna, knowledge of the Supreme Reality, and Vijñāna, knowledge of the pluralistic manifestation of that reality. The region of Brahmā-Prajāpati is the region of transcendence so far as the lower regions of 'Parameṣthī', the sun, the moon, and the earth are concerned. But with reference to Prajāpati itself, of which it is just a branch, it remains relative,

[1] G. N. Jha, *Śaṁkara Vedānta*, pp. 29–30.
[2] *Ibid.*, p. 130.

and is hence a region of activity of the soul, though not of the body, mind or intellect. The higher state of self-realization is therefore gradually attainable through physical, mental and intellectual activity—the acceptance of the pluralistic nature of the spatio-temporal world and also the activistic philosophy of differentiated behaviour (Viṣama Varttana) based on the transcendental metaphysics of intuitive oneness (Sama Darśana). The Vedas have undoubtedly propounded both these views, which later on were wrongly supposed to be antagonistic to each other due to a travesty of circumstances created by the negligence of scholars towards Brāhmaṇic literature.

The interrelation of the Mīmāṁsā and the Advaita Vedānta ought to be recognized both from the theoretical and practical points of view. It does not contradict the basic notion of the Vedānta or that of the Mīmāṁsā. That is why I have tried to support the view of Maṇḍana Miśra. Before we proceed with the ethical implications of Śaṁkara's Vedānta, I would like to sum up the interrelation of these two schools with the following quotation from Dr Jha's *Śaṁkara Vedānta:*

'Thus according to this view, the knowledge derived and perfected by means of meditation and other forms of Upānsana is higher than that derived only from the Vedānta texts. This idea of the older Vedānta would appear to be supported by the order in which we find Shravaṇa, Manana and the rest mentioned in the well-known texts: where "Shravaṇa", standing for verbal knowledge, comes first and is followed by contemplation, leading to final direct self-realization.'[1]

The Aim of the Advaita Vedānta

From the preceding discussion it is quite evident that the aim of the Vedānta, like that of the Mīmāṁsā, is the attainment of the state of self-realization, which brings about Jivanmukti, or a here and now state of spiritual existence, and Videh-mukti, or final liberation hereafter. It goes without saying that the non-dualism of Śaṁkara has a moral and spiritual basis and a moral and spiritual aim. Unjust critics have misunderstood the purpose of his philosophy, and have therefore drawn wrong conclusions from transcendental metaphysics. Not only does his school

[1] G. N. Jha, *Śaṁkara Vedānta*, p. 1.

of pure non-dualism refute the nihilistic metaphysics of the Buddhistic school, but it emphasizes the need of conviction in spiritual values and a firm faith in the existence of God, who from the practical and pragmatic point of view is the creator, the sustainer, and the destroyer of the universe, and at the same time is Satyam, Jñānam, Anantam (truth, knowledge and infinity) from the transcendental (Pārmārthika) point of view. The moment we overlook the aim of Śaṁkara's philosophy we are bound to misconstrue it as a pessimism and an escapism. Such a biased view has been responsible for various allegations against this great and unique philosopher, moralist and mystic who is at once highly intellectual in his analysis, practical in his outlook, firm in his faith, and open to conviction and reason in his philosophical views. Refuting the charge of pessimism, asceticism, and illusionism against Śaṁkara, Dr V. H. Date has remarked:

'The Vedānta of Śaṁkara stands for courage and strength of character, for optimism and hope, for a life which being in touch with the Real, is full of activity, contemplation, joy, knowledge, contentment and service to mankind. . . . Disinterested and altruistic action, meditation, prayer and consequent attainment to Godhood, or the Absolute through the grace of God, are but the different aspects of this ethico-spiritual discipline. Jñāna, then, means the realization of Brahman and not merely an intellectual understanding about it.'[1]

If we study Śaṁkara's system carefully and dispassionately we shall conclude that he is neither an agnostic metaphysically nor a pessimist ethically. There is no doubt that his ethics is inseparably connected with his metaphysics and cannot be rightly understood without the right perspective of the latter. Hence a word about his metaphysical notion of Maya and the world is not only necessary but unavoidable before we proceed with the ethical aspect of his philosophy. Apart from the evidence from his commentaries on the Brahma Sūtra, the Bhagavadgītā, and the Upaniṣads, the very fact that Śaṁkara ardently worked throughout his short span of life to expel Buddhistic nihilism (Śunyavada) from philosophy and Buddhistic pessimistic ethics from Indian life is enough to prove that his

[1] V. H. Date, *Vedānta Explained*, Vol. II, pp. 447–8.

aim of propounding the Advaita Vedānta was ethical and spiritual.

Śaṁkara's Notion of Māyā and the World

At the outset I would like to point out that nowhere in his commentaries has Śaṁkara made any statement that might lead us to conclude that the world is unreal. On the contrary, his aim from beginning to end has been to remove the misunderstanding that the world is unreal and liberation (or Nirvāṇa, as the Buddhists term it) is non-existence, or Sūnya. He has drawn our attention to the two Mahāvākyas (great statements of the Upaniṣads) which appear to be contradictory but are really complementary and coherent. These two Mahāvākyas are 'Brahman satyam jaganmithyā', i.e. The Absolute is real and the world is illusory; and 'Sarvam khalvidam Brahman', i.e. Everything that exists is the Absolute.

The unitiated may rightly object to accepting both statements as valid simultaneously. But analysis and logical explanation of these statements removes the doubt. The first statement refers to the transcendental aspect of Brahman, whereas the second one refers to its immanent aspect. The Upaniṣads clearly state that God or Brahman is the immanent cause, source, and the goal of the cosmos. All things spring from Brahman, they thrive on Brahman, and ultimately merge into Brahman. In this sense Brahman is the all pervasive, omniscient, omnipresent and omnipotent, invisible basis and background of the entire visible universe. It is both the material as well as the efficient cause of the cosmic creation. The spatio-temporal world is rooted in Brahman, and, as such, it must be Brahman in its ultimate analysis. The same existence, consciousness and bliss (Saccidānanda) which sleeps in the non-living and dreams in the vegetable kingdom, becomes conscious in animals, and attains self-consciousness in man.

But at the same time, this infinite cause of the finite universe, the unmoved mover of its motion, the invisible basis of the visible universe, the impersonal and objective spiritual consciousness of the personal and subjective minds (Jivas), cannot be said to be coterminus with the universe, however vast and extended it may be. In order to guard the aspirant against this error, the Upaniṣads state that Brahman is neither time nor space; neither cause nor effect; neither motion nor rest; neither light nor darkness; neither heat nor cold; neither pleasure nor pain, in short, not limited by any qualities whatsoever. It cannot be seen, although it is the very cause of our seeing; it cannot be heard, although it is the very cause of our hearing; it cannot be touched, although it is the very cause of our actual knowledge; it cannot be tasted, although it is the very cause of our taste; and it cannot be smelled, though it is the very cause of the olfactory sensation.

This negativistic explanation of the immanent and transcendent reality is indicative of the unique nature of Brahman, which cannot be reduced to verbal expression, but which, at the same time, is a real, positive existence, consciousness and bliss so far as its experiential aspect is concerned, and which is truth knowledge and infinity so far as its essential nature (Svarūpa Lakṣaṇa) is concerned. In order to banish mere scepticism and mere nihilism, the Upaniṣads in their pithy dialogues identify this immanent and transcendent objective Brahman with the subjective Ātman, which is the doer, seer, enjoyer, and experiencer, and the existence of which, as such, automatically becomes indubitable and self-evident. This attempt of the Upaniṣads, which is expressed in the oft-repeated and popularly accepted universal statement, 'Tat, tvam asi' (that thou art), has a special significance in this context and requires a detailed discussion. In my opinion this statement is the keynote of Śaṁkara's theory of Māyā and his notion of the relative reality of the world based on that theory.

'That thou art', implies the identity of objective reality and the subjective self on the one hand, and the influence of Avidyā (illusion-producing-ignorance) of the aspirant on the other. Had the aspirant been aware of the identity of Ātman and Brahman, this statement would have been gratuitous and meaningless. The identity of the self and Brahman is already there as an accomplished fact. Knowledge of it is something like the discovery of a necklace round the neck of the wearer which she has lost sight of due to forgetfulness. But the wearer being unmindful of the presence of the necklace would not be able to discover it and confess her forgetfulness unless someone else reminds her of it. In like manner the statement, 'That thou art', is uttered by the instructor, and the ignorance of the aspirant is suddenly dispelled. It would not be out of place here, to refer to this dramatic act of self-realization as it is described in the Chāndogya Upaniṣad.

Uddālaka Aruṇī, a learned Brahmaṇa, finds that his son, Śvetaketu, is arrogant after returning from his preceptor on the completion of his education. He therefore feels that his son is unaware of the knowledge of Brahman and the identity of the same with the Ātman. When he is convinced of his son's ignorance he takes the responsibility of imparting the knowledge of the ultimate Reality to his son. He first of all explains to Śvetaketu that Brahman is the all-pervasive, immanent cause of the cosmos and that it is infinite, immutable, unchanging, basic reality, untouched by the changing, moving, evolving, physical, biological and mental processes, which go on in the world and in the individual. While referring to the transcendental nature of Brahman, Uddālaka uses negative terms, and lest his son misconceive Brahman to be a non-entity he suddenly and dramatically identifies that very Brahman with the Ātman of his son, Śvetaketu. M. Hiriyanna mentions this episode of the Chāndogya Upaniṣad in the following passage: 'Uddālaka begins by postulating an Ultimate entity, which is to be regarded as mental or spiritual, because it is stated to have thought (Aiksata) and which he terms Sat, or Being. He then proceeds to describe how the whole universe is a manifestation of it . . . What is made out by this is that the spiritual entity postulated in the beginning is all comprehensive and that whatever is, has sprung from it. Then suddenly and with dramatic swiftness, the original Sat is identified with the self of Śvetaketu: "Tat tvam asi, Śvetaketu." The purpose of the identification is obviously to bring home to the mind of Śvetaketu the undoubted reality of the postulated source of the universe.'[1] There is no doubt that the notion of one's own self does not require any external proof, and is therefore indubitable and self-evident. Hence the observation that Uddālaka compares the certitude of the objective Brahman with the certitude of the subjective Ātman is justified. It should be remembered that Uddālaka Aruṇi himself has realized the existence of Brahman, whereas the young Śvetaketu is a novice in the science of spirit. Hence the identification of Brahman with the self of Śvetaketu is of great aid in convincing the son of the real existence of the objective, immanent and transcendent Brahman. I submit that the father, who has self-

[1] M. Hiriyanna, *Outlines of Indian Philosophy*, pp. 58–9.

realization, also wants to banish the ignorance of Śvetaketu, who has so far been taking his physical, biological, mental or intellectual self to be the Ātman. It is here that the concept of Avidyā or Māyā is required to give intellectual support to the existence of an unchanging and immutable reality, behind the changing, evolving and mutable world process. How can the physical, mental and intellectual self of Śvetaketu be Brahman? Śvetaketu is aware of his being limited, spatio-temporal, individual person. Uddālaka has already attained self-realization and he makes an attempt to awaken the immortality and immutability hidden in the self of Śvetaketu.

Such awakening of the spiritual consciousness was possible because of the mutual personal contact of the preceptor and the pupil during the Upaniṣadic period. But during Śaṁkara's period the forest universities (Aśram) that imparted Ātma-vidyā ceased to exist. It was the age of debate and intellectual tournament between the highly learned philosophers and thinkers. Hence, Ṣaṁkara hit upon the concept of Māyā or Avidyā, which could solve the riddle of the reality of the world and also of the infinite aspect of the finite and the limited self. Śaṁkara therefore regards Māyā as the illusion-producing power of Brahman or God, which can be compared to the power of a magician who makes one coin appear as many. As long as the effect of the illusion of the magician lasts the spectators continue to see many coins instead of one. But a person who comes to know the trick of the magician sees one coin only. If the magician withdraws his 'power', the layman would also come to see that the coin is one and not many. Similarly, Māyā makes a man perceive the world as many instead of as one. The one comos appears transformed as a manifold universe, just as a snake is the transformation of a rope into a snake when we experience an illusion (Bhrama). Just as the snake is a superimposition (Vivarta) on the rope, which is behind it, similarly the manyness of the world is superimposition (Vivarta) on the oneness of Brahman behind the world. That is why Śaṁkara's view is known as Vivartavāda (illusionism) as opposed to Rāmānuja's view of the world as a real transformation like the change of milk into curds. Rāmānuja's view, therefore, is an evolutionism (Parināmavāda) whereas Śaṁkara's view is Vivartavāda (illusionism). The world is real because it is rooted in Brahman, just as the snake of an illusion is real because it is rooted in the rope, which is real.

What Śaṁkara tries to point out is that the world as the Vivarta of Brahman is neither absolutely real because it is just a Vivarta nor is it absolutely unreal because it is not imaginary like the horns of a hare or like the son of a barren woman. It is therefore relatively real. As compared with the imaginary entities like the horns of a hare it is real, but as compared with the Absolute Reality of Brahman it turns out to be as false as the snake appears to be false when the man under the illusion becomes conscious of the underlying reality of the rope. Māyā according to Śaṁkara has the twofold function of concealing the reality (Avaraṇa) from our view, and of distorting (Vikṣepa) the reality so that it may appear to be what it is actually not. 'Sarvam khalvidam Brahman' is appropriate because even the illusion of the snake is real, as the cause of its appearance is the real rope. The manyness of the universe is real because it is the distortion (Vikṣepa) of the one Brahman. 'Brahman satyam, jaganmithyā' is also appropriate because the manyness of the world disappears the moment the effect of Māyā disappears and knowledge of the Brahman dawns upon the perceiver, just as the snake disappears the moment the effect of ignorance is over and knowledge of the underlying rope dawns forth. Thus the world is neither absolutely unreal nor absolutely real, but it is relatively real.

Thus Śaṁkara's notion of Māyā reconciles the statement, 'Everything is Brahman' and 'The Brahman is true and the world is illusory', on the one hand, and gives an explanation of the identity of Ātman (self) and Brahman (universal self), on the other. The gist of Śaṁkara's metaphysics is that the Brahman combined with Māyā is the manifold world, and the same Brahman under the influence of Avidyā is Ātman, or the individual self. The empirical world, which is the objective appearance of the Absolute, and the empirical self (Jiva), which is the subjective experience of the Absolute, are both identical with Brahman. They are both the modes or transformations of the same Ultimate Reality; they originate from it, and they must ultimately merge into it. Avidyā or Māyā alone is the cause of the limitation of the world and also of the empirical self. Ethics is concerned with the resurrection of the empirical self as it aims at bringing the pristine spiritual glory back to the self. The self, which is potentially infinite and essentially consciousness, existence and bliss, suffers from the afflictions of the world, simply because it has lost sight of the spiritual potentiality in it on account of Avidyā (ignorance), which conceals and distorts the basic reality of Brahman residing in the innermost recess of the empirical self. It is therefore evident that the knowledge of this infinite potentiality, the awareness of the latent absoluteness and recognition of the accomplished fact of spiritual perfection, would lead to the attainment of Mokṣa, which, according to Advaita Vedānta, consists in the merger of the self (Ātman) with Brahman. But before the merger, which takes place after the annihilation of the physical body, the individual does attain Jīvanmukti, even when the self continues as mortal. This much acquaintance with the ethical implications of Śaṁkara's theory of Māyā, which is the pivot of the Advaita metaphysics, is sufficient for our purpose of entering upon the study of the ethics of this system.

The Ethics of Śaṁkara

In order to do full justice to the ethical views of Śaṁkara, it is necessary for us to be constantly mindful of his metaphysical views as expressed above, because his ethics as well as his religion are permeated with his metaphysical standpoint. We have noted that the nature of the world according to Śaṁkara is real from the empirical or Vyāvahārika point of view, and unreal from the transcendental or Pārmārthikā point of view. In like manner, from the empirical point of view God or Brahman is immanent, the physical as well as the efficient cause of the creation, preservation, and destruction of the universe, and it is Satyam, Jñānam, Anantam (truth, knowledge and infinity) without any attributes (Nirguna Brahman) from the transcendental point of view. Similarly, self or Ātman is the empirical, limited, individual personality (Jīva), which experiences the manyness of the world and the plurality of selves (Jīvas) from the Vyāvahārika (empirical) point of view; and the same self Ātman, is the spiritual, infinite, universal Brahman from the transcendental point of view. We have already discussed in the last chapter how man is both a specialized, particularized individual who must recognize plurality in his behaviour from the scientific (Vaijnanika) point of view, and is also the universal, non-dualistic self who must experience unitive knowledge (Samadarśana) from the intuitive (Jñānatmaka) or transcendental point of view. My contention is that Śaṁkara's view of metaphysics and ethics is quite in keeping with our thesis that man is the highest reality; that his essential characteristic is that he can and should behave in accordance with the realistic and the pluralistic nature of the world; and that he can and should realize (see) the underlying (spiritual) unity of the visible pluralistic universe. The divorce between realism and mysticism, between pluralism and monism, and between pragmatism and spiritualism, the sole cause of the partial and unbalanced development of human personality, is not committed either by the Vedas, by the Mīmāṁsā, or by the Advaita Vedānta of Śaṁkara.

The moment we lose sight of this synthetic and integrated aspect of Indian philosophy we misunderstand, misinterpret and misrepresent it. Let us therefore be impartial in our interpretation of the ethics of Śaṁkara. Such impartiality will consist in keeping in view the difference between the empirical and the transcendental points of view, a distinction which has been recognized right from the time of the Vedas. A word of caution about overlooking this distinction appears necessary here particularly because precisely this fallacy has been responsible for the gross misunderstanding, misinterpretation and misrepresentation of the Vedic thought and culture.

The Vedic hymns give explanations of the constitution and function of nature from three points of view, namely, (1) The perceptual point of view, based on the common man's perception of nature (Driṣti Mūlā Sriṣṭi); (2) the empirical or scientific point of view, based on the relative stability of the sun as the centre of the solar system (Sthiti Mūla Sriṣṭi); and (3) the transcendental point of view, based on the all-pervasiveness and pure, all-pervasive stability of the Prajāpati (Sriṣṭi Mūlā Sriṣṭi). From the perceptual point of view, the viewpoint of the man on the street, who has nothing to do with the scientific explanation of natural phenomena, the earth is believed to be stationary and the sun is believed to be in motion from east to west. From the scientific (Vaijñānika) point of view, the sun is a fixed centre around which the earth and the other planets revolve. From the transcendental point of view the solar systems, including suns and galactic systems, are all revolving around Svayambhu Prajāpati, the centre of centres. Thus when Śaṁkara adopts two points of view, i.e. the empirical or scientific Vyāvahārika point of view, and the transcendental (Pārmārthika) point of view in explaining the nature of the world, self and God, he does not make a departure from the Vedic style. On the contrary, he points out that only the layman's point of view, being unscientific, is unsound and unimportant, where the scientific as well as the transcendental points of view have an equal value for philosophy. When Śaṁkara lays down the rules of conduct he gives equal weight to the ethical duties which are necessary for material progress (Abhyudaya) of the individual and of society, and to spiritual duty necessary for the attainment of Mokṣa. Most scholars of Indian philosophy overlook Śaṁkara's empirical ethics and mistake him as anti-ethical and anti-social so far as the social and individual development of life is concerned. We shall, however, first tackle Śaṁkara's honest views about the spiritual aspect of human life, and later discuss his views about the practical application of morality to life.

Mokṣa is the supreme good and its attainment means the shedding of the individual personality, the merger of Ātman in Brahman, eternal consciousness, eternal existence and eternal bliss. Śaṁkara is emphatic that the 'knowledge' of Brahman, which amounts to self-realization, is the sole gateway to Mokṣa. Dr Radhakrishnan refers to Mokṣa as the supreme good accepted by Śaṁkara as follows:

'To realize Brahman is the end of all activities . . . Brahmatmaikatva, or the realization of the identity with the infinite reality, is the final end of life . . . and the only supreme value. Until it is reached the finite soul is at unrest with itself. . . The only object that can give us permanent satisfaction is the experience of Brahman (Brahmānubhava). It is the supreme state of joy and peace and the perfection of individual development.'[1]

The word Brahmānubhava, which means the experience of Brahman, is worth noting carefully. Śaṁkara uses this term frequently, thereby indicating that self-realization is not merely a concept or an ideal beyond the empirical pale, but is rather and more exactly an actual experience which the individual undergoes. This fact also explains the acceptance of Jīvanmukti by Śaṁkara. Mokṣa, therefore, is ethico-spiritual and is neither

[1] S. Radhakrishnan, *Indian Philosophy*, Vol. II, p. 613.

merely ethical nor merely spiritual or metaphysical. Since it has to be achieved here and now, it is evident that the effort to achieve it is an ethical effort. Similarly it is a state free from 'relative' experience and, as such, it is a unique spiritual existence by the attainment of which the individual transcends his empirical level of consciousness. Even here Śaṁkara admits the synthesis of the empirical and the transcendental, or the ethical and the metaphysical aspects of life.

The longing for intuitive knowledge of Brahman is the starting point of Śaṁkara's commentary on the Brahmasūtra. The very first Sūtra says 'Athāto Brahman Jijnasa', i.e. 'Now therefore the desire to know the Brahman'. We should not overlook the significance of the word 'now'. It signifies that the knowledge of Brahman is a consequent event, which ought to have been produced by some other event. Śaṁkara explains that the antecedent conditions without which no one is authorized to enter upon the knowledge of Brahman, are four. The first prerequisite for a spiritual aspirant is designated 'Sadasad Viveka', i.e. discrimination between the permanent and the impermanent nature of things. The second qualification is freedom from attachment to sensual pleasures whether here in the material world or hereafter. The third qualification is the cultivation of virtues like peace of mind, self-control, endurance, alertness and faith (Sraddhā). The fourth prerequisite of an aspirant is a strong desire, or yearning for Mokṣa. This explanation of Śaṁkara is usually overlooked by those who wrongly believe that he derides or derogates action or morality in comparison with the knowledge of Brahman. The very fact that discrimination (wisdom), self-devotion, self-control and desire to attain Mokṣa are accepted as the qualifications of the students of the Vedānta is enough to prove how a virtuous life is necessary for the seeker of the ultimate reality. Incidentally, these four prerequisites correspond to the four cardinal virtues advocated by the ancient Greek philosophers, wisdom, justice, temperance and courage.

To be able to discriminate, to manifest discretion concerning what is abiding and what is not abiding is evidence of great wisdom in man. The word Viveka, which literally stands for discretion, is purposely used by Śaṁkara because a person without discretion is not fit to attain the highest knowledge (Jñāna), having attained which nothing else remains to be known. All the mystics in India have remarked the need of wisdom for following the spiritual path. But the difference between mysticism and non-dualism lies in the fact that whereas the mystics consider discretion the result of the grace of God which comes to the man who surrenders himself entirely to the Divine Will, the non-dualist (Advaitavādin) believes that wisdom precedes not only faith, but even the spirit of renunciation and the ethical virtues. Mystics like Tulsi Das would assert:

Binu satsaṅga viveka nà hoū,
Hari kṛipā binu sulabha na soū[1]

'Discretion is not possible without the company of good people, and the company of good people is not possible without the grace of God.'

Śaṁkara's viewpoint is intellectual and hence ethical, for ethics and virtue, according to the Vedic philosophy, are the offshoots of, as well as the goals or the ideal of intellect. A rationalist and a dialectical thinker, Śaṁkara elevates intellect, and considers faith the consequence of reason, whereas the mystics subordinate reason to faith.

When a person first realizes that the soul is permanent and body and mind are transitory; that the spiritual aspect of human personality is abiding; that physical as well as mental aspects are non-abiding, only then does he realize that sensual enjoyments though soothing and pleasing are temporary and ultimately painful. Hence his intellect revolts against the unlicensed satisfaction of sensual desires, and compels the individual to do justice to himself by not being misled by temporary pleasures whether in the mundane world or in heaven. This virtue of justice to oneself is responsible for detachment and the spirit of renunciation and self-devotion. Thus the second qualification of the aspirant is based on the virtue of justice, which means that neither the blind satisfaction of desires nor the suppression of desires, but the harmonization of desires should be taken to be the ideal of an aspirant.

The third qualification, which enjoins upon the seeker of Mokṣa, the cultivation of good habits of peace of mind, self-control, alertness and faith can be easily summed up as temperance, if we adopt the Western terminology of virtues pro-

[1] *Tulsi Rāmāyana*, 1st Canto.

pounded by Plato and Aristotle. There can be no peace of mind without the power of toleration, forbearance and endurance; and all this is possible only when a person has self-control and leads the life of temperance and moderation. This very attitude of balance and equilibrium brings faith and conviction in the mind of the aspirant, and conviction alone leads the individual to become courageous enough to sacrifice transitory pleasures and enjoyments for the sake of the eternal bliss and peace. Thus the third qualification of the aspirant awakens in him the fourth one, the longing for eternal existence, which we can compare with the golden mean of courage. Thus the four qualifications of the new entrant of the Advaita Vedānta, as explained by Śaṁkara, can be favourably compared to the four cardinal virtues of wisdom (prudence), justice, temperance and courage respectively.

This analysis of Śaṁkara's commentary on the very first aphorism (Sutra) of the Vedānta Sūtra is the proof of the ethical attitude of Śaṁkara with regard to the knowledge of Brahman. Śaṁkara did not only approve the ethical virtues and moral conduct, but he regarded morality to be the unavoidable antecedent of the knowledge of Brahman. Moreover we should not forget that Śamkara calls self-realization Brahmānubhava, the spiritual experience, and not merely a theoretical knowledge of the Absolute. The Upaniṣads clearly state that the 'knower of Brahman becomes verily the Brahman itself' (Brahmavit Bramaiva bhavati). This means that the goal of the Vedānta is not mere knowledge, but a concrete state of existence in which the knower and the known, the subject and the object, the cognizer and the cognition, the good person and the goodness, merge into one complete whole—the Absolute truth, knowledge and infinity. The use of the word Brahmānubhava (spiritual experience) is the highest experience and 'the highest reality' ever cognized by man. This explains why he says at the end that he bows down to the experience of self-realization (Atmānubhūtaye Namah). His preference to the experience of the self over formal worship and formal ethical adherence (Karma Kānda) shows his innermost urge towards the ethical and the moral regeneration of man which, according to him, is the only prerequisite for the uplift of the fallen humanity and the ascent of the soul to the loftiest heights of Mokṣa. Thus the four principles to be followed by the aspirant for the knowledge of Brahman are indicative of the four ethical virtues which must be cultivated by all normal individuals.

The Need of Relative Morality

The fact remains that the stage of Jīvanmukti is the final and the ultimate stage, the last step. But this does not mean that Śaṁkara abolishes the stages preceding the final one. When he draws our attention to the transcendental level of spiritual existence, he wants us to know that, as compared with the Absolute, relative morality has no significance, for the individual at this (highest) level has already practised and surpassed relative morality. But he emphasizes again and again the need of practical morality, which is the means of the attainment of the highest stage. Dr G. N. Jha refers to this significance of the practical morality in Śaṁkara by quoting Sūtra 2.1.14 from the commentary of the great Ācārya as follows:

'All worldly activities are practically real until oneness with Brahman has been realized; just as all dream-activity is real so long as the dream lasts. So long as the true unity of the self has not been realized, it is not right for any one to regard as unreal all the worldly activities based upon the notions of means of cognition, objects of cognition, and results of cognition and such other things. Consequently prior to the realization of this oneness with Brahman all the worldly activities, as also the activities based upon the Vedic injunctions, are quite justified.'[1]

Śaṁkara states very clearly that it is only at the highest stage that the distinctions of the knower and the known and the doer and the act vanish, and that non-recognition of duality at the practical level would amount to foolishness. This explains why Śaṁkara time and again refers to the utility of morality and meditation (Karma and Upāsanā) for the aspirant. Since the approach to the spiritual state of eternal existence is by way of intellect, moral life, which is the only means of the intellectual development of the individual, cannot be and should not be forsaken altogether. Although Śaṁkara did overemphasize the need of knowledge (Jñāna), as compared with the performance of acts, he could not afford to be domestic in this matter. In his

[1] G. N. Jha, *Śāṁkara Vedanta*, p. 45.

commentary on Brahma Sūtra 3.1.7. he does show his tendency towards the synthesis of knowledge and action. He holds that 'Those persons, who confine themselves entirely to the performance of acts and do not turn their attention to true knowledge are ignorant of the true self. This does not apply to those persons who combine in their practice both knowledge and action'.[1]

Śaṁkara never derided the performance of sacrifice and of the rituals enjoined by the Vedas. Rather, he says that 'The performance of all acts like sacrifice and the like is dependent upon right conduct. Without right conduct, a man cannot be entitled to the performance of such acts. Even though right conduct is an end in itself attained by man and as such, has no direct bearing upon sacrifices, its influence is felt at the time of appearance of the results of those sacrifices'.[2] These remarks of Śaṁkara point out that he did not consider morality to be self-contained only, but also a means to the attainment of desirable results. He distinctly states that right conduct has both absolute as well as relative value. It has absolute value for the aspirant who performs action without any selfish attachment. But for a layman, who does not adopt the absolute value of right conduct, this morality is necessary because it brings about desirable results and leads him Mokṣaward gradually as he passes through various graduated births in an ascending order.

It is evident from the discussion so far that morality is accepted by Śaṁkara as the necessary means of attaining true knowledge of the self. The acceptance of the duties meant for different stages (Aśramas) of life further proves Śaṁkara's emphasis on the adoption of ethical life as the means for the attainment of liberation. It appears to be necessary to cite evidence to prove the acceptance of Aśrama Dharmas by Śaṁkara. Dr Jha, quoting Śaṁkara in this connexion, writes: '3.4.19. The duties laid down for the various Aśramas have to be performed as declared in Chāndogya Upaniṣad, 2.23.1. . . .'.

The same Upaniṣad speaks of man in the three earlier stages of student, householder and hermit, as going to 'pure regions', and of the remaining one 'renunciate' as becoming 'immortal'. The reason given for this is that the renunciates incur no sin

[1] G. N. Jha, *Sāṁkara Vedanta*, p. 49.
[2] *Ibid.*

by renouncing action, while people in other three stages incur sin by neglecting the duties laid down in the scriptures. 'It will not do for one to say—"I am a Renunciate, I shall renounce all duties." That would be self-deceptive, and renunciation is not for all and sundry; it is for the very few; and that also after one has passed through the other Aśramas and duly performed the duties attaching to each.'[1]

Not only is complete renunciation meant for a chosen few, but those few must also have passed through the other three stages of life meant for normal human beings. The integrated scheme of life, based on the Varnaśrama Dharmas and aiming at spiritual-realization, was accepted by Śaṁkara with the same emphasis it was given by the propounders of the other orthodox schools. Śaṁkara recognized the distinction between Samadarśana and Visamavarttana (unitive knowledge and differentiated behaviour) in the sense we have indicated in the previous chapter. The four-fold scheme of life with four chief values, the four stages for the performance of individual duties, and the four divisions of society for the fulfilment of social development was the scheme recognized and responded to by all the philosophers of ancient India, because they knew that the essence of Indian culture lay in this ethico-social and ethico-spiritual plan which aimed at the well-being of humanity. It appears that Śaṁkara had fully recognized that Vijñāna, or the scientific knowledge of the Vedas, which advocated the adoption of the Aśrama Dharmas, was conducive to Jñāna, or the intuitive knowledge of Brahman. Śaṁkara himself admitted this in the following simple statement: 'The performance of the duties of the Aśramas is needed in the bringing about of true knowledge.'[2]

Similarly in his commentary on the Upaniṣads, Śaṁkara clearly states that the path of action and the path of renunciation are to be accomplished conjointly by one and the same person. He advocates the performance of the Agnihotra sacrifice and other acts enjoined by the Vedas, and considers such performance conducive to the knowledge of Brahman. While commenting upon the Bṛhidāranyaka Upaniṣad Śaṁkara says 'In as much as knowledge and action are the means leading up to the acquiring of another body and undergoing experiences,

[1] G. N. Jha, *Śāṁkara Vedanta*, pp. 53–4.
[2] *Ibid.*, p. 57.

it is only right that one should have recourse only to such knowledge and action as are right'.[1]

What Śaṁkara has tried to make explicit is the fact that when action is performed with the knowledge of the Brahman, it brings about liberation and has absolute value. Virtues like self-control, charity, compassion, etc., are means to the attainment of true knowledge, as accepted by Śaṁkara in his commentary on the Brahma Sūtra. He also regarded these very virtues to be helpful for Abhyudaya, or prosperity, besides being of assistance in worship and meditation. In his commentary on Bṛihadārankya Upaniṣad Śaṁkara writes: 'Self-control, charity and compassion are necessary preliminaries to all forms of worship and meditation. It is only when one has acquired self-control, charity and compassion that one becomes entitled to the performance of the various forms of worship and meditation that have been set forth. These are just those actions that lead to prosperity that have to be set forth in connexion with the conditioned self.'[2] The crux of the whole problem is that ethical principles which are the outcome of intellect are conducive not only to worldly prosperity, but are also the right means of attaining true knowledge, ending in Mokṣa. Man is a peculiar combination of the material and the spiritual aspects of the same reality, but this peculiarity changes into a harmony when he connects material and the social progress with spiritual evolution through the concept of 'Dharma' or duty, which is the only connecting link between Abhyudaya, mundane prosperity, and Nihśreyasa, spiritual perfection. Man's intellect, which is at the root of his material as well as his spiritual effort, is a wonderful instrument at his disposal. It is through intellect that he brings about a reconciliation between Artha (wealth) and Kāma (fulfilment of desire) on the one hand, and Mokṣa (liberation) on the other. It is through intellect that he grasps the significance of virtues as means of social progress and also as means of self-realization. Again, it is through intellect that man can follow the ideal of Niśkāma Karma Yoga, which exhorts him to perform action without longing for its results, and to maintain equilibrium of mind. Śaṁkara is of the opinion that when we follow the principle of complete self-surrender to God, so far as the fruits of our actions are concerned we can do so most effectively when

[1] G. N. Jha, *Śāṁkara Vedanta*, p. 66.
[2] *Ibid.*, p. 67.

we have knowledge of the identity of the self, or Ātman, with Brahman.

It is evident from the discussion that in accepting the importance of duty from the social and the spiritual point of view, Śaṁkara keeps constantly alive the ultimate aim of duty, or action, and knowledge, or self-realization, but at the same time he always cautions us against the folly of neglecting the performance of actions, even when one has attained the highest state of Jivanmukti. Commenting on the sixteenth verse of the third chapter of the Bhagavadgītā Śaṁkara says:

'The upshot of this chapter is that until a man has attained true knowledge he should continue to perform actions until he has attained the capacity to enter upon the higher discipline of pure knowledge. One should even for that purpose continue to perform actions.'[1]

We should keep in mind the fact that the Advaita Vedānta accepts the theory of Karman and the transmigration of souls according to the Karman accumulated by them. The individual attains the final state of liberation after passing through various incarnations gradually, and hence the performance of duties that fall to the lot of an individual in life is regarded as the means of attaining Mokṣa. At no stage of life, not even for a minute, should a person cease to act. The attainment of true knowledge expedites the approach of the final stage. It is, therefore, not antagonistic to action but complementary to it. We shall return to the importance of selfless duty in the next chapter. Here it will suffice to say that Śaṁkara agrees with the activistic spirit of the Bhagavadgītā and Mīmāṁsā. This is evident from Śaṁkara's commentary on the thirteenth verse of the fourth discourse of the Bhagavadgītā:

'You should perform action; you should neither sit idle, nor renounce action. Not having reached true knowledge of self you should do acts for purifying yourself. If you have attained true knowledge, then also you should continue to perform acts for the purpose of the benefit of the people.'[2]

[1] G. N. Jha, *Saṁkara Vedanta*, p. 71.
[2] *Ibid.*, pp. 72–3.

The fact remains that the interpreters of Śaṁkara in their over-zealousness in giving the highest place to his transcendental metaphysics generally have not cared to see that he was also an ethical philosopher, and that he favoured both transcendental and practical aspects of ethics and moral life. This neglect of his moral views is perhaps the outcome of the misunderstanding that transcendental metaphysics is antagonistic to ethics. Indian philosophy right from the Vedic period to the classical schools adhered to its unique ideal of the synthesis of the moral and the spiritual aspects of life, and never divorced religion from philosophy, ethics from metaphysics, and science from spirituality. Śaṁkara is not an exception to the general trend of Indian philosophy. We need not be apologetic in this respect, and we need not try to put forward any argument to hide the fact that Śaṁkara overemphasized transcendentalism to strike at the root of Buddhistic nihilism, which had caught the imagination of an average Indian. This he did by drawing the attention of the masses towards the fact that the concept of Suṇya put forward by the Buddha was a perversion of the concept of the transcendent Brahman. It was the need of the hour to present a positive notion of the individual self and to prove that this empirical self was in fact the manifestation of the cosmic Brahman, which was both immanent as well as transcendent. Hence man, the replica of Brahman, ought to develop his empirical, as well as the transcendental self. Thus adherence to personal duties (Āśrama Dharmas) and to social duties (Varṇa Dharmas) was accepted by Śaṁkara. But he pointed out that the duties, as well as the intuitive knowledge of the Brahman, ultimately aimed at the merger of Ātman with Brahman. Similarly, Kāma (desire) according to him should be sublimated and transmuted into longing for the union with Brahman on the part of the individual. Thus for him the only Purusārtha to be realized was that of Mokṣa and the other three ought to be subordinated to it. While advocating this attitude he pointed out that only a chosen few could afford to rise above the empirical level.

However, his repeated statements with regard to the performance of duties on the part of each and every individual, and the emphasis he laid on adherence to Niṣkāma Karma (action without attachment) even on the part of the man who has attained Jivanmukti, and whose actions would not bind him to the world, amply prove that the highest goal of life was the sublime state of selfless service, universal love, and freedom from selfishness and narrowmindedness. He never advocated seclusion and inactivity even for the Sanyāsin or the Renunciate. The central feature of the ethics of the Advaita Vedānta is that it advocates a cosmopolitan outlook on life, and explodes the traditional rigidity of the caste system by preferring the life of spirit to that of custom. Summing up the ideal of life advocated by Śaṁkara, Dr Radhakrishnan remarks, 'It is life in the spirit full of meekness and peace, holiness and joy, and not sinking into a state of contemplative inertia'.[1]

The life of spirit is the life of fullness and perfection; it is the life of self-sacrifice as well as that of self-realization. It leads necessarily to the progress of the individual and society, both from the material and the spiritual point of view. This ideal of life is expounded in the Bhagavadgītā, the song divine, which advocates toleration, universal brotherhood and coexistence of all people and all religions. Hence we shall proceed with the ethics of the Bhagavadgītā in the next chapter.

[1] S. Radhakrishnan, *Indian Philosophy*, Vol. II, p. 619.

CHAPTER XII

THE ETHICS OF THE BHAGAVADGĪTĀ

The Place of the Bhagavadgītā

In the ethical history of Indian philosophy the Bhagavadgītā occupies the central place. It is the quintessence of Hindu culture and the sum and substance of Indian philosophical theory and practice, metaphysics and ethics, and religion, mysticism and tradition. To millions it is the gospel of Truth, the message of Divine Life, and an inspiring and exhilarating ideal for the conduct of life. Any person in any walk of life, belonging to any sex, religion, or society can derive practical guidance from it. Although most scholars highly regard it and consider it the essence of the Upaniṣads, it would be a mistake to neglect the originality of this great and unique work, which in my opinion has an intrinsic value because it views man as an integrated whole of physical, mental, intellectual and spiritual aspects, and sees human nature as a synthesis of knowing, willing and feeling, or thought, action and intuition. This threefold nature or psychological constitution of man prompted the author of the Bhagavadgītā to propound a practical philosophy of knowledge (Jñāna), action (Karma), and devotion (Bhakti). None of the three paths mentioned above can singly be regarded as sufficient, nor can any one of them be permanently isolated from the other two. If man is an organic whole, all three paths of Jñāna, Karma and Bhakti must be followed for the complete normal development of character and personality.

The message of the Gītā, which literally means a divine song (Bhagavadgītā), is so simple and so straightforward that it may be grasped by a man without any philosophical background, and yet it is so subtle and so difficult to practise strictly that the most intelligent and scholarly persons may falter in following its mandate in critical situations. However, the importance of the Bhagavadgītā lies in the fact that if followed, it is an unfailing guide to truth and goodness in the darkness of doubt, despondency and indecision. The song celestial has been read, recited, and heard by millions of people over the past millennia, and numberless persons have adopted the way of life propounded in it. Almost all prominent thinkers and scholars of Indian philosophy have ruminated over the ideas expressed in the great work and have arrived at their own conclusions with regard to the practical application of the philosophy of the Bhagavadgītā. From ancient times to the contemporary period this epitome of Indian philosophy and culture has inspired men of India to assimilate, interpret and practise the ideas expressed in the 700 verses which comprise this work, and each has confessed that every time the Bhagavadgītā is read in the original it gives rise to new ideas and associations and that every reading appears to be novel and fresh. The great philosophers like Saṁkarācārya, Rāmanujācārya and Nimbārkācārya in the past, and Lokmanya Tilak, Mahatma Gandhi, Dr Radhakrishnan and Pandit Motilal Shastri in the contemporary period have been greatly inspired by the Bhagavadgītā, and their life and work indicate the indelible impression of its philosophy on them. Hence the ethics of the Bhagavadgītā, the basis of the life and practice of the Indians for ages, has unique importance in the history of Indian philosophy.

The many and various interpretations of the Bhagavadgītā do not reflect any basic ambiguity or laxity of doctrines propounded in it. Rather they suggest and speak to the depth and pithiness of the ideals it sets out for the conduct of life. Moreover, the fact is that the metaphysics, cosmology, psychology, religion and ethics which are interwoven in the Bhagavadgītā have two sources: (1) Śruti (literally, 'conviction'), represented by the Upaniṣads, Brāhmaṇas and Vedic hymns, and (2) Smṛiti (literally, 'reason'), represented by Dharma Sāstra, or the Hindu law books. What the Bhagavadgītā points out is that there is no conflict between Śruti and Smṛiti, or between conviction and reason. Wherever dogmatism and conservatism take hold of the human mind a degeneration of ethics and stagnation of logic automatically follow. The catholicism of the Bhagavadgītā warns against such a perversion of ideas and lethargy toward right action. On the one hand it advocates a life of action and moral duty; on the other it makes the aspirant rise above the relative level of empirical experiences to attain what is called the state of the stability of intellect (Sthitaprajñatā), or equanimity and mental equilibrium. To some, the philosophy of the Bhagavadgītā inspires detachment from material pursuits and the attainment of true knowledge, which abolishes the distinction between knower and known, right and wrong, and even between good and evil. To others, it gives a message of relentless activity, without the expectation of any fruit; of hope; of goodwill; a life of dynamism and progress, material, social and spiritual, leading to self-purification and self-realization. To still others, the philosophy of this gospel is through and through based on the religious experience, and its sole purpose is to awaken the spark of divinity latent in every individual, to prompt him to seek self-realization in self-surrender, and to attain salvation through deep devotion to God and constant meditation on Him so as to invoke His grace. It is held that this process prompts the realization that man becomes God only when he understands that he is an instrument for the fulfilment of the great purpose set before him by the omniscient, omnipotent, and omnipresent Almighty Power. All these interpretations have their own justification, and in the last analysis all of them turn out to be complementary to one another.

The Concept of Dharma in the Bhagavadgītā

That the philosophy of the Bhagavadgītā is the synthesis of all the orthodox schools of Indian philosophy and of Vedic and Upaniṣadic thought has now been acknowledged by various scholars, although no systematic attempt has been made to expound those basic principles of the Bhagavadgītā that are the basis and background of the six systems of Indian philosophy. As a matter of fact the Bhagavadgītā is historically prior to the classical schools of Indian philosophy, and it is the former which supplies not only the material but much of the inspiration to the latter, and which also more truly represents the synthetic philosophy of the Vedas, which, in turn, as we have seen, lay down a monistic metaphysics and a pluralistic (astro)-physics. The Bhagavadgītā itself represents a continuation of the organismic philosophy of the Vedas, and fully endorses the latter's ethical views as well as its metaphysical notions. However, being posterior to the Vedas, it clarifies the distinction between empirical ethics and absolute ethics, and develops the thought that neither extreme material well-being or mundane prosperity in the spirit of self-aggrandizement, nor extreme other worldly well-being with radical asceticism and in the spirit of cynicism is desirable. Neither the path of indulgence (Pravritti Marga) nor that of asceticism (Nivṛitti Mārga) is desirable. Indulgence in the enjoyment of the pluralistic spatio-temporal world without insight into its spiritual monistic basis is as harmful, anti-social, and anti-ethical as indulgence in a lower pantheism and equating good with evil without recognition of the pluralistic nature of the empirical world is disastrous. The Bhagavadgītā follows the philosophy of Samadarśana (the unitive view of the Ultimate Reality) and Visamavarttana (differentiated behaviour in the empirical world) to the core.

The situation, which gives rise to this synthetic view of ethics and metaphysics, is peculiar, but it is a real situation which in some form or other vexes every normal individual. A brief analysis of it appears necessary before we proceed to explain the main ethical doctrines of the Bhagavadgītā, for the problem posed in the very first chapter of the Bhagavadgītā is both general and particular, and centres around the conflict of the empirical and the spiritual aspects of human personality. How this conflict can be resolved by adhering to Dharma, or morality, which is the connecting link between the secular and spiritual domains will be clearer in the conclusion. But what I wish to point out here is that the opening scene of the situation that leads to the formulation of the philosophy of the Bhagavadgītā is one which presents and poses an ethical problem (Dharma Saṅkata) and the scene itself is enacted on the field of battle, designated the field of duty (Dharma Kṣetra) in the first verse of the first chapter of the Bhagavadgītā.[1]

The author of the Mahābhārata, the great sage Vyasa, who declared that 'There is nothing superior to man in the cosmos', begins the first chapter of the Bhagavadgītā by putting these words in the mouth of the great king Dhṛitarāṣṭra (one who holds the nation):

Dharmakṣetre kurekṣetre samavetā yuyutsavah;
Māmakāh paṇḍavāścaiva kimakurvata sanjaya!

'O Sanjaya! What did my sons and the sons of Paṇḍu do, having gathered in the field of battle, the field of righteousness (duty) with the desire of war?'

[1] Bhagavadgītā I, 1.

The battlefield is referred to as the field of righteousness or duty here for two reasons. The first is historical, or mythico-historical, and the second is philosophical. It is worth recalling that the five Pāṇḍavas, first cousins of the sons of Dhṛitarāṣṭra, had been denied their right to property because they had voluntarily given away their kingdom to the Kauravas, having lost everything in a game of dice owing to the trick played by Shakuni, the maternal uncle of the Kauravas. Dharmarāja (the king of duty) Yudhiṣṭhira and his younger Pāṇḍava brothers had left the kingdom for thirteen years on the explicit understanding that their territory would be returned to them at the end of their exile. The dispute arose when the Kauravas backed out of their promise and appropriated the entire kingdom of the Pāṇḍavas, who held that they were the rightful owners of the territory which they entrusted to the Kauravas thirteen years ago. But the Kauravas, particularly Kauravas Duryodhana, the eldest son of the blind king, Dhritarāṣṭra, would not accept the claim, and would not grant even five acres of land to the Pāṇḍavas for their subsistence. Thus Duryodhana claimed to be right, holding that the Pāṇḍavas had lost their kingdom at the game of dice; and Yudhiṣṭhira claimed to be right, because in spite of being tricked at dice, he had fulfilled the promise of remaining in exile for thirteen long years. When all the negotiations broke down, and when Duryodhana ignored arguments, law and justice, both parties decided to settle the issue by resorting to war at Kurukṣetra, the battlefield; hence the battlefield was called the field of Dharma (duty).

The philosophical reason for calling the battlefield the field of duty is obvious. We have all along pointed out that all the orthodox systems of Indian philosophy, and the Vedas and Upaniṣads, unequivocally accepted Varṇāśrama Dharmas, or socio-individual duties, as necessary and unavoidable for the ethico-spiritual development of individuals and society. Each and every individual must attend to his duties according to his social status, psychological inclination, and the profession adopted by him. What Bradley called 'My station and its duties' is exactly what Indian philosophy means by Varṇāśrama Dharmas. We stated earlier that the Varṇa or caste of an individual is not determined by birth, but by psychological inclination and the profession voluntarily adopted by him. In the Bhagavadgītā this fact is clarified by the great Yogin

Krishṇa, who, having attained true knowledge of Brahman, and thus having identified himself with God, says:

Cāturvarṇya mayā sriṣṭam guṇakarmavibhāgaśah[1]

That is,

'The four divisions of society have been created by me on the basis of inclination and profession.'

It is evident from this statement and from other statements referring to the abolition of spiritual differences between the high caste Brāhmaṇa and the low caste Cāṇḍāla that until the time of the Bhagavadgītā there was no rigidity in the caste system, and the classification was based not on birth, but on the profession or the occupation voluntarily chosen by a person. In the very first chapter of the Bhagavadgītā we find that Duryodhana approaches the field-marshal, Droṇācārya, who is a Brāhmaṇa by birth, to acquaint him with the strategic organization of the army of the Pāṇḍavas. The name of Aśvatthāmā, the son of Droṇācārya, is mentioned as one of the notable warriors. All these facts support our contention that the classification of castes was entirely based on profession and the bent of mind of an individual during the epic period. Once a person had adopted a particular profession, it was necessary for him to adhere to the duty enjoined upon that profession even at the cost of his life. Referring to this devotion to duty, it has been remarked in the Bhagavadgītā that one should prefer death, while performing one's own Dharma to a change of professional duty.[2]

Svadharme ninhanam śreyad, paradharmo bhayāvahah.

Not only this, but the opportunity of laying down one's life while performing one's duty is regarded as a golden chance for attaining liberation. This opportunity, particularly the Kṣatriya's opportunity of dying on the battlefield, is considered very rare and is regarded equivalent to the opportunity of entering

[1] Bhagavadgītā, IV, 13.
[2] *Ibid.*, III, 35.

into the open gates of heaven, as it were.[1] Thus when king Dhṛitarāṣṭra refers to the battlefield as the field of Dharma, he has in mind this background of the duty of courting death as the highest duty for a Kṣatriya.

Deviation from Dharma is regarded as the most hateworthy and heinous crime, both by Arjuna, the pupil, and by Krishṇa, his preceptor and the propounder of the philosophy of the Bhagavadgītā. In the first chapter Arjuna is perturbed, especially because war leads to the massacre of men, and the mass killing of men leads to the corruption of women, which would ultimately result in the destruction of all the ancient Dharmas. While exhorting Arjuna to muster courage and to perform his duty of fighting against injustice, Krishṇa points out to the former that if he adopts asceticism and runs away from the battlefield, people would dub him a coward, and that the disgrace and defamation that would ensue as a result of his deviation from duty would be worse than death. The importance of duty is stressed throughout the dialogue between Krishṇa and Arjuna in this great treatise of ethics and philosophy.

We should mention that even here both the empirical and spiritual aspects of Dharma are enunciated, and both views of duty are regarded as equally worthy, ennobling and divine. It would be as erroneous to overlook the instrumental value of social and professional duties as to neglect the highest spiritual value of complete self-surrender to God. The Bhagavadgītā holds that courting death is better than deviation from one's social and professional duty, and it also emphasizes the idea that the aspirant should ultimately take refuge in God. But the ultimate stage of Jivanmukti would not be attainable without the performance of one's duty according to one's profession and occupation. We shall refer to this point again in the discussion of the path of devotion in the sequel. What we should note here is that the opening verse of the Bhagavadgītā indicates that the main purpose of the work is to resolve the conflict of duties which is bound to arise in the life of a conscientious and ethical individual.

With this much introduction to the situation that gives rise to the philosophy of the Bhagavadgītā and its purpose of resolving ethical conflict, we can proceed with the interpretation of its main doctrines. It has been admitted at all sides that the

[1] Bhagavadgītā, II, 32.

Bhagavadgītā enunciates both metaphysics (Brahma Vidya) and ethics (Acāra Śāstra). In our language it would be accurate to call it an ethico-metaphysical work. At the cost of repetition I must remind the reader that throughout this work I have tried to express the ethico-metaphysical nature of Indian philosophy. We have seen that no system or branch of any system of Indian philosophy is devoid of this characteristic, and that this very special feature makes Indian philosophy unique, because it aims at, and even brings about, a reconciliation between intellect and intuition, the former giving rise to ethics and the latter affirming the non-dualism of the Ultimate Reality, which though beyond intellect, lies within the reach of human experience. Thus the approach to unitive knowledge is via intellect. The Bhagavadgītā endorses this view of ours throughout, and our task in this chapter is to point out how the three-fold path of knowledge, action, and devotion comes to our rescue in establishing this contention which we have held while analysing the ethical views of all the important systems of Indian philosophy. For want of space, it is not possible to enter into all the details of the ethics of the Bhagavadgītā, which demands an independent volume to itself. But we shall discuss in this chapter four main doctrines which appear to be the sum and substance of the ethics of the Bhagavadgītā. I will first take up (1) the concept of the Sthitaprajña, which is equivalent to the concept of Jivanmukti of the other systems, and then proceed to discuss the ethical significance of (2) the path of knowledge, (3) the path of action, and (4) the path of devotion respectively. This four-fold treatment, I presume, will provide an insight into the ethical standpoint of the dialogue between Krishṇa and Arjuna.

The Idea of Sthitaprajña

The ideal of Sthitaprajña, or stable intellect, is meant to provide some guidance for the common man when he is overpowered by emotions and faces a conflict of sentiments and duties which appears insoluble. This was the case with Arjuna, who being overwhelmed by sentiments for his kin, was not able to decide whether he should fulfil his duty as a warrior and attack the opponents, or become a recluse to avoid the bloodshed and death of his brothers, uncles, grand-uncles, etc. He could not entertain the idea of attacking venerated persons like Bhīshma, his grand uncle, and Droṇācārya, his preceptor and trainer in the art of war, because they ought to have been 'worshipped by him with flowers and not overpowered by the shower of arrows'.[1] His affection for his blood-relations was aroused to the extent of rationalizing his decision to avoid the battle even if he were tempted to fight on the promise of becoming the ruler of gods. The weakness of his heart deluded him so much that he was unable to decide what course of action was right for him. Hence he said to Krishṇa, 'I have been deluded on account of the feeling of feeble-mindedness, therefore I request you, because I am unable to discriminate between right and wrong, to tell me definitely what course is desirable for my well-being; I am your pupil, and as such I seek your guidance'.[2]

Krishṇa, being a great Yogin himself, discerned that Arjuna had lost sight of the fact that by killing the persons who had sided with injustice and untruth he would not be doing any damage to their soul, which is eternal and immortal. He was going to commit the blunder of confusing the physical body with the soul, and was going to behave toward the differentiated, embodied individuals equally (Sama Varttana), when actually the bond of unity among the individuals was neither body, nor mind, nor intellect, but Ātman, which he could not see without the intuitive knowledge of the oneness of reality (Samadarśana). Instead of Samadarśana and Viṣamavarttana (monistic philosophy and pluralistic behaviour), he was putting the cart before the horse, entertaining Visama Darśana (pluralistic philosophy), and Samavarttana (monistic or uniform behaviour) with all individuals, irrespective of their differences inculcated or embodied in the evil deeds they committed. Arjuna had lost the balance of his mind and he had to be awakened from his ignorance, which was possible only by bringing stability to his intellect. But before acquainting him with the ideal of Sthitaprajña, Krishṇa thought it necessary to give Arjuna an insight into the nature of the Ultimate Reality to prepare him to rise to the higher level of a balanced mind and a balanced intellect.

Therefore, Arjuna is reminded of the fact that in spite of his apparent sensible talk, he shows a lack of intellect because he worries about the changeable and destructible physical bodies.

[1] Bhagavadgītā, II, 4.
[2] *Ibid.*, II, 7.

Wise persons do not bother about the passing away of physical bodies. It therefore becomes necessary for Krishṇa to clarify the point that physical death is no death at all, and that

Dust thou art to dust returnest
Was not spoken of the soul,

as Longfellow observed. The Bhagavadgītā is most emphatic about the immortality of the soul and the indestructibility of the ultimate stuff on which the entire universe of names and forms, of matter, life, mind, and intellect is based and grounded. Unless a fearlessness towards physical annihilation were advocated, emotionally disturbed and mentally unbalanced Arjuna could not be brought back to normalcy, nor could he be exhorted to follow the ideal of the Sthitaprajña. Hence Krishṇa emphasizes that no individual (Jīva) can perish absolutely, and that the soul continues to exist eternally, although it passes through various incarnations. The courageous person is not deluded by the fear of death, because death is nothing but a change, just like the change of childhood into adolescence, of adolescence into youth, and of youth into old age.'[1] If the physical coil of the soul is changeable and destructible, then man is not wise who indulges in the transitory sensual pleasures of life, or who is pained by bodily or sensual affliction. On the contrary, a truly wise man is one who takes the experience of cold and heat, and pleasure and pain to be a temporary phase of life. These short-lived, passing, fleeting pleasures should be accepted by the aspirant to be the most unabiding temporary phases which ought to be tolerated by the aspirant.[2] Krishṇa declares that if a person is not perturbed by momentary pleasures and pains, if he remains balanced and never gives up courage, he should be considered worthiest to attain immortality. Further, he holds that whatever exists must have its being, and that there can be no existence without reality. Basic reality must necessarily be all-pervasive and indestructible. It is such a lasting reality that in spite of the destruction of the body, mind and senses it continues to exist. Hence the soul cannot be identified with any of the lower levels of existence like life, body, mind or intellect. On

[1] Bhagavadgītā, II, 13.
[2] *Ibid.*, II, 14.

the contrary, the soul remains when bodies perish, and the soul changes old bodies for new as a man changes his old dress for a new one.[1] It cannot be destroyed by any power or element like fire, weapons, wind or water, etc. in any way whatsoever.[2]

Thus one who wants to become a person of stable intellect should realize that this unitive principle, Ātman, self, or soul, is the unmanifest reality, and as such is unthinkable; but at the same time it is manifested when it takes up form, when it dwells in a living body. Even if the incarnation of the soul, and births and deaths are supposed perpetual, one need not worry about physical death, because 'To one who is born, death is certain; and to one who dies, rebirth is certain'.[3] The fact remains that beings are unmanifest before birth and unmanifest after physical annihilation. Since they become manifest only in the 'middle', the wise man is he who recognizes the indestructibility of the self. If the self is eternal and the basic reality of the entire cosmos is indestructible (Avināśi), then the wise should look at pleasure and pain, loss and gain, and victory and defeat equally, because these activities affect only the manifested aspect of the self, i.e. body, mind, and intellect, and not its unmanifested aspect of self-luminosity, pure consciousness, pure intelligence and bliss.

But the question arises how to reconcile the empirical aspects of the experiences of pleasure and pain, etc. on the one hand, and the blissful state of the transcendent soul on the other. The answer is that one should behave in a differentiated manner according to the plural nature of the spatio-temporal world, but at the same time one should continue to acknowledge the basic spiritual unity of the self and the Brahman. Though our intellect gives us the empirical knowledge of the physical world, it is also closest to the spiritual self. Hence if we can control intellect, if we can make it stable, the reconciliation between the material and the spiritual, between the relative pairs of opposites and the absolute oneness of the Brahman is not only possible but certain. The intellect is the connecting link between the material and the spiritual world, and hence is the best means to the attainment of a balanced state of mind, the prerequisite of Jivanmukti. It is the intellect which makes us understand the difference between Jñāna and Vijñāna, and

[1] Bhagavadgītā, II, 22.
[2] *Ibid.*, II, 23. [3] *Ibid.*, II, 27.

which testifies to the need of both of them. Again, it is the intellect which discriminates between true and false, right and wrong, beautiful and ugly. In short, intellect is the very foundation of descriptive judgments as well as of value judgments, of philosophic reflection and metaphysical speculation. From the Indian point of view, Dharma, as we have already seen a number of times, is the means of intellectual development and of Mokṣa. The concept of the Sthitaprajña confirms this contention, because the ethical discipline advocated for the Sthitaprajña ultimately leads him to attain Brāhmīsthiti, or the divine state, in which a person is never deluded and ultimately attains Nirvana or merges with Brahman.

However, a Sthitaprajña must have a firm determination. A strong will is necessary for one who aims at the attainment of the highest state. Determination here means conviction in the truth of self-realization, or the identity of the self with the Brahman. When the aspirant aims at this highest goal of unitive experience, attainable through intuitive knowledge, only then can he rise above the three Guṇas, expounded in the scientific aspect (Jñāna-pakṣa) of the Vedas, and only then can he transcend qualities and establish himself permanently in goodness (Sattva), without caring for acquisition (Yoga, in a relative sense) and preservation (Kṣema).[1] It is quite evident from the idea expressed in the forty-fifth verse of the second discourse of the Bhagavadgītā, which I have just cited, that the qualities (i.e. the pluralistic nature of the universe as expounded in the Vedas) are not to be repudiated but to be transcended. What does transcendence mean here? Our contention throughout has been that the aim of attaining oneness with the Brahman can be fulfilled when we accept the plurality of the empirical world. But once we understand the non-dual aspect of reality and have reached the stage of self-realization, then and only then the pluralistic aspect of nature expressed in the Vedas becomes secondary for us. The next verse of the same discourse of the Bhagavadgītā may be quoted here to support our view:

Yāvanartha udapāne sarvatah samplutodake;
Tavān-sarveṣu vedeṣu brāhmaṇasya vijānatah.

[1] Bhagavadgītā, II, 45.

That is,

'All the purpose that small reservoirs serve is served by a vast lake entirely filled with water. Similarly the purpose that all the Vedas serve is attained by a man of realization.'[1]

It is noteworthy here that a man of realization, i.e. a man who has realized Brahman, finds that realization is a better substitute for the Vedas; but a layman cannot do this. The very fact that the man with self-realization considers knowledge of Brahman a better substitute, and does not declare the Vedas to be meaningless, shows that the Bhagavadgītā, in propounding the ideal of Sthitaprajña, aims at reconciling and showing the compatibility of knowledge (Jñana) of Brahman and the acceptance of manyness (Vijñāna), as was acknowledged by Mīmāṁsā and Vedānta.

The Bhagavadgītā is quite clear with regard to the nature and the possibility of this reconciliation. It states emphatically that actions in accordance with the dual nature of the empirical world should not be and cannot be altogether dismissed. But they can be and should be performed without expectation of the result (whether good or bad) on the part of the wise man, i.e. the man who knows the oneness of the Brahman. The 51st and 52nd verses of the second discourse, which lead to a further description of the characteristics of a Sthitaprajña, are worth quoting in this connexion, because they very distinctly state that when a person has shed his delusions in favour of wisdom, only then does he rise above contradictions, not earlier. The verses are as follows:

Karmajaṁ buddhiyuktā hi phalaṁ tyaktva manīṣiṇah;
Janmabandhavinirmuktāh padaṁ gacchantyanāmayaṁ.
Yadā te mohakalilaṁ buddhirvyatitariṣyati;
Tadā gantāsi nirvedaṁ śtrotavyasya śrutasya ca.[2]

That is,

'Endowed with wisdom, giving up the fruit resulting from action, attaining self-realization, and freed from the bondage of

[1] Swami Vireśwarānanda, *Srimad-Bhagavadgitā*, II, 46 (p. 60).
[2] *Ibid.*, II, 51, 52, pp. 64–5.

birth, verily, they go to that abode which is free from evil. When your understanding will get beyond the maze of delusion, then you will have attained indifference to what is to be heard and what is heard.'

It would be nothing short of foolishness to disregard the importance of good and evil as opposites under the influence of the imaginary recognition of oneness in the empirical world. The state of Yoga brings about a reconciliation of empirical and spiritual experiences, Yoga here standing for knowledge of truth in the sense of intuiting it. This Yoga is attainable only when a person's understanding or intellect has been stabilized. The very next verse of the same discourse therefore says:

Śrutivpratipannā te yadā sthāsyati niścalā;
Samādhāvacalā buddhistadā yogamavāpsyasi[1]

That is,

'When your understanding (now) perplexed by hearing will rest in Samadhi (the Lord), unswerving and steady, then you shall attain Yoga.'

If the Bhagavadgītā is the quintessence of the philosophy of the Vedas and the Upaniṣads, the concept of the Sthitaprajña must be regarded as the quintessence of the Bhagavadgītā. A person whose knowledge is true, who performs action without the expectation of fruit, and who constantly meditates on God attains the state of Sthitaprajña. In other words, all these disciplines of knowledge (Jñāna), action (Karma), and devotion (Bhakti)—when followed in an integrated manner, lead a person to the state of established wisdom, or intellect. This fact becomes quite clear when we analyse the characteristics of a person attaining Sthitaprajña as developed in the Bhagavadgītā.

The first prerequisite of Sthitaprajña is giving up the desires of mind (sensual desires or base animal desires) and delighting in one's own self (Ātman). This latter characteristic should not be misunderstood as selfishness. On the contrary, a person delighted in the self knows that the self is not his body, mind, or intellect, but the universal Brahman which resides in all and which prompts him to love all and be just to all.

[1] Swami Vireśwarānanda, *Srimad-Bhagavadgītā*, II, 53.

The second characteristic of Sthitaprajña is forbearance, which means courage to stand against all the odds of life. This prerequisite is in fact Tapasyā, or endurance, in the sense of behaving equally in adversity as well as in prosperity. According to the Bhagavadgītā, 'He who is undisturbed in misery and free from desires amidst pleasures, who is devoid of all attachment, fear and anger, that sage is said to be of steady wisdom'.[1] A person who has forbearance is not one to lose heart when confronted with sudden calamity, nor one to be over-elated at prosperity. This kind of penance is a spiritual discipline which leads to the true knowledge of the Ātman.

The third prerequisite of a Sthitaprajña is akin to forbearance because it requires him to be free of attraction towards pleasure and free of distraction in the presence of pain. The fifty-seventh verse of the second discourse of the Bhagavadgītā explains this quality as freedom from affection and from hatred, or, rather, from favour and jealousy. One who behaves the same when compliments are paid to him, who does not retaliate for injury done to him, or flatters those who do good to him is a person with stable intellect.

The fourth and the most essential characteristic of the person with steady wisdom is self-control. This quality is explained fully in the Bhagavadgītā with illustrations and with the warning that the absence of self-control leads to the total destruction of the character of an individual. It is pointed out that 'When he completely withdraws his senses from sense objects, even as tortoise its limbs, (then) his wisdom is steady'.[2] It should be remembered that this qualification of the Sthitaprajña is not a negative attitude of the mind but rather a positive exercise of reason, withdrawing the mind from sensual objects and at the same time concentrating it on God or the Supreme Spirit to reach the highest state of bliss in this life. This fact is clearly stated in the fifty-ninth verse of the second discourse, where it is suggested that mere abstinence from sensual objects is not enough, because by mere withdrawal of mind from sensual objects the objects may fall away, yet the desire to enjoy them may continue to be present unconsciously. But when the aspirant realizes the presence of Brahman, i.e. when he gets a flash of the Supreme Reality in his own self, then

[1] Swami Vireśwarānanda, *Srimad-Bhagavadgītā*, II, 56.
[2] *Ibid.*, II, 58.

by contrast every longing for sensual satisfaction disappears. It is admitted that in spite of great efforts on the part of man the mind by its very nature is driven towards sensual pleasures. But the best way to control the senses, to attain the state of the stability of intellect, is to meditate on God or to turn one's attention towards God. That is why it is said that when a person controls all his senses and concentrates his mind on God he is a person with stable intellect.[1]

The aspirant is forewarned in the second discourse of the Bhagavadgītā against the consequences of lack of self-control. Even 'mental indulgence' in the objects of senses sets up a vicious circle which ultimately brings about the breakdown of the individual's character. I cannot resist quoting the two more important verses of the second discourse in this connection:

> *Dhyayāto visāyanpuṅsah sangasteṣupajāyate;*
> *Sangātsañjāyate kāmāh kāmātkrodho-bhijāyate.*
> *Krodhādbhavati saṁmohah saṁmohātsmṛitivibhramah;*
> *Smṛitibraṁśadbuddhināśo buddhināśātpraṇaśyati.*[2]

That is:

'While mentally indulging in sensual objects, a person comes to be associated with them; the association leads to desire for the sensual objects; desire or attachment brings about anger (when the desired object is not available); anger leads to delusion; delusion brings about the confusion of memory; the confusion of memory leads to the destruction of intelligence, and the destruction of intelligence results in the total annihilation of the character.'

Self-control leading to equanimity is regarded as the prerequisite of a Sthitaprajña, because without it not only would there be no spiritual outlook but, on the contrary, there will occur a gradual deterioration of the mind of the person, ultimately ending in mental chaos and intellectual disintegration.

Serenity and calmness of mind is not possible without the exercise of self-control. One who has no control over his senses and mind can neither have knowledge nor resort to meditation;

[1] Swami Vireśwarānanda, *Srimad-Bhagavadgītā*, II, 61.
[2] *Ibid.*, II, 62–3.

a person devoid of meditation can have no peace; and a person who has lost peace of mind must constantly be miserable. Psychologically and logically, it is accepted by all hands that once a person yields to animal instincts and relaxes rational control over mind and senses, he is bound to lose the power of discrimination and fall to the level of a brute. Hence it is emphasized again and again that only a person whose senses are completely under control is one who can be said to have a stable intellect or wisdom.

However, a Sthitaprajña is neither a recluse, who follows asceticism to the extreme extent of suppressing all desires, nor is he over-indulgent and indiscreet, so far as the satisfaction of his animal desires is concerned. On the contrary, he follows the mean between the two extremes of asceticism or self-mortification and licentiousness or self-indulgence. Having the spiritual background and the glimpse of the Ultimate Reality, he is different from the common man. In the words of the Bhagavadgītā, 'That which to all creatures is night, is when the man of self-control is wide awake, and that in which (all) creatures are wide awake, is night to the sage who sees'.[1]

The most important point here is the expression 'The sage who sees', which means the person who has intuitive knowledge of the oneness of Brahman. He is considered wide awake while others are asleep, because when others give up action on account of their ignorance, he remains active. He does not delude himself by imagining that since the entire cosmos is one he need not resort to action. In other words, he does not entertain the false maxim of Samavarttana, behaving equally in all situations, without paying heed to the pluralistic nature of the empirical world. That is why he wakes (has true knowledge) while others are asleep (are ignorant). Similarly, while ignorant persons indulge in sensual pleasures, believing that the pluralistic empirical world is the ultimate reality, and believing that there is no underlying spiritual unity, their activity, which is ordinarily supposed to be the result of their awakening, is in fact an inactivity indicative of their unconsciousness or ignorance. Hence they are actually labouring under an illusion while they feel they have true knowledge.

A Sthitaprajña therefore is one who synthesizes action and knowledge (Karma and Jñāna), passion and reason, psychology

[1] Swami Vireśwārananda, *Srimad-Bhagavadgītā*, II, 69.

and logic, intellect and intuition, thereby systematising all desires, instead of either suppressing them or becoming a slave to them. This unshakable character of the Sthitaprajña is beautifully depicted at the end of the second discourse of the Bhagavadgītā:

'He attains peace into whom all sense objects enter, even as rivers enter an ocean, which is unaffected though being overfilled, and not he who is desirous of enjoyments.'[1]

Such an ideal is not only helpful for attaining liberation, which though it may be regarded as something not empirical by some people from the practical point of view, has great significance.

The heart of the man with mental equilibrium overflows with love and compassion for all living beings, irrespective of friend and foe. Hence such a person can never retaliate even when he is victimized by an aggressor. The sublimation of the emotions attained through self-control enriches life and promotes harmony, bringing about the healthy development of the individual and the happiness of family life. Modern psychologists have repeatedly pointed out that the emotions of anger and fear are not only harmful for bodily health, but they even prove fatal when uncontrolled. The emphasis on self-control, indifference to depressing and the elating situations, and freedom from the emotions of fear and anger advocated as the characteristics of the Sthitaprajña, are undoubtedly useful from the point of view of maintaining bodily health and cheerfulness, ingredients of success in practical life. A well-known American author approached a healthy ninety-year-old man and wanted to know the cause of his worldly success and extraordinary health. The old man is said to have answered briefly, 'Words don't hurt me'.

The Path of Knowledge

As I have already stated, the sole purpose of the teaching of the Bhagavadgītā is the solution of the conflict of duties which arises in everybody's life at some time or other. The solution offered is in fact a combination of knowledge, action, and love. The three-fold path propounded by the Bhagavadgītā is therefore known as the Jñāna Mārga, or the path of knowledge;

[1] Swami Vireśwarananda, *Srimad-Bhagavadgītā,* II, 70.

Karma Mārga, or the path of action; and Bhakti Mārga, or the path of devotion. Although these paths are discussed separately in separate chapters of the work, and are indicative of the different types of people to whom they are suited, yet it would be wrong to consider them mutually exclusive. Knowing, feeling, and willing are the basic constituents of human nature, and the paths of knowledge, devotion and action respectively correspond to them. Psychological researches have discovered that pure types of personality are very rare, and that most persons are of mixed type. In other words, it is very rare to come across a person who is either predominantly cognitive, or predominantly emotive, or predominantly conative. Cognition, affection and conation; or knowledge, feeling and action, exist simultaneously and in an interrelated manner in the normal individual. That is why Jñāna, Karma and Bhakti are regarded as equally important in the Bhagavadgītā. Though some scholars have tried to prove that the path of knowledge is primary, others have given premium to the path of action, and still others to that of devotion, yet we should not lose sight of the inseparability and the interdependence of all the three paths. We should never forget that man is an integrated whole of all three constituents, and that the teaching of the Bhagavadgītā aims at the development of the personality of the individual in an integrated manner. It is only for the sake of convenience that we are dealing with the ethical significance of these three paths separately. That is why, without adhering to the sequence of the discourses of the Bhagavadgītā (which starts with the path of action) we shall deal with the path of knowledge first. However, this line of action adopted by us is quite in keeping with the purpose of the Bhagavadgītā. The ideal of Sthitaprajña, in fact, is the starting point of the ethics of the Gītā, and in this ideal knowledge of ultimate reality is discussed first.

For want of space, it is not possible to discuss the path of knowledge in detail, and hence we shall omit whatever has already been said about the importance of the knowledge of Ātman, the basic reality. The very word Jñāna Mārga indicates that this path requires true knowledge, which discriminates between what is permanent and what is impermanent. But the path of knowledge shows that this knowledge should be regarded as the redeeming feature of man's nature. When once a person has come to know—rather, to see, intuitively—that neither his body, nor his mind, nor his intellect is Ātman, or the abiding principle, he must rid himself of the ego-feeling. He must give up the false notion that he is the doer or the subject, because his real self is above the activities of the body, the senses, the mind and the intellect. However, the higher knowledge does not abolish the existence of the body, the senses, the mind and the intellect. Rather, it makes one aware of the fact that Ātman transcends duality and manyness in its real state of self-luminous existence. The ego is a manifestation of the unmanifest soul, and so are the body, the senses, the mind and the intellect. Although these are intimately related, and the grosser depends upon the subtler, yet the subtlest of all is the soul (Ātman), the central and the pivotal element in human personality. The senses are said to be subtler than, and hence superior to, their objects; the mind is subtler than (and superior to) the senses; the intellect is subtler than (and superior to) the mind; and self (Ātman) is subtler than and superior to the intellect.[1] This is the main point to be understood by an aspirant.

This supreme knowledge causes a person to give up ordinary attachments and to perform action without any expectation of its fruits. The goal of the path of knowledge is self-realization, or the identity of the self with the ultimate reality, i.e. Brahman. Hence knowledge of the transcendental nature of the self which is to be realized makes an individual indifferent to selfish desires and eliminates all impurities of mind. One who has this knowledge is free from all evil consequences of action which bind the ignorant. The nineteenth verse of the fourth discourse, entitled the 'Path of Knowledge', states: 'He whose actions are all free from the hankering for desires, whose actions have been burnt by the fire of knowledge, him the wise call a sage.'[2] Though engaged in action, such a person is in fact not doing anything, because he is always contented and does not worry about the consequences. His actions are like the offerings of a person to the fire of knowledge. Such a person is said to be engaged in performing the sacrifice of knowledge (Jñāna Yajña). It has therefore been said that, 'He who is devoid of attachment, free, whose mind is established in knowledge, and who does work as a sacrifice (for the Lord)—his entire action melts away'.[3] We should keep in mind that the melting away of

[1] Swami Vireśwārananda, *Srimad-Bhagavadgītā,* III, 4.
[2] *Ibid.,* IV, 19. [3] *Ibid.,* XII, 13–14.

action does not mean the repudiation of action or resorting to inactivity, but stands for destruction of the evil *consequences* of action.

This path of knowledge might appear to be a mere ideal at first sight, and one might very well say that giving up the notion of being a doer, which amounts to eschewing personal responsibility, at least spiritually, is not what we require today. But some study of contemporary problems would reveal that the path of knowledge is a solution of many problems of suffering humanity. Whereas the contemporary age of freedom of thought, feeling and action has ushered in an era of 'equality, liberty and fraternity' in every walk of life, and has enhanced the dignity of man by recognizing his fundamental rights all over the globe, it has also resulted in the emergence of an individualism of an extreme type, which overemphasizes freedom and self-determination. The fall of the feudalistic system of society and the rise of an international economic community has compelled man the world over to widen his outlook and to recognize the whole human race as one family. But in actual practice contemporary humanism and international fellowship have turned out to be mere slogans. We are still trying to outrace each other in the area of atomic power, for example. International organizations, whose sole purpose is to infuse the spirit of fellow feelings and universal brotherhood, have turned out to be cockpits of struggle between power blocs. Man today is faced with a great ethical crisis; doubt and suspicion is rife all over the world. The danger of push-button war haunts the average citizen today, and humanity at large, in spite of the astonishing success of science, appears to have been oppressed by its marvellous conquest over nature.

The present is an age of mental torture, psychological maladjustment, divided families, divorce, disillusionment, double personalities, disintegrated societies. All these symptoms suggest that man has lost his balance of mind and that his scientific knowledge has become a handicap in the march towards peace and prosperity. Our argument has suggested that what is missing in all this is true knowledge of the underlying oneness of the universe. What we lack today is not scientific knowledge of the plurality of the physical universe, but the intuitive knowledge of the monistic and non-dualistic Brahman. This deficiency cannot be made up by overemphasizing science, by over-asserting egoism, and by giving unlicensed freedom to man in every walk of life. On the contrary, our emphasis today should be on self-control, duty and self-realization, which makes the socialization, nay, even the divinization of man possible, and infuses in him love not only for his fellow beings, but for all living creatures and even for the entire cosmos. This is possible only when the path of knowledge leads the individual to realize that in spite of being physically insignificant in the vast cosmos, where his native planet is comparatively less than an atom in extension, he is the miniature cosmos and virtual Absolute, because the indwelling spirit of the universe is most truly manifested in his personality alone.

There is little doubt that the path of knowledge as developed in the Bhagavadgītā fulfils the needs of contemporary crises. In the domestic, social, national or international areas of life there is dire need for enlightened persons, awakened souls and balanced minds who can infuse the spirit of self-devotion and self-sacrifice in each and every individual by imparting this true knowledge to satisfy the urgent craving for self-control, duty and social well-being instead of the clamour for unlimited freedom and individual rights. The path of knowledge would not deny the rights of man, but would dignify them and make man capable of enjoying these rights with greater zest than ever before. It would not crush freedom or political equality, but it would give man an insight into the nature of real freedom, which is liberation and real spiritual equality.

How this path brings about a synthesis of material progress and the spiritual development of human personality will be evident in showing that the Niṣkāma Karma Mārga, or the path of renunciation in action, which prompts man to be most actively engaged in social and empirical pursuits, is in fact the necessary corollary of the path of knowledge. Let us therefore proceed with the detailed study of the path of action, or Karma Yoga.

The Path of Action

If the path of knowledge demands that an aspirant exercise self-control, to know the distinction between the abiding Ātman and the non-abiding ego, so as to give up the notion of a doer, there is likely to be doubt in the mind of a person whether this amounts to renouncing all activity. But this doubt is dispelled by the Bhagavadgītā which advocates the path of action (Karma Yoga) as strongly as the path of knowledge. Insight into the nature of reality does not abolish the need of an active life, without which an aspirant can neither continue to live successfully nor can he adopt either self-control or the worship of God for attaining Mokṣa. The enunciation of Karma Yoga in the Bhagavadgītā is the most convincing proof of the acceptance of the scientific or the empirical aspect of the Vedic philosophy as the means of attaining liberation. The entire discussion of the Karma Yoga in the third discourse centres on the idea that the concept of the various Devatās, or physical entities, given in the Vedas is intimately associated with diversity of action (Visamavarttana) which a man must adopt in order to be successful in his practical life and in order also to attain liberation.

To avoid confusion between the significance of the Jñāna Yoga and the Karma Yoga, which are ultimately inseparable though distinguishable, the author of the Bhagavadgītā first points out that the path of knowledge is meant for the followers of Śaṁkhya, i.e. persons whose minds have been prepared by true knowledge and self-control, and the path of action is meant for the Yogins, i.e. persons who attain true knowledge through action or duty performed without any selfish end. Both paths aim at self-purification and lead to the same goal. The two paths may be adopted by persons with different bents of mind. But just as disinterested action as a spiritual discipline leads to true knowledge, similarly true knowledge of Brahman and also of the world prompts the wise man not to give up action, but to give up attachment towards action.

If a person thinks that by giving up activity or by renouncing duty one reaches a state of inactivity, he would be labouring under a delusion. The mere renunciation of activity can never make a person attain perfection.[1] The fact is that inactivity is not at all possible as long as man exists physically, because the physical world, which is generated by Prakṛiti, is continuously active in view of the constant interaction of the three Guṇas belonging to the Prakṛiti. No one can exist even for a moment without performing activity of some kind or other.[2] Hence a person who gives up activity altogether is inferior to the Karma

[1] Swami Vireśwārananda, *Srimad-Bhagavadgītā*, III, 4.
[2] *Ibid.*, III, 5.

Yogin, who, in spite of adopting self-control, continues to perform all actions through his organs of action without being attached to those actions. Performing one's daily duties is regarded by the Bhagavadgītā as unavoidable both for the attainment of gradual liberation (Karma Muktī), and for the maintenance of one's bodily existence.[1]

In order to support the unavoidability of performing action for the successful conduct of life in the pluralistic physical world, the Bhagavadgītā quotes the Vedic injunction which requires men to derive all physical benefits from the gods (i.e. the physical elements), by performing sacrifices, i.e. by analysing the physical phenomena and by yoking nature to enjoy physical pleasures.[2] When the Bhagavadgītā urges that men and gods should both attain the supreme good by mutual give and take, what is meant is that man, being intelligent, should utilize scientific knowledge about the material world for the ultimate purpose of attaining perfection. We have mentioned that man should enjoy the benefits he receives from nature by engaging in activity and by rendering service and self-sacrifice. If a person enjoys worldly pleasures without performing his duties and sacrifices towards gods, i.e. without making offerings of his action towards nature, he should be considered a thief.[3]

The performance of sacrifice towards gods also means sharing the benefits received from natural forces with our fellow men. A spiritual communism was accepted by the Indian sages who declared that a person who does not share his meals with others, and who cooks only for filling his own belly was a criminal and sinful. This utilitarianism is beautifully expressed in the following verse of the Bhagavadgītā: 'The good who partake of the remnants of a sacrifice are freed from all sins; but those sinful persons, who cook for their own sake, partake of sin.'[4] By declaring selfishness and hoarding as sin, the Bhagavadgītā advocates an ethics which favours co-operation and humanitarianism. The recognition of the necessity of performing constant action, with a view to produce wealth and food to bring about material prosperity for the human race, shows that non-attachment to action means the performance of one's duty, not merely for the sake of duty but for social well-being. This aspect of Niṣkāma Karma Yoga indicates

[1] Swami Vireśwārananda, *Srimad-Bhagavadgītā*, III, 9.
[2] *Ibid.*, III, 10. [3] *Ibid.*, III, 12. [4] *Ibid.*, III, 13.

that unattached action is not to be identified with Kant's 'will that wills nothing', but it has a wide motive and a nobler purpose to be fulfilled than the selfish motive of satisfying sensual desires.

We have to interpret the oft-quoted verse of the Bhagavadgītā, which exhorts us to renounce the fruits of the action we perform in the light of the above discussion. The verse says:

Karmaṇyevādhikārāste mā phaleṣu kadācana;
Mā karmaphalaheturbhūrma te sāngo-stu akarmaṇi.[1]

That is,

'Your only right is to continue to work; but not to expect results: do not perform actions with the motive of some future benefit; but do not (at the same time) attach yourself to inactivity.'

Two points are noteworthy in the context of the unattached performance of action. The first point is that Niṣkāma Karma Yoga does not advocate renunciation of action, but it simply propounds renunciation in action. That is why we have categorically stated that one should not give up action in any case. Secondly, when this ideal exhorts us not to have any motive of future benefit while performing the action, and not to bother about good or bad consequences of the action, it does not falsify human psychology, according to which no action can be motiveless. What it commands is that one should give up attachment to the motive, in the sense of remaining unperturbed by the success or the non-success of the action. If motiveless action is a psychological impossibility, then Niṣkāma Karma Yoga, which literally means engaging in action without desire, would have no significance at all. But the fact remains that Niṣkāma Karma Yoga recognizes the motivation of action. What it points out is that the motive of one's action should not be the transitory satisfaction of sensual desire, but rather the highest motive of self-realization. We have already stated that only in comparison with the higher stage of self-realization, knowledge of the empirical world (as expounded in the Vedas) is to be considered of lower status. Niṣkāma Karma Yoga has two motives, one of

[1] Swami Vireśwārananda, *Srimad-Bhagavadgītā*, II, 47.

which must be tacitly accepted by the aspirant. The first is Ātmaśuddhi, or cleansing the heart; the second is subserving the purpose of God (Iśvara). The aim of the first motive is self-conquest, and that of the latter is self-surrender to God, to become free from all fears (Abhaya). If a person accepts the first motive, he must sacrifice his personal interest for that of the society as a whole and bring about social well-being even at the cost of his own life. If the second motive is accepted, the aspirant must go on working for the well-being of all living creatures, taking himself to be an instrument in the hands of God. Thus self-realization and God-realization are the two goals, one of which is accepted by the aspirant when he performs actions without any personal motive.

The climax of human culture and the zenith of civilization that the human race was supposed to have reached by adoption of the scientific modes of thought and investigation cannot be regarded important as long as dejection and despondency, denial and disbelief, and danger and death continue to haunt the human soul. A dispassionate analysis of the situation would make every rational individual see that what man needs most today is a sense of duty, a feeling of self-devotion, self-sacrifice and self-denial. Such a sense of duty and devotion to the well-being of humanity can be aroused and achieved by the adoption of the Niṣkāma Karma Yoga, motivated by the stimulus of self-purification. Pragmatic modern man would not accept an empty ideal. Hence, the ideal of performing duty without personal interest yet pregnant with the possibility of the enhancement of one's personality by self-purification on the one hand, and of the well-being of humanity on the other, is most appealing to the modern mind.

The Path of Devotion

While appreciating the pragmatic value of the path of action, we have thrown sufficient light on the motive of self-purification and on the importance of the goal of self-realization. But we purposely avoided detailed discussion of the motive of subserving God and the goal of God-realization because the analysis of this motive and the corresponding goal belongs to the Bhakti Yoga, or the path of devotion. However critical and antagonistic the science-ridden, empirically deluded, and pragmatically fanatic modern man may be towards God or religion, he cannot, even on intellectual grounds, discard and disprove the existence of God and the spiritual power centred and magnificently manifested in man's mind. Scientists, sages, and philosophers in all ages and climes have asserted and experienced the presence of the Divine in man as well as in nature. On his death-bed, Plotinus is said to have addressed his physician as follows: 'I was waiting for you before that which is divine in me departs to unite with itself, the Divine in the Universe.' This expression is exactly similar to the statements of the Upaniṣad which declare that 'Ātman is Brahman', i.e. 'the self is God'. 'That thou art', 'I am Absolute', 'Everything in the universe is verily the Brahman', are similarly indicative expressions. The presence of the indwelling spirit which permeates the universe and enshrines the human heart has been felt by the greatest thinkers, scientists and mystics all over the world at all times. In India, which is the land of spiritualism and sages, research in spiritual matters has been carried out most meticulously and systematically, and the technique of God-realization has been most elaborately laid down.

We use the word 'God-realization', not 'seeing God', because it is not only the personal God who is the object of devotion, but also the immanent Brahman. The Personalness of God is not denied, but his real nature is explained in Indian philosophy. He is accepted as the creator, the preserver and the destroyer, where creation, preservation and destruction are the three functions of the personal God and also the three aspects of the power or motion which resides in Brahman. God as a personal being is worshipped and propitiated, because the omnipotence of God or Brahman does not deny the possibility of the appearance of personal God to the devotee. The Bhagavadgītā does advocate deep love and devotion to God. But it clearly points out that this Father, Doer and Master, Almighty God, is all-pervasive, and as such resides in every individual. God-realization therefore means the actualization of the divine potentiality of man. The words, Paramādhama, the supreme place of the refuge of the devotee, indicate that the state reached by the devotee ultimately is the Divine State. However, when a devotee strongly desires to see God face to face and remain near Him for worship and meditation, deriving utmost joy, power and inspiration, he is granted that choice by the Almighty.

The spiritual potentiality in man can be made manifest and actual by following the path of knowledge, action and devotion. The threefold path is the spiritual discipline without which the unlimited power of the soul cannot be experienced by the individual. Thus the experience of religious consciousness can be had by a common man, provided he chooses to have it. God, therefore, is not a theoretical concept, but an actual empirical reality, the Divine presence, which can be felt by a sincere devotee. There is no need of formalities, but of an attitude of mind, an honest urge and firm conviction in the Power, Presence and Potentiality of the Divine. This conviction can be aroused by a certain ethical discipline, by the knowledge of the Supreme Being, and by the Grace of God which showers forth when a person surrenders himself to the Almighty and dedicates all his thoughts, feelings and actions to Him, making himself an instrument for the fulfilment of the Divine Purpose. Those who deny the existence of God or ridicule the idea of Divine Grace are generally those who have never made efforts to experience the potential power which resides not outside, but inside their own hearts. They forget that we cannot have a direct experience of any potentiality without bringing that potentiality under some striking or drastic conditions. As laymen we believe and take it for granted that water is liquid. But science tells us that it is only a combination of gases. Now the gaseous nature of the water is its potentiality. If the scientist is challenged with regard to the gaseous nature of water, he would take the doubter to the laboratory, pass an electric current through the water, and we should see with our own eyes how the liquid is changed into gases. Similarly, the infinitude, transcendence, immanence, indestructibility and omnipresence of the soul are potentialities which can be made manifest when the spiritual discipline laid down in the Bhagavadgītā is practically followed. Unless a person submits himself to this discipline and to the drastic conditions of the paths of knowledge, action, and devotion, he will not experience the Divinity in him. He will never know the reality of the immanence and the transcendence of the spirit. But he has no right to deny the existence of the Supreme Power, or God, just as a person who has never witnessed the change of water into gases in a laboratory has no right to deny that fact. One who says that he does not believe in the existence of God, nor would he adopt the spiritual discipline, and yet would like to know or to see God would be acting like a man who wants to learn the art of swimming without actually entering the water.

This is the reason for the great emphasis on conviction in the Bhakti Yoga. A firm conviction (Sraddhā) is an unavoidable pre-condition of God-realization. The Bhagavadgītā clearly says that only a man with firm conviction attains true knowledge, whereas a doubter perishes. Once a person is firmly intent upon following the spiritual path, he makes spiritual progress, and the power acquired by him during the course of his effort (Sādhanā), expels his doubt. A Yogin is he who worships God with full faith and devotion. The best Yogins are those who are ever devoted and are endowed with supreme faith.[1] But at the same time, those who worship the indestructible, indescribable, unmanifest, inconceivable, changeless, immovable and eternal Brahman by self control, are also regarded as devotees who attain God.[2] Since the meditation on the unmanifest Brahman is tedious and difficult, the followers of the Niṣkāma Karma Yoga, who are attached to God instead of being attached to the fruits of action, do attain God. A person not able to meditate should practise Niṣkāma Karma with full faith in God, and in that manner would attain God. Self-surrender to God makes Niṣkāma Karma psychologically justified and practicable. Without the aim of God-realization the path of action would either turn into an empty doctrine or lead the individual to indulge in sensual pleasures. Similarly the central object of the Jñāna Yoga, which requires an aspirant to give up the notion of a doer, would not be possible to attain if a man were not to accept the will of God as supreme, and his personal will as the instrument to fulfil the Divine purpose. Hence we find that the path of devotion makes possible the success of the path of knowledge and also the path of action, because of the faith in the Supreme God, which is necessary for the execution of the Yoga, or the way of uniting oneself with the Supreme Reality.

The path of devotion is the easiest but the most efficacious path, for it leads to the knowledge of the Supreme Reality and also makes a Yogin capable of exercising self-control because of God's Grace. That is the reason why after expounding various philosophies of life and after acquainting Arjuna with various

[1] Swami Vireśwarānanda, *Srimad-Bhagavadgītā*, XII, 2.
[2] *Ibid.*, XII, 3 and 4.

kinds of Yajñas, or sacrifices, that lead a person to Mokṣa, Krishṇa, who has identified himself with God, ultimately says to his disciple, 'Fix your mind on Me, be devoted to Me, worship Me and bow down to Me; then you shall come to Me. Truly I promise to you, for you are dear to Me'.[1] This promise is most inspiring and elevating. God is ready to go to all lengths to embrace His devotee if the latter has true devotion and love for the Supreme Person. The path of devotion has a great advantage because it makes a person fearless, and God never fails to save his dear devotees. The Bible says that whosoever believeth in Christ and God will not perish. The Bhagavadgītā also declares that the devotee of God never meets destruction. All the mystics in the East and the West have spoken in the same strain, and have behaved in the same fearless manner when they are God-intoxicated. A person who is truly in love with God must rise above all the formalities of caste, creed and sect, and must transcend all the relative differences between man and man and between religion and religion. It is in this sense that a true devotee who is intoxicated with the love of God is exhorted to give up all relative duties. The Bhagavadgītā says that 'Giving up all duties, the aspirant should take refuge in God, because He will liberate him from all sins and relieve him from all grief'.[2]

However, it would be erroneous to hold that the path of devotion frees a man from his moral responsibility. There is no doubt that a true devotee keeps the love of God higher than all the relative behests of society and ethics, but this does not mean that he should become immoral. On the contrary, a true devotee, who is the lover of God, and who is in return loved by Him, is one who is non-envious, friendly and compassionate towards all beings, free from ideas of possession and ego-consciousness, sympathetic in pain and pleasure, forgiving, always contented, contemplative, self-controlled, of firm conviction and with his mind and intellect dedicated to God.[3] Krishṇa, while addressing his disciple Arjuna, and while identifying himself with God, says, 'From whom the world gets no trouble, and who gets no trouble from the world, who is free from elation, jealousy, fear and anxiety—he is dear to Me. Independent, clean, dexterous, indifferent, untroubled and discarding all

[1] Swami Vireśwarānanda, *Srimad-Bhagavadgītā*, XVIII, 65.
[2] *Ibid.*, XVIII, 66. [3] *Ibid.*, XII, 13–14.

endeavours—such a devotee of Mine is dear to Me'.[1] The fact remains that knowledge, action and love go hand in hand, and a person who is intoxicated by the love of God cannot be oblivious to true knowledge and duty, both of which are equally necessary for the aspirant. This fact is summed up by Mrs Annie Besant in her introduction to the Bhagavadgītā in the following manner: 'Of all the songs of the great poem of Mahābharāta, there is none so rare and precious as this, the Lord's song [Bhagavadgītā]. Since the time it fell from the divine lips of Lord Krishṇa and quelled the surging emotions of his disciple and friend, how many troubled hearts has it quieted? How many weary souls has it led to Him? It is meant to lift the aspirant from the lower levels of renunciation to the loftier heights, where desires are dead, and where the yogin lives in deep contemplation, while his body and mind are engaged in discharging the duties that fall to his lot in life.'[2] The crux of the whole problem is that the ethics of the Bhagavadgītā, like all the ethical philosophies of India, does not divide religion from secular life, nor does it divorce true knowledge from action or from love. It is truly ethico-metaphysical and spirituo-empirical.

[1] Mrs Annie Besant, *Bhagavadgītā*, Introduction.
[2] *Ibid.*, XII, 15–16.

CHAPTER XIII

CONTEMPORARY INDIAN ETHICS: TAGORE'S UNIVERSALISTIC PERSONALISM

Introductory

We have so far provided a critical survey of the ethical philosophies of India on the basis of the original doctrines propounded in the Vedas, the Upaniṣads, the heterodox and the orthodox systems, and last but not least, in the philosophy of the Bhagavadgītā. We concluded the path of devotion by citing a passage in which it was mentioned that the ethics of the Bhagavadgītā, particularly that of the paths of love and action, has inspired numberless aspirants and has brought them solace, peace and bliss. Although historically the doctrines of the Bhagavadgītā are even older than those of the classical schools, they are ever new and ever inspiring, because the philosophy propounded in this work is the cream of the entire philosophical tradition and cultural development of this country. When we think of contemporary Indian philosophy, we cannot mention the name of any great original thinker, whether a technical philosopher or an active political and social reformer, who has not been influenced by the ideology of the Bhagavadgītā in his reflection as well as in his practical life. That is the reason we purposely departed from the chronological arrangement of Indian ethics in giving a setting to the ethics of the Bhagavadgītā.

The terms 'contemporary Indian philosophy', and for that matter 'contemporary Indian ethics', are rather vague, and critics hold different views with reference to the problem of 'Contemporary Indian Thought'. Some persons hold that there is no 'Contemporary Indian Philosophy' worth the name, because thinkers like Tagore, Bhagvandas, Mahatma Gandhi, Radhakrishnan, and others, have only tried to rationalize the ancient Indian philosophy of the Vedas, the Upaniṣads, the Bhagavadgītā, the classical schools of Buddhism and Vedānta, etc. Others refuse to call the thought of such philosophers 'contemporary philosophy', because they hold that no philosophy can be termed 'contemporary' unless it takes the findings of contemporary science to be the basis of all thought and culture. Still others dismiss the whole of 'Indian thought' from the field of philosophy, and even go to the extent of saying that the Indians never had any philosophy but mysticism. With due respect to such critics, I submit that such observations only reveal ignorance of the depth of Indian philosophy.

It is true that history has not recorded the lives of great philosophers after the Vedantins, like Śaṁkara, Rāmānuja Vallabha, and Nimbārka, but this does not mean that the development of Indian philosophy had ceased altogether after the establishment of the various schools of the Vedānta. Indian philosophy never suffered from stagnation, as some contemporary writers have wrongly believed. The Indian mind is most critical and reflective, and it is always open to conviction. That is one good reason why Indian philosophy presents a vast panorama which includes materialism, idealism, dualism, monism, and realism as well as mysticism. If Indian philosophy is not accepted as philosophy because it looks to the Vedas and the Upaniṣads as its perennial sources, then even Western philosophy should also not be regarded 'philosophy', for more than one writer has remarked that it is nothing but a commentary on Plato, the father of Western philosophy. The continuity of thought is not a sign of stagnation, but of life and dynamism. Indian philosophy is a continuous flow of thought, an incessant growth and development of ideas and culture reflected in the thought and behaviour of great personalities like Rsabha Krishṇa, Vyāsa, the Buddha, Mahāvīra and Śaṁkara in ancient times, and Tagore, Bhagvandas, Gandhi, Radhakrishnan and Nehru in the contemporary period. If the ancient thinkers laid the foundation of different systems and grounded them on logic and reason, the contemporary thinkers have re-examined those grounds in the light of the impact of Western culture, and have been able to prove that the synthesis of the Indian and the Western thought and culture is not only possible but essential for the emergence and evolution of one world-culture, i.e. human culture. Thus the evolution of Indian philosophy, which is predominantly concerned with the practical conduct of life, has been creative and progressive throughout.

As we have seen, originally the ethico-social organization of the Hindus was based on individual and social duties, and it aimed at an all-round development of the personality of the individual and the well-being of society. But due to political vicissitudes, theory and practice of philosophy in India fell apart, and the result was that the import of the synthetic view of life was lost sight of. The traditional and the conventional aspects of the caste system predominated over the spiritual, psychological and ethical aspects, and the social evils of untouchability—prohibition of inter-caste marriages and taboos on co-dining of different castes, etc.—crept in and the masses of India followed only conventions. Spiritualism was reduced to forms and ceremonials. Because of foreign domination, research in Indian philosophy and indigenous culture was thwarted, and highly valuable books dealing with scientific and philosophic topics were burnt to ashes by hostile and bigoted aggressors. By the time the British conquered India, ethical degeneration and lack of intellectual and philosophical initiative had reached the lowest ebb. The British government and the British-Indian bureaucrats took no interest in research on Indology, and devoted all their energies to establishing strong foreign rule in the country. But willy-nilly they had to educate Indians even in the interest of strengthening the roots of British imperialism with the help of mercenary educated employees. Hence the education of Indian people by the English, whose sole purpose was at first to produce clerks and to create hatred on the part of Indians towards their own culture, ultimately turned out to be a blessing in disguise. It led to the awakening of the Indian mind, and in the long run brought about a renaissance in India, the impact of which resulted in the reorientation of Indian philosophy and the emergence of a synthetic humanistic outlook which accommodates and reconciles Eastern and Western culture.

This renaissance had both negative and positive aspects. Negatively, it led to severe criticism towards the apparent other-worldliness, the pessimistic trend of overlooking mundane and material progress, and the artificial barriers of caste and creed which has assumed a most rigid form. This criticism came from believers in religions other than the Hindu religion, who aimed at converting the downtrodden castes to Christianity or Islam, as well as from social reformers like Raja Ram Mohan Roy and Swami Dayananda, the great architects of Brahmasamāja and Ārya Samāja, respectively. Positively this renaissance, instead of generating dislike and offence against the ancient Hindu culture, which had now fallen on evil days, gave inspiration to great minds to find out the causes of moral deterioration and to instil a spiritual regeneration and conviction in the dignity of man, who had been declared in the Upaniṣads to be the highest reality. The twofold influence of the renaissance ultimately brought about a cultural and national consciousness in India, and this consciousness has been responsible for the emergence of contemporary philosophy and of the reorientation of spiritual values in India. This ethical reorientation I term 'contemporary ethics'. In this chapter I propose to throw light on the ethical ideas of Dr Rabindra Nath Tagore, who I think was the foremost propounder of the cultural synthesis of the East and the West. From a cultural and philosophical point of view we can say that the ethical notions of Rabindra Nath Tagore have great significance because they have given inspiration to his contemporaries and successors in the fields of ethics and philosophy. From the national point of view, as also from the point of view of political philosophy, Mahatma Gandhi is undoubtedly the pioneer of contemporary ethics. If Tagore laid the foundation of a universalistic personalism, emphasizing the spiritual power in man, Gandhi applied the spiritual power to the practical conduct of life in the struggle for independence, and proved that the transcendental element of value in man enables him to overcome all obstacles in the way of the integrated development of his personality and his society. Hence in treating contemporary ethics I will first give a brief analysis of Tagore's ethical views based on universalistic personalism, and then discuss the Gandhian ethics based on his pragmatic idealism. It would not be out of place here to mention that Dr Radhakrishnan in the philosophical field developed and elaborated the synthesis of the Eastern and the Western culture by propounding what I dare to call Spiritual Humanism, whereas Jawaharlal Nehru has given us an ethics, which though a continuation and elaboration of Gandhism, is based on what I have called Realistic Idealism. Hence while dealing with contemporary Indian ethics, I will discuss the ethical notions of the above-mentioned four contemporary Indian thinkers, Dr Rabindra Nath Tagore, Mahatma Gandhi, Dr S. Radhakrishnan and Pandit Jawaharlal

Nehru. My selection of these thinkers is based on the reasons given above, and I trust that the ethical ideas of these four contemporary stalwarts of Indian thought and culture will give us the cream of contemporary Indian philosophy.

Tagore as a Philosopher

Dr Rabindra Nath Tagore, master mind of the contemporary world, preceptor, sage, great poet and unique literary giant, was to my mind primarily a philosopher, a sage and a seer whose versatility, strengthened by deep insight into human nature, is hard to find in the East or West. His songs and poems, his prose and stories are permeated with highly philosophic ideas, all aimed at awakening slumbering humanity from the sleep of material drunkenness to the life of dynamism and spiritual existence. While emphasizing the need of spiritual awakening in this machine age Tagore writes,

'Purely physical dominance is mechanical and modern machines are merely exaggerating our bodies, lengthening and multiplying our limbs. The modern mind in its innate childishness delights in this enormous bodily bulk, representing an inordinate material power, saying: "Let me have the big toy and no sentiment which can disturb it." It does not realize that in this we are returning to that antediluvian age which revelled in its production of gigantic physical frames, leaving no room for the freedom of the inner spirit.'[1]

Every sentence in this statement reveals the philosophic mind of Tagore who warned us of the mad material pursuit, and who cautioned us that overemphasis on physical development at the cost of mental, intellectual and spiritual aspects of human nature would lead to self destruction. Although Tagore did not live to see and hear the havoc caused by the atomic bombs dropped on Hiroshima and Nagasaki, yet he warned mankind of the possibility of annihilation and extinction if man did not pay any heed to the regeneration of spirit and mind. He pointed out again and again that the extinction of the race of huge reptiles and lizards was sufficient to teach the lesson that if man still continued to pursue physical development at the cost of the

[1] Rabindra Nath Tagore, 'On the Religion of an Artist,' *Contemporary Indian Philosophy* (eds. S. Radhakrishnan and Moore), p. 28.

development of the spirit he would totally extinguish himself, as did the huge reptiles in the hoary past. He therefore emphasized the need of the ideal and the predominance of the spirit over the body. In his words,

'All great human movements in the world are related to some great ideal. Some of you may say that such a doctrine of spirit has been in its death-throes for over a century and is now moribund; that we have nothing to rely upon but external forces and material foundations. But I say, on my part, that your doctrine was obsolete long ago. It was exploded in the springtime of life, when mere size was swept off the face of the world and was replaced by man, brought naked into the heart of creation, man with his helpless body but with his indomitable mind and spirit.'[1]

It is evident that in the long drawn-out battle between the philosophies of materialism and idealism, Tagore not only favoured the latter, but put forward a very strong and factual argument to disprove materialism and to show it illogical and untenable. If the facts of evolution are considered we shall have to admit that nature's great experiment with life has proved beyond doubt that the purpose of evolution is to evolve higher and subtler aspects of spirit or mind and not the grosser aspects of the physical body. Thus Tagore points out that nature itself decided millions of years ago that spirit is mightier and hence more real than matter. As I have already hinted, Tagore, an uncompromising spiritualist, gives a new impetus to idealism and derogates the brute, illogical and hence illusory doctrine of materialism by appealing to the facts of evolution. Such an attempt cannot be made by a non-philosopher.

Besides this, Tagore is a philosopher who is not merely a theorist, but one who loves philosophy and realizes the presence of the indwelling spirit in the innermost recess of his heart. He is not one who simply professes a formal religion, but one who practises spirituality in his everyday life. Referring to this aspect of his own personality, Tagore writes, 'I have already confessed that my religion is a poet's religion; all that I feel about it is from vision and not from knowledge. I frankly say that I cannot

[1] Rabindra Nath Tagore, 'On the Religion of an Artist,' *Contemporary Indian Philosophy* (eds. S. Radhakrishnan and Moore), pp. 28–9.

satisfactorily answer questions about the problem of evil, or about what happens after death. And yet I am sure that there have come moments, when my soul has touched the infinite and has become intensely conscious of it through illumination of joy'.[1] The contrast between knowledge and vision is significant: being highly intellectual Tagore could not have used a poor epithet. He appropriately uses the word 'vision', which is connected with seeing and implies the presence of the seer, or Ātman. He not only supported the doctrine of the oneness of the self with the Brahman but verified it through self-realization. Although he tried to express what in reality is beyond speech, he emphatically agrees with the Upaniṣads regarding the ineffability of the spiritual experience. As he says: 'It has been said in our Upaniṣads that our mind and our words come away baffled from the supreme Truth, but he who knows that, through immediate joy of his own soul, is saved from all doubts and fears.'[2] This expression of the inexpressible based on the immediate spiritual experience could come only from a true philosopher who attained the state of self-realization and intuited the unitive knowledge of the non-dualistic reality (Sama Darśana). He is an idealistic, spiritualistic, non-dualistic philosopher who believes both in the theory of monism and the practice of ethical life to attain self-realization. He does not value the human body because it is the container of life, but because it personifies the impersonal and infinite universal spirit, or Brahman. This view of his is what I have called universalistic personalism. Tagore himself says:

'All that is inert and inanimate is limited to the bare fact of existence. Life is perpetually creative, because it contains in itself that surplus which ever overflows the boundaries of the immediate time and space, restlessly pursuing its adventure of expression in the varied forms of self-realization. Our living body has its vital organs that are important in maintaining its efficiency, but this body is not a mere convenient sack for the purpose of holding stomach, heart, lungs and brains; but it is an image—its highest value is in the fact that it communicates its personality.'[3]

[1] Rabindra Nath Tagore, 'On the Religion of an Artist,' *Contemporary Indian Philosophy* (eds. S. Radhakrishnan and Moore), p. 34.

[2] *Ibid.*, p. 34. [3] *Ibid.*, p. 35.

Self-realization according to Tagore, therefore, means the realization of the universal spiritual self. It stands for that transcendental, spiritual element in man which is the very essence of his personality. Personality for Tagore is nothing but the limitation of the unlimited, the finitization of the infinite for the purpose of creation. In his own words 'Limitation of the unlimited is personality; God is personal where he creates'.[1] This outlook of Tagore is undoubtedly indicative of his being a creative idealist so far as the practical aspect of philosophy is concerned. He admits that personality is a limitation, but this limitation has the purpose of creation. It is not a handicap but an advantage. Thus he eliminates pessimism and scepticism from the domain of spiritualism. His sole purpose of philosophizing was to reconcile spiritualism with empiricism, and mysticism with realism. This he could bring about successfully, in consequence of his mastery of expression and his unique intellectual conviction—hence my contention that Tagore was a philosopher of a high order.

The Ethical Views of Tagore

As a poet-philosopher and as a Upaniṣadic spiritualist Tagore's ethical views are almost bound to be perfectionist, and in fact he advocated harmony and equilibrium as the ideal to be achieved by an ethical person. But at the same time Tagore is realistic and does not believe in an imaginary idealism. He does not attempt to shut his eyes to the concrete facts of life. A perfect artist and faithful to the ideal that 'Beauty is truth, truth beauty', he sets just such an ethical ideal for the individual and for society: all ugliness and evil, imbalance and discord, and disharmony and disproportion should give place to beauty and goodness, balance and equilibrium, and unity and symmetry in an ideal individual and an ideal society. Unity, of course, is the keynote of the philosophy of Tagore, and he considers spiritual unity to be the basis of the physical universe as well as that of human life. There is harmony and unity at the root of the physical universe. Only human spirit can find that unity because human personality is a universalistic personality in the

[1] Rabindra Nath Tagore, 'On the Religion of an Artist,' *Contemporary Indian Philosophy* (eds. S. Radhakrishnan and Moore), p. 37.

sense that it is the limitation of the unlimited and the finalization of the infinite, and hence a dynamic and creative entity, as opposed to the bare matter of fact, inorganic world. Tagore regards colour, shape and movement of the physical body to be superfluous and the personality or the transcendental aspect of imagination, which represents the spiritual element, as the centre of the creation out of superfluous matter over which the spirit presides. Tagore agrees with the Vedic view that the world is an expression of the central spirit. He says: 'Brahma is boundless in his superfluity which inevitably finds its expression in the eternal world process. Here we have the doctrine of the genesis of creation, and therefore of the origin of art. Of all living creatures in the world, man has his vital and mental energy vastly in excess of his need, which urges him to work in various lines of creation for its own sake. Like Brahma himself, he takes joy in productions that are unnecessary to him and therefore representing his extravagance and not his hand to mouth penury.'[1] Although the material creation is a superfluity, yet it implies the presence of spirit in man, and the spirit in fact is the creator, the doer, the enjoyer and the seer. This spirit alone is the harmonizer. Hence self-realization means the awakening of this element of unity and harmony in man. Creative art leads us to self-realization; beauty or harmony brings about goodness. In the words of Tagore: 'This living atmosphere of superfluity in man is dominated by his imagination, as the earth's atmosphere by the light. It helps us to integrate desultory facts in a vision of harmony and then to translate it into our activities for the very joy of its perfection; it invokes in us the Universal Man who is the seer and the doer of all times and countries. The immediate consciousness of reality in its present form, unobscured by the shadow of self-interest, irrespective of moral or utilitarian recommendation, gives us joy, as does the self-revealing personality of our own.'[2]

The ethical ideal according to Tagore is therefore self-realization, i.e. the realization of the Universal Man in art. When spiritual awakening takes place, man is bound to rise above self-interest and give up narrow-mindedness and selfishness altogether. Tagore clearly states that self-realization,

[1] Rabindra Nath Tagore, 'On the Religion of an Artist,' *Contemporary Indian Philosophy* (eds. S. Radhakrishnan and Moore), pp. 34–5.

[2] *Ibid.*, p. 35.

which means rising above relative one-sided personal selfishness, though utilitarian, cannot be said to have been inspired by a utilitarian ideology. On the other hand it is self-born and self-created. Tagore's notion of beauty as truth links aesthetics with ethics through metaphysics. Truth, Beauty and Goodness are the eternal values made manifest in the thinking, feeling and willing of man, and if man is a miniature universe, these very values which sponsor in him the apprehension of truth, the appreciation of beauty, and the realization of goodness must also bring him in direct contact with the ultimate reality. Truth, beauty and goodness are values as well as the three forms of the same non-dualistic absolute reality. That is why the seeker of truth declares that self-consistency or reason when applied to life leads us to realize our real self; the artists feels that creation and appreciation of beauty which exhorts us to lead a harmonious life brings us self-realization; and the moralist, who lays emphasis on duty for the sake of duty without any self-interest, argues that the attainment of the supreme good means the identification of the self with the ultimate reality. Thus truth, beauty and goodness are values from the practical point of view, and they represent the basic reality or truth from the metaphysical point of view. Facts in themselves have no value, but they are converted into value by man who is the meeting-point of facts and values, as well as of ethics, science and metaphysics. This is the greatness of man as a rational being. This is the transcendental or spiritual aspect of life which is most highly developed in his personality, and it is the reason Tagore regards human personality as the principle of unity. It is not individuality but universality. It is this view of Tagore I call universalistic personalism, to distinguish it from individualism. Tagore is very clear about this notion of personality when he declares, 'The personality in me is a self-conscious principle of a living unity; it at once comprehends and yet transcends all the details of facts that are individually mine, my knowledge, feeling, wish and will, my memory, my hope, my love, my activities and all my belongings. This personality which has the sense of One in its nature realizes it in things, thoughts and facts made into units. The principle of unity which it contains is more or less perfectly satisfied in a beautiful face of a picture, a poem, a song, a character, or a harmony of inter-related ideas or facts and then for these things become intensely real and therefore joyful'.[1] We experience this bliss only when a datum, whether it is a physical object, or a mental fact, appeals to us so intensely, it becomes so real for us that we identify ourselves with it or become one with it. In our empirical life the only reality which is more real or indubitable for us is the reality of our own self. When we are so much absorbed in an object through sight, sound, touch or smell that we identify ourselves with it so that we become oblivious of everything else around us, we are certainly enjoying that object. It is in this sense that Irving defined joy: 'Self-forgetfulness is the essence of enjoyment.' Forgetting physical surroundings or ideas in a bid to be absorbed in something more urgent and more absorbing is a sure sign of transcendence and the enjoyment of the self within its own self. This is the highest state of equilibrium, peace and bliss.

Tagore points out that the creation and the enjoyment of art indicates that the world process is the Līlā, or play of 'The Supreme Person', and this play is a 'rhythm' through which it is revealed to us. He regards God or Brahman as a great Māyāvin (artist) who expresses his Māyā, or art of rhythm, in the form of the world process. Since rhythm 'is the movement generated and regulated by harmonious restriction' and is a creative force, so the world is not an illusion but a harmony. Thus matter, life, and mind are all rhythmic expressions of the spirit which creates and generates the rhythm. Although the materials of the world are the accessories by means of which man creates harmony and enjoys life we should not forget that man is higher than the material. It is his spirit which is the creator, doer, and enjoyer. In his attempt to acquire more and more material for enjoyment, modern man has lost sight of the creative force of the spirit—even of life itself—and hence, he cannot enjoy the perfect harmony of the soul with matter, of the individual person with the Ultimate Reality or the Supreme Person. Tagore supports this harmonious and rhythmic aspect of reality by pointing out that even modern science has postulated rhythmic motion or energy as the cause of the differentiated and pluralistic world of objects. 'So life is maya, as moralists love to say, it is and is not. All that we find in it is the rhythm, through which it shows itself. Are rocks and minerals any better? Has not

[1] Rabindra Nath Tagore, 'On the Religion of an Artist,' *Contemporary Indian Philosophy* (eds. S. Radhakrishnan and Moore), pp. 36–7.

science shown us the fact that the ultimate difference between one element and another is only that of rhythm? The fundamental distinction of gold from mercury lies merely in the difference of rhythm in their respective atomic constitution like the distinction of the king from his subject, which is not in their different constituents, but in the different meters of their situation and circumstances. There you find behind the scene the Artist, the Magician of Rhythm, who imparts an appearance of substance to the unsubstantial.'[1]

Therefore Tagore is most explicit about the underlying unity of the spirit and empirical plurality. But in advancing a theory of spiritual unity he does not advocate an impersonal absolutism which would cut off spirit from matter and the creator from the creation. Hence he opposes extreme absolutism on the ground that it would ethically imply puritanism or asceticism. On the one hand he accepts the universalistic and the unitive aspect of human personality, that is, the spirit; on the other hand, he also accepts the notion that man is a limited Brahman, and that the finitude of the individual is the real play of the infinite spirit or Brahman. Hence the ideal of man's ethical life is not asceticism or puritanism nor indulgence in sensual enjoyment. It is the adjustment of our individual self to our universal self. In our language it is the synthesis of the one and the many, the monistic spirit and the pluralistic world. We must have Samadarśana, intuitive knowledge of the oneness; we must also have Visamvarttana, the recognition of empirical distinctions in the pluralistic material world of objects and individuals. Thus the great poet, philosopher and the sage arrives at the ethics of equilibrium, synthesis, harmony and perfection by recognizing 'beauty as truth' and by making art the instrument to attain spiritual liberation. He declares that all evils are simply indicative of 'Want of adjustment of our individual self to our universal self?[2] The spirit of unity of the self with nature and with all human beings prompts us to rise above narrow-mindedness and selfishness, and to demolish artificial barriers between man and man. Man and nature are both expressions of the universal spirit, and this invisible spirit is the centre of attractions in all objects and individuals. One can obtain endless joy the moment

[1] Rabindra Nath Tagore, 'On the Religion of an Artist,' *Contemporary Indian Philosophy* (eds. S. Radhakrishnan and Moore), p. 38.

[2] D. M. Dutta, *Chief Currents of Contemporary Philosophy*, p. 527.

one adjusts one's individual self to the universal spirit. This is made practical by the inculcation of love for all human beings. Tagore's message for mankind is the message of love, harmony, peace, universal brotherhood, and spiritual unity.

Tagore's ideal thus sees as equally necessary and important the science and practical efficiency of the West on the one hand, and the spiritualism of India on the other. He has therefore made a great contribution to the possible synthesis of the Eastern and the Western cultures. He derides narrow nationalism and has always advocated internationalism. He also points out that in spite of the marvellous achievements of science and its conquest of nature, the West attempts to enjoy wealth and material amenities without conquering selfishness because it has neglected the unitive aspect of spirit in man. In India, however, the sages have taught us from the time of the Upaniṣads that wealth and material things should not be considered ends in themselves. They must be enjoyed and utilized as the means to the final end of the adjustment of the individual self with the universal self, which is equally present in all human beings and which is the strongest bond of unity between men in spite of artificial differences created by physical, geographical, political, social, religious and ideological diversities. The conquest of nature and the conquest of the empirical self must go hand in hand. The development of empirical knowledge through science and technological research must also be accompanied by the development of intuitive knowledge through spiritual discipline and self-realization. The oriental heritage of spiritual philosophy and the occidental achievement of empirical science must bring about harmony in the life and culture of the Eastern and the Western hemispheres and thus evolve one human culture.

CHAPTER XIV

CONTEMPORARY INDIAN ETHICS. THE SPIRITUAL HUMANISM OF RADHAKRISHNAN

Dr Radhakrishnan, whose life and works reflect the true spirit of Indian culture and philosophy, has sounded a clarion call to awaken mankind from its slumber of doubt and despondency. The vividness of his thought, the unique lucidity of his expression, and a rare original expression of the universal doctrines evolved in consequence of his penetrating insight into Indian and Western cultures, foreshadowing an era of one-world culture, are some of the qualities responsible for the acknowledgement of his ideas in East and West. Commenting on one of his most important works in 1936, the well-known British thinker, the late Professor J. H. Muirhead, wrote:

'India stands at the opening of a new era in her history which requires above all things, along with an abiding admiration of her past achievements, a forward looking faith in the power of the soul of her people to rise as high as, and perhaps even to excel, the greatest of them.'[1]

Much has happened since then, and India's leadership—political, ethical and spiritual—is recognized all over the world today. Radhakrishnan has contributed towards the greatness of India by his honest attempt to bring East and West together culturally and philosophically, and by his effort to frame a synthetic and comprehensive philosophy and ideology that might lead to the integration not of one country or continent but of the whole world. He has repeatedly pointed out that culture crosses geographical frontiers, and that narrowmindedness and conservatism have no place in the new humanism that is bound to emerge out of the mutual understanding of East and West. In his words:

[1] S. Radhakrishnan, *Contemporary Indian Philosophy*, p. 16.

'The supreme task of our generation is to give a soul to the growing world-consciousness, to develop ideals and institutions necessary for the creative expression of the world soul, to transmit these loyalties and impulses to future generations and train them into world citizens.'[1]

Radhakrishnan holds that the evolution, or, rather, the expression of the world soul is possible only when we shed our national narrowmindedness and make relentless efforts to bring about international understanding through intellectual mobilization: 'In the life of mind and spirit we cannot afford to display a mood of provincialism. At any rate a mobilization of the wisdom of the world may have some justification at a time when so many other forms of mobilization are threatening it.'[2]

This statement emphasizes the need of a catholic outlook and the precaution to be taken to protect mankind from self-destruction, which may perhaps be imminent if an intellectual effort is not made to evolve a humanistic ideology. Of course, Radhakrishnan is not the propounder of humanism, nor can any other single thinker be regarded as such. Broadly speaking, humanism may be defined as that intellectual attitude which aims at manifesting the greatness of man and enjoins upon him the use of all his potentialities and powers for the attainment of his freedom. In other words, humanism points out that science and philosophy, art and literature, in short everything that man has achieved as the result of his rational thinking and intellectual acumen, must aim at the well-being of man.

Types of Humanism

No one will dispute the adoption of humanism as a philosophy of life in the general sense indicated above. But difficulties arise when a narrow view of this ideology is adopted, or when a particular type of it—positivistic humanism, communistic humanism, etc.—is advocated as the solution to all human problems. Positivistic humanism holds that the highest level of the development of the human mind is its capability to perceive positive relations of the events of the world as causes and effects, and as such man should not embark upon any scheme

[1] S. Radhakrishnan, *Eastern Religions and Western Thought*, p. viii.
[2] *Ibid.*

of knowledge which does not directly benefit him. This view is narrow and rules out the advancement of knowledge as an intrinsic value, banishing metaphysics, religion and even speculative thinking in favour of pure physics and mathematics. Communistic humanism claims to cure all human ailments by reducing the individual to a mere cog in the social machinery, thereby thwarting his freedom of thought, speech and action. Consequently, man should 'live by bread alone' without satisfying his religious urge and spiritual restlessness. Both these types of humanism turn out to be anti-religious, anti-metaphysical, and anthropocentric in the narrow sense of making biological man 'the measure of all things'.

One result of the positivistic attitude of the West is the ideology of pragmatism, according to which the reality of everything including the values of truth, beauty and goodness, should be recognized in proportion to its practical utility. American humanism, or rather, Americanism, which is named capitalism by the communists and hailed as democratic humanism by its supporters and admirers, is largely based on the pragmatic approach to life. 'Practical utility' is its motto, and it claims to aim at human freedom, thereby giving birth to a universal humanism that should embrace humanity. The question arises whether this claim is justified and whether the American people who have adopted this ideology are fully satisfied with its results. The answer to this question would decide whether a pragmatic humanism would lead to the evolution of a world culture in which the apparent antagonism between the oriental and the occidental cultures would be resolved. Before Radhakrishnan's solution to this knotty problem is presented, the opinion of an American thinker may be cited. Commenting upon the imperfection of the pragmatic attitude, W. E. Hocking remarks:

'Generally speaking, the pragmatic and realistic temper of the West takes the things of experience at their face value as real. It treats its physical objects and commercial credits as realities in the full sense of the word. It believes that its "progress" is largely due to this realism. It does indeed remind itself occasionally that these things are not final, and that there is a mystery behind the overt facts; but having recognized the existence of a mystery, perhaps once a week, it then proceeds to treat the world as though the mystery were of no practical importance.'[1] The same thinker acknowledges the superiority of oriental philosophy, for unlike Western philosophy it is not only an intellectual pursuit but has practical significance in advocating not merely a theoretical viewpoint but an actual mode of life.

In spite of its unprecedented material progress, which is undoubtedly a great contribution towards human well-being, the Western way of life, with its tendency to separate theory and practice, and fact and value by adhering to crude pragmatic standards, does not recognize or supply that unifying force which prefers love to economic gain and brotherhood to cut-throat competition. This has resulted in the emergence of a commercialized culture which tends to neglect humanitarianism and fellow-feeling, measuring human affairs with the yardstick of gold and dollars. Surplus stocks of products and foodstuffs are destroyed in some Western countries to keep up prices when millions of people in other parts of the country and of the world suffer from want and hunger. This extreme individualism and commercialism is the natural outcome of the ideology of pragmatic humanism.

Spirit in Man

In the face of these facts, when one type of humanism in its zeal to dignify man and magnify his rights turns out to be an extreme individualism, and the other with its uncompromising fanaticism for communistic ideology tends to be a totalitarianism, what remedy can possibly be suggested for the redemption of the human race? Here we need the guidance of Dr Radhakrishnan, who combines oriental wisdom with occidental alertness of intellect, and about whom Professor G. P. Conger of America writes, 'Never in the history of philosophy has there been quite such a world figure. With his unique dual appointment at Benares and Oxford like a weaver's shuttle he has gone to and fro between East and West carrying a thread of understanding, weaving it into the fabric of civilization. . . . Except for an occasional Marcus Aurelius, philosophers never will be kings, but sometimes a philosopher wields among his contemporaries an influence which any king might envy'.[2] His influence is the

[1] Charles A. Moore, *Philosophy East and West*, pp. 4–5.
[2] Burnett, E., *This is My Philosophy*, p. 344.

result of continued reflection on the problem of bringing about the cultural integration of East and West by providing a firm foundation on which an edifice of humanism can be built. He has remarked as one of the chief causes of confusion and one-sidedness in Western thinkers their failure to recognize that 'The soul is the actuality of the organic body in man, even as vision is the actuality of the eye'.[1] The central point in Radhakrishnan's philosophy is the assertion of the presence of spirit in man as the basis of unity in diversity, similarity in difference, and harmony in discord. It is worthy of note that Radhakrishnan's notion of spirit is not anthropomorphic or supernatural, notions which would not be tolerated by either the pragmatists or by the Marxists. Nor is it abstract like the Hegelian notion of spirit, which has been responsible for the rise of positivistic and communistic brands of humanism, both of which are anthropocentric. He does not regard spirit as a substance, for such a notion would be both unscientific and unrealistic. He identifies spirit with life, which is 'something in itself and by itself, and cannot be compared to any substance, subjective or objective'.

Spirit in man is the central reality, the basis of his physical existence, biological growth, mental development and intellectual evolution. Radhakrishnan's notion of spirit appeals to the modern mind because it does not contradict science and is logically consistent and intelligible. Defining spirit in man he says, 'It is not the physical body or the vital organism, the mind or the will, but something which underlies them all and sustains them. It is the basis and background of our being, the universality that cannot be reduced to this or that formula'.[2]

Radhakrishnan emphasizes the point that our negligence of the power of spirit in man, and our assumption that intellectual and moral qualities exhaust the nature of man, have led to the formulation of the mistaken notion that scientific or secular humanism can rebuild the world. His criticism of the positivistic attitude is not destructive, however, but constructive, in the sense that it aims at eradicating selfishness and radical individualism, which are the correlates of such a sceptical attitude. He has raised his voice against the evil effects of secular humanism, whether positivistic or communistic, because he feels strongly that the solution to human problems lies elsewhere.

[1] S. Radhakrishnan, *An Idealist View of Life*, p. 226.

[2] *Ibid.*, p. 205.

He sums up the plight of modern society in the following lines: 'We have a world of rationalist prophets, of selfish individualists, of a monstrous economic system compounded out of industrialism and capitalism, of vast technical achievements and external conquests, of continual craving for creative comforts and love of luxury, of unbridled and endless covetousness in public life, of dictatorship of blood and brutality, anxious to make the world a shambles drippling with human blood, of atheism and disdain for the soul, a world in which nothing is certain and men have lost assurance.'[1]

The Intuitive Method

It would be wrong to regard this as a note of pessimism. Rather, it is merely a factual description of the existing state of affairs, the outcome of a commercialized culture man has adopted as a result of his assent to secular humanism. Radhakrishnan therefore argues that peace of mind will remain inaccessible as long as he adheres to a superficial look at physical facts and as long as he does not make an attempt to penetrate the mystery of spirit. He suggests this is possible through intuition, which is beyond reason though not against reason, and which, being dynamically continuous with thought pierces through conceptual knowledge, to living reality. Radhakrishnan corrects positivism by pointing out that intellect is not the highest level of human knowledge, and that the underlying unity in the diversity of the physical world can be discerned only through the method of intuition. Intuition is regarded higher than the discursive process of thinking, because it is attained only after arduous study and analysis. Thinkers like Plato, Spinoza, Bradley and Bergson have admitted that a direct knowledge of reality can be attained through intuition. Radhakrishnan declares that intuition is not imagination but real apprehension of truth. In his words, 'The deepest things of life are known only through intuitive apprehension, we recognize their truth, but do not reason about them. In the sphere of values we depend a good deal on this kind of knowledge.' It is intuition alone that can give us direct knowledge of right and wrong, beauty and ugliness, and even truth and falsehood.

In the realms of value and worth—in appreciation, aesthetics

[1] Radhakrishnan and Muirhead (eds.), *Contemporary Indian Philosophy*, p. 264.

and ethics—intellectual analysis and pragmatic judgment cannot be our true guide. Humanism deprived of values would not be humanism at all. As we have seen, pragmatic and communistic humanism cannot explain values satisfactorily since both regard biological man as 'the measure of all things'. They neglect the spiritual and the central aspect of human nature without the knowledge of which integrated development is not possible either for man or for society as a whole. Thus the spiritual element of man, which is the unitive and the universal element, and its intuitive realization alone can inculcate universal love and brotherhood in each and every human individual. It can thus bring about a synthesis of man's material progress and spiritual development. Material progress, which symbolizes Western culture, is the outcome of the positivistic method of science. Spiritual development, which symbolizes the East, is the result of the intuitive method. Dr Radhakrishnan always urges the adoption of both these methods and has warned us not to forget that 'the religion of spirit will give purpose to life, which will not demand any aversion or ambiguity, which will reconcile the ideal and the real, the poetry and the prose of life, which will speak to the profound realities of our nature and satisfy the whole of our being, our critical intelligence and our active desire'.[1] This I designate the spiritual humanism of Radhakrishnan, which aims to blend the oriental and the occidental cultures, thereby paving the way for a universal human culture. This humanism accommodates science as well as religion, reason as well as faith, individual freedom as well as social well-being, discipline as well as desire, and self-sacrifice as well as self-realization. It promotes a life of equipoise which brings about health, happiness, holiness and harmony both of the individual and society.

It is evident from the foregoing that Radhakrishnan is a perfectionist like Bradley and Green in his ethical views. He repudiates the mad pursuit of material pleasures, but he is not a cynic. He spurns an arbitrary suppression of desires, but he is not a hedonist or an epicurean. Even though he is an advocate of absolutism in his metaphysical leanings, yet he is not a fatalist or a determinist. His ethics combines a conviction concerning the freedom of will, a faith in spiritual progress through human

[1] Radhakrishnan and Muirhead (eds.), *Contemporary Indian Philosophy*, p. 275.

effort, and an ideal of life which aims at the well-being of humanity irrespective of caste, creed and sex and with a full emphasis on the quality of man socially, intellectually and spiritually. He does not believe in superstition, yet he has the conviction that the traditional morality of India when pruned of its crudeness and credulity can bring about an ethico-social reorganization of society, and lay down the foundation of a world fellowship and universal brotherhood.

He considers religion the inseparable and indispensable counterpart of ethics. In his words,

'Religion is, in essence, experience of or living contact with ultimate reality. It is not a subjective phenomenon, not mere cultivation of the inner life, but the apprehension of something that stands over against the individual. . . . Though religious experience is analogous in some respects to the other manifestations of spiritual activity, such as scientific genius, artistic creation or moral heroism, it cannot be identified with any of them. It is unique and autonomous. The spirit is at home with itself in religion and its life satisfies every side of our being.'[1]

Since spiritual life is the highest life, and since morality is just one manifestation of spiritual activity, the life of spirit is the basis as well as the goal of ethics. The life of spirit is the truest and the most desirable life. It leads to the attainment of a state of perfection or self-realization, the highest state that can ever be arrived at by man. In his words:

'Spiritual geniuses possess the highest that man can possess, constant contact with the creative principle of which life is the manifestation, coincidence with the divine will, serene calm, inward peace, which no passion can disturb, no persecution can dismay.'[2]

The absence of faith and conviction in the spiritual power that man possesses is responsible for religious doubts. But the vacuum created by this doubt has not been filled in spite of man's efforts to substitute religion by other creeds and convictions like atheism, socialism, pragmatism, etc. Referring to the failure of these substitutes for religion Radhakrishnan says,

[1] Radhakrishnan and Muirhead (eds.), *Contemporary Indian Philosophy*, p. 492.

[2] *Ibid.*, p. 275.

'Their one lesson is that, notwithstanding the transformation of life, the shifting moral values and preoccupations of the time, the primal craving for the eternal and abiding remains inextinguishable, unbelief is impossible. Along with a deep discontent with standard forms of religion, there is a growing seriousness about it. The forms are dissolving but the needs persist. The millions who neither dare to have a religion nor do without one are rushing hither and thither seeking for direction.'[1] An overwhelming majority of people today feel the absence of any purpose in life. They seek an aim or an ideal for the achievement of which they would strive with zeal and fervour to extinguish the monotony and barrenness that has entered their lives.

Radhakrishnan emphasizes the need of conviction in the spiritual powers of man, for without such conviction neither the spiritual development of man's personality is possible, nor can he penetrate the depth of reality, the surface of which is imperfectly investigated by empirical science. Science besides being sceptical in its attitude (which is diametrically opposed to the attitude of faith and conviction necessary for the life of spirit) lacks moral appeal and ultimately turns out to be pessimistic. The pessimism so generated by science leaves little scope for virtue, morality and religion, without which man cannot survive socially and culturally. The successes of science in the field of physics, chemistry and technology have led some enthusiastic philosophers to naturalism, which claims to be a philosophy of science. Although the sciences disclaim having any philosophy and deny that naturalism is their philosophical theory, yet naturalists do base their world-view on the established results of science. The main thesis of naturalism is that nature is the only reality and that there is nothing behind nature, beyond nature, or other than nature. Therefore it explains all the events of the world in a negative manner and denies everything that appears contradictory to its notion of nature. According to this philosophy, nature is a continuity of causes and effects; it is vast, relentless, indifferent to human weal or woe, ultimately unconscious and unintelligent, although it has accidently given birth to a self-conscious and intelligent creature like man. Man's achievements, scientific, moral and cultural; his amazing civilization, his almost unlimited power and conquest of time and space are all a temporary aspect of

[1] S. Radhakrishnan, *An Idealist View of Life*, p. 82.

the unlimited cosmos, which being originally unconscious and purposeless will one day crush life and consciousness forever. This is the final picture of life and the universe depicted by the philosophy inspired by science and built on the scientific empirical method, which is necessarily sceptical on account of the changeability and unpredictability of natural phenomena, the study of which is the sole business of this method.

Naturalism denies the existence of God, rejects the offering of prayers, disbelieves in soul, reduces man to a thinking machine by denying the freedom of will, and asserts that consciousness is just an accidental and temporary phase of nature. This fancy for making matter superior to spirit, this craze for preferring unconscious to conscious, and non-living substance to life; this extreme pessimism, born of its love for a sceptical approach, is responsible for the moral and spiritual degeneration of man and the atmosphere of distress and dismay rampant in the world. Radhakrishnan sees the causes of this distress and has remarked: 'The world is passing through a period of uncertainty, of worldless longing. It wants to get out of its present mood of spiritual chaos, moral aimlessness and intellectual vagrancy.'[1] He is, however, not disheartened by this adverse state of affairs and believes that the darkest hour is nearest the dawn. To quote Radhakrishnan once again: 'In spite of all appearances to the contrary, we discern in the present unrest the gradual dawning of a great light, a converging life endeavour, a growing realization that there is a secret spirit in which we are all one, and of which humanity is the highest vehicle on earth, and an increasing desire to live out this knowledge and establish a kingdom of spirit on earth.'[2] Spiritual humanism is an answer to the pessimistic attitude and the grave situation generated by it. It not only proposes an ideal for the development of the individual, leading him to moral heights and infusing in him moral courage, but also advocates a universal standard of human life which would bring about an integrated development of the whole human race, and solve all human problems arising out of the narrowmindedness and shortsightedness born out of ignorance of the power of spirit.

The highest ethical ideal, which is not merely a theoretical

[1] S. Radhakrishnan, *Contemporary Indian Philosophy*, p. 265.
[2] S. Radhakrishnan, *Eastern Religions and Western Thought*, pp. 33–4.

concept, is Mokṣa, or spiritual realization. The ethics which aims at Mokṣa affirms that: 'Man does not live by bread alone, nor by his work, capital ambition or power or relations to external nature. He lives or must live by his life of spirit. Mokṣa is self-emancipation, the fulfilment of the spirit in us in the heart of the eternal. This is what gives ultimate satisfaction and all other activities are directed to the realization of this end.'[1] His repeated emphasis on spiritual realization as the supreme good of life is indicative of his conviction that the invisible and unmanifested eternal which is the cause of the visible manifested physical world is at once the basis as well as the goal, the beginning as well as the end, and cause as well as the culmination of the individual, society and the cosmos. Even if we accept the process of evolution to explain the nature of the world, we have to admit that matter, life, mind or consciousness, and self or self-consciousness have sprung up gradually, and that they are the visible manifestations of the invisible spirit. In this hierarchy of evolution, the subtle is the higher reality and controls the lower, of which it is the basis and explanation. This reinterpretation of the Upaniṣadic theory of the Pañcakośa, in which the spirit is regarded as the central principle of intellect, mind, life and the physical body, is the most interesting as well as valuable contribution of Radhakrishnan to philosophy in general, and to the comparative study of Eastern and Western philosophy in particular. If man is an integrated whole of matter (Annamayakośa), life (Prāṇamayakośa), mind (Manomayakośa), intellect (Jñānamayakośa) and spirit (Anandmayakośa), and if body depends on life, life on mind, mind on intellect and intellect on spirit for regulation and development, then it is evident that Radhakrishnan's emphasis on spiritual development is justified. The highest freedom is attainable only through spiritual realization.

Hence the originality of Dr Radhakrishnan lies in formulating a synthetic system of philosophy of life which brings about a reconciliation of ethics and metaphysics without resorting to authority or blind faith. This achievement has been responsible for the wide acknowledgement and appreciation of his thought, which is idealistic as well as logical, spiritualistic as well as realistic, and transcendental as well as pragmatic. He has brought home to Western thinkers the fact that Indian ethics

[1] S. Radhakrishnan, *The Hindu View of Life*, p. 81.

is not authoritarian, but pragmatic though transcendental, in the sense of being absolutistic. Spiritual realization, which is the state of existence in which the individual can rise above the contradictions of life, is attained through morality, and the intuitive knowledge of the reality is reached through intellect. The empirical world with all its pleasures of sense is not to be discarded but transcended, and liberation (Mokṣa) is not the isolated existence of the soul, but a displacement of a false outlook by a true one, Avidyā by Vidyā. This outlook does not make the individual selfish, but inspires him to be altruistic. Radhakrishnan once again brings to light the humanistic aspects of Indian philosophy and points out that the ideal of Mokṣa, far from being antagonistic to social well-being, is not only conducive to it but is the very basis of it. The antagonism between religion and material progress, and between spiritualism and secular well-being disappears the moment it is realized that 'The liberated soul is not indifferent to the welfare of the world. It is related of Buddha that when he was on the threshold of Nirvāṇa he turned away and took the vow never to cross it so long as a single being remained subject to sorrow and suffering.'[1]

Detachment from the relative and the transitory, from the false and finite, means attachment to the absolute and eternal and devotion to the true and the infinite. Dharma, which stands for righteous action, is the same as the Ṛita or right order of the universe, which means 'the truth of things as well as the law of evolution'. Among contemporary Indian philosophers Radhakrishnan has given the widest and the truest connotation of Dharma, and only such a definition can make it acceptable to each and every individual irrespective of his or her caste or creed, faith or nationality, status or sex. I will therefore conclude his ethics based on spiritual humanism with the following definition of Dharma held by him: 'Dharma, formed from the root, dhṛi, to hold, means that which holds a thing and maintains it in being. Every form of life, every group of men has its dharma, which is the law of its being. Dharma or virtue is conformity with the truth of things; adharma or vice is opposition to it. Moral evil is disharmony with the truth, which encompasses and controls the world.'[1]

[1] S. Radhakrishnan, *The Hindu View of Life*, p. 92.

[1] *Ibid.*, p. 78.

L

CHAPTER XV

CONTEMPORARY INDIAN ETHICS: GANDHIAN ETHICS BASED ON PRAGMATIC SPIRITUALISM

M. K. Gandhi's Place in Philosophy

Among contemporary thinkers of India the name of Mahatma Gandhi will ever remain high, not because of his philosophic acumen or his depth of insight into the nature of the ultimate reality, but because of the simple and straightforward views which he preached and practised without swerving from truth at every moment during his long career as a social reformer, a political leader, a saint, a true lover of humanity and an apostle of peace and non-violence. Never in the history of the world have millions of men been so directly influenced by the impact of a living philosopher. They have adopted spiritual paths of truth and sublimity in hordes, facing guns and cannon fearlessly, suffering the tortures of imprisonment and courting death with a smile on their faces under the leadership of this greatest sage and philosopher, who is rightly claimed today to belong not only to India but to the whole world and mankind.

Besides being an original thinker, Mahatma Gandhi was the first Indian after Aśoka the Great to apply non-violence to politics and spiritualize India's struggle for independence. Truth and non-violence form the crux of his philosophy and represent the metaphysics and ethics he preached and practised. By applying these two maxims to the practical life of the millions of Indians, and by identifying truth with God and non-violence with love, he has given a pragmatic proof of the success of spiritualism. Hence I prefer to call Gandhi's philosophy pragmatic spiritualism, pragmatic because his philosophy was not a mere intellectual pursuit or an abstract theory, but an applied idea which inspired millions of Indians to be awakened and to cast off the fear of death to fight the battle of truth by adopting the non-violent method. 'As a specialist in Ahiṁsa and Truth,

Gandhi has made the world his debtor, by his actual demonstration of the moral equivalent of war. Specifically, so far as India was concerned, he made a fear-ridden people fearless. The prison houses and the gallows which used to awe the people were transformed into holy shrines. He endowed non-violence with power. He taught the virtue of self-discipline and self-purification to the individual, and disciplined organized action to the masses for overcoming social, economic and political ills.'[1]

The entire life history of Mahatma Gandhi was an experiment with truth, and this experiment ultimately proved the victory of truth over untruth, of love over violence. He had abiding faith in the power of non-violence and his followers demonstrated the application of his ideology during the mass movements of Satyāgraha (non-violent protest) against the high-handedness of the British government in India. The courage and forbearance shown by the marchers of truth (Satyāgrahīs), who defied the ban of the British government to prepare salt in 1930, is a unique example of the successful application of non-violence to politics. Hundreds of thousands of people were thrown in jail and thousands of them underwent atrocities by the police. During this movement two thousand five hundred volunteers led by Mrs Sarojini Naidu and Manilal Gandhi near Bombay showed undaunted courage in not even raising a hand to ward off the blows of the police. A well-known correspondent of the United Press, Webb Miller, reported this event in the following words:

'In complete silence Gandhi men drew up and halted a hundred yards from the stockade. A picked column advanced from the crowd, waded the ditches and approached the barbed wire stockade. . . Suddenly at a word of command, scores of native policemen rushed upon the advancing marchers and rained blows on their heads with their steel-shod lathis. Not one of the marchers even raised an arm to fend off the blows. They went down like ninepins. From where I stood I heard the sickening whack of the club on unprotected skulls. The waiting crowd of marchers groaned and sucked in their breath in sympathetic pain of every blow. Those struck down fell sprawling, unconscious or writhing with fractured skulls or broken shoulders. . . .

[1] H. T. Muzumdar, *Mahatma Gandhi Peaceful Revolutionary*, p. 98.

The survivors, without breaking ranks, silently and doggedly marched on until struck down.'[1]

The same treatment was meted out to all the groups of thousands of volunteers. The fearlessness of the marchers was unsurpassed. Everyone was prepared to embrace death to uphold the honour of his country, and to show the world that hatred could be rooted out not by hatred but by love. Referring to this fearlessness Webb Miller wrote:

'Although everyone knew that within a few minutes he would be beaten down, perhaps killed, I could detect no signs of wavering or fear. They marched steadily with hands up, without the encouragement of music or cheering or any possibility that they might escape serious injury or death. The police rushed out and mechanically beat down the second column. There was no fight, no struggle, the marchers simply walked forward till struck down.'[2]

It is now admitted by all that the bloodless revolution led by Mahatma Gandhi was a unique example for the world torn asunder with hatred to learn the lesson of love and brotherhood. He could not have exerted such an influence on the teeming millions of India had he not himself lived the life of a true lover of mankind. Albert Einstein, the well-known scientist-philosopher, called Mahatma Gandhi 'a leader of his people, unsupported by outward authority . . . a victorious fighter who has always scorned the use of force; a man of wisdom and humility armed with resolve and inflexible consistency, who has devoted all his strength to the uplifting of his people and the betterment of their lot; a man who has confronted the brutality of Europe with the dignity of the simple human beings and thus at all times risen superior. . . . Generations to come will scarce believe that such a one as this ever in flesh and blood walked upon this earth.'[3] Einstein's remarks are quite justified because such great men appear very rarely. But the life and work of Gandhi is a constant reminder to the world that non-violence, the creed of the brave and the courageous, is a practical mode of life and not

[1] Louis Fischer, *The Life of Mahatma Gandhi, Part II*, p. 22.
[2] *Ibid.*, p. 22.
[3] H. T. Muzumdar, *op. cit.*, p. 96.

a mere theory or a dogma. In the words of Louis Fischer, 'Gandhi rejected the atom and grasped the sermon on the Mount. He was a nuclear infant and an ethical giant. He knew nothing about killing and much about living in the twentieth century'.[1] That Mahatma Gandhi was pragmatic is quite evident from his utterances and actions, his considered opinions and his practical life. He never hated anyone and lived up to his ideals under all circumstances. His firm faith in the power of love is due to his conviction that even the meanest of the human species is capable of cultivating virtues because man is essentially spiritual and divine. That is why I have called Gandhi's philosophy a pragmatic spiritualism. If this ideology is practically followed there is no reason why man should not be able to bring about lasting peace on this earth. Mahatma Gandhi was sure that love alone could be victorious over hatred. In 1946 expressing his opinion on the dropping of the atom bomb, he wrote:

'The moral to be legitimately drawn from the supreme tragedy of the bomb is that it will not be destroyed by counter bombs, even as violence cannot be destroyed by counter violence. Mankind has got to get out of violence only through non-violence. Hatred can be overcome only by love.'[2]

The Meaning of Non-Violence

If the philosophy of M. K. Gandhi were to be summed up in one word that word would be 'non-violence'. But this term, as used by Gandhi, has a very wide connotation, and stands for the love born of the universal element of spirit in man. The concept of non-violence (Ahiṁsā) is very old so far as Indian philosophy is concerned. It is at least as old as the Vedas, because the command of the Veda, 'Mā himsyāt sarva bhūtāni', means 'Do not kill any living being'. The Jaina Tīrthaṅkara Mahāvīra and the Buddha both advocate Ahiṁsā as the highest virtue. Jainism placed it higher than truth and regarded adherence to truth as the necessary corollary of non-violence. The Buddha identified it with universal compassion. But both these great teachers advocated the practice of Ahiṁsā in the religious sphere with

[1] Louis Fischer, *op. cit.*, p. 100.
[2] *Harijan*, July 7, 1946.

the sole purpose of leading suffering individuals towards a painless state of Mokṣa. They were undoubtedly religious teachers and as such they did not apply this virtue as a secular value. Mahatma Gandhi, on the other hand, was a man of the masses, interested in the social, economic, political and mundane well-being of the people. His sole purpose was to bring down heaven on earth by spiritualizing secular life. Gandhi was no doubt the first to apply the concept of Ahiṁsā to practical life and to give it the widest possible connotation by identifying it with truth or God. He was led to this conclusion not merely by deliberation but by following the path of non-violence, and thus by gradually realizing its true significance through experience. Non-violence is a way of life, which is the means as well as the end of the spiritual realization. It is the means because it brings about universal love, compassion, fellow-feeling and a sense of justice. It is the end because absolute non-violence is the highest ideal, the attainment of which would convert a man to God. Though the word is negative, yet it has a positive import. In the words of Mahatma Gandhi: 'Ahimsā means love in the Pauline sense and yet something more than love defined by St Paul, although I know St Paul's beautiful definition is good enough for all practical purposes . . . Besides love in the English language has other connotations and so I was compelled to use the negative word.'[1] Gandhi advocated the cultivation of truthfulness, humility, tolerance and loving kindness as the necessary prerequisites of the votary of non-violence. Non-violence as such is the soul force, which is the potential law of human nature and which can be made manifest through the virtues of truth, tolerance, humility and love. 'Non-violence is the law of our species as violence is the law of the brute. The spirit lies dormant in the brute and he knows no law but that of physical might. The dignity of man requires obedience to a higher law to the strength of the spirit.'[2] It is therefore evident that for Gandhi non-violence is neither a negative attitude of non-aggression towards the aggressor, nor does it merely mean avoiding injury to tiny living beings, but it 'is an active force of the highest order. It is soul force or the power of Godhead within us.'[3]

[1] *Harijan*, March 14, 1936.
[2] *Young India*, Aug. 11, 1920.
[3] *Harijan*, Nov. 12, 1938.

Metaphysical Basis of Non-Violence

Usually the metaphysical aspect of non-violence is lost sight of, and people are misled to believe that Gandhi preached the pacifistic philosophy of meekness and non-resistance. If somebody slaps you on the left cheek, turn your right cheek towards him. There is no doubt that Gandhi was influenced by Christian ethics and that he was a true living Christian in one sense. But he was more a mystic in the practical sense and had realized through experience that non-violent behaviour, when inspired from the innermost recess of the human personality, is mightier than the mightiest weapons on the face of the earth because then it rises from the central force, the spirit of man, which is in fact the central reality and the central truth, God. That is why he identified non-violence with truth and the truth with all-pervasive God. If God as truth is the basis and the background of the universe and man, the only way to Godliness is the life of non-violence and love, and hence God, Life, Truth and Love are identical, and all are again the ultimate Good. This conviction of God was the greatest strength in the personality of Mahatma Gandhi and grew in him gradually through experience. Gandhi did try to give expression to his belief in the existence of God and said,

'There is an indefinable mysterious Power, which pervades everything. I feel it; though I do not see it. It is the unseen Power, which makes itself felt and yet defies all proof because it is so unlike all that I perceive through my senses. It transcends senses . . . But it is possible to reason out the existence of God to a limited extent . . . There is an orderliness in the universe, there is an unalterable law governing everything and every being that exists or lives. It is not a blind law, for no blind law can govern the conduct of human beings . . . That law then which governs all life is God . . . I do dimly perceive that whilst everything around me is ever changing, ever dying, there is underlying all that change a living Power that is changeless, that holds all together, that creates, dissolves and recreates. That informing Power or Spirit is God . . . In the midst of death life persists, in the midst of untruth truth persists, in the midst of darkness light persists. Hence I gather that God is life, Truth and Love. He is Love. He is the Supreme God.'[1]

[1] Louis Fischer, *op. cit.*, p. 51.

This statement of Gandhi puts his philosophy, his metaphysics, his ethics and his religion in a nutshell. It leads us to conclude that what the Vedic Ṛsis had propounded through the intuitive experience and meditation was endorsed by Gandhi through his own experience and reason. The identification of non-violence as the ideal of conduct with Truth, the central reality, leads one to necessarily conclude that Gandhism is undoubtedly an ethico-metaphysical system. The moment we lose sight of the metaphysical aspect of Gandhi's ethics, we are bound to misunderstand it as an apologetic ethics. But a study of Gandhi's thought and conviction proves that the same maxim of Samadarśana (unitive knowledge) of the underlying spirit, and Visamavarttana (differentiated behaviour with regard to the empirical world to distinguish between good and evil), was reasserted by Gandhi. Gandhi embodies the spiritual culture and practical ethics of India. Instead of entering into intellectual discussions of metaphysics and ethics he has applied the central truth to concrete life. He has pointed out that evil must be hated because it is due to the malevolent tendency and ignorance of the evildoer. Hence we must behave differently towards the evildoer and the benefactor because of their differences of conduct (Visamavarttana). But at the same time we should never hate the evildoer, because the doer in every individual is not the body, or the mind, or the intellect, but the spirit. We should look at friend and foe alike without hating their person (Samadarśana), but we should not behave neutrally toward both so far as our judgment of good and evil is concerned. We should not imitate evil. Not only this, we should neither hear anybody's evil, nor see it, nor speak about it. Thus we must have Visamavarttana towards good and evil. But we ought to love all human beings, whether they are good or bad, kind or cruel, broadminded or selfish, because the spirit, central in them (Prajapati), is the unitive force. Thus Gandhi believed that even the meanest person was capable of being reformed because 'man is the image of God'.

The universality of ethics is defended by Gandhi on metaphysical grounds. When the central reality or God is all-pervasive, and religion creates no barriers between man and man, then the denial of freedom and equality to all human beings is not only politically unjust but spiritually sinful. Gandhi says: 'It is a first-class human tragedy that peoples of the earth, who claim to believe in the message of Jesus, whom they describe as the Prince of Peace, show little of that belief in actual practice. It is painful to see sincere Christian divines limiting the scope of Jesus's message to select individuals. I have been taught from my childhood, and I have tested the truth by experience, that primary virtues of mankind are possible of cultivation by the meanest of the human species. It is this undoubted universal possibility that distinguishes the human from the rest of God's creation.'[1] He advocated the law of love and regarded that law as objective as any other physical law of nature. This attitude of Gandhi is entirely due to his firm conviction that the soul force or the spirit is universally present in man and in nature, and that it is given to man to develop this soul force by practising virtue, the highest and most pervasive form of which is non-violence. Armed with this conviction, in truth, Gandhi was able to follow the path of non-violence courageously and fearlessly. It is true that without strong conviction in the eternality of the soul and the omnipresence of the Truth non-violence as a mode of life turns out to be a fiction. We shall now proceed to discuss briefly the ethical application of this synthesis of truth and non-violence, of love and service, and of freedom and justice, for the individual, society and mankind as a whole. In other words we shall discuss briefly the application of Gandhian ethics in the life of the individual, the nation, and the community of nations to judge how far the gospel of truth and non-violence can contribute towards the well-being of humanity and the establishment of eternal peace in the world.

Non-Violence and the Individual

Gandhi, true to his convictions, was replete with deep love for all human beings because he actually lived up to his ideals which identified love with truth and truth with God. His aim in life, so far as his own person was concerned, was God-realization. Therefore the application of non-violence to the individual, according to Gandhi, was God-realization, or getting nearer the truth or God, who is the source of human spirit. This aim of life is religious, but this religion is the religion of humanity, of love, of dedication, of social service and self-devotion. Gandhi wrote:

[1] *Harijan*, May 16, 1936.

'I am being led to my religion through Truth and non-violence, i.e. love in the broadest sense. I often describe my religion as Religion of Truth. Of late, instead of saying God is Truth I have been saying Truth is God, in order more fully to define my Religion. I used at one time to know by heart a thousand names of God . . . But nowadays nothing so completely describes my God as Truth. Denial of God we have known. Denial of Truth we have not known. The most ignorant among mankind has some truth in him. We are all sparks of Truth. The sum total of these sparks is indestructible, as-yet-Unknown Truth, which is God. I am being daily led nearer to it by constant prayer.'[1]

It is evident from this statement that the aim of the path of non-violence, which is, in fact, the path of love, is the merger of the individual self into the universal self or God. This contention of ours can be supported with reference to Gandhi's notion about death. In a note of consolation to a friend he wrote:

'I am sorry for your loss, which in reality is no loss. "Death is but a sleep and a forgetting". This is such a sweet sleep that the body has not to wake again and the dead load of memory is thrown overboard . . . When the isolated drops melt, they share the majesty of the ocean, to which they belong. In isolation they die but to meet the ocean again.'[2]

Gandhi never explained his notion of liberation or Mokṣa, because his aim, like that of the Buddha, was not metaphysical exposition, but practical eradication of suffering, the well-being of humanity. But it goes without saying that he believed in the infinite existence of the soul after physical death, and that his ethics was on the one hand, based on the concept of the immortality of soul, and on the other, it aimed at the merger of the finite individual self with the universal infinite Truth or God.

This aim of the path of non-violence seems to be otherworldly. But we know that Gandhi was pragmatic. As such he did say that the practical aim of non-violence was self-purification. Enunciating the five characteristics of non-violence, he says:

[1] S. Radhakrishnan and Muirhead (eds.), *Contemporary Indian Philosophy*, p. 21.

[2] Louis Fischer, *op. cit.*, Vol. II, p. 89.

'(*a*) Non-violence implies as complete a self-purification as is humanly possible.

'(*b*) Man for man, the strength of non-violence is in exact proportion to the ability, not the will of the non-violent person to inflict violence.

'(*c*) Non-violence is without exception superior to violence, i.e. the power at the disposal of a non-violent person is always greater than he would have if he was violent.

'(*d*) There is no such thing as defeat in non-violence. The end of violence is surest defeat.

'(*e*) The ultimate end of non-violence is surest victory—if such a term may be used of non-violence. In reality when there is no sense of defeat, there is no sense of victory.'[1]

Self-purification, which is the essential characteristic of non-violent conduct, ultimately leads the individual to attain a state of equipoise and equilibrium, at which time he rises above the contradictions of defeat and victory. The spiritual development of the personality is therefore the pragmatic purpose of the path of non-violence. Non-violence is not the creed of the coward or the weakling, but that of the brave and the courageous. It makes a person fearless and absolutely indifferent to physical death. Unless he musters that much courage he cannot follow the path of non-violence, and unless he is non-violent and truthful to the core, he cannot attain spiritual strength. Gandhi did accept the ideal of Sthitaprajña of the Bhagavadgītā as the ideal. He actually practised it and came to the conclusion that self-restraint ultimately leads to self-purification.

The Application of Non-Violence to National and International Life

Gandhi asserted most emphatically that adherence to non-violence was not restricted to the personal sphere of an individual. A life of truth and non-violence is essentially the life of dedication to the service of fellow beings. The goal of non-violent conduct is self-purification on the one hand, and social well-being on the other. Since Gandhi's religion is the religion of humanity, based on the conviction that every man has the spark of truth, non-violence or love in him, and since the best way to

[1] *Harijan*, Oct. 12, 1935.

overcome evil is not to kill the evildoer but to change his heart by refusing to retaliate, it is evident that this religion has a social bearing. In the words of Gandhi,

'The bearing of this religion on social life is, or has to be seen in one's daily social contact. To be true to such religion one has to lose oneself in continuous and continuing service of all life. Realization of truth is impossible without a complete merging of oneself in, and identification with, this limitless ocean of life. Hence, for me, there is no escape from social service, there is no happiness on earth beyond or apart from it. Social service here must be taken to include every department of life. In this scheme there is nothing low, nothing high. For all is one, though we seem to be many.'[1]

Self-realization always implies self-sacrifice, because it means the realization of the higher or the universal self by sacrificing or neglecting the lower or the individual self. 'Individuals or nations, who would practise non-violence, must be prepared to sacrifice all except honour.'[2]

The technique of non-violence lies in suffering—suffering with a view to purify one's ownself on the one hand, and to change the heart of the aggressor or the evildoer on the other. The following six prerequisites or presuppositions, as Gandhi termed them, are essential for the votary of non-violence:

(1) It must be taken for granted that non-violence is the law meant for the rational beings and is thus preferable to brute force, which is the law of the jungle.

(2) The votary of non-violence must have a living faith in God.

(3) Non-violence should be taken to be the best defence of one's self-respect and should not be used as the means to protect one's property or wealth.

(4) Non-violence implies self-sacrifice and hence presumes the possession of other people's property and countries to be an immoral act.

(5) The power of non-violence is available to all, irrespective

[1] M. K. Gandhi, 'On the Bearing of his Religion on Social Life,' in S. Radhakrishnan, *Contemporary Indian Philosophy*, p. 21.

[2] M. K. Gandhi, *Towards Lasting Peace*, A. T. Hingorani (ed.), p. 9.

of caste, creed and age, provided that one has an abiding faith in the God of love. It should thus be accepted as the law of life.

(6) The law of love—non-violence, which is the law of life, is equally pragmatic in the case of community and in the case of the whole humanity.

Thus Gandhi's non-violence implies a classless society and a world without economic, political or social disparities. If the law of love is applied to the life of the individuals and of communities, there is no reason why it should not bring about lasting peace to mankind. Gandhi pleaded that the application of non-violence to society could lead to great results provided people did undergo the requisite sacrifice. Gandhi wrote:

'Modern science is replete with illustrations of the seemingly impossible having become possible within living memory. But victories of physical science would be nothing against the victory of the Science of Life, which is summed up in Love, which is the law of our Being. I know that it cannot be proved by argument. It shall be proved by persons living it in their lives in utter disregard of consequences to themselves. There is no real gain without sacrifice, and since the law of love is the realest gain, sacrifice too must be the greatest required.'[1]

Gandhi proved the efficacy of the law of love by actually practising it. There is little question that whenever one resorts to violence, one does so because one has lost faith in the dignity of man and has transgressed the duty of respect for life. As long as organized violence and race for armament persist in the world we cannot boast of humanism, whether that humanism is supposed to be based on democracy or on communism. The presence of violence is undoubtedly the proof of the bankruptcy of reason, the transgression of humanitarianism, and the predominance of animal instinct over the spiritual urge of man. There can be no hope in rescuing humanity from atomic suicide unless world politicians recognize the supremacy of the law of love and unless they actually adopt it in their political dealings. Gandhi wrote in 1936:

'If recognized leaders of mankind, who have control over engines of destruction, were wholly to renounce their use with full knowledge of implications, permanent peace can be obtained.

[1] M. K. Gandhi, *Towards Lasting Peace*, A. T. Hingorani (ed.), p. 15.

This is clearly impossible without the great powers of the earth renouncing their imperialistic designs. This again seems impossible without these great nations ceasing to believe in soul-destroying competition and to desire to multiply wants and, therefore, increase their material possessions.'[1]

Gandhism, therefore, is a golden mean between the two extremes of individualism, based on a capitalistic outlook of the exploitation of the labour of others, and communism, which reduces an individual to a mere cog in the social machinery and has no respect either for the spirit in man or for fundamental human rights. The path of non-violence advocated by Gandhi rises above all artificial barriers of caste, creed, religion and nationality, and yet raises the dignity of man in all spheres of life. The greatest proof of the success of such a way of life lies in actually living it, as Gandhi emphasized more than once. Unless people adopt the law of love, as Gandhi did in his life, there can be no hope for the elimination of war and destruction. But faith in the divine element of human nature is essential for the promotion of lasting peace. 'Not to believe in the possibility of permanent peace is to disbelieve in the godliness of human nature. Methods hitherto adopted have failed because rock bottom sincerity on the part of those who have striven has been lacking. Not that they have realized this lack. Peace is unattainable by part performance of conditions, even as chemical combination is impossible without complete fulfilment of conditions of attainment thereof.'[2]

Just as the proof of the cake lies in its eating, the proof of the efficiency of the path of non-violence lies in adopting it. The inherent goodness in human nature has to be provoked, and the only way to do it is to adopt the spiritual discipline, the code of non-violence, which automatically arouses love in man and brings about the victory of love over hatred, of truth over untruth, of light over darkness, of righteousness over unrighteousness, and of immortality over death. Gandhism is the path of spiritual discipline, which can be adopted by all individuals, all communities and all nations the world over. It is the message of love and peace, a ray of 'kindly light amidst encircling gloom', and the last hope of the survival of human-kind in the dark and

[1] M. K. Gandhi, *Towards Lasting Peace*, A. T. Hingorani (ed.), p. 1.
[2] *Ibid.*

dismal hour of doubt and despondency. How far the ideals advocated by Gandhi can be applied to national and international affairs of men will be made more explicit when we study the thoughts and achievements of Jawaharlal Nehru, who is the successor of Mahatma Gandhi so far as the application of the path of non-violence to practical life is concerned. If Gandhi showed the way towards peace, national and international, it was left to Nehru to march towards the goal courageously facing all the odds and obstacles, and to prove that if a sincere effort is made, the goodness of man can be invoked and practical problems at the national and international levels can be solved by adhering to the principles of truth, non-violence, justice and peaceful co-existence.

As we shall see later, in spite of his reluctance to accept non-violence as a creed or as a dogma, Nehru did not discard the philosophy of non-violence. But being compelled by political problems of a peculiar nature, he preferred relative violence to inertia and inactivity. Nehru has always been impressed by the efficiency of non-violence and has accepted the dynamics behind non-co-operation and civil disobedience, which were apparently negative terms and which implied the positive force of non-violence. This attitude of Nehru towards the peaceful revolution led by Mahatma Gandhi has been expressed by Dr Das in the following manner:

'In spite of the abundance of "nons" in the Indian revolution, such as non-violence, non-co-operation, etc., it was not a negative or a passive affair. It was an active, dynamic, energizing drive, which lifted a whole nation out of a morass of demoralization and helplessness, the inevitable result of a long period of subjection. Nehru never regarded it as "a kind of pious and static pacifism" but always as a "forceful method of enforcing the mass will".'[1]

The difference between Nehru's realism and Gandhi's pragmatism will become apparent as we proceed with the former's view in the next chapter. However, it will suffice here to say that Gandhi as well as Nehru are equally opposed to aggression and violence on the part of individuals and nations. The last two world wars and the disastrous consequences of their deadly

[1] M. N. Das, *The Political Philosophy of Nehru*, pp. 61–2.

weapons have touched the hearts of both these peace-loving humanists. So long as there is organized violence present in the world, so long as man continues to believe in brute force as the means of solving national and international problems, we cannot justly claim to be civilized and cultured in spite of the marvellous progress of science and technology. Although science is a search after truth, it is a specialized and partial search. It tries to remain indifferent to human weal and woe and is thus anti-humanistic. Commenting upon the Gandhian notion of truth and non-violence Louis Fischer writes: 'Truth is identification with God and humanity. From Truth non-violence is born . . . "There is nothing wrong in every man following Ruth, according to his lights", says Gandhi from Yervada Mandir. Each person must be true to his own Truth. But if the seeker after Truth began to destroy those who sow Truth in their way, he would recede from Truth. How can one realize God by killing or hurting? Non-violence, however, is more than peacefulness or pacifism; it is love, and excludes evil thought, undue haste, lies or hatred.'[1] Both Gandhi and Nehru are the ardent seekers of Truth and strong upholders of the path of non-violence. They deride the use of force in politics and strongly believe in the possibility of changing the heart of the aggressor through negotiation and reasoning. An organized non-violence which would bring a reign of love and peace appears to be the only remedy against organized violence, which during the first half of the twentieth century has twice given unlicensed freedom to hatred, disorder and destruction.

[1] Louis Fischer, *The Life of Mahatma Gandhi*, p. 54.

CHAPTER XVI

CONTEMPORARY INDIAN ETHICS: HUMANISTIC ETHICS: NEHRU'S REALISTIC IDEALISM

Humanistic Ethics

The title of this chapter might appear odd to the reader, for I have already stated that Nehru is the successor of Gandhi and a political philosopher, and hence his ethics must necessarily be the ethics of non-violence. However, the point of calling Nehru's ethical views humanistic is only to bring home to the reader the humanistic implications of Gandhian ethics. All ethics is humanistic; its goal is the well-being of humanity. Indian ethics, as we have seen, is humanistic through and through. So is Western ethics. But a dispassionate study of the various ethical philosophies of India reveals that Indian ethics has emphasized humanism to the extent of divinizing man and thereby making him God. Man is accepted as one with reality because of the presence of spirit in him. This spirit is designated as part of Truth by Gandhi, as the bond of unity by Dr Radhakrishnan, and as the centre of rhythm by Tagore. Nehru, though apparently opposed to religion in the sense of blind faith, does believe in the power of spirit and even in the immortality of soul. Whereas I have said that Gandhi's ethics is based on pragmatic spiritualism, I am not inclined to say the same with regard to the ethical views of Jawaharlal Nehru. Nehru has been deeply influenced by Gandhi, but he has his own notions about religion, God and spirituality. For these reasons it appears desirable to describe the ethical views of Nehru as humanistic. Since Nehru does have his own philosophical views, it will be evident from the ensuing discussion in this chapter that Nehru has based Gandhian ethics on what I have dared to call Realistic Idealism.

Nehru as a Philosopher

W. E. Hocking has suggested that 'Philosophy is a set of beliefs by which we live'. If this definition of philosophy is accepted, it would be evident that each and every rational being is a philosopher, because man as a thinking animal conducts his life not blindly but purposively. Every one of us has some vague notion about the purpose of human life and the duty of man as a social animal. We have more or less explicit ideals which we cherish and strive to achieve.

In fact our behaviour in the home, in society and in national or international politics bears the stamp of our conscious or unconscious philosophy. In this sense no one can avoid being a philosopher. It is in this sense that one Western scholar remarked, 'The choice given to us is not between philosophy and no philosophy, but it is between a good philosophy and a bad philosophy'.[1]

Mr Nehru is a philosopher not only in this general sense but also as an original thinker and critical scholar who has seriously pondered the philosophical aspect of human life. It is true that he has not propounded a metaphysical theory of the universe or an ethical system which could be termed Nehruism. But his reflections on philosophical topics, though not academically philosophic, are in fact the visions and flashes of his inner self. If his views are thoroughly analysed and dispassionately examined, one can conclude that Nehru's philosophy is a sort of synthesis of realism on the one hand and idealism on the other. Thus he appears to be a realistic idealist, which indicates that his philosophy is a synthesis of the realistic attitude of Western science and the idealistic or the spiritualistic urge of Indian philosophy. Such a philosophy can bridge the gulf between the oriental and the occidental cultures and can help to promote a new humanism which may ultimately lead to the unity of mankind and foster international understanding, goodwill and peace.

The fact that Nehru's life has been greatly influenced by his Western education from his early childhood, and by the views of Mahatma Gandhi, the greatest spiritual and ethical leader of our times, cannot and should not be overlooked. If we want to discover the philosophy in Nehru we shall have to refer to his writings, which are the truest expression of his real self. He himself is wonderstruck when he reads his own works, as is evident from his following remarks in the *Discovery of India*:

[1] William James, *Pragmatism*, chapter I.

'I have a strange sensation when I read something that I had written some time previously . . . I recognize it of course, but not wholly; it seems almost that I was reading some familiar piece written by another, who was near to me and yet who was different.'[1]

This expression clearly indicates that his views, which are the unconscious product of the Western scientific outlook and the Gandhian spiritualistic and ethical philosophy, are the flashes and visions of a changing, growing mind, a mind never quite satisfied with itself, constantly examining, testing and retesting its conclusions against the outer world of hard fact and the inner world of adamant spirit.

Philosophy may also be conveniently defined as the study of the nature of the universe as a whole and of the purpose of human life. The former aspect of philosophy, often termed theoretical philosophy, has always led the greatest thinkers of the world to delve into metaphysical problems like the existence of God, the unity or diversity of the Ultimate Reality and the immortality of the soul. The second aspect of philosophy, which often is designated practical philosophy, raises the problem of right and wrong, of good and evil, of truth and falsehood, and of beauty and ugliness. But both the theoretical as well as the practical aspects of philosophy are so interrelated and interdependent that reflection on one invariably leads us to the implications of the other.

The chief method of approach in both types of philosophy is reason or intellectual apprehension. Since analysis and synthesis are the functions of the intellect, every great philosopher is prompted to relate metaphysics and ethics, theory and practice, speculation and life. However, many great philosophers, like the Buddha, have not only neglected metaphysical problems but have purposely evaded their discussions because they often turn out to be abstract and abstruse, thereby becoming complex and confusing for a person who wants to tackle the concrete problems of life successfully.

A refusal to enter the arena of metaphysics on the one hand, and an emphasis on humanistic problems on the other on the part of a thinker, do not justify excluding him from the fold of philosophers. On the contrary, much contemporary Western

[1] Jawaharlal Nehru, *Discovery of India*, Introduction.

philosophy prides itself in condemning metaphysics as a fruitless pursuit. Mr Nehru, who is out and out scientific in his outlook and predominantly objective in his approach, is a philosopher who puts a premium on ethics over metaphysics and on humanism over abstract analysis. It would, however, be erroneous to say that he has no metaphysical notions at all. Though his activism and his practical bent of mind prompt him to devote his thought and action to the solution of concrete human problems, he does not possess the urge to delve deep into the mysteries of life. In one place he says 'Often, as I look at this world, I have a sense of mysteries of unknown depths. The urge to understand it in so far as I can, comes to me, to be in tune with it and to experience it in its fullness.'[1] These words indicate in Indian philosophy 'Brahman Jijñāsā', curiosity to know or realize ultimate reality. This tendency of the finite to know the infinite, of the limited to merge into the unlimited is regarded by some as proof of the existence of the imperishable Absolute. It is, however, worth mentioning here that Mr Nehru prefers the objective approach to knowledge of ultimate reality. But he himself admits that there is no such thing as true objectivity. Consequently he remarks: 'If the subjective element is unavoidable and inevitable, it should be conditioned, as far as possible, by the scientific method.'[2]

This attitude of his is surely justified and every serious student of philosophy will agree with him. Contemporary Western philosophy has derided religion and condemned metaphysics because of the presence of anthropomorphic tendencies in them. But the Indian system of the Vedānta, which is a unique monistic metaphysical theory, is neither anthropomorphic like theism nor anthropocentric like positivistic or materialistic humanism, but is a mean between the two. It is, if I may be permitted to use the term, spiritualistic humanism, which eliminates extremist tendencies of anthropomorphism and anthropocentrism. It would be desirable here to explain this view-point at some length.

Auguste Comte, the great French philosopher, propounded a theory popularly known as Positivistic Humanism. Comte is of the opinion that man today has reached a stage when his power of understanding is no more theistic or metaphysical, but positivistic. He points out that the human mind has three stages or

[1] Jawaharlal Nehru, *op. cit.*, chapter I. [2] *Ibid.*, chapter I.

levels of development, namely, theistic, metaphysical and positivistic. At the theistic level, when man wanted to explain the events of the world, he attributed them to gods or supernatural beings who possessed wills like human beings.

This stage of the development of the mind was succeeded by the metaphysical stage at which he substituted entities for gods in explaining the events of the world. The final stage of the human mind is the positivistic at which stage it explains the events of the world with reference to its true causes and effects scientifically. He therefore concludes that since man has crossed the stage of infancy when he required the notion of personal God to protect him from all dangers, and since he has reached the positivistic stage of adulthood, he no more requires a parental God. Moreover, the notion of God, being an abstract, metaphysical notion, cannot inspire man any longer. Comte suggests that man is in bad need of an object of worship that should inspire him. That object should be positive 'humanity'. He says that all men's thoughts should be devoted to the understanding of humanity, all his feelings to the love of humanity and all his actions to the service of humanity.

Comte remarked that 'Heaven declares the glory not of God, but of Kepler and Newton'. He believes science should be studied and advanced only for the benefit of mankind. There is no need of a disinterested search for truth, no need of any metaphysics, and no need of any science like astronomy, which is concerned with objects remote from the human pale. Thus positivistic humanism would ban the study of astrophysics and would not allow scientists to encourage interplanetary travels.

Pringle-Pattison has rightly remarked that Comte commits the mistake of a man, who being enamoured of the beauty of the bubble in a river, forgets the stream of the great river which generated the bubble. Positivistic humanism, in its anxiety to condemn the anthropomorphic tendency of Western theism, itself commits the fallacy of extreme anthropocentrism. When positivism is divorced from the inner and spiritual aspect of man, it either turns into anthropocentrism or into the disinterested callousness of scientific progress. Mr Nehru has referred to this tendency of science in the following manner:

'Or again, perhaps, the very progress of science, unconnected with, and isolated from, moral discipline and ethical considerations, will lead to the concentration of power and the terrible instruments of destruction, which it has made, in the hands of evil and selfish men seeking domination of others and thus to the destruction of its own great achievements. Something of this kind we see happening now, and behind this war there lies internal conflict of the spirit of man.'[1]

Thus Comte's philosophy neglects the spiritual aspect of human personality, and for an abstract notion of God it substitutes an abstract notion of 'humanity', which, without the acceptance of the continuity of evolution and of the unity of Ultimate Reality, hangs in mid-air. It is therefore evident that philosophy or science cannot overlook the claims of metaphysics.

The monistic theory of the Advaita Vedānta, which rejects the notion of a personal God, which emphasizes the spiritual oneness of the cosmos, and which is not anthropomorphic or anthropocentric appeals to Mr Nehru, who says:

'Any idea of a personal God seems very odd to me. Intellectually, I can appreciate to some extent the conception of monism, and I have been attracted towards the Advaita (non-dualist) philosophy of the Vedānta, though I do not presume to understand it in all its depth and intricacy, and I realize that merely an intellectual appreciation of such matter does not carry one far.'[2]

This intellectual appreciation of monism and the tendency to accept the non-dualism of the Vedānta is indicative of the realistic idealism of Mr Nehru, which is neither anthropocentric like Comte's humanism which would divorce science from metaphysics and man from the universe, nor anthropomorphic like western theism with a predominance of supernatural elements. He does not commit the blunder of overemphasizing analysis and of dividing philosophy and science into watertight compartments. His loyalty to realism compels him to arrive at the impartial conclusion that the microcosm and macrocosm cannot be drastically separated.

Dwelling upon this point he adds:

[1] Jawaharlal Nehru, *Discovery of India*, Ch. I.
[2] *Ibid.*

'More recent researches into the nature of matter, the structure of the atom, the transmutation of the elements and the transformation of electricity and light, either into the other, have carried human knowledge much further. Man no longer sees nature as something distinct from himself. Human destiny appears to become a part of nature's rhythmic energy.'[1]

In the same strain he compares some of the latest conclusions of science with the non-dualistic philosophy of the Vedānta, and quotes Karl K. Darrow to support his contention that 'the latest developments in physics have gone a long way to demonstrate a fundamental unity of nature'.[2]

There is no doubt that no humanism can stand without the notion of unity among men, and no unity among men is conceivable without believing in the unity of nature, all the more so if science supports such a contention. Mr Nehru has drawn the attention of students of philosophy towards the possibility of the verification of the monistic conception of the Ultimate Reality through scientific method. He also accepts intuition as the means of knowledge, but being a positivist he prefers experimental and scientific verification of the conclusions drawn by the sages through intuition. Thus while accepting the metaphysical basis of the spiritual unity, he finds no place for blind faith and dogmatism. But he does recognize the possibility of the invisible world, and he advocates 'the application of the scientific method to emotional and religious experiences', thereby bringing science and metaphysics and religion and philosophy into unity.

Nehru's contribution to philosophy is to see that the intellectual interpretation of the nature of the universe and the scientific approach to metaphysics and religion can lead to the emergence of a world philosophy, which is metaphysically monistic and ethically humanistic, a philosophy which is realistic because it is not other-worldly; idealistic because it is not mechanical; and universalistic because it is secular and cosmopolitan.

The Ethical Aspect of Nehru's Philosophy

It virtually goes without saying that every independent thinker and, more particularly, a person who dedicates his life to a general cause, is bound to follow fundamental principles which

[1] Jawaharlal Nehru, *op. cit.*, Ch. 1. [2] *Ibid.*

he accepts and endorses as unavoidable or desirable for the conduct of life. Mr Nehru relinquished comforts and embraced a hard life; he sacrificed his family happiness, his wealth and what-not to improve the lot of millions of his countrymen, to lead a constant and tough fight against British imperialism, and to break the shackles of slavery of a great but helpless country. India had lost its ancient glory and its eminence as the most cultured and most civilized nation of the world because of political vicissitudes. His resolve to dedicate his life to this noble cause, his patriotic passion, his urge to free the ignorant and innocent millions from the clutches of hunger and penury, and his determination to achieve all this under the guidance of the great saint and philosopher, Mahatma Gandhi, makes it quite evident that what favourably struck Jawaharlal Nehru in his early years was not a hedonistic philosophy of life, but an altruistic spirit of self-sacrifice, restraint, and service in behalf of suffering humanity.

Interested in action toward this end which was quite natural and necessary under the circumstances and made Shri Nehru give up a life of comfort in his youth, it was not possible for him to work out abstract questions of metaphysics. He himself agrees that 'Some vague or more precise philosophy of life we all have, though most of us accept unthinkingly the general attitude of life which is characteristic of our generation and environment'.[1] He reports that though he had some attraction towards metaphysical speculation, yet he never had 'a taste for vague speculation'.

If we compare his philosophical attitude to the thinkers of ancient India, particularly the India of the sixth century before Christ (since during that period India abounded in philosophy of life), we can find a parallel in the Buddhistic philosophy which appears to have influenced both Mahatma Gandhi and his rightful successor, Nehru. His passion for truth and non-violence, and his unique manner of tackling international problems by offering solutions with reference to his ideology of 'Pañcaśīla', are indicative of his inclination towards a spiritual philosophy of life based on love and non-violence. This practical, or rather, pragmatic philosophy is necessarily indifferent towards eschatological, or other-worldly conceptions. The Buddha declared at the end that he had purposely avoided reference to

[1] Jawaharlal Nehru, *op. cit.*

metaphysical problems because it would have obstructed his mission of ethical emancipation of the people. Mr Nehru, in referring to his philosophy of life has remarked, 'Essentially, am interested in this world, in this life, not in some other world or a future life'.[1] He believes in solving human problems and hence he declares that 'The real problems for me remain problems of individual and social life, of harmonious living, of a proper balancing of an individual's inner and outer life, of an adjustment of the relations between individuals and between groups, of continuous becoming something higher, of social development, of the ceaseless adventure of man'.[2] These words come from the core of the heart of a thinker who believes in a dynamic, active, and selfless philosophy of life. Thus his utterances and his practical life offer us a pragmatic and altruistic philosophy of life, which demands a sense of responsibility from each and every member of the society, and a spirit of self-sacrifice with a view to uplift humanity economically, socially, morally and spiritually.

As an ethical thinker Nehru firmly believes in Gandhi's notion of justifying the means to justify the ends. He has always admired and adopted the method of Satyagraha for the attainment of freedom. Gandhi rightly designated the movement of protest against the foreign rule as Satyagraha, the truthful protest, or rather, 'the insistence on truth'. Freedom is the 'birthright of every individual' and the crushing of human freedom by the British imperialists in India was undoubtedly untruth. Satyagraha, which also consisted in non-co-operation with the foreign government to rule millions of unwilling Indians and whose wealth was exploited by the British for centuries, was the most justified means for the just end of gaining political independence for India. Nehru emphasizes the worthiness of the means both from the theoretical as well as from the practical point of view. In his autobiography he writes, 'A worthy end should have worthy means leading up to it. That seemed not only a good ethical doctrine, but sound, practical politics, for the means that are not good often defeat the end in view and raise new problems and difficulties.'[3] It should not be forgotten that Nehru is concerned mainly with the practical application

[1] Jawaharlal Nehru, *op. cit.* [2] *Ibid.*

[3] Jawaharlal Nehru, *An Autobiography with Musings on Recent Events in India*, 1958, p. 73.

of theories. He accepts the nobility of the means, sincerity of purpose or 'good will' as the best means, not merely because various thinkers and philosophers have put forward the intuitive theory of morality based on the intrinsic goodness of the goodwill, but because good results cannot possibly be achieved without the right means and goodwill. He is essentially humanistic, and morality, or right, for him is the means for the well-being of humanity. For him nothing is more important than man, and hence man is an end in himself. Kant, the most influential moral philosopher of the modern age declared that man should be treated as an end in himself, but as a theorist he did not consider anything of intrinsic worth or value but 'good will'. All intuitionists, including Gandhi, in spite of their humanistic outlook, consider goodwill an end in itself. But Nehru has always remained a utilitarian in the sense that he considers morality the means for the betterment of man and not an end in itself. Kant's kingdom of ends was a mere theory, and his 'duty for the sake of duty' ultimately turned out to be empty. Hence we cannot say that Kant was a humanistic philosopher. A truly humanistic view, though moral, must essentially regard man—concrete man—to be the meeting ground of all values. We should not forget that man has generated the concept of value and that value has meaning only for man. It is this humanistic attitude towards philosophy, ethics and religion, which predominates in the thought of Nehru and prompts him to declare that 'God we may deny, but what hope is there for us if we deny man and thus reduce everything to futility'.[1] We have already stated that Indian philosophy from the Vedic period asserted the dignity of man, and declared him to be superior even to God because he is embodied Brahman. The body, or Nāma Rūpa (name and form) as it is called, is declared to be true in the Brāhmaṇa Granthas which declare 'Nāma rūpe satyaṁ', that is, name and form contain reality or Truth. Contemporary Indian thinkers have reasserted faith in man. A profound contemporary thinker, Shri G. C. Chatterjee, while throwing light on the intrinsic aspect of value, writes:

'The question is to some extent purely academic, for I believe that things at any rate, of great intrinsic value are all connected with experience or are the subjects of experience, but at the

[1] Jawaharlal Nehru, *Discovery of India*, p. 445.

same time I hold that mind is itself embodied and if the corporeal aspect of mind is divorced from it, I believe that the value of such wholes would greatly diminish . . . For example, I believe that love between persons is one of the greatest goods, but all the persons whom I love have a body, and I cannot myself differentiate between my love for their bodies and my love for their spiritual personalities. That I should love a person's spiritual being and at the same time hate or be indifferent to that person's physical being, seems to me an impossibility.'[1] This realistic attitude is present in Nehru's thought throughout and is responsible for his emphasis on improving the material lot of human beings.

Nehru's realism prompts him to adopt the humanistic approach to all problems and to subordinate all interests to the main interest of human well-being. Hence it is natural for him to be more a utilitarian than an intuitionist, to lay more emphasis on concrete consequences than on the abstract motive. He is therefore not a mere speculator but a practical thinker. He accepts the power of spirit, but this power, according to him, has been made active and effective because man has always put up a brave struggle against the odds of life. He says: 'How amazing is this spirit of man! In spite of innumerable failings, man throughout the ages has sacrificed his life and all he held dear for an ideal, for truth, for faith, for country and honour. That ideal may change, but the capacity for self-sacrifice continues, and, because of that, much may be forgiven to man, and it is impossible to lose hope for him. In the midst of disaster, he has not lost his dignity or his faith in the values he cherished.'[2] His faith in the self-sacrificing capacity of man, which in fact is the real 'dignity' of man, is unshakable. If Kant was a moralist par excellence and if Gandhi was alone, Nehru can be rightly called a humanist par excellence. A rigorous ethics ends in asceticism and self-torture, but a humanistic ethics always upholds man as the highest reality and puts a premium upon human well-being rather than upon formal and ideal principles, which sometimes are to be sacrificed on humanitarian grounds. Nehru lays a great emphasis on a human approach. We have already stated in this chapter that he derides the absence of the human

[1] G. C. Chatterjee, 'Commonsense Empiricism', in *Contemporary Indian Philosophy* (ed. by S. Radhakrishnan and Muirhead), p. 106.

[2] Jawaharlal Nehru, *op. cit.*, p. 18.

approach in science, although he admires science and the scientific method. Wherever he disagrees with the idealism of Gandhi, or favours relative violence to absolute non-violence, he does so because of his extreme humanism.

The Ethics of Pañcaśīla—The Five Principles of Conduct

However, Nehru is a pacifist to the core and abhors war and the use of deadly weapons for the destruction of mankind. He has been applauded the world over as the greatest upholder of peace and promoter of the policy of non-violence in international politics. Proof for his adherence to the policy of non-violence in international relations is the fact that Nehru has banned the production of atom bombs in his own country, although its scientists are now capable of making them. Besides the practical application of the policy of non-violence with regard to India's diplomacy envisaged in his attitude of non-alignment, Nehru has positively contributed to the promotion of the world peace. He has laid down the five ethical principles, or Pañcaśila, as they now have been popularly acknowledged the world over.

These five principles of peaceful co-existence of the nations are:

(1) Respect for the territorial integrity and sovereignty of other nations.

(2) Non-aggression, i.e. eschewing armed attack on other nations.

(3) Non-interference in the domestic affairs of other nations.

(4) Maintaining equality and mutual benefit with regard to trade and commerce with other nations.

(5) Peaceful co-existence, i.e. toleration for the ideology of other nations.

Nehru enunciated these broad principles of conduct for all the nations with a view to allow political freedom to all nations, to give them equal opportunities to thrive and prosper materially, and to enjoy the blessings of peace. These five principles were first of all officially accepted by China in 1954, when she entered into a mutual agreement with India, and within a year they were adopted by more than thirty countries. There is little doubt that if these principles are accepted and strictly followed in the conduct of political affairs by all the nations of the world, the mutual distrust and doubt, fear and frustration and coercion and the cold war of the so-called power blocs would disappear, and a distressed humanity would revive hope and happiness in its life.

Incidentally, the five universal principles, which are meant for the conduct of nations and hence for the national and the international evolution of society, correspond to the five principles of restraint (Yamas), which aim at the spiritual development of the individual. These five yamas of the Yoga, viz. (1) Truth, (2) Non-violence, (3) Continence or celibacy, (4) Non-stealing and (5) Non-possession, have also been accepted by Jainism. Respect for the territorial integrity and sovereignty of each other on the part of two nations is in fact the recognition of the truth of frontiers and the sovereign power with which each state is invested. The second, Śīla, or the principle of national behaviour, non-aggression, evidently corresponds to the principle of the adoption of non-violence, which positively means love for all living beings. According to Mahatma Gandhi, the law of non-violence, or love, is the law of our being.

The third principle of peaceful co-existence, non-interference in the domestic affairs of other nations, corresponds to the individual code of continence, which in the case of a married man means confining his conjugal relation only to his own wife. If a nation does not interfere in the internal affairs of the other nation, it means that it is not committing adultery. Interference in the internal matters of a state by an external power amounts to adultery. The wife is the symbol of domestic life. Continence means not interfering in the domestic life of others. Hence the third principle of peaceful co-existence is based on the Yama of continence, or Brahṁacarya.

The fourth principle of peaceful co-existence demands the maintenance of mutual benefit with regard to trade and commerce, and this code appears to me to be equivalent to the restraint of non-stealing. Asteya, or non-stealing, demands that an individual should not appropriate the property of others. Mutual benefit in trade and commerce between two countries is possible only when the countries remain honest in their dealings and do not resort to misappropriation. Hence my contention is that the fourth tenet of Pañcaśīla corresponds exactly to the restraint of non-stealing.

The fifth Śīla or universal principle of conduct advocated by

Nehru is undoubtedly the highest. Peaceful co-existence alone can lead to universal peace and all-round prosperity of the human race. Co-existence means 'unity in diversity' and 'harmony in discord'. It stands for toleration of the ideology or way of life of other nations. Whether a country follows the democratic way of life or a communistic form of government, the foremost duty of an ideal nation is not to force its own ideology on its neighbours. A democratic nation should not preach its ideology in a communist country, and vice-versa. When a nation wants to thrust its own form of government on its neighbours in an imperialist manner, it means that it wants to spread its ideology outside its geographical and political limits. This intention, or act, amounts to violation of the restraint of non-possession, which demands that one should be satisfied with one's limited resources. Thus the fifth Śīla or universal principle clearly corresponds to the fifth principle of restraint, viz., non-possession or Aparigraha.

This interpretation of the Pañcaśīla of Nehru is entirely my own. But it appears convincing to me because individual and society, man and nation, are so intimately related and organic to each other that their basic principles of conduct must necessarily be uniform. Moreover this interpretation of mine confirms my contention that Nehru's ethics is thoroughly humanistic and realistic. There is no doubt that if the world is ever to get rid of the fear of the wholesale destruction of humanity and the total annihilation of the cultural achievements of man, the leaders of this globe shall have to admit that the only alternative to co-existence is co-destruction.

CHAPTER XVII

CONCLUSION: THE CONTRIBUTION OF INDIAN ETHICS TO HUMAN WELL-BEING

Mysticism versus Realism

In the light of our thesis, according to which 'unity in diversity' and 'harmony in discord' are regarded as the ideal and the truth in the case of the individual, society and the cosmos, Gandhi's pragmatic spiritualism and Nehru's realistic idealism, both of which emphasize morality, are equally important. Both Gandhi and Nehru agree that means should justify ends, so that the right and the good should be harmonious. Both thinkers are humanistic, lovers of peace and non-violence. Gandhi laid more stress on the spiritual method, the inner voice, faith in God, whose grace must be invoked through prayers to gain spiritual strength so as to follow truth and non-violence absolutely in all the spheres of life, social, economic or political. He therefore laid more emphasis on intuition, and had the firm faith that a life of suffering and self-sacrifice which minimizes wants, even to the extent of eliminating machine-made goods, could infuse spiritual oneness and universal love in each and every individual. He therefore over-emphasized a sort of asceticism as the means to the removal of evil and suffering, and advocated non-violence as a creed, and a religion—a passion. Nehru, though a votary of non-violence and truth, lays greater emphasis on scientific method and wants to apply scientific analysis even to the life of emotion and religion. He has greater faith in the material achievements of science, though sometimes he is disgusted with the indifference of scientific research towards human weal and woe. He therefore lays more emphasis on intellectual acumen and feels that there is the possibility of a scientific humanism. He does not show that same conviction—at least that depth of conviction—in the power of spirit and the possibility of intuitional realization of the oneness of the individual with the cosmos, or absolute, or God, present in Gandhi.

He therefore regards non-violence as an expedient means towards the peace and prosperity of the human race. He does not repudiate the utility of machines and does not favour asceticism and the reduction of wants. Gandhi himself attained a super-state of mind, which made him free from science and technology, and he thought that each and every individual could rise above material wants and higher standards of living. Thus Gandhi was too spiritualistic in his outlook. But Nehru, being in the thick of practical life, realized that in the atomic age no nation and no society can bring about social well-being without the services of science and technology. Thus Gandhi over-emphasized the intuitive method, and Nehru advocated the superiority of the scientific attitude.

The fact remains that both intuition and intellect are equally important for the integrated development of man. The spirit in man cannot be abstracted from the body and the body cannot exist without the soul force. Spiritual conviction and material advancement must go hand in hand. Firm faith in God, as the indwelling spirit and as the unitive force of the pluralistic universe, and intellectual confidence in the progress of science must co-exist in the human breast. We should neither be agnostical with regard to the existence of the spiritual, invisible and unmanifested central reality, nor should we be too sure of the intellectual conclusions in the domain of science, which is always open to modification and change. An attitude of certainty with regard to the subjective, immanent and transcendental self and an honest scepticism with regard to the changing, pluralistic and manifold objective universe are admissible and even essential.

Spiritual conviction can be attained through the intuitive method, the method of Jñāna, and this method enjoins upon us a spiritual discipline, i.e. Yoga, either in the form of intellectual knowledge of truth (Jñāna Yoga), or in the form of unattached engagement in active life (Karma Yoga), or in the form of love of God (Bhakti Yoga). All the three types of Yoga can be followed simultaneously and can thus lead to the integrated development of the individual. Gandhi combined in himself all three, but he was predominantly a mystic. Nehru combined in himself the path of knowledge (scientific conviction), the path of selfless action, and the path of love for humanity. But in him intellectual conviction predominates to the extent of concealing his spiritual aspect. If Gandhi was a mystic, Nehru is a realist; if Gandhi followed intuition and emphasized rightness in morality and spiritual oneness in metaphysics, Nehru follows the empirical method and emphasizes goodness in morality and material manyness in metaphysics. Gandhi believed in the intuitive approach to truth, as Nehru believes in the intellectual approach. Gandhi would spiritualize science and subordinate material to the spiritual, flesh to reason. Nehru believes in scientific humanism and is lukewarm with regard to the power of spirit. But the mysticism of Gandhi with its spiritual bias must be synthesized with the realism of Nehru with its secular bias. It is true that abstract spiritualism is empty, but at the same time it must be remembered that secular humanism is blind. Mysticism and realism are not opposed to each other; spiritual growth is certainly compatible with material advancement. We have demonstrated the truth of the synthesis throughout our study of Indian ethics. A dispassionate survey and critical analysis of the ethical philosophies of India forcibly leads us to the conclusion that intuitive knowledge (Jñāna) of the underlying oneness of Brahman, of soul, of the Holy, of the invisible ultimate cause of the manifested universe, and the scientific knowledge (Vijñāna) of the manifest plurality of the universe, the visible effect of the unmanifested Power, are both compatible and complementary to each other. Hence the right and the good can be synthesized in man, who is capable of gaining intuitive oneness with the spirit, thereby experiencing universal love, and of recognizing the pluralistic nature of the universe, so as to yoke natural power to human well-being. Hence man can be inspired by the 'rhythm', as Tagore would say; by the intuitive apprehension of the spirit, as Radhakrishnan has held; by non-violence as the law of Love, as Gandhi has advocated; to be actively engaged in the material, mental and moral well-being of the human race, which is the ultimate aim of the activistic philosophy of Nehru as well.

Capitalism versus Communism

We have just mentioned that contemporary Indian philosophy, particularly Gandhism, aims at the reconciliation of individual freedom and social well-being and thus strikes a mean between two extremes. Throughout our discussion we have tried to throw light on the practical bearings of Indian ethics on life and have repeatedly pointed out that the notion of 'unity in diversity' is not merely an ideal, but a practical plea. In the present age of the power of the press and propaganda, both right and wrong notions, constructive and destructive ideologies, and messages of love and hate reach the common man in no time in all the nooks and corners of the world. From this point of view contemporary society is better organized than at any previous time. But at the same time it is also in danger of being constantly disrupted because erroneous, confused and destructive notions as well spread like wildfire and cause havoc, particularly when a way of life or ideology adopted by one nation or group of nations is constitutionally and philosophically opposed to that adopted by another nation or group of nations. Much has been said about the gross differences between a democratic form of government which it is alleged makes capitalism thrive freely, and the communist form of government which is alleged to crush individual freedom of every kind. It is normally believed that capitalism and communism, democracy and totalitarianism, and individual freedom and social regimentation are two completely opposing ideologies, and that the two power blocs vying with each other in the nuclear race cannot co-exist.

The purpose of this book is purely ethical, but ethics has direct bearing on practical life and practical problems. Although in this work we are not primarily concerned with the merits and demerits of capitalism and communism, yet we must briefly assess the ethical value of both these great ideologies, and then decide whether and how Indian ethics can help us to reconcile these two ways of life. Capitalism, which is the outcome of the recognition of the respect for property, believes in free enterprise in its broadest sense. But when this freedom leads to the concentration of wealth in a few who grow extraordinarily rich, and keeps the overwhelming majority poor, this system degenerates and brings about social evils in its wake. The capitalists can capture political power and purchase votes in a democracy. They can monopolize trade and grow richer, while the poor become poorer in spite of the usually constant development of industry and commerce in a capitalistic country. All the abuses of wealth, overspending in luxuries, drink, debauchery and the like are likely to crop up in not only the materially most favoured classes, but in consequence of emulation in all classes. This happens when wealth comes to be considered the highest value in a society. Ultimately ethical values are subordinated to the mad pursuit for wealth, and humanitarianism gives place to formalism. Art, literature, science, philosophy, in short the entire institutional fabric of the society and state, is under the sway of an ideology which corrupts men and curbs their freedom of thought, feeling and action. This economic slavery of man in a capitalistic country spreads gradually, and for centuries the people who fall victim to it often do not realize that their spirit is being subordinated to flesh and their conscience to callousness. Free enterprise raises the material standards of living by increasing the wants of society, by providing every individual with the amenities and the comforts of life, and by giving him the opportunities to 'eat, drink and be merry', even to the point of eating, debauching, and drinking to death. But at the same time it dulls the human spirit, murders morality, kills love, dismembers family life, disrupts social institutions, fosters fastidious divorces, increases personality disorders, neuroses, complexes and suicides, thereby creating an unconscious hatred for man in the minds of citizens. The outward glamour of life is accompanied by inner gloom.

Ethical Implications of Communism

Though communism is a political institution and a particular way of organizing a society or state, yet it is certainly an ideology and a way of life which has been adopted by millions of Europeans and Asians. The basis of communism is the Marxist philosophy of dialectical materialism. Karl Marx was the first to lay down the theoretical foundation of what is now popularly known as communism. He held that the basic changes in society are a process of revolution. There has always been class war in society and the class which came first has to be 'negated' and opposed by the next one so as to wipe out the former. Dialectical materialism, which is just the reverse of Idealism, states that the world process is a constant material change of thesis, antithesis and anti-anti-thesis.

According to Hegel, who gave Marx his main clue, the world process and hence all reality, whether material, biological, mental or intellectual, follows the thought process. The thought process begins with a positive proposition or affirmation followed by a negative proposition or negation, and ultimately by a synthesis of affirmation and negation. Thus Idealism believes in thesis, anti-thesis, and synthesis, or affirmation, negation, and the resultant combination of the two, bringing about a harmony. But according to dialectical materialism, we have affirmation, negation, and lastly, negation of negation. From the idealistic point of view the state has evolved and will evolve into a harmonious whole where the contradictions or clashes of different interests of individuals and communities will be resolved and synthesized. But from the Marxist point of view the state, nay, even the entire human society, from the very beginning has been following the process of dialectical materialism of affirmation, negation, and the negation of negation. In other words, one class, say, landlords, came into existence, then that class was opposed by the industrialist class, which wiped out the former class. The industrialist class becomes the capitalistic class and it is being opposed by the labour class which must extinguish the class of the industrialists. Communism therefore believes that the victory of the proletariat or the working class, over the bourgeoisie, or the capitalistic class, would bring about a classless society. It aims at economic equality by declaring that the entire wealth and material resources of a country belong to society or the nation as a whole. This great experiment in communism was begun in Russia after the Revolution. Many other European countries and China have adopted communism. However, we are not concerned here with the material achievements or the political implications of communism but only with its ethical interpretation.

Whether Russia or Yugoslavia or China has succeeded in establishing a classless society and in curing all social evils and solving all economic problems and moral issues is very difficult to assess. However, whether communism is accepted as a theory of human well-being or considered an ideology we shall have to admit that it is one-sided even in its aims of redeeming suffering humanity. Even economically none of the communist countries has been able to bring about an equalization or even 'levelling down' of human society. Human beings are not merely material products; minds cannot be lumped together and made quantitatively equal and proportionate. Even if every individual were to have an equal share of material wealth, irrespective of his being a doctor or a professor, a labourer or an engineer, no one with a sane head on his shoulders would say that they would be equally happy. Happiness cannot be identified with wealth or even with position or status. Moreover economic equality, the equal distribution of loaves and fishes, is not possible in a state where political power is concentrated in only a chosen few. Communism may succeed in abolishing the difference between man and man by drastically taking charge of the entire wealth of a country and by distributing it equally among its citizens; but it creates a political capitalism by concentrating power in a few leaders and ultimately fosters totalitarianism.

In a communist régime where wealth alone is supposed the ultimate end of life, individual freedom of thought, feeling and action is thwarted, religion is suppressed, spiritualism is deadened, and the individual is reduced to a mere cog in the social machinery. There is no political freedom, no party system, because one party is supreme. There is no possibility of genuine difference of opinion, discussion, exchange of ideas and hence of a natural growth of thought and culture. Man is reduced to an automaton, life to a mechanical routine, matter is subjugated to matter, individual freedom to the mechanical laws of the commune, and parental affection towards children to the husbandry of the state.

Communism like capitalism is based on and fosters an exaggerated, one-sided view of man and neglects the inner urge of the spirit of man. Capitalism gives unlicensed freedom to the individual with regard to the acquisition and use of wealth and thus creates a superiority complex in man, making him feel that his individual ego is all in all. It thus isolates man from the world, from the nation, from society and even from the family. Excessive sumptuary freedom also results in frustration and maladjustment, especially when the spirit is starved in consequence of the indulgence of the individual in personal sensual pleasures, merry-making and revelry. Thus capitalism, in exaggerating the theory of human rights makes the individual forget his moral duties and spiritual obligations. Communism on the other hand, forcibly yokes the individual to the material well-being of society without giving him the opportunity even to dwell upon the mental, intellectual and spiritual aspects of his personality. Too much restriction, which amounts to asceticism, is as harmful to the integrated development of personality as the unlicensed freedom to satisfy all desires. Capitalism and communism forget that man as an integrated personality has an inner unity of spirit and an outer diversity of social status, a professional occupation and moral code different for the persons occupying different positions in society and state. Man and society both express 'unity in diversity'. Man is potentially free, spiritually divine, and morally sublime. But he is empirically limited, materially bound, and socially restricted. What Indian ethics points out is that the unity of spirit must be recognized, developed, practised and realized by following a spiritual discipline which is neither drastic like a forced communist code, nor absolutely lax to the extent of reducing freedom to caprice and impulsiveness. Indian ethics exhorts man to tolerate the external forms of religion, society and state. But at the same time it reminds him to recognize the reality of the unitive spirit and to turn its potentiality into an actuality, which would bring about a synthesis of the individual and society, of faith and reason, of religion and secularism, and of national interests and internationalism, thereby binding the whole of humanity by the silken thread of love, brotherhood, and toleration—political, economic, religious and social—and of fellow-feeling, amounting to the spirit of self-devotion and self-sacrifice.

Positively, the tenets of Indian ethics lead us to what I have called spiritual humanism, which is neither abstract or purely theoretical, nor grossly indulgent to the neglect of the ideal element of human personality as in communism. If the human race with all its diversities of physical form, mental acumen and intellectual achievements has to exist on this planet, we shall have to admit that the only way to do it is to preserve all that is good and real, beautiful and harmonious, and spiritual and rational in human nature. This spiritual regeneration however, does not imply the suppression of the material progress achieved by man through science and technology, yet it certainly prohibits the misuse of scientific knowledge and the perversion of political ideologies. We have said more than once that Indian ethics, being ethico-metaphysical, or ethico-spiritual, combines in itself truth and goodness. As such it is idealistic as well as pragmatic, and spiritualistic as well as humanistic. It neither overdoes spirit nor matter, but it certainly subordinates the lower reality to the higher one so that man, the combination of spirit as well as matter, might develop his personality in an integrated manner.

With a view to achieve this it is necessary to practise equanimity and mental equilibrium as advocated by the ethics of the Bhagavadgītā, which accommodates all religions, all philosophies and all ethical opinions, in one gospel of universal Truth. The recognition of the universality of Truth, the presence of that very Truth in each and every individual, and the possibility of reawakening this potential universality through spiritual discipline, particularly through self-control, has been the key-note of Indian ethics right from Vedic times to the contemporary period.

One reason for emphasizing self-discipline in man is that its practice alone indicates the superiority of man to all other living creatures, who by their very nature are incapacitated to exercise will power and discretion which are the fundamentals of self-control. It is the rationality or insight in man that prompts him to rise above the instinctive level of animality and to subordinate his passion to reason, his emotion to intellect, and his impulse to discrimination. This constitutes the supremacy of man in the biological world, which has inspired great thinkers and prophets to declare that 'Man is the crown of all creation' and the 'image of God'. Reason or discretion as the distinctive feature of human nature is depicted in a Sanskrit verse which has it that hunger, sleep, fear and sex are common tendencies to men and animals, but reason alone is a superior quality in men. Those who are devoid of reasoning are not different from animals. In the words of Bertrand Russell: 'The civilized man is distinguished from the savage mainly by prudence, or to use a slightly wider term, forethought. He is willing to ensure present pains for the sake of future pleasure, even if the future pleasures are rather distant . . . True forethought only arises when a man does something towards which no impulse urges him, because his reason tells him that he will profit by it at some future date.'[1] Thus, psychologically speaking, prudence, reason or insight in man is responsible for his self-control.

We can add two further reasons which impel man to resort to self-control, the first of which is pragmatic and the second one is the spiritual urge of attaining infinitude or liberation. As we now know, man with a balanced mind is called a Sthitaprajña

[1] Bertrand Russell, *A History of Western Philosophy*, p. 33.

(one possessing a stable intellect) in the philosophy of the Bhagavadgītā. A man with a stable intellect is one who behaves equally in pleasure and pain, praise and blame, heat and cold, loss and gain, and in prosperity as well as in adversity. He is not perturbed by evil, nor does he feel elated over a windfall; he is indifferent to fear and anger. Such a person neither flatters others, nor does he blame them; he behaves equally with friend and foe, with young and old, high and low.

Such an attitude of mind is not indicative of cowardice or escapism. On the contrary, it requires great courage and self-reliance for an individual to forgive the offender instead of adopting vengeful behaviour and retaliation. Mahatma Gandhi's creed of non-violence is not the creed of defeatist, but that of the brave and courageous. Gandhi's life and his glorious death are testimony to the undaunted courage and fearlessness of the great saint, philosopher, reformer and nationalist. The calmness and smile on the face of Mahatma Gandhi, when the assassin fired the revolver, and his refusal to save himself by any physical effort at the fatal juncture, proved that spiritual power is mightier than physical force.

It may be said that Gandhi was an extraordinary person so far as self-control was concerned; but a dispassionate study of his life would indicate that he acquired this attitude of equilibrium by practising the principle of non-violence and by inculcating the qualities of a Sthitaprajña in him gradually and constantly. If men in power and politics were to follow the example of Mahatma Gandhi even to the extent of forbearance for the ideology of their adversary, there is no reason why international understanding and goodwill should fail to make every citizen of the world a lover of humanity and therefore a staunch supporter of everlasting peace. Great consequences are bound to ensue if mental equilibrium is attained by great statesmen, administrators and leaders of eminence.

There is no doubt that a balanced attitude towards life is not child's play. But if human experience testifies that this is the royal road to health and happiness, harmony and holiness, there is no reason why a rational being should not adopt it and thereby attain the status of a superman. Supermanhood is not something which is infused in an individual by some magic. It is nothing but the spiritual potentiality of man actualized, and made manifest by ethical discipline and spiritual exercise.

In the medieval period, the Western world accepted the theological definition of man as a religious creature. During this era it was believed that the most essential element in man was adherence to his tenets which he should not forsake even at the cost of his life. But this definition of man, as we all know, led to fanaticism of an extreme type, which resulted in the crusades, internecine armed conflicts in the name of religion, and the merciless treatment of innocent people, who were subjected to physical tortures and ultimately burnt alive in public places. It is quite evident that the definition of man as a religious animal instead of bringing about love and harmony in society led to hatred and discord, and thus it proved pragmatically false and theoretically unsound, being narrow and one-sided.

With the advent of the Renaissance and Reformation, a new spirit of freedom of thought overtook the Western world, and thinkers made attempts to turn the tables, to overthrow dogmatism and to shake off the fetters that shackled man, who though born free, was bound by the religious, social and political ties, which divided society into rich and poor, high and low, and ruler and the ruled. This revolutionary spirit declared that man was not a religious being, but was essentially a political animal whose liberation lay in 'liberty, equality and fraternity'. This definition of man, based on the political aspect of his personality, was expected to bring about peace and harmony to the human race. But unfortunately it first led to the Civil War in France, culminating in the reign of terror and then to the Napoleonic wars, which were based on political differences between the two great countries of England and France. Not only did this definition of man bring about havoc during the eighteenth and the nineteenth centuries but its destructive influence has since been very effective. The First World War was the outcome of the political differences between England and Germany, and the Second World War was an open conflict between the two political ideologies of totalitarianism and democracy. Thus the definition of man as a political animal has also brought about distrust, discord, and disturbance in human society instead of the expected harmony and peace.

The more recent definition of man as merely an economic animal has given rise to the Marxist philosophy which forgets that 'man does not live by bread alone', and that his distinctive features are not biological needs and instinctive urges, but intellectual understanding and spiritual realization. If eating and drinking had been the only essential requirements of human life, then man would never have risen above the brutish level, and there would never have been any progress in science, art, culture and philosophy to redeem man from the mechanical monotony of a factual environment, and to lift him to the sublime normative level of apprehending truth, appreciating beauty, and realizing goodness. The Marxist definition of man discards religion, neglects ethics, transgresses the individual freedom of man, reducing him to a mere cog in a machine, and suppresses whatever is sublime and spiritual in his personality. That is why in spite of relentless efforts of international leaders to seek a solution to the problem of an everlasting peace, and in spite of the emergence of the world organizations like UNO, UNESCO, WHO, etc., the net result has been the cold war between the power blocs, the indiscriminate use of the veto, and mutual distrust in the matter of disarmament and control over nuclear weapons. Unless a comprehensive definition of man is accepted and adhered to, with a view to bringing about an integrated development of his personality and society, it will not be possible to infuse in him the true spirit of fellow feeling and human brotherhood, which are most essential for the success of any international movement.

It is evident that Western thinkers have from the very beginning laid more emphasis on the material and external aspects of human personality than upon the inner self. On the other hand, India is known to have overemphasized the spiritual or inner aspect of men. But this does not mean that Indians have neglected physical needs and the emotional satisfaction of man. On the contrary, Vedic thought has from time immemorial defined man as an integrated whole of body, mind, intellect and soul. This definition is most comprehensive and it does not leave out any essential aspect of human personality. The physical body is under the control of mind, which is subtler than matter; the intellect, which is subtler than mind, controls it; and soul, the subtlest of all the aspects is regarded as the representative of the central reality, Prajāpati, the invisible and all-pervasive cause of the visible universe.

Indian thinkers and philosophers found self-control essential to develop the soul to such an extent as to make its unlimited potential powers actual and effective for the development of human personality. If the body is kept healthy for soundness of mind, and mind is kept in equilibrium by the exercise of intellect, spiritual realization takes place, and the person at this level rises above all antimonies and contradictions that vex ordinary man and that are the source of suffering and torture. The road to spiritual development is outside inward, starting from the physical, passing through the mental and intellectual route to the central reality. That is why ancient Indian sages propounded the four Purusārthas or the ends of life: (1) Artha, or wealth, (2) Kāma, or love, (3) Dharma, or morality and (4) Mokṣa, or spiritual perfection. Wealth is the economic value, which is instrumental for the healthy development of the body; love is the emotional value conducive to mental growth; morality or virtue leads to the development of intellect, and Mokṣa, the supreme good attainable in this life, is the highest level of spiritual existence of the individual.

We shall have to admit that even in India, which boasts of this integrated scheme of life, people have wrongly laid emphasis on one or two of the four ends of life, thereby taking a narrow and onesided view of Indian philosophy and culture. Whenever we overemphasize one end at the cost of others, we are bound to evolve a sectarian attitude harmful to the normal growth of personality. The West today is in bad need of the spiritual development, the methods of which have been elaborately developed by the Indian sages. The East, particularly India, is equally in bad need of material development which can be achieved only by the scientific technique which she has to learn from the West. Thus the combination of spiritual growth, attainable through mental equilibrium, and material progress, possible through the empirical methods of science, would not only lead to the prosperity of India, but would undoubtedly bring about a synthesis of the oriental and the occidental cultures, thereby resulting in a world culture, a thoroughly universal human culture.

SELECTIVE BIBLIOGRAPHY

BAIJNATH. *Hinduism; Ancient and Modern*. Meerut, 1905.

BARUA, B. M. *A History of Pre-buddhistic Indian Philosophy*. Calcutta, 1921.

BERGSON, HENRY. *Creative Evolution*. London, 1954.

BERNARD, THEOS. *Hindu Philosophy*. New York, 1947.

BESANT, MRS ANNIE. *The Bhagavadgītā*. Adyar Madras, 1957.

BHANDARKAR, R. G. *Vaisnavism, Saivism, and Minor Religious Systems*. Strassburg, 1930.

BLOOMFIELD, M. *Life and Stories of the Jaina Savior Pārçvanātha*. Baltimore, 1919.

BRADLEY, F. H. *Ethical Studies*. Oxford, 1952.

BURNETT, W. *This is My Philosophy*. London, 1958.

BURTT, E. A. *The Teachings of the Compassionate Buddha*. New York, 1955.

Chandogya Upaniṣad (original Hindu scripture).

CHATTERJEE, G. C. *Introduction to Indian Philosophy*. Calcutta, 1960.

CHOPRA, C. M. *A Short History of the Terapanthi Sect of the Śvetāmbara Jainas*. Calcutta, N.D.

CUNNINGHAM, G. W. *Problems of Philosophy*. Calcutta, 1956.

DAS, A. C. *Studies in Philosophy*. Calcutta, 1962.

DAS GUPTA, S. N. *A History of Indian Philosophy*. Cambridge, 1922.

DAS, M. N. *The Political Philosophy of Nehru*. London, 1961.

Daśavaikālika Sūtra (Jaina scripture).

DATE, V. H. *Vedanta Explained*. Bombay, 1959.

DATTA, D. M. *The Chief Currents of Contemporary Philosophy*. Calcutta, 1950.

FISCHER, LOUIS. *The Life of Mahatma Gandhi*. London, 1957.

GANDHI MAHATMA, M. K. *Buddha Aura Ahiṁsā*.

Towards Lasting Peace (ed. A. T. Hingorani). Bombay, 1956

GHANDI, VIR CHAND. *The Karma Philosophy*. Bombay, 1913.

GUṆABHADRĀCĀRYA. *Mahāpurāna*. Bhāratiya, Kāśī, 1954.

HARIDAS AND MAZUMDAR. *Mahatma Gandhi Peaceful Revolutionary*. New York and London, 1952.

Harijan (Journal). October 12, 1935; March 14, 1936; May 16, 1936; November 12, 1936; July 7, 1946.

HIRIYANNA, M. *Essentials of Indian Philosophy*. London, 1949.

Outlines of Indian Philosophy. London, 1951.

HOPKINS, E. W. *Ethics of India*. New Haven, 1924.

The Religions of India. Boston, 1895.

JACOBI, HERMANN. *Studies in Jainism* (ed. Mani Jinvijaya). Ahmedabad, 1946.

JAIN, CHOTE LALL. *Jaina Bibliography*. Satish Chandra Śeal Bhāratī. Jaina Parisat, Calcutta, 1945.

JHA, G. N. *Shānkara Vedanta*. Allahabad, 1939.

KANT, IMMANUEL. *Foundation of the Metaphysics of Morals*. Chicago, 1958.

KAPADIA, H. R. *A History of the Canonical Literature of the Jainas.* Gujarati Press, Bombay, 1941.
KEITH, A. R. *The Karma Mīmāṁsā.* Calcutta, 1921.
An Exposition of the Nyāya and Vaiśesika Systems. Oxford, 1921.
LALL, ĀCĀRYA JAWAHAR. *Saddharma Mandanam.* Tansakhdas Phusraj, Sardarshahar, 1932.
MACKENZIE, J. S. *A Manual of Ethics.* London, 1948.
MAJUMDAR, AKSHOY KUMAR. *The Hindu History from* 3000 BC *to* AD 1200 (2nd edition). Dacca, 1920.
MAL, MUNI NATH. *Ahiṁsā Aura Uske Vicāraka.* Ādarśa Sāhitya Saṅgha, Sardarshahar, 1951.
MARITAIN, JACQUES. *True Humanism.* London, 1954.
MONTGOMERY, JAMES A. *Religions of the Past and the Present.* Philadelphia and London, 1918.
MOORE, C. A. *Philosophy East and West.* London, 1946.
MOORE, G. E. *Principia Ethica.* Cambridge, 1954.
NAGRAJ, SWAMI. *Ācārya Bhikshu Aura Mahatma Gandhi.*
NAHAR, P. C. *An Epitome of Jainism.* Calcutta, 1917.
NEHRU, JAWAHARLAL. *Discovery of India.* London, 1951.
An Autobiography with Musings on Recent Events in India. London, 1949.
OTTO, RUDOLPH. *The Idea of the Holy.* London, 1936.
PARGITTER, F. E. *Ancient Indian Historical Tradition.* London, 1922.
PATTISON, PRINGLE. *Idea of God.* Oxford, 1930.
POUSSIN, M. *The Way to Nirvāna.*
PRABHAVANANDA, SWAMI AND FREDERICK MANDRESTER. *The Spiritual Heritage of India.* London, 1962; New York, 1963.
AND CHRISTOPHER ISHERWOOD. *Bhagavad Gītā. The Song of God.* Sri Ramakrishana Math, Mylapore, Madras, 1954.
PRASADJI, BRAHMACHARI ŚITAL. *A Comparative Study of Jainism and Buddhism.* Jaina Mission Society, Madras, 1932.
RADHAKRISHNAN, DR S. *Bhagavadgītā.* London, 1949.
Indian Philosophy. (8th Impression). London and New York, 1958.
An Idealistic View of Life. London, 1947.
Eastern Religion and Western Thought. London, 1940.
The Hindu View of Life. London, 1949.
RADHAKRISHNAN, DR S. AND MOORE, C. A. (eds.) *A Source Book in Indian Philosophy.* London, 1957.
RADHAKRISHNAN, DR S. AND MUIRHEAD. (eds.) *Contemporary Indian Philosophy.* London, 1936.
RAJ, MUNRI NAG. *Ācāraya Bhiksu-Aura Mahatma Gandhi.* Ādarśu Sāhitya Saṅgha. Sardarshahar, 1953.
RAJU, P. T. 'Humanistic Transformation', *The Aryan Path.* June, 1951.
RUSSELL, BERTRAND. *A History of Western Philosophy.* London and New York, 1945.
SANGHVI, PANDIT SUKH LAL. *Tattvartha Sutra.* Wardha, 1952.
SHASTRI, D. *A Short History of Indian Materialism.* Calcutta, Allahabad, Patna, 1930.

SHASTRI, PANDIT MOTILAL. *Bharatīya Dristi se Vijñāna Śabda Kā Samanvaya*. Jaipur, N.D.

Culture and Civilization. Jaipur, N.D.

STEVENSON, MRS SINCLAIR. *The Heart of Jainism*. London, Edinburgh, Bombay, New York, Toronto, Melbourne, Oxford University Press, 1915.

SURI, AMITAGATI. *Dvātrinśatikā*. Panna Lal Chondhri, Kāśī, 1926.

SŪTRA, ŚRĪ ĀCĀRĀṄGA. *Sthanakavāsī Jaina Conference*. Bombay, 1938.

The Sacred Books of the East. (S.B.E.) Vols. XLIV–XLV. Clarendon Press, Oxford, 1895.

THILLY, FRANK. *A History of Philosophy*. New York, 1951.

TULSI, ACARYA. *Jaina Siddhanta Dipika*.

UPADHYE, A. N. *Pravacansāra of Kunda Kunda Ācārya*. Bombay, 1935.

Śrī Yogīndu Deva's Paranātmāprakāśa and Yogāsara. Parama-Śruta Prabhāvaka-Mandala, Bombay, 1937.

VIREŚWĀRANANDA, SWAMI. *Srimad-Bhagavadgītā*. Mylopore, Madras, 1929.

WERKMEISTER, W. H. *Theories of Ethics*. Nebraska, 1961.

WINDLEBAND, W. *History of Western Philosophy*. New York, 1901.

ZIMMER, H. *Philosophies of India* (ed. Joseph Campbell). New York, 1951.

INDEX